Perspectives on
AKIRA KUROSAWA

Perspectives on
FILM

RONALD GOTTESMAN
University of Southern California
and
HARRY M. GEDULD
Indiana University

Series Editors

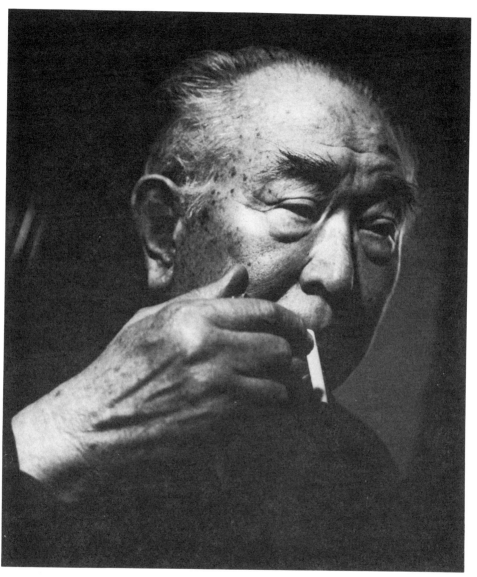

Akira Kurosawa, Tokyo, June 1991.
Photograph by James Fee

Perspectives on
AKIRA KUROSAWA

edited by
JAMES GOODWIN

G. K. Hall & Co.
An Imprint of Macmillan Publishing Company
New York

Maxwell Macmillan Canada
Toronto

Maxwell Macmillan International
New York   Oxford   Singapore   Sydney

G.K. Hall & Co.
An Imprint of Macmillan Publishing Company
866 Third Avenue
New York, NY 10022

Maxwell Macmillan Canada, Inc.
1200 Eglinton Avenue East
Suite 200
Don Mills, Ontario M3C 3N1

Macmillan Publishing Company is part of the Maxwell Communication Group of Companies.

Library of Congress Catalog Card Number: 94-1222

Printed in the United States of America

Printing Number
1 2 3 4 5 6 7 8 9 10

Library of Congress Cataloging-in-Publication Data

Perspectives on Akira Kurosawa / [edited by] James Goodwin.
     p.   cm. — (Perspectives on film)
    Filmography: p.
    Includes bibliographical references and index.
    ISBN 0–8161–1993–7 : $50.00
    1. Kurosawa, Akira. 1910–   —Criticism and interpretation.
I. Goodwin, James, 1945– . II. Series.
PN1998.3.K87P47   1994
791.43'0233'092—dc20

                                94–1222
                                  CIP

for Ron,
mentor and valued friend

Contents

Illustrations Follow Page 142

Series Editors' Note

THIS SERIES is devoted to supplying comprehensive coverage of several topics: directors, individual films, national film traditions, film genres, and other categories that scholars have devised for organizing the rich history of film as expressive form, cultural force, and industrial and technological enterprise. Each volume essentially brings together two kinds of critical and historical material: first, previously published reviews, interviews, written and pictorial documents, essays, and other forms of commentary and interpretation; and, second, commissioned writings designed to provide fresh perspectives. Each volume is edited by a film scholar and contains a substantial introduction that traces and interprets the history of the critical response to the subject and indicates its current status among specialists. As appropriate, volumes will also provide production credits, filmographies, selective annotated bibliographies, indexes, and other reference materials. Titles in this series will thus combine the virtues of an interpretive archive and a reference guide. The success of each volume should be measured against this objective.

Professor Goodwin has brought together an extraordinary array of commissioned, translated, and reprinted writings commensurate with the status of Akira Kurosawa as the most universally revered living filmmaker. The first group of these pieces, "Film Artists on Kurosawa," offers admiring and acute observations by several generations of film directors, producers, actors, screenwriters, and editors from every corner of the globe, reminding us of Kurosawa's worldwide appeal and international recognition as a master of the film form. The second section, "Kurosawa on Kurosawa," helps us to understand Kurosawa's development as a director from his youthful fascination with film artists such as Keaton, Eisenstein, Buñuel, and Murnau, to his mature reflections on the way film directing requires a firm grasp of all the other arts as well as the arts of life. Kurosawa's intense devotion to his chosen form of expression, his deep learning, and his profound under-standing of the human spirit are made clear in this section. The final section, "Film Critics on Kurosawa," offers commentary on and analysis of Kurosawa's widely acknowledged masterpieces such as *Rashomon, Seven Samurai, Yojimbo, Ikiru, Throne of Blood, Red Beard, Dodeskaden, Dersu Uzala, Kagemusha,* and *Ran* to his more recent productions *Dreams* and *Rhapsody in August* (and most of his other films as well). Virtually every major critic—French, Japanese, and Americans among them—is included, and together they shed light on Kurosawa's persistent themes, his defining styles and techniques, his capacity to utilize popular and high cultural forms, and the steady deepening of his social and philosophic outlook in the course of more than fifty years of engagement with the art of film. By artful selection, wise commissioning of original essays, and by elegant arrangement, Professor Goodwin has created a volume that does honor and justice to an artist whose life work is one of the proudest creative achievements of the twentieth century.

Publisher's Note

PRODUCING A volume that contains both newly commissioned and reprinted material presents the publisher with the challenge of balancing the desire to achieve stylistic consistency with the need to preserve the integrity of works first published elsewhere. In the Perspectives series, essays commissioned especially for a particular volume are edited to be consistent with G. K. Hall's house style; reprinted essays appear in the style in which they were first published, with only typographical errors corrected. Consequently, shifts in style from one essay to another are the result of our efforts to be faithful to each text as it was originally published.

Preface

Wᴵᵀᴴ ᴛʜᴇ use of Japanese terms and names here, in a collection of criticism whose audience will include the general reader, the system of macrons used among specialists in Asian studies is not employed. Traditional Japanese name order, with the family name first and given name second, is retained in those essays that follow this style. In all other cases, Japanese names are rendered according to the Western custom of given name followed by family name. The practice in foreign film scholarship of providing a transcription of the original release title is followed for the first citation of Kurosawa's films in my Introduction and my contribution as in a few other essays that are collected here.

Discussions on Japanese film history and on Kurosawa films with Michael Baskett and Professor Mikiro Kato of Kyoto University have contributed significantly to my knowledge of these subjects. In addition to the excellent new translations of Japanese essays that he prepared, Michael Baskett provided invaluable research assistance, particularly with the filmography. Help with matters of Japanese language and culture was kindly extended by Matthew Bills, Saori Hirata, and Hiromi Kinjo. Ronald Gottesman, to whom this volume is dedicated, has contributed greatly over the years to my understanding of film. My wife Andrea and my daughter Lonnie have provided loving encouragement and support.

I am grateful for research funds and a travel grant from the Committee on Research of the Academic Senate, University of California at Los Angeles. The Center for Japanese Studies at UCLA has substantially supported my work on this book through the Sasakawa Fund. The Toshiba International Foundation helped with the permissions cost for Keiko McDonald's essay. The portrait of Akira Kurosawa is provided courtesy of the photographer James Fee. I thank David Desser for the contribution of his important essay to the collection. I owe a general debt of gratitude to the authors, journals, publishers, and academic presses that provided permission to reprint material at no cost or for a nominal fee.

My research with published materials was facilitated by librarians and staff at the Theater Arts Library and the University Research Library at UCLA, the Academy of Motion Picture Arts and Sciences Library, the University of Southern California libraries, the Museum of Modern Art Library, and the Japan Film Center at the Japan Society, New York. Sharon Farb of the UCLA Theater Arts Library and Akira Tochigi and Kyoko Hirano at the Japan Society were particularly helpful. The Museum of Modern Art has granted permission for the use of photographic illustrations from its Film Stills Archive. Frame enlargements have been made from prints distributed by Audio Brandon Films. My research with film materials was aided by the UCLA Film and Television Archive and the UCLA Instructional Media Center. Carol Prescott at the UCLA Media Center and Robert Silber provided much technical assistance.

INTRODUCTION

Introduction

JAMES GOODWIN

IN JANUARY 1992 Akira Kurosawa announced plans for his new film entitled *Mada Da Yo* (Not Yet!), an exclamation associated with the children's game of hide-and-seek. The production, undertaken in the eighty-second year of Kurosawa's life, is the thirtieth film directed, edited, and co-written by this preeminent figure in world cinema. "Mada da yo" also expresses Kurosawa's own longevity and fortitude as an artist at an age when most individuals are retired and inactive. The film story concerns the closing phase of a writer's life (based on the experiences of the Japanese essayist Hyakken Uchida) and his relationship with former students. It depicts the survival of the writer's wit and dignity and the resilience of his ideas and values in the face of personal loss. The same strengths of character are to be found in Akira Kurosawa over the course of a career dedicated since 1936 to the art of film.

By the year of Kurosawa's birth, 1910, the new medium was only fifteen years old. His father, Yutaka Kurosawa, was receptive to motion pictures in spite of denunciations against them as a harmful Western influence by many educated, traditional Japanese. The father often took the Kurosawa family to the American and European motion pictures exhibited in Tokyo. On these outings they viewed popular imported action serials, slapstick comedies, and entertainment features. By age nine, in 1919, Kurosawa began to attend movie theaters on his own, following the recommendations of his older brother Heigo. Heigo became in young adulthood a disciple of modern European thought and culture. By the end of the 1920s Heigo wrote on the art of foreign cinema and performed as a silent film narrator, or *benshi*.[1]

Kurosawa's experiences in childhood and youth as a film spectator were formative. The personal narrative Kurosawa recorded for his book *Something Like an Autobiography* (*Gama no Abura*, 1982) lists about 100 films he remembers having seen for the first time between ages nine and nineteen. Included on his list are works by the directors Luis Buñuel, Charlie Chaplin, Cecil B. DeMille, Sergei Eisenstein, John Ford, D. W. Griffith, Rex Ingram, Buster Keaton, Fritz Lang, Ernst Lubitsch, F. W. Murnau, V. I. Pudovkin, Jean Renoir, Victor Sjostrom, Josef von Sternberg, Erich von Stroheim, and King Vidor.[2]

Kurosawa's initial artistic goals were set, however, as a painter. With the support of his liberal-minded father, Kurosawa received formal training in both the ancient art of calligraphy and the modern, Western school of landscape painting. Receptive to its political ideals and to its populist cultural program, Kurosawa joined the Proletarian Artists' League in 1928. Contrary to his expectations, Kurosawa found that the League's agitational-propaganda art diminished his passion for painting. He separated from the group in 1932 and directed his energies toward the development of a personal style as a painter. He aspired to the "intensity of realism" he admired in Courbet and the autonomy of vision he found in the paintings of Cézanne and van Gogh (*Autobiography*, 77). Ironically, the influence of these artists was so strong that it left Kurosawa unable to develop an independent style. To pay for canvas and paints in these years, he free-lanced as a commercial artist, producing magazine illustrations and cartoons.

In 1935, Kurosawa responded to a classified advertisement for assistant-director trainees at P.C.L. (Photo Chemical Laboratory), a new company formed to produce sound films. P.C.L. had rapidly established an audience by hiring skilled film directors like Mikio Naruse and Kajiro Yamamoto. (P.C.L. was later absorbed into Toho, the production company for which Kurosawa made thirteen films in the period 1943–1958 and which distributed five Kurosawa productions in the years 1960–1965.) One of 500 applicants for five available positions as assistant director with P.C.L., Kurosawa was surprised by his successful passage through the elaborate process of examinations and interviews. He began the training program in 1936.

Reflecting on this turn of events forty-five years later, Kurosawa wrote:

> It was chance that led me to walk along the road to P.C.L. and, in so doing, the road to becoming a film director, yet somehow everything that I had done prior to that seemed to point to it as an inevitability. I had dabbled eagerly in painting, literature, theater, music, and other arts and stuffed my head full of all the things that come together in the art of the film. Yet I had never noticed that cinema was the one field where I would be required to make use of all I had learned. I can't help wondering what fate had prepared me so well for this road I was to take in life. (*Autobiography*, 90)

Unexpectedly, the first months of training proved unstimulating and Kurosawa considered resigning the position. Once he was assigned to the production unit led by Kajiro Yamamoto, however, Kurosawa made a lifelong commitment to filmmaking.

Kurosawa esteems Kajiro Yamamoto as "the best teacher of my entire life" (*Autobiography*, 90). In the course of his distinguished career, Kurosawa has acknowledged the influence of many additional film artists on his imagination and on his own concepts of cinema. Among those artists within Japanese cinema, he names Kenji Mizoguchi, Mikio Naruse, Yasujiro Ozu, Yasujiro Shimazu, and Sadao Yamanaka most prominently. Within American cinema, he admires Frank Capra, John Ford, Howard Hawks, George Stevens, and William Wyler. Among other figures in world cinema, Kurosawa has expressed professional respect for directors as different as Abel Gance and Michelangelo Antonioni.

Of his favorite directors from the classic Hollywood studio era, Kurosawa has noted: "From the very beginning I respected John Ford. I have always paid close attention to his films."[3] The first meeting between Kurosawa and John Ford took place in the fall of 1957 when the Japanese director attended the London Film Festival, where Ford, Vittorio de Sica, and other eminent filmmakers were being honored. On this occasion, Ford recounted that he had visited the sound stages of Toho studios while Kurosawa was engaged in the production of *The Men Who Tread on the Tiger's Tail* (*Tora no O o Fumu Otokotachi,* 1945). Kurosawa had been too busy with the filming to meet Ford in 1945 and he did not receive the personal greeting the American director had meant to convey through an assistant. To make up for that missed opportunity, Ford invited Kurosawa in 1957 to the set of *Gideon's Day* (1958), which the American director was filming at the MGM Studios in London.[4] In the preface to *Something Like an Autobiography* Kurosawa expresses the personal desire to maintain in old age the same dignity and humility possessed by Jean Renoir and John Ford. Unquestionably, Akira Kurosawa has done so. Accepting an Honorary Academy Award in 1990 Kurosawa promised, in a statement reprinted in this collection: "From now on I will work as hard as I can at making movies, and maybe by following this path I will achieve an understanding of the true essence of cinema and earn this award."

FILM ARTISTS ON KUROSAWA

Many distinguished artists from the worlds of theater and cinema have paid homage to Akira Kurosawa. While their professional admiration for Kurosawa's work comes as no surprise, what does surprise is the diversity in the personal backgrounds, cinematic styles, and social interests of the film artists who honor Kurosawa. In the tributes to Kurosawa reprinted for this volume, the reader encounters prominent figures from the national cinemas of England, Japan, India, the Soviet Union, and the United States who possess vastly different sensibilities and who represent distinctive filmic traditions.

Early acclaim in the West for Kurosawa came from Tony Richardson and Lindsay Anderson, two important participants in the Free Cinema movement that flourished in Great Britain during the 1950s. Like many filmmakers in the Free Cinema, both directors evolved in their work from documentaries on contemporary urban life to fiction films in the manner of working-class social realism. Tony Richardson is the original stage and screen director of plays by John Osborne, whose theater world is marked by social protest and psychological revelation. Richardson is particularly appreciative of the detached, analytical treatment of behavior and emotions in Kurosawa's *Rashomon* (*Rashomon,* 1950) and *Seven Samurai* (*Shichinin no Samurai,* 1954). Lindsay Anderson, best known for his film adaptation of the novel *This Sporting Life* (1963) and for the anarchically comic *If...* (1968), values the wholeness of vision in Kurosawa's cinema, a quality more common to the epic realist novel than to the feature-length film.

Kurosawa's use of the Shakespeare play *Macbeth* in his film *Throne of Blood* (*Kumonosu-jo*, 1957) has gained the profound respect of two other important directors of British stage and screen, Peter Brook and Peter Hall. One of the most significant figures in contemporary world theater, Peter Brook has also directed the films *Lord of the Flies* (1963), *Marat/Sade* (1966), and *King Lear* (1971). For Brook, the greatness of *Throne of Blood* lies in its conception of a historical, Japanese context based on the *Macbeth* plot without attempting to adapt the Shakespearean dialogue to the screen. Peter Hall formed the Royal Shakespeare Company in 1960 and was subsequently appointed head of the National Theater; he is also a principal director for the Royal Opera House. Like Brook, Peter Hall has experience in bringing Shakespeare to the screen with *A Midsummer Night's Dream* (1968). In Hall's estimation, Kurosawa's achievement in *Throne of Blood* comes through reduction of the text of Shakespeare, in order to reach an essential vision of the drama and imagery at the core of the play.

One of the most memorable features of *Throne of Blood* is the performance of Toshiro Mifune as Washizu, the Macbeth figure. In 1946, at the time of Mifune's audition for Toho studios, Kurosawa observed the actor's unique adroitness: "Mifune had a kind of talent I had never encountered before in the Japanese film world. It was, above all, the speed with which he expressed himself that was astounding. . . . The speed of his movements was such that he said in a single action what took ordinary actors three separate movements to express. He put forth everything directly and boldly" (*Autobiography*, 161). Kurosawa first cast Mifune in his own films in 1948 as the tubercular criminal in *Drunken Angel* (*Yoidore Tenshi*, 1948).

Toshiro Mifune performed leading roles in all but one of the director's next fifteen films during the years 1949–1965. Their collaboration is as important to film history as other great pairings of actor with director, such as those of Lillian Gish with D. W. Griffith, John Wayne with John Ford and with Howard Hawks, and Jean Gabin with Marcel Carné and with Jean Renoir. Their professional and personal relationship was ruptured, and it has remained so, with the release of *Red Beard* (*Akahige*, 1965) whose lengthy production extensions caused Mifune to break obligations to other projects. In the 1960s, Mifune reflected that in his career "there is nothing of note I have done without Kurosawa, and I am proud of none of my pictures but those which I have done with him."[5]

In the interview "Mifune Talks: A Story of a Man Called Red Beard," translated by Michael Baskett for this volume, the actor honors Kurosawa above all for his intense commitment through the entire production process, a quality that endows the finished film with beauty and emotional power. Twenty years after they had ceased working together, Mifune continued to acknowledge Kurosawa as a great director who has innovated new methods in Japanese acting: "Whatever I'm able to do as an actor I learned from him. My best work is all in Kurosawa-*sensei*'s films."[6] *Sensei* conveys the compound meaning of master, teacher, and mentor; it is a term that combines affection with respect.

Through his films, Kurosawa has served as a *sensei* to many distinguished directors in world cinema. *Rashomon* exerted an indelible impact on Satyajit Ray, a Bengali director whose *Apu* trilogy—*Pather Panchali* (1955), *Aparajito* (1956), and *The World of Apu* (1959)—brought the cinema of India to the world's attention much as *Rashomon* had for Japanese cinema at the start of the decade. Writing about *Rashomon* fifteen years after first seeing it, in an article excerpted for this collection, Ray vividly recollects his initial impressions. He values the film as exemplary of the artistic potential within cinema. It realizes cinema's potential not only through visual composition but through the actors' performances, the editing, and the audiovisual structure. At the time of his death in 1992, Satyajit Ray had achieved international stature as a humanist of the cinema in the company of directors like Jean Renoir and Akira Kurosawa.

Grigori Kozintsev is an important Soviet theater and film director whose career in the cinema began in the 1920s with the artistic avant-garde that flourished over that decade. Before his death in 1973, Kozintsev became best known for his screen adaptation of the literary masterworks *Don Quixote* (1957), *Hamlet* (1963), and *King Lear* (1971). Understanding the complex problems involved in adapting a recognized classic to the screen, Kozintsev finds inspiration in Kurosawa's film of the nineteenth-century Russian novel *The Idiot* by Feodor Dostoevsky (*Hakuchi,* 1951). Kozintsev commends Kurosawa's radical decision to treat the material as a contemporary story, transposing the novel's setting in Petersburg of the 1860s to Japan of the late 1940s. The transposition has enabled the director to represent directly the inner, passionate drama of the novel and to convey its ideas and spirituality with none of the mustiness of a period piece. Kozintsev recognizes further influences on Kurosawa's cinema from the classic Russian authors Nikolai Gogol, Leo Tolstoy, and Maxim Gorky.

Andrey Tarkovsky, who chose to live outside the Soviet Union from 1983 until the time of his death in 1986, defines cinema as a process of "sculpting in time." Tarkovsky's films—notably *Andrey Rublev* (1966), *Solaris* (1972), and *The Sacrifice* (1986)—are meditative, visionary explorations of human experience. In his opinion, while most commercial films do not possess the poetic capacity to represent the actuality of life, such a quality is to be found in Kurosawa's cinema. Tarkovsky offers a shot from the climactic battle scene in *Seven Samurai* as the ideal of a concentrated, poetic image on film.

Filmmakers who have achieved success in Hollywood are equally appreciative of Kurosawa's artistic accomplishments. Three of Hollywood's most popular directors—George Lucas, Steven Spielberg, and Francis Ford Coppola—offered crucial support and financial guarantees that made it possible for Kurosawa to create *Kagemusha* (*Kagemusha,* 1980) and *Dreams* (*Yume,* 1990) in a period when Japanese studios cut back on their investment in his work. George Lucas is best known as director of *American Graffiti* (1973) and *Star Wars* (1977); he has also worked as executive producer on several films directed by Steven Spielberg. Lucas has acknowledged the debt *Star Wars* owes in story and style to Kurosawa's comic adventure epic *The Hidden Fortress* (*Kakushi Toride no San-Akunin,* 1958). In his statements on the occasions of the release of *Ran* (*Ran,* 1985) and of the 1990 Honorary Academy Award, Lucas praised the epic scale of Kurosawa's vision and its tragic insight. On the same occasions, Steven Spielberg acclaimed the universal human appeal of Kurosawa's films and his artistic dedication to the medium.

The last tribute published in this volume comes from Stuart Baird, film editor for many major Hollywood productions including *Superman* (1978), *Altered States* (1980), and *Gorillas in the Mist* (1988). Baird esteems Kurosawa for his consummate artistry and for the "accomplishment, in a medium that has always been more of a business than an art form, to have produced, with such consistency of vision and purpose, a body of work that has reflected his own philosophy." The Academy of Motion Pictures Arts and Sciences has awarded an Oscar for outstanding foreign language film to Kurosawa's work twice, for *Rashomon* and *Dersu Uzala* (*Dersu Uzala,* 1975).

In 1966, Kurosawa signed a contract with Twentieth Century Fox studios. He proposed to direct his new script *Runaway Train,* an American story that he wanted to shoot in upstate New York during winter. The project was intended to be his first color film, though by design the winter light would greatly mute the color range. When weather conditions caused protracted delays on location, however, Fox terminated the project. Kurosawa is credited with the story idea for the 1985 American feature under the same title, directed by Andrei Konchalovsky. Soviet-born, Konchalovsky collaborated with Tarkovsky as a scriptwriter and directed the award-winning *Siberiad* (1978) before emigrating to the United States to make films, including *Maria's Lovers* (1984). In making *Runaway Train,* Konchalovsky prized the original story concepts: "The design is still Kurosawa's. The concentration of energy and passion, the existential point of view, and the image of the train as something—perhaps civilization—out of control. I was extremely cautious in protecting Kurosawa's main design.... [The story's conclusion is] not very familiar to the Western mind. We tend to love winners, and we don't like losers."[7] With *Dodeskaden* (*Dodeskaden,* 1970), Kurosawa transformed the image of the train as a metaphor for a runaway civilization. In that film, an imaginary trolley is the spiritual refuge of a retarded young man.

In responding to *Ran,* Francis Ford Coppola has placed the film among the ranks of sublime works in the visual and performance arts: "When you look at a masterpiece of a film, it is the same as when you look at a great play or painting in that it should have the same qualities such as power, humanity, emotion, strength, philosophy, and humor. In the history of world films, Kurosawa's are those few that have these qualities in a genuine sense."[8] Lawrence Kasdan, the screenwriter and director of *Body Heat* (1981), *The Big Chill* (1983), and *The Accidental Tourist* (1988), has found professional guidance and wisdom in a theme central to Kurosawa's film stories: "Kurosawa, the greatest director who ever lived, said that villains have arrived at what they're going to be... that's their flaw, but that heroes evolve—they're open to change and growth. I want to be evolving."[9] In 1992 Kurosawa received the D. W. Griffith award, in recognition of his career achievement, from the Directors Guild of America. Kurosawa joined a distinguished company of directors previously honored by the Guild for their careers in film: John Ford, William Wyler, Alfred Hitchcock, Frank Capra, George Cukor, John Huston, Orson Welles, Billy Wilder, Elia Kazan, and Ingmar Bergman.

The same professional esteem for Kurosawa is to be found among independent, noncommercial filmmakers. Jonas Mekas, who moved to New York City from Europe in 1949 after spending the war years in a German labor camp, became a central figure in the American avant-garde cinema movement. Mekas founded *Film Culture* magazine in 1955 and was a principal organizer of the Filmmakers Cooperative and Anthology Film Archives. In the mid-1950s he began to keep his own personal diary in moving picture form. Mekas also wrote as a featured film critic for the *Village Voice,* where he reviewed many Kurosawa releases. In Meka's estimation: "Any Kurosawa film digs deep into the heart of our times. When one sees *The Lower Depths* [*Donzoko,* 1957] one cannot avoid comparisons with the best modern statements in other arts—[Jack Gelber's play] *The Connection* or [Samuel Beckett's] *Waiting for Godot,* for instance."[10] Equally powerful are Kurosawa's visual treatment and handling of the performers: "Kurosawa's imagery is always exciting. That is one part of good cinema. The acting is a mixture of Kabuki, commedia del l'arte, and free improvisation. Only Orson Welles can beat Kurosawa on casting, on digging out the weirdest faces—rich, rugged, plump, evil, all tremendously expressive."[11]

During the production of *Ran* the French filmmaker Chris Marker shot and narrated a documentary entitled *A. K.* (1985). Marker is an experimental filmmaker whose work includes the remarkable *La Jetée* (1964), a futuristic narrative constructed of still photographs. His documentary on Kurosawa and the making of *Ran* contemplates the director's stature as a *sensei:* "Sensei: 'Master.' In all disciplines, from flower arrangement to the martial arts, the Sensei is one who imparts a kind of spiritual gift in attaining technical perfection. The tide of respect that surrounds and protects Kurosawa has nothing to do with the dread that some men, who do not have his genius, are believed to exert in order to reign on high. And as in the past with grand masters of the Sword, Sensei avoids abstraction. He talks of craft, he thinks about facts and about experience."[12]

A witness to Kurosawa's inventive procedure of shooting epic scenes on location, Marker comments: "During the days that follow, the combat between the film production and the fogs turns into guerrilla warfare. Sensei keeps his troops ready even when one cannot see farther than one meter. A fair period, and shooting begins. Sometimes he improvises; on clear days he makes use of a passing mist that resembles smoke. He extracts his film from the raw material of an environment that he creates, like a sculptor."[13] The analogy Marker has invoked in order to describe Kurosawa's creative process is remarkably consistent with Tarkovsky's poetics of cinema.

Akira Kurosawa's example for and influence on other artists are by no means confined to the film world. From the literary world one notable instance is Gabriel García Márquez, the novelist who received international acclaim with the publication in 1967 of *One Hundred Years of Solitude*, a magic realist fiction. Formerly a reporter and film critic for the press in Bogota, Colombia, Márquez recorded a lengthy and genial conversation with Kurosawa upon the release of the director's *Rhapsody in August (Hachigatsu no Kyoshikyoku,* 1991). That film, like many of his previous works, adapts its story from a literary original. Márquez expresses admiration for Kurosawa's sensitive and intelligent treatment of literary sources: "You have made stupendous adaptations of great literary works, and I have many doubts about the adaptations that have been made or could be made of mine."[14] The novelist, who esteems *Red Beard* as one of the great films in the history of cinema, testifies, "I owe a large measure of my own faith in humanity to Kurosawa's films."[15]

KUROSAWA ON KUROSAWA

The selections from interviews, statements, and personal accounts reprinted in this section present Kurosawa's views on his filmmaking experiences and on film art generally. In the first reprinted statement, excerpted from a 1981 interview conducted by Tony Rayns, Kurosawa recalls the beginnings of his film career, as assistant director and writer with the Toho company in the 1930s and 1940s. Kajiro Yamamoto's professional affiliation with Kurosawa is remembered as a familial mentorship, like that of an older brother to a younger one. While Kurosawa gained experience in the chief technical and production facets of filmmaking, the core of his training under Yamamoto's guidance was in script writing and editing. He wrote original film scripts in the war period (1937–1945), but censors blocked many of them from production. In part as a retreat from the political realities of this period, Kurosawa began a serious study of traditional Japanese crafts and arts that continues into the present.

In an interview conducted by Donald Richie, Kurosawa savors the memory of his first film as director, *Sanshiro Sugata (Sugata Sanshiro,* 1943). Though he judges the film to be an entertainment piece, Kurosawa avoided the plain style common to Japanese narrative cinema of the day. The story in

Sanshiro Sugata remains simple and exemplary, but the visual treatment through composition and editing is innovative and exuberant. As a first film, it ranks in the company of inspired debut films by masters such as Luis Buñuel (*Un Chien andalou,* 1928), Sergei Eisenstein (*Strike,* 1925), and Orson Welles (*Citizen Kane,* 1941). In Kurosawa's estimation, he achieved the first full sense of his potential in film art with *Drunken Angel* in 1948. A fictional treatment of real social issues, *Drunken Angel* belongs to the broad category in Japanese cinema of the *gendai-mono,* or drama of modern life. Kurosawa created nine *gendai-mono* in the years 1946–1955.

Kurosawa gained international attention with the honors given to *Rashomon* at the 1951 Venice Film Festival and the American Academy Awards. *Rashomon*'s story and setting fall into the other principal category in Japanese cinema, the *jidai-geki* or period drama. But Kurosawa's approach to the story does not conform to the traits of costume drama, action adventure, or romantic period piece common to the genre. Through a use of several fragmentary and unreliable narratives, *Rashomon* is modern and inventive in its telling. An Italian distribution agent working in Japan had submitted *Rashomon* to the Venice festival. The chief executive at the production studio Daiei had not thought to do so because he had found the film nearly incomprehensible.

Kurosawa concludes the account of his life and career in *Something Like an Autobiography* with events surrounding the reception of *Rashomon.* Though he finished the composition of his autobiography in 1981, the narrative in the book extends only to events in 1951. The reprinted "Epilogue" offers a rationale for this discrepancy. Kurosawa observes that both he and his autobiography are, like the characters in *Rashomon* and the Daiei president who later claimed credit for the film's success, "incapable of talking about themselves with total honesty." Kurosawa believes that there is more honesty when a life story is conveyed through a person's work: "There is nothing that says more about its creator than the work itself."

Throne of Blood is considered by many film artists and critics as one of the most powerful adaptations ever of Shakespeare to screen. In an interview with Tadao Sato, Kurosawa explains that he selected *Macbeth* as story material on the basis of its similarity to a period of civil wars in Japan of the fifteenth and sixteenth centuries.[16] That period is also the age in which Noh theater originated. For the design and direction of the film, Kurosawa adopted Noh styles in speech, movement, and characterization. To distill personality traits and motivations, Kurosawa instructed each principal actor to study a Noh mask appropriate to the role. For the composition of action and its editing, he utilized the distinctive tempo of Noh, which alternates between "quietness and vehemence."

Asked by an interviewer from *Cinema* magazine about the possible influences of the American film genre of the Western on his *jidai-geki,* Kurosawa distinguishes between the latter's specific Japanese contexts and the general appeal of the mythic heroism and film grammar utilized in the American genre. In a later interview with Yoshio Shirai, Hayao Shibata, and Koichi Yamada published in *Cahiers du Cinéma,* Kurosawa explores the variations over his film career between historical stories and modern ones. The two categories are ultimately not exclusive, however, since a historical story such as *Rashomon* can be presented in modern fashion. And the action-adventure storyline typically associated with period material can be adapted to the moral and social concerns of a modern story such as *Ikiru (Ikiru,* 1952). Kurosawa expresses deep appreciation for the timeless, universal quality found in the nineteenth-century Russian novel, particularly in the work of Tolstoy and Dostoevsky.

In the interview "Making Films for All the People," Kurosawa emphasizes the importance of the writing process for the film director. Looking back, in 1986, over his scripts, Kurosawa perceives a shift from the direct protest about a social problem of a film like *Ikiru* to a more general, philosophical concern for humanity in later films. For *Kagemusha,* as Kurosawa commented to Tony Rayns, the writing process crystallized around an enigma in the historical record on the Battle of Nagashino, when all the *taisho* (generals) of one clan died in combat. While production on *Kagemusha* was in progress, Kurosawa had already begun work on a script that entailed parallels to the Shakespeare tragedy *King Lear,* but that project was not completed until 1985, with the release of *Ran.*

Speaking with Peter Grilli about *Ran,* Kurosawa clarifies the relationship of the *King Lear* plot to his film story. Where the play leaves unexplained the sources of the power that the king relinquishes, *Ran* seeks to imagine the ruler's political and family past. The interview with John Powers discloses a historical source for the film's portrayal of the fool Kyoami. Kurosawa bases the relationship between warlord and fool on records from the early samurai era that document emotionally intimate, and sometimes homosexual, relations between samurai and attendant. In the same interview, Kurosawa recounts the circumstances behind his shift to making films in color, starting with *Dodeskaden.* Through such innovations and discoveries Kurosawa's enthusiasm for cinema has been renewed over the duration of a long career.

Both the *Cahiers du Cinéma* and John Powers interviews refer to Kurosawa as "the Emperor." Journalists have conferred this epithet upon Kurosawa in their characterization of his demeanor on the movie set as autocratic. In truth, the epithet amounts to a popularized, reductive caricature of the film director at work. Among peers in the medium, as each tribute in the previous section attests, Kurosawa is a *sensei,* a respected mentor. Kurosawa's own immense respect for the medium suffuses his "Notes on Filmmaking." There, he defines cinematic beauty in terms of the "kiln changes" that occur in the course of creating a film. His reflections provide great insight into all phases of filmmaking, from story structure and set design to audiovisual composition.

FILM CRITICS ON KUROSAWA

Film criticism has deployed a host of approaches in the discussion of Kurosawa's cinema. These critical approaches range from traditional areas of thematic interpretation, stylistic analysis, and auteur study to newer fields of genre study, gender issues, semiotics, and deconstruction. Collected in the present volume are representative commentaries from each of the most important scholars and critics who have written on Kurosawa. Patricia Erens, *Akira Kurosawa: A Guide to References and Resources* (Boston: G. K. Hall, 1979) provides a valuable annotated bibliography of writings about Kurosawa—primarily in English, French, and Japanese—over the period 1951–1977.

Tadao Sato, one of Japan's most prominent analysts of media and culture, is well known in the West for his book *Currents in Japanese Cinema.* The reprinted excerpt "Kurosawa's Fathers" examines the thematic patterns of relationship between father and son, or between their surrogate figures. The father stands as *sensei* to his son in Kurosawa's 1942 unproduced film script *All Is Quiet* (*Shizuka Nari*), a story written in the wartime spirit of service to the nation. The role of father as noble mentor, Sato finds, is consistent in *Sanshiro Sugata, No Regrets for Our Youth* (*Waga Seishun ni Kuinashi,* 1946), *The Quiet Duel* (*Shizukanaru Ketto,* 1949), and *Stray Dog* (*Nora Inu,* 1949). The relationship is problematized through human failings, social realities, and the inescapability of death in *Drunken Angel* and *Ikiru.* Such conflicted relations between father and son create a dimension of tragic nobility in Kurosawa's cinema.

Audie Bock notes the correlation of heroism and humanism in Kurosawa's work in her survey *Japanese Film Directors.* In the selection reprinted, she examines the individual's quest toward enlightenment in several Kurosawa films of the 1940s. The drama and imagery of progress toward spiritual self-knowledge contribute to a cultivation of individuality that Kurosawa considers important for Japanese society. Returning years later to assess this same concern, Bock argues that the moral interpretation of human experience that animates his masterworks has declined to didactic moralizing in Kurosawa's recent films.[17]

Reviewing *The Men Who Tread on the Tiger's Tail* fifteen years after it was made, and upon its general release in the United States, John McCarten recognizes the parodic and political purposes of Kurosawa's revisions in adapting a solemn story from the traditional Kabuki repertory. Though the plot is largely preserved, its meaning is transformed through the addition of a character, a commoner whose behavior is eccentric and whose outlook is decidedly modern.

Over the course of his career, Kurosawa has benefited from long productive relationships with collaborators such as scenarists, art directors, production designers, composers, and sound specialists. One of the most fertile collaborations was with the composer Fumio Hayasaka, which began in 1948 with *Drunken Angel* and continued until his death in 1955. The essay "Working with Fumio Hayasaka" by Masaaki Tsuzuki, translated here for the first time, amply quotes Hayasaka and Kurosawa on the subject of their artistic relationship. Beyond film music, Hayasaka contributed ideas on story development, editing, performance, and audiovisual montage. Tsuzuki's essay also provides analysis of the principal musical motifs in *Seven Samurai* and of their thematic correlations to the film drama.

Barbara Wolf in "Detectives and Doctors" examines Kurosawa's *gendai-mono* from *Drunken Angel* through *Red Beard*. Each of these modern film stories entails either crime or illness as a compelling condition for characters. Each narrative is shaped as an investigation or an examination that probes beneath the prosaic and orderly appearances of modern life. The detective and doctor protagonists struggle to bring a form of redemption into a world afflicted by vice and disease. Wolf focuses on their moral, romantic revolt against the dispirited conditions of modern existence. *Red Beard* is a synthesis of these themes. The doctor Red Beard is a healer of both body and spirit whose selfless efforts instruct others in heroism. In "Kurosawa's Detective-Story Parables" Norman Silverstein draws attention to the process of moral instruction in two films, *Stray Dog* and *High and Low* (*Tengoku to Jigoku,* 1963). Silverstein proposes analogies to a variety of Western contexts, from John Milton's *Paradise Lost* to the cinema of Ingmar Bergman, in order to argue that Kurosawa has shaped two Christian parables on the triumph of good over evil.

Stanley Kauffmann, one of America's foremost film and theater critics, gives full account of the importance of *Rashomon* to film history. His essay provides the central contexts—from its place in Kurosawa's career to its reception in the West—necessary for an understanding of the film's impact. The film has many affinities with other modernist versions of relativism, such as the Japanese stories by Ryunosuke Akutagawa, on which it is based, and the theater of Pirandello. At the same time, the film possesses the immediate appeal of American popular movies in the tradition of John Ford or Frank Capra. After tracing the film's multiple versions of truth, Kauffmann identifies three intrinsic sources of its artistic power: the intensity in acting; the contrastive textures of its principal settings; and the visual momentum and mobility in the presentation of the characters' stories. The only distracting element for this critic is the choice of Ravel's *Bolero* for the soundtrack as a prominent musical motif. Kauffmann can forgive this lapse in light of the film's visual and narrative integrity and of the honesty and seriousness in its themes.

For André Bazin, who remains since his death in 1958 one of the most influential figures in film criticism, the example of *Rashomon* induces humility in the critic. The European debut of *Rashomon* in 1951 revealed mastery and innovation in film language from a national cinema unknown to the West. Bazin celebrates the film's assimilation of a foreign technical medium without loss to a Japanese style and worldview. He praises it further for achieving a tragic tone seldom reached in Western cinema. Bazin's admiration is tempered, however, by the intuition that this single example does not fully represent the artistry of Japanese cinema, which was as yet largely unseen by Western viewers. Indeed, the reception given to *Rashomon* would provide incentive for the exhibition of works by the masters Kenji Mizoguchi and Yasujiro Ozu in Europe and the United States during the early 1950s.

In "Kurosawa's Women," a section from Joan Mellen's book *The Waves at Genji's Door: Japan Through Its Cinema, Rashomon* and films that follow are examined for representations of gender within Japanese culture. In them, Mellen finds clichéd characterizations of women and a simplification of social issues. She concludes that the female characters fall flatly into two broad categories—angel and demon—and that only masculine passion is respected in the film stories. Elsewhere, Mellen has studied the projection of the masculine issue of moral commitment onto an epic plane in Kurosawa's cinema. The outcome of moral struggle for his epic heroes most often brings change at the individual level while failing to change society.[18]

The selection from Dennis Giles's essay "Kurosawa's Heroes" analyzes *Ikiru* for the drama of an individual's emergence into self and into action. Giles clarifies this process through references to philosophical categories of potentiality, negation, freedom, projection, and transcendence. In these contexts, the film's ethos is recognized as materialist and existential rather than idealist. In the face of his own terminal cancer, the protagonist Watanabe comes to life only by acting upon the social world, not by abstractly contemplating it. Unlike Joan Mellen, Giles believes that such representative acts of individual heroism lay a basis for social change.

While remaining somewhat cautious in his assessment of Kurosawa's true standing within world cinema, André Bazin nonetheless acknowledges the director's mastery in *Seven Samurai*. Bazin admires the ingenuity of the film's structure, the direct power of its visualizations, and a richness of detail that is novelistic in its amplitude. By comparison to John Ford's "glorious examples" of the Western, *Seven Samurai* surpasses the American genre in the epic depiction of humanity. With his essay "The Circumstance of the East, the Fate of the West," Bert Cardullo contends that the nature of conflict in *Seven Samurai* is epic without being tragic. The force of social and historical circumstances is ultimately greater than the power of individual will or action in the film. While the samurai act nobly, the changing technology of warfare clearly signals the eventual demise of the swordsman as the ideal warrior. Unlike the operation of *fate* in a tragedy, which isolates individual suffering, the course of circumstances develops collective human identity. To make such distinctions, Cardullo draws comparisons between Kurosawa's worldview and that of Shakespearean tragedy.

In his book *The Samurai Film,* Alain Silver examines the Kurosawa *jidai-geki* of the 1950s and 1960s in the context of a samurai genre. The

genre approach entails comparative study with other directors like Mizoguchi and within Kurosawa's own samurai films in order to uncover his variations and innovations with the cultural material. Kurosawa develops the
samurai's dramatic conflicts on a personal level rather than on one of social
institutions, as in the *jidai-geki* of Masaki Kobayashi. In the section
reprinted, Silver provides a reading of the iconic and symbolic codes in
Yojimbo (*Yojimbo*, 1961) and *Sanjuro* (*Tsubaki Sanjuro*, 1962) and demonstrates the samurai's heroism of negative capability and romantic alienation
in these two Kurosawa films. David Desser, in *The Samurai Films of Akira
Kurosawa* (Ann Arbor: UMI Research Press, 1983), explores an intercultural
exchange from West to East that contributes to theme and imagery in Kurosawa's *jidai-geki*. His book is particularly interested in Kurosawa's adaptation of American popular formulas to Japanese contexts.[19]

My own essay "Akira Kurosawa and the Atomic Age" turns to three *gendai-
mono* to consider Kurosawa's representations of the legacy of Japan's defeat
in 1945 through the American deployment of atomic weapons. Kurosawa first
directly engaged this issue with *Record of a Living Being* (*Ikimono no
Kiroku*, 1955) and he has returned to it recently in *Dreams* and *Rhapsody
in August*. *Record of a Living Being* is remarkable for its insights into the
social psychology of living under the cold war threats of atomic devastation.
The common acceptance of this condition in Japanese society of the 1950s
leads Kurosawa to treat the matter in a paradoxical and absurdist manner.
Two episodes in *Dreams* imagine an apocalyptic end to the atomic era when
nuclear radiation overwhelms the island nation. *Rhapsody in August* considers what legacy remains from the 1945 atomic bombs for contemporary Japan
and particularly for the youngest generation. Like *Dersu Uzala*, this film story
is concerned with the processes of memory and it is told in a reflective mode.

Noël Burch's book *To the Distant Observer: Form and Meaning in the
Japanese Cinema* (1979) reinvigorated the discussion of Japanese film in the
West and it has established new critical considerations.[20] Adopting a method-
ology of deconstructing the text drawn primarily from the critical practices of
Roland Barthes and Jacques Derrida, Burch contends that Japanese cinema in
1930–1945 perfected a unique film language that has more affinities with classical Japanese culture of the Heian era (794–1185) than with conventions of
cinema in the West. Kurosawa stands apart from this Japanese cultural heritage in having thoroughly assimilated Western modes of representation in
the narrative and visual media. In doing so, Kurosawa surpassed his models
to develop an individual style. In the reprinted discussion of *The Lower
Depths* and *Throne of Blood*, Burch offers penetrating analysis of the films'
screen geometry, narrative construction, and dramatic stylization.

In an article on the making of *Throne of Blood*, translated here for the
first time by Michael Baskett, Japanese critic Yoshio Shirai details the use of
three cameras for each shot on the film's set. A process that Kurosawa
started when he made *Seven Samurai*, the method contributes to the dis-

tinctive screen space he creates through composition and editing. In writing about his experience as a movie extra on location, Shirai also captures the director's perfectionism and the Noh tradition of "watching with a detached gaze" that Kurosawa describes in "Notes on Filmmaking."

Vernon Young, in *"The Hidden Fortress:* Kurosawa's Comic Mode," proposes a wealth of comparisons in assessing this comic, action-adventure *jidai-geki.* The film combines the immediate gratification of the Hollywood entertainment epic with the moral complexity of Joseph Conrad's fiction and the dynamic montage of Eisenstein's cinema. The film's two peasants, induced by greed to participate in the epic action, figure in the comedy as a parodic version of heroism. Young explains that Kurosawa has intensified conventional traits of the samurai genre for the purpose of representing essential traits within humanity. This vision is consistent with an ancient, philosophical tradition of comedy.

David Desser places Kurosawa's cinema within a context of traditional Japanese narrative modes in his essay "Narrating the Human Condition: *High and Low* and Story-Telling in Kurosawa's Cinema," written for this volume.[21] Desser's contextualization yields many insights into Kurosawa's experimental adaptation of story-telling traditions. In the process, Kurosawa has innovated cinematic modes of narration and has constructed an authorial identity within his own cinema. Desser concludes that the consequence of such narrative experiments is not a deconstruction of cinematic representation, as Noël Burch claims for other Japanese directors. Rather, the experiments directly render the thematic issues of ethical choice with which Kurosawa films are identified. The moral dilemma narrated in *High and Low,* Desser persuasively demonstrates, is reiterated through compositional devices of framing and perspective.

Keiko McDonald's *Cinema East* contains chapters on *Rashomon, Throne of Blood,* and "Images of Son and Superhero in Kurosawa's *Red Beard,"* the one reprinted for this volume.[22] McDonald focuses on Kurosawa's expression of social and moral concerns. In these three films, according to her thesis, Kurosawa constructs the narrative so as to explore a problem central in a general definition of human nature and to dramatize an individual's choice of action in defining the meaning of his own existence. Through a careful study of visual composition and character types, McDonald explains the ways in which *Red Beard* prescribes heroic altruism as a course of action. In the heroic doctor and *sensei* Red Beard she finds, as Tadao Sato has observed in the case of early Kurosawa films, an idealized patriarch linked to a surrogate son who at first rebels.

Philip Strick, in reviewing *Dodeskaden,* remarks that Kurosawa's new film depicts social chaos without any promise of redemption at the hands of a superhero.[23] Nevertheless, the fictional slum world still contains individual, exemplary acts of compassion. The review by Strick also notes the powerful contrasts between naturalism and expressionism in Kurosawa's first uses of color for a film story. A profile of Kurosawa written by Lillian Ross for *The New Yorker* in 1981 recounts the director's concern with capturing accurately on film the specific hues and color range traditional to Japanese society.[24]

The title *Kagemusha* means literally "shadow warrior," and Marsha Kinder clarifies precisely the film's representation of double and substitute identities. To do so, her essay applies semiotics, or the science of human signs, and in particular Charles Peirce's three categories of the sign: index, icon, and symbol. Meaning in *Kagemusha* derives from the selection and interaction of semiotic relationships among these three types. Political events are directed by the ruler's control over cultural signs; when sovereign control is lost, disorder and defeat ensue. The narrative alternates between scenes of action and scenes of interpretation. The viewer's experience of the film is inseparable from a reflexive process of signification that occurs both in a dimension of historical representation and in one of the film work's own creation.

For Frances M. Malpezzi and William M. Clements, in their essay "The Double and the Theme of Selflessness in *Kagemusha*," the film's major theme lies in a conflict between individual will and social responsibility. They find that the film contrasts a Western narrative pattern of personality formation and individual identity with a characteristic Japanese ethic of self-sacrifice. While the warlord's son exemplifies the first pattern, the thief who doubles for the warlord embarks upon a course of action that leads to fulfillment of a heroic ideal of selflessness. This shadow warrior's experience reveals that the individual's social role possesses more value and meaning than any act of self-assertion. Loss of self serves a greater good: integration of the social whole.

Pauline Kael, when she reviewed *Kagemusha* for *The New Yorker*, maintained that the film fails in its epic purpose because of its contradictory effect as "a movie about immobility." She termed the work "a schoolmaster's fable" on account of what she perceived as its detached tone, static and ceremonial pace, and lifeless formalism.[25] Kael evaluated *Kagemusha*'s view of history as merely aesthetic and abstract, particularly in comparison to the modernity and immediacy exemplified in *Seven Samurai* or to the satiric force of *Yojimbo*.[26] *Ran* later elicited Kael's grudging admiration: "This epic is static, but it deepens, and it has its own ornery splendor."[27] Still, she identified as a failing in *Ran* the impersonal detachment of its dramatic perspective. This quality leads to characterizations that are symbolic and generic rather than complexly human. *Ran* won her praise as a work of conceptual art, not as a historical epic.

For Jan Kott, one of our foremost commentators on Western theater from classical Greece to contemporary absurdism, *Ran* occupies a place alongside other great works of tragic art. Kott's review, reprinted in this collection, applauds the genius of Kurosawa's interpretation of Shakespeare and of his adoption of Japanese theater traditions. In the reprinted essay "*Ran* and the

Tragedy of History," Brian Parker compares Kurosawa's film with the screen adaptations of *King Lear* directed by Grigori Kozintsev and Peter Brook. While Kozintsev and Brook largely agree over a film language appropriate to the tragedy, the Soviet director interprets the play as a social parable and the British director interprets it as an existential event. *Ran* contrasts with these two interpretations by virtue of its approach to the dramatic material as a historical chronicle, and Parker invites comparisons of *Ran* to Shakespeare's history plays. In analyzing its style, his essay invokes a range of aesthetic contexts, from the musical structure of a sonata to Japanese scroll painting. On a thematic level, Parker considers the response to tragedy in *Ran* to be based in an ethos of Buddhism and *bushido,* the samurai code.

Terrence Rafferty's review of *Dreams* cautions that the film does not reveal the director's dream life or subconscious self. Instead of a confessional tone, the film possesses the solemnity of an impersonal ceremony. Of the eight episodes in *Dreams,* Rafferty judges only the first four to be worthy expressions of Kurosawa's artistic genius. These four episodes are conceived on the grand scale of his visual imagination and they are based in an immediate experience of vision rather than in moral instruction. Vincent Canby, in a review of *Rhapsody in August* from the 1991 Cannes film festival, admires the continued integrity of Kurosawa's style and outlook. *Rhapsody in August* considers the effects of the Nagasaki atomic bomb through a method of indirection and reflection rather than through any re-creation or images of the catastrophe. Canby praises the director's austere treatment of his subject matter, which avoids concessions to sentimental identification.

The five reprinted essays that conclude this volume provide overviews of the important thematic, stylistic, and structural properties that distinguish the cinema of Akira Kurosawa. In "Zen and Selfhood: Patterns of Eastern Thought in Kurosawa's Films," Stephen Prince examines the director's rejection of the social norms that sustain Japan's feudal heritage. On the one hand, Kurosawa's story pattern of the individual's heroic confrontation with forces of reaction and oppression is a familiar plot for Western audiences. On the other, his characterization of the samurai warrior in terms of a selfless ideal is based in Zen Buddhist precepts. In the way of Zen, knowledge is acquired through action. The goal of personal conduct and the ideal of beauty become one in a reverence for nature and a desire for harmony. The role of the Zen master is not to instruct directly but to point out a path toward self-discovery. Prince concludes that the connections of Kurosawa's themes to Zen thought are ultimately dialectical. While they draw upon the above principles, his themes contest other Zen precepts such as passivity and resignation in the face of fate. Prince's essay also contains a detailed explanation of how Kurosawa's moral concepts are given form through his camera and editing styles.

The selection "Method, Technique, and Style" is excerpted from Donald Richie's book *The Films of Akira Kurosawa,* which from the time of its first publication in 1965 established the standard for auteur treatment of Kurosawa. Auteur criticism, in its most basic form, maintains that the film director devotes a career to creating variations on an essential, integral concept and vision. Richie applies this premise in asserting: "All Kurosawa films are about the same thing:... character revelation." His study focuses on *bushido*, the way of the samurai, as the unifying principle in Kurosawa's life and cinema. Accordingly, Richie discusses each film in terms of the shared attributes of an ethos of action, a humane recognition of man's imperfections, a passion for reality, and an intolerance for illusion. Unity of form is evident to Richie through the distinctive stylistic traits in Kurosawa's story structure, compositional geometry, and editing rhythm.

With "Akira Kurosawa," Noël Burch resumes his critique of the emphasis in film commentary on artistic technique as merely a mode for the transmission of themes and values—on form as the servant of content, in other words. Burch makes an unexpected correlation between the cinema of Kurosawa and that of Eisenstein in their emphases on the discontinuous properties of the shot-change. During the 1940s Kurosawa mastered the transparent style in shot construction and editing common to cinema in the West. *Rashomon* and *Ikiru* mark a shift in his filmmaking practices of the 1950s toward an obvious disclosure of formal devices such as the shot's frameline and editing construction. Burch values the films' contradiction of any normative assumptions that formal properties only function in service to other orders of meaning on narrative, dramatic, or thematic levels. "Textual awareness" is as important to an understanding of Kurosawa's cinema as are humanist messages. Such textuality is apparent in the hard-edge wipe, which Kurosawa often uses as a transitional sign in preference to the dissolve, a relatively unnoticeable editing device. For films Kurosawa made in 1950–1963, turning points in the dramatic structure are often visibly marked by textual interventions such as the wipe cut.

Gilles Deleuze, in his books *Cinema 1: The Movement-Image* and *Cinema 2: The Time-Image*, adapts Henri Bergson's ideas on perception and Peirce's categories of the sign for his own philosophical investigation into film structure.[28] The reprinted excerpt "Figures, or the Transformation of Forms" concerns the distinctive visual images and narrative discourse of Kurosawa's cinema. Deleuze finds his shot compositions of lateral movement to be so singular as to constitute the director's "personal signature." The compositions are also a configuration that reiterates Kurosawa's thematic preoccupation with life at the high and low reaches of society. Deleuze recognizes a remarkable affinity of Kurosawa to Dostoevsky in the representation of the interrelation between situation and action as an urgent, profound matter.[29] For both artists, a story's momentum traces the process of a protagonist's immersion in a situation and his engagement with an issue much larger than the initial situation itself. In closing, Deleuze's essay differentiates Kurosawa's almost exclusively masculine world from the feminine universe created in the cinema of Mizoguchi.

Stephen Prince's *The Warrior's Camera: The Cinema of Akira Kurosawa* greatly extends our understanding of the worldview developed in the films. From Prince's perspective, Kurosawa's career in cinema developed as a cultural project influenced by the forces of transformation in Japanese society since World War II. The structural dynamic that underlies visual form and narrative treatment among the films over his career is the evolution of a cinema that is both politically engaged and popular. In the reprinted section, Prince starts from *Something Like an Autobiography* as he seeks the cultural sources for Kurosawa's ideal of the warrior spirit, with its qualities of discipline, honor, and stoicism.[30] Moving beyond an obvious level of individual heroism, Prince traces the films' compelling relation of self to the human nexus back to roots in Buddhist thought.

Akira Kurosawa's films frequently dramatize a process of inner awakening and enlightenment. When asked to reflect on his life in film, Kurosawa often refers to this process. In accepting the 1990 Academy Award for life achievement, for example, he remarked that the honor comes too early in his career for he is still in the learning stages of his art. Through further work in cinema, he explained, "I will continue to devote my entire being to understanding this wonderful art." In this statement, made without false humility at age eighty, Kurosawa expresses the belief that filmmaking is his path toward knowledge. The reflections, tributes, and commentaries gathered in this book increase our understanding of the engaging and enduring search for knowledge Akira Kurosawa has created through his films.

Notes

1. The biographical and cultural contexts to Kurosawa's cinema are examined at length in my book *Akira Kurosawa and Intertextual Cinema* (Baltimore: Johns Hopkins University Press, 1994), from which I draw some material for this Introduction.

2. Akira Kurosawa, *Something Like an Autobiography,* trans. Audie E. Bock (New York: Vintage, 1983), 73–74; hereafter cited in the text.

3. Quoted in Donald Richie, *The Films of Akira Kurosawa,* rev. ed. (Berkeley: University of California Press, 1984), 227.

4. Yoshio Shirai, "John Ford to Kurosawa Akira" ("John Ford and Akira Kurosawa"), *Kinema Jumpo,* April 1963, special issue *Kurosawa Akira: Sono Sakuhin to Kao* (Akira Kurosawa: His Films and Face): 84–85.

5. Quoted in Richie, *Films of Kurosawa,* 222.

6. Quoted in Peter Grilli, "Civil Samurai," *Film Comment* 20, no. 4 (July-August 1984): 66.

7. Quoted in "An Out-of-Control Train Courtesy of Kurosawa," *New York Times,* 29 November 1985, C 8.

8. Quoted in *Kurosawa Eiga no Bijutsu* (Kurosawa's Film Art) (Tokyo: Gakushu Kenkyusha, 1985), 10.

9. Quoted in Elaine Dutka, "Lawrence Kasdan's Grand Balancing Act," *Los Angeles Times,* 24 December 1991, F 5.

10. Jonas Mekas, "Movie Journal," *Village Voice,* 8 February 1962, 11.

11. Jonas Mekas, "Movie Journal," *Village Voice,* 25 October 1962, 13.

12. From Chris Marker's narration to *A. K.,* first published in *Positif,* no. 296 (octobre 1985): 50–51; translation by James Goodwin.

13. Ibid., 52.

14. "The Conversation: Kurosawa and García Márquez," *Los Angeles Times Calendar,* 23 June 1991, 28.

15. Ibid., 29.

16. Another version of this interview is translated and published in Roger Manvell, *Shakespeare and the Film* (London: Dent and Sons, 1971), 102–4.

17. Audie Bock, "The Moralistic Cinema of Kurosawa," in *Kurosawa: Perceptions on Life, An Anthology of Essays,* ed. Kevin K. W. Chang (Honolulu: Honolulu Academy of Arts, 1991), 16–23.

18. Joan Mellen, "The Epic Cinema of Kurosawa," *Take One* 3, no. 4 (March-April 1971): 16–19.

19. Two articles draw specific comparisons between the Hollywood Western genre and Kurosawa's samurai films: Joseph L. Anderson, "Japanese Swordfighters and American Gunfighters," *Cinema Journal* 12, no. 2 (Spring 1973): 1–21; and David Desser, "Kurosawa's Eastern 'Western': *Sanjuro* and the Influence of *Shane,*" *Film Criticism* 8, no. 1 (Fall 1983): 54–65.

20. The critical discussion initiated by Burch's book is represented by David Bordwell, "Our Dream Cinema: Western Historiography and the Japanese Film," *Film Reader,* no. 4 (1979): 45–62; Robert Cohen, "Towards a Theory of Japanese Narrative," *Quarterly Review of Film Studies* 6, no. 2 (Spring 1981): 181–200; and Scott L. Malcomson, "The Pure Land Beyond the Seas: Barthes, Burch and the Uses of Japan," *Screen* 26, no. 3–4 (May-August 1985): 23–33.

21. His essay adapts some material from the previous publication, David Desser, "Narrating the Human Condition: *High and Low* and the Dilemma of Personal Responsibility," in *Kurosawa: Perceptions on Life,* 6–15.

22. Keiko I. McDonald, *Cinema East: A Critical Study of Major Japanese Films* (Rutherford, N.J.: Fairleigh Dickinson University Press, 1983).

23. For other perspectives on *Dodeskaden,* see the *Cinema* (Los Angeles) 7, no. 2 (Spring 1972) issue, which contains an interview with Kurosawa, 14–17; Masahiro Ogi, "Kurosawa, *Dodeskaden* and Japanese Culture," trans. Haruji Nakamura and Leonard Schrader, 18–19; and Joan Mellen, "*Dodeskaden:* A Renewal," 20–22.

24. Lillian Ross, "Kurosawa Frames," *The New Yorker,* 21 December 1981, 51–78.

25. Pauline Kael, "Victims," *The New Yorker,* 2 February 1981, 88–95.

26. For her laudatory reviews of these two earlier films see Pauline Kael, *I Lost It at the Movies* (Boston: Little, Brown, 1965), 119–24, 239–45.

27. Pauline Kael, "Macro, Micro, Stinko," *The New Yorker,* 13 January 1986, 64–68. A similar assessment of *Ran* is made in Stanley Kauffmann, "A Grand Finale," *The New Republic,* 6–13 January 1986, 26–28.

28. Gilles Deleuze, *Cinema 1: The Movement Image,* trans. Hugh Tomlinson and Barbara Habberjam (Minneapolis: University of Minnesota Press, 1986); *Cinema 2: The Time Image,* trans. Hugh Tomlinson and Robert Galeta (Minneapolis: University of Minnesota Press, 1989).

29. An early comparative study of the two artists is Donald Richie, "Dostoevsky with a Japanese Camera," in *The Emergence of Film Art,* ed. Lewis Jacobs (New York: Hopkinson and Blake, 1969), 328–35.

30. Linda Ehrlich, "Kurosawa's Fragile Heroes: Another Look at the *Tateyaku*," in *Kurosawa: Perceptions on Life*, 34–45, finds the subtext of a survivor mentality within Kurosawa's idealized male characters.

FILM ARTISTS ON KUROSAWA

Seven Samurai

TONY RICHARDSON

I N *The Seven Samurai,* and in the light it throws back on *Rashomon,* Kurosawa's method and personality emerge clearly. He is, above everything else, an exact psychological observer, a keen analyst of behaviour—in a fundamentally detached way. His handling of the young lovers is typical of this. He notes and traces with precision and truth their first, half-terrified awareness of each other sexually, the growth of mutual attraction, the boy's *gauche* admiration, the girl's aching and almost frantic abandonment; what he fails to do is to convey any feeling for, or identification with, the individuals themselves. . . .

In this it is not unrewarding to compare Kurosawa with [John] Ford—by whom, report has it, he claims to have been influenced. There are many superficial resemblances—the reliance on traditional values, the use of folk ceremonies and rituals, the comic horseplay—to Ford in particular and to the Western in general. The fast, vivid handling of the action sequences, the staccato cutting, the variety of angles, the shooting up through horses rearing in the mud, are all reminiscent of recent films in this genre. But the difference is more revealing. The funeral of the first samurai, killed in a preliminary skirmish, is exactly the sort of scene to which Ford responds, with all his reverence and honour for times past and the community of beliefs and feeling which they embodied. Kurosawa uses the scene in two ways, first as a further observation of the character of the "crazy samurai"—who, in a defiant attempt to satisfy his own feelings of frustration and impotence, raises the flag the dead man has sewn—and secondly, as an effective incident for heightening the narrative tension: the bandits launch their first onslaught during the funeral. One of the love scenes is used in a similar way, and in both cases one feels an ultimate shying-away from any direct, committed emotion—except anger.

Of course, to say Kurosawa is not Ford is critically meaningless; the comparison has value only in so far as it is a way of gauging the film's intentions, and its realization of them. What made *Rashomon* so unique and impressive was that everything, the subject, the formal structure, the playing, even perhaps the period, allowed for this exterior approach to behaviour. In *The Seven Samurai* Kurosawa is striving for something different, a re-creation, a bringing to life of the past and the people whose story he is telling. . . .

Excerpted and reprinted from *Sight and Sound* 24, no. 4 (Spring 1955): 195–96, by permission.

Kurosawa is a virtuoso exponent of every technique of suspense, surprise, excitement, and in this he gives nothing to his Western masters. Only in his handling of the series of battles is there a hint of monotony. He knows exactly when to hold a silence; how to punch home an extraordinary fact with maximum effect; and his use of the camera is devastating—dazzling close-ups as the village deputation, overawed and desperate in their quest for samurai, scan the crowded street, or wild tracking shots as the drunken Mifune stumbles after his assailant. Visually the film makes a tremendous impression. Kurosawa can combine formal grace with dramatic accuracy, and many scenes create a startling pictorial impact. The raid on the bandits' hideout, when their slaughtered bodies are hurled, naked and haphazard, into the muddied pools outside their burning hut, is not unworthy of the Goya of *Los Desatres*. The final effect indeed of *The Seven Samurai* is not unlike that of *Salammbo* [a historical novel by Gustave Flaubert, published in 1862], a triumph of rage and artifice; and one's final acknowledgement is not of the intrinsic fascination of the material but the wrested skill of the artificer.

[*Ikiru*]

LINDSAY ANDERSON

I⊤ ɪꜱ in the work of these Japanese directors that we see at its richest and most developed a conception of cinema where the relationship of the artist to his public is far nearer that of the novelist to his reader than that of the *metteur-en-scène* to his audience. This is not quite the same thing as being "literary." Imagine, when you have seen *Ugetsu Monogatari* or *Chika-matsu Monogatari*, an *Anna Karenina* filmed by Mizoguchi. It is not merely that he is a finer artist than the Western directors who have taken the subject; it is that the method, the *wholeness* of his vision can create a whole world, in which detail and atmosphere are as significant (contribute as much to the "movement") as the characters-in-action, the plot.

Probably of all these directors, Kurosawa is the most Western in his attitude—one might almost say the most modern (without implying that the others are old-fashioned in any pejorative sense). And presumably this is why he has been the first to become anything like a celebrity in Europe. But his *Ikiru [Living]...* comes as a fascinating revelation after the more brilliantly-surfaced *Rashomon* and *Seven Samurai*. It is a modern story, and we start simply, directly, without dramatisation. The screen is filled with an X-ray photograph of the principal character's chest. He has got cancer, a voice tells us. And we see him, an elderly, desiccated little man, a civil servant, sitting behind his desk, methodically applying his seal to a pile of papers—which obviously arouse in him not the slightest attention or interest. Deliberately and in detail this man's situation and story are explored....

What is richly suggestive is the whole method of the film; the bare force of its style, the awareness and relevance of a whole social background, the edge and sharpness of its characterisation. Perhaps most striking is Kurosawa's conception for the last half of the picture. Instead of being recounted as a straight narrative, the process of the park's construction (naturally, once it is completed everyone gets the credit for it except the true originator) is pieced together in flashbacks from the dead man's funeral, where his family, colleagues, and superiors sit ceremoniously together, discussing him in varying terms of hypocrisy, misunderstanding, or (in one case only) sympathy. Here Kurosawa's clear-sighted, analytical view of human nature is at its most telling, and the deliberate, piecemeal tempo at which the reconstruction is taken is completely at variance with conventional ideas of "How to Construct a Screenplay." In comparison with *Living*, in fact, *Umberto D.* seems

---

Excerpted and reprinted from "Two Inches off the Ground," *Sight and Sound* 27, no. 3 (Winter 1957–1958): 131–33, 160, by permission.

29

hardly experimental at all. It is almost incredible that films of this serious-ness and weight can be produced within the framework of a commercial industry. Too often, it is clear, the cinema is credited with limitations which are in fact not the limitations of the medium at all, but simply the limita-tions of the cultures within which western film-makers have had to work.

[Shakespeare and Kurosawa]

PETER BROOK

THE SAD history of Shakespeare on the screen—which is really pretty pitiful if you think about it—is that apparently over a hundred films have
been made of his plays, and most of them are unspeakably bad. What this
sad history does is to recapture some of the history of Shakespeare on the
stage through its worst periods. There is no golden beginning in the Elizabethan theatre: you start in the worst nineteenth century tradition of big
spectacle. It's incredible the number of Shakespeare subjects that were used
between 1900 and 1910, all because they gave the opportunity for the cinema
to show that you could have crowds of people, masses of costumes, great
epic shots, and so forth.

Then they moved on to Recording the Star Performance. So one has films
designed to show off people like Barrymore, Bernhardt, Forbes-Robertson.
These are recordings of big actors' solos, following the nineteenth century
idea that there are these big moments in Shakespeare, and therefore—
wrong conclusion—that this is what Shakespeare is all about. . . .

It was exactly the same in the cinema. The producers looked for the big
situations, and between the wars the cinema was dominated by big stars
who all wanted to crown their careers with prestige, and all had a go at
Shakespeare: Douglas Fairbanks, Mary Pickford, Elisabeth Bergner, Leslie
Howard, Norma Shearer. Again it's mid-nineteenth century acting, by sec-
ond-rate, well-loved actors who want a go at the big parts. Artistically, it's
not worth considering. . . .

The great masterpiece, of course, is the Kurosawa film, *Throne of Blood,*
which doesn't really come into the Shakespeare question at all because it
doesn't have the text. Even though Kurosawa follows the plot very closely,
transposing it into Japan in the Middle Ages and making Macbeth a samurai,
he has new Japanese dialogue and is really doing another *Seven Samurai.* It
doesn't matter where the story comes from: he is doing what every filmmaker has always done, which is to construct a film out of an idea and get
the appropriate dialogue to go with it. It doesn't tackle the problem of how
you make a film of Shakespeare which is a movie and yet uses the fact that
you've got a text which is continually changing gear.

The problem in filming Shakespeare is, how can you change gears, fluc-
tuate between gears, styles, and conventions as lightly and as deftly as the
mental processes inside a person, which can be reflected by blank verse but

Excerpted and reprinted from Peter Brook, interviewed by Geoffrey Reeves, "Shakespeare on
Three Screens," *Sight and Sound* 34, no. 2 (Spring 1965): 66–70, by permission.

not by the consistency of each single image? It is the same problem that every film-maker has to face in relation to all filming now, thirty-five years after the invention of sound. Sound stopped the cinema right in its tracks. People thought at the time that it took away the mobility of the camera. Well, very rapidly they found a way back to the full mobility of the camera, but the mobility of *thought,* which the silent cinema had, is only just being recaptured in the cinema.

[Shakespeare and Kurosawa]

PETER HALL

IT'S TRUE that Shakespeare's structural rhythms, the counterpoint between scenes, often work in the same way as good film editing. But in a more important respect, Shakespeare is no screen writer. He is a verbal dramatist, relying on the associative and metaphorical power of words. Action is secondary. What is meant is said. Even his stage action is verbalized before or after the event.

This is bad screen writing. A good filmscript relies on contrasting visual images. What is spoken is of secondary importance. And so potent is the camera in convincing us that we are peering at reality, that dialogue is best under-written or elliptical.

There have been some great Shakespeare films. But it is interesting to study how much text they have jettisoned in order to reach the cinema. . . .

The pressure on the filmmaker is to convey pictures rather than words, and the one precludes the other. Not only do they conflict; there isn't time for both. Olivier's battle of Agincourt; Orson Welles riding across Macbeth's misty moors; the Russian Hamlet striding through the well-boned court—these are what the filmgoer remembers. The directors have in fact set out to capture the general image of the play, its story and its mood, with a deliberate simplification of the text. From this point of view, perhaps the most successful Shakespeare film ever made was the Japanese Macbeth, *Throne of Blood*. This had hardly any words, and none of them by Shakespeare.

Excerpted and reprinted from "Why the Fairies Have Dirty Faces," *The Sunday Times* (London), 26 January 1969, 55, by permission of the author.

Mifune Talks: A Story of a Man Called Red Beard

TOSHIRO MIFUNE

I FIRST met Mr. Kurosawa at a pre-screening of *To the End of the Silver Mountains* (*Ginrei no Hate*, 1947). The director was Senkichi Taniguchi and Kurosawa was the screenwriter and editor. During location shooting I kept getting orders to retake certain scenes and add other ones—all from Kurosawa, who was doing the editing as we filmed. I remember thinking that he was a man of many orders. . . .

Finally with *The Drunken Angel* (1948) we were able to do our first job together. Since that time we have had a long acquaintance of over fifteen years. For myself, I don't really recognize any changes in him. Other than during filming, Kurosawa isn't the type of person who tediously gives advice to people. However, because he can really cut you to the core with just one or two words, it can really affect those who are on the receiving end. Young actresses are usually the ones most affected.

As for direction, since we do so many rehearsals there aren't so many problems, but we are people and he is a person so inevitably there are going to be points of difference with the director in interpretation. But, since it is only right for an actor to adjust to the director's way with his own, this is a situation where we have to compromise.

However, even with the long shooting period, the many rehearsals, the multiple cameras and all, the production proceeds one cut by one cut. If Kurosawa wasn't in charge of everything, he couldn't stand it. But, I often think that if he doesn't delegate some of the responsibility he physically won't be able to last. Actually, part of the way into this film [*Red Beard*] he made himself sick. But that is Kurosawa's good point; bringing the sense of responsibility to a point of beauty. Especially now that he has become the "international" Kurosawa in both name and fact, he is alone in the world. Matters have reached the level where he cannot overlook one small prop or the movement of one supporting actor. On this point, I feel that I would like to direct someday to find out just how demanding a job being a director is, and also to understand some of Kurosawa's suffering. If you have to do all of that, being an actor is far easier.

This time we were able to finish up *Red Beard,* and in making any good film the staff has to become a circle, each person must fulfill his part sufficiently. If they do, the center (the director) will pull everything together, and if we can make a good film, the people will come to see it. Holding this conviction is important to doing anything, for us and for all people, I think.

Translated by Michael Baskett for this volume from "Mifune Toshiro wa Kataru: Satsuei Genba de Jitakude Shaberu Akahige to yu Otoko no Hanashi," *Kinema Jumpo,* 5 September 1964 (special issue no. 10): 93–95. Printed by permission of *Kinema Jumpo* and Toshiro Mifune.

[Akira Kurosawa]

SATYAJIT RAY

THE EFFECT of [*Rashomon*] on me, personally, was electric. I saw it three times on consecutive days and wondered each time if there was another film anywhere which gave such sustained and dazzling proof of a director's command over every aspect of film making. Even after fifteen years, whole chunks of the film come vividly back to mind in all their visual and aural richness: the woodcutter's journey through the forest, shot with a relentless tracking camera from an incredible variety of angles—high, low, back, and front—and cut with axe-edge precision; the bandit's first sight of the woman as she rides by, her veil lifted momentarily by a breeze, while he lolls in the shade of a tree, slapping away at mosquitoes; the striking formality of the court scene with the judge never seen at all; the scene of witchcraft with the medium whirling in a trance, and the wind blowing from two opposite directions at the same time. . . .

"I am the kind of person," says Kurosawa, "that works violently, throwing myself into it. I also like hot summers, cold winters, heavy rains and snows, and I think most of my pictures have that. I like extremes because I find them most alive."

This seems to me the direct opposite of Ozu and Mizoguchi. But this does not necessarily make Kurosawa less Japanese. As even a cursory study of their history shows, the Japanese are by no means a simple people lending themselves to easy categorization. Contradictory traits abound. The national character reveals markedly militarist tendencies throughout history, although the arts have all along maintained a serenity achieved through a rigid formalism. . . .

Even the lesser works of Kurosawa show a grasp of technique which is truly astonishing. He is, first, of all, a master of cutting. "For me," says Kurosawa, "shooting only means getting something to edit." While we need not take this as literally true, Kurosawa's very method of shooting suggests his deep concern about continuity (the "flowing quality," as Kurosawa says) in both its physical and emotional aspects. He shoots his films in sequence—an expensive procedure which few directors can afford. He also shoots with multiple cameras—another expensive method—which automatically solves some of the more taxing continuity problems. His sound track—always composed with meticulous care—also adds to the feeling of fluency.

Excerpted and reprinted from *Our Films, Their Films* (Calcutta: Orient Longman Limited, 1976), 180–83, 185, by permission of the publisher.

[The Greatness of Cinema]

GRIGORI KOZINTSEV

K UROSAWA'S *The Idiot,* I thought, was a miraculous transformation of a classic on to the screen. Dostoevsky's pages came to life, words—the subtlest definitions—took shape. I saw Rogozhin's eyes on the screen, wild flaming, burning coals of fire—exactly the eyes that Dostoevsky described.

But Toshiro Mifune (the actor who played Rogozhin) had slanting eyes. And the action of the film takes place in contemporary Japan. Everything is different. A steamer instead of a train, a buddha instead of a cross, every custom is typical of another people, bearing no resemblance to Russia.

And indeed at first, when the first shots appeared, I was half amazed, half embarrassed: how unfamiliar it all was. Whatever anyone says, we all watch foreign productions of Russian classics with suspicion. Or at least we watch them with suspicion to start with. But I soon forgot about the way of life; the facial characteristics of another race became normal.... I found myself in Dostoevsky's world, among his heroes; this was the complex and fantastic collection of his characters—their strange encounters and partings; it was all outwardly different and yet completely the same in its inner action, the same world that the author created....

What did Kurosawa manage to grasp which was fundamental, much more important than the external objects, and why was it he and he alone who succeeded in overcoming this difficult problem? He was able to express on screen that "fantastic reality" about which the author wrote so persistently.

Here all the external details were different and yet they reminded one of the core of the work, the link between one thing and another. The life of the film contained at the same time a contemporary reality, and a kind of ancient religious element, the strange peace of Prince Myshkin's spiritual world, and Rogozhin's inflamed conscience....

The Russian classics have influenced much of Kurosawa's work. I do not just mean the production of *The Idiot, The Lower Depths,* but other films as well. In *Ikiru* ... it is not difficult to find a similarity between the mummy-like official and Gogol's Bashmachkin, [and] traits from *The Death of Ivan Ilych.*

Kurosawa is perhaps one of the most daring innovators. He has not been afraid to refute everything that was considered to be the basis of cinematographic art. In *Throne of Blood,* ... taken from the story of *Macbeth,* he

---

Excerpted and reprinted from *King Lear: The Space of Tragedy,* trans. Mary Mackintosh (Berkeley: University of California Press, 1977), 9–11, by permission of the Copyright Agency of Russia.

refused to have any close-ups. The most tragic scenes were taken in long shots; the actors sat for a long time in silence on mats. The décor was sometimes no more than a patch of mould on a paper wall. The Noh Theater had migrated to the screen: Lady Macbeth was made up like a mask; the actors' walk made one think of the ritual step; the movement of fingers like a dance; the asymmetrical arrangement of figures on the bare stage—the style itself belonged to ancient times.

But when the samurai horses burst out of the mist and one saw the ferocious eyes and black threatening weapons—the signs of death and the signs of greatness, and the fighters circled round the same place eight times, powerless to break out of the mist—one caught one's breath at the greatness of Shakespeare and at the same time the greatness of cinema.

Sculpting in Time

ANDREY TARKOVSKY

I WANT to make the point yet again that in film, every time, the first essential in any plastic composition, its necessary and final criterion, is whether it is true to life, specific and factual; that is what makes it unique. By contrast, symbols are born, and readily pass into general use to become clichés, when an author hits upon a particular plastic composition, ties it in with some mysterious turn of thought of his own, loads it with extraneous meaning.

The purity of cinema, its inherent strength, is revealed not in the symbolic aptness of images (however bold these may be) but in the capacity of those images to express a specific, unique, actual fact.

A shot from *The Seven Samurai.* A medieval Japanese village. A fight is going on between some horsemen and the samurai who are on foot. It is pouring with rain, there is mud everywhere. The samurai wear an ancient Japanese garment which leaves most of the leg bare, and their legs are plastered with mud. And when one samurai falls down dead we see the rain washing away the mud and his leg becoming white, as white as marble. A man is dead; that is an image which is a fact. It is innocent of symbolism, and that is an image.

Excerpted and reprinted from *Sculpting in Time: Reflections on the Cinema,* trans. Kitty Hunter-Blair (Austin: University of Texas Press, 1989), 72–73, courtesy of Random House, Inc., copyright © 1989.

Kurosawa and *Ran*

GEORGE LUCAS

ONE OF my favorites among Kurosawa films is *Seven Samurai.* It was the first Kurosawa film I had seen. It was a long time ago when I started learning film-making at school. I've seen it many, many times since, and it was an extremely powerful film. It was a powerful experience for me. I'd never seen films like that before in my life, and it was a profound experience. It was one thing when I saw a real film, and this was really exquisite film-making, and I knew enough about film-making at that point to appreciate it.

As a film-maker Kurosawa is a genius. As a man, he is a wonderfully nice man to be around, very funny, and a very good human being.

When you are ready to make films, better than the last one, then you look at the master, and Kurosawa is very definitely one of the masters. More than anything else, he is inspirational; he makes you want to make movies.

I think the costumes in Kurosawa's new film, *Ran,* are gorgeous. There's no question that this kind of attention to detail that Kurosawa puts into a movie is almost a lost art. There are very few film-makers nowadays who are able to command the resources or to insist on the attention to detail that Kurosawa does. As a result we get these very very beautiful costumes. They say that only in Hollywood in the thirties and forties could they spend this much time and money and attention on that kind of detail. So, I'd say, in that sense, too, that it's pretty rewarding to see that happen again. Besides Kurosawa only David Lean and Stanley Kubrick could do this.

Reprinted from *Kurosawa Eiga no Bijutsu* [Kurosawa's Film Art] (Tokyo: Gakushu Kenkyusha, 1985), 14, by permission of the publisher and George Lucas.

Kurosawa, My Teacher

STEVEN SPIELBERG

M Y FIRST encounter with a Kurosawa film was *Throne of Blood.* In my opinion the film's power lies in its nobility, and the arrangement of beautiful images.

Akira Kurosawa is the most exquisite gift Japanese culture has given the world of motion picture lovers. His appeal is crosscultural. He celebrates mankind as heroes and villains and does this with a rare compassion that has won the respect of film-makers in every country on this planet.

Out of all the Kurosawa films, the best three would be: *The Hidden Fortress, Throne of Blood,* and *Ikiru.*

What I expect from his works are: beauty, agony, love of life, loss of life, rebirth, lessons learned, betrayal, visual metaphors, action, sweep, epic scope, delicate nuance, dreams, nightmares, children, wisdom, doom, and hope.

My message to Akira Kurosawa is: Please never stop teaching us. Retire at one hundred.

Reprinted from *Kurosawa Eiga no Bijutsu* [Kurosawa's Film Art] (Tokyo: Gakushu Kenkyusha, 1985), 18, by permission of the publisher and Steven Spielberg.

Honorary Academy Award to Akira Kurosawa

STEVEN SPIELBERG AND GEORGE LUCAS

STEVEN SPIELBERG: This year the Academy's Board of Governors has voted an Honorary Award to a man who many of us believe is our greatest living filmmaker, and all of us know is one of the few true visionaries ever to work in our medium. Akira Kurosawa has made 27 films in his 47 years as a director. Among them, such indisputable classics as *Rashomon, Ikiru, Throne of Blood, Seven Samurai,* and *Ran.*

GEORGE LUCAS: Someone once asked Mr. Kurosawa if his movies have a common theme. His answer was that they ask the common question: why can't people be happier together? He has put that question in contemporary terms, and in films of epic historical sweep. But [he has] always answered it in a way that intensifies and finally transforms our shared human reality into a thing of awesome and often tragic beauty.

AKIRA KUROSAWA [assisted by translator Audie Bock]: I am very deeply honored to receive such a wonderful prize. But I have to ask whether I really deserve it... I'm a little worried. Because I don't feel that I understand cinema yet. I really don't feel that I have yet grasped the essence of cinema. Cinema is a marvelous thing, but to grasp its true essence is very, very difficult. But what I promise you is that from now on I will work as hard as I can at making movies, and maybe by following this path I will achieve an understanding of the true essence of cinema and earn this award. George— Steven— Thank you.

Presented at the 62nd Academy Awards (for 1989). © Copyright Academy of Motion Pictures Arts and Sciences, 1990. Used with permission.

A Tribute to Akira Kurosawa

STUART BAIRD

AKIRA KUROSAWA . . . supremely stylish, technically a master of the medium, but above all a great storyteller of humanity and compassion; for me his name conjures up, as few others, everything that the cinema can and should be.

Although wonderfully entertaining, there is nothing trivial or small about a Kurosawa film. He aims high and even his more obviously commercial films, such as *Yojimbo* and *Sanjuro,* remain a celebration of Kurosawa's values. The heroes in his films are modest men who uncompromisingly search for personal enlightenment and self-knowledge. Reflecting those heroes, Kurosawa has consistently and fearlessly traveled the same path.

As one who believes in the value of cinema, and who also believes in the positive virtues of the human spirit, how can I not stand in awe before the creator of *Rashomon, Ikiru, The Seven Samurai, Throne of Blood, The Bad Sleep Well, High and Low, Red Beard, Dersu Uzala,* and *Ran?* Kurosawa's life's work is an inspiration, a testament to the human spirit, a celebration of humanity as well as the cinema. I admire him not because of his ability to create an image that will live in the mind's eye forever, such as the image of the blind man tapping his way on the three-sided precipice at the end of *Ran;* nor for his skill to track and zoom and pace and cut these images into fireworks of dynamic filmmaking that are unsurpassed in all of cinema, as in the battle sequences in *The Seven Samurai;* nor for his ability to invent camera moves of scintillating excitement, such as the accelerating tracking shot through heavy foreground that suddenly is pulled to a jarring halt, choreographed to the drama of the action; nor because he *never* forgets the wide shot in his films, with the landscape and changing elements always a presence; no, not because of the wonderful vocabulary of filmmaking skills that Kurosawa wields so magically in all his films, but because it is wielded so tactfully, with such integrity. No cheap tricks for him, but a subjugation of technique in service of his story and his characters—and such characters! He loves people, he loves humanity, and his films celebrate this. There is nothing nihilistic or pessimistic in a Kurosawa film. I feel better about being a human being after seeing his films, but not in a sentimentally Capra-esque way. Even in *Ran,* which means "chaos" and may seem pervaded by a sense of total despair, Kurosawa faces up to the reality he sees in today's human condition, but it is not pessimism to refuse to turn your eyes from the truth.

This tribute was written specifically for this volume and is published here for the first time with the permission of the author.

These themes can be recognized from his very first film, *Sanshiro Sugata*. It is an amazing accomplishment, in a medium that has always been more of a business than an art form, to have produced, with such consistency of vision and purpose, a body of work that has reflected his own philosophy—but to fight the good fight has not been without cost.

In Japan, he was for decades a prophet without honor. From his first international success with *Rashomon* he has been accused of directing his films toward popularity abroad—and even of betraying his own culture for this acclaim. Do we in the West admire the films of Kurosawa because they are more accessible to us than those of other Japanese directors? They do have the pace and vitality which make them certainly more palatable to Western tastes than Ozu or Mizoguchi. Possibly the strangeness and exoticism of their Japanese subjects has something to do with their popularity abroad. It is certainly the reason the Japanese critics believe he has achieved his international reputation. If so, this is only partly true. His films always deal simply and truthfully with the great puzzles of the human condition and these concerns cross all boundaries of culture and language. They stand the test of time as masterpieces of the cinema without any need to rest on the appeal of exoticism. In some ways, however, his films do seem more Western than Japanese. Kurosawa greatly admired American cinema and was influenced by its style and technique, which he has adapted to his own. He has been compared to John Ford, and indeed they have many similarities. Kurosawa admired Ford and they both express a love of people and basic human values in their films. They both had a close association with an actor who portrayed for each of them a very similar hero figure; John Wayne in Ford's case and Toshiro Mifune in Kurosawa's. They also shared a supreme talent as storytellers and a masterly visual flair for composition. Kurosawa started as a painter and his roots shine through his films. Kurosawa *designs* his films, the sets, the costumes, sometimes even the makeup of his main characters. He also always writes or co-writes his scenarios and *always* edits his own films. There is never an editor credited on a Kurosawa film. In fact, he is more renowned in Japan as the great editor than as the great director. I personally don't believe it can be said that a film is truly *directed* without a total control of the editing process. From the very first, as an assistant to the Japanese director Kajiro Yamamoto, his obsession with every detail became legendary. Kurosawa has said he sees everything in terms of cinema, and indeed he is the complete filmmaker—the credit "A Kurosawa Film" for once really has some validity. Perhaps only Chaplin has had more control over his films. As a boy, Kurosawa was brought up on silent films, and he has said he still refers back to silent movies to remind himself to eliminate any unnecessary dialogue from his own work. Together with the essential element of music, he believes that the narrative and emotions of his films should be powerfully enough expressed to be understood, as far as possible, in purely visual terms—and this is as it should be. Films began and blossomed as a new art form without need of the spoken word. They created an international language that was able to cross all cultural boundaries. It is against the masterpieces of the silent era that all films that have followed must be judged, and Kurosawa's films supremely pass this test.

In possibly the most difficult medium of all the arts for a man to express a personal vision, Kurosawa has consistently held to his own path and has never lowered his standards. During the making of *Beauty and the Beast*, Jean Cocteau wrote peevishly in his journal that "a million dollars can't be art," complaining of all the distractions and pressures of budget, schedule, and collaboration that are an inevitable part of making feature films. Even now at over eighty, Kurosawa has always had the strength of vision and purpose to overcome these obstacles and has proved Cocteau wrong many times over. There was a dark period of despair in the 1970s when he found himself totally unable to raise finances for his projects—and this prospect of life without his work drove him to attempt suicide—but thanks to the Soviet film industry and subsequently his admirers George Lucas and Francis Coppola, Kurosawa has been able to continue. The results, for me, have been some of his greatest films—the wonderful *Dersu Uzala*, followed by *Kagemusha* and *Ran*. He is for me a truly heroic figure, a true artist of the cinema, and that can be said of very few.

KUROSAWA ON KUROSAWA

[The 1930s and the 1940s]

INTERVIEW WITH TONY RAYNS

K<small>UROSAWA</small>: People sometimes speak of "apprenticeship" as a characteristic of the Japanese film system, and there may be some directors who experienced their training as such, but in my case it was emphatically not so. In the 1930s, I did work as assistant to Yamamoto Kajiro, but I was completely free to do whatever I wanted. Our relationship was less that of a teacher and pupil than that of elder and younger brothers. Yamamoto's greatness was that he tried to accept all sorts of talents. At that time, the PCL company itself was very small *(Kurosawa gestured towards the Toho Studio buildings outside the window)*—only two buildings over there, and very little ground space. The company's policy was to regard assistant directors as cadets—a kind of élite-to-be. Assistants were supposed to involve themselves in every stage of production; then they would be promoted to chief assistant, whereupon they were supposed to learn leadership, how to guide a team in one direction. A chief assistant had to do every imaginable kind of job, including that of producer.

There were two pillars in Yamamoto's training policy: scenario writing and editing. He considered that a good director must be a scenario writer too, and let me write a lot—scenarios were my main source of income. He also let me do a lot of editing; in the later part of his career, I edited almost all his films. That was immensely helpful to me.

When I worked as Yamamoto's chief assistant, I was especially impressed by his ability to direct actors—the way he'd tell them that such-and-such was right or wrong. I hardly noticed details of performance myself at the time, and began to think I lacked the capability or talent to become a director. Yamamoto reassured me. He pointed out that he'd written the scenario himself, and thus had a mental image of the whole thing—he could see it all clearly before he started. He said it was natural that I, as chief assistant, shouldn't notice such matters. I wasn't convinced at the time, but when I began directing myself, I found myself standing beside the camera saying things like "Very good, go ahead" and so on. I suddenly realised that everything was very clear to me too.... During the war years, I was mainly writing scenarios. I presented a lot of them to the company, but internal censorship was very strong, and many of my ideas were ruled out. It made me very angry, and I tried to put up a strong resistance. It was a long time before I succeeded in shooting *Sugata Sanshiro (Judo Saga)*. I didn't enjoy those

Excerpted and reprinted from "Tokyo Stories: Kurosawa," *Sight and Sound* 50, no. 3 (Summer 1981): 170–74, by permission.

struggles at the time, but, looking back, I see that they were a good preparation for later struggles against the company's money-men.

There was no freedom of expression during the war. All I could do was read books and write scenarios, without having any real outlet for my own feelings. *Dersu Uzala* was one of the ideas that came to me then. Like other ideas, it underwent a process of fermentation and maturing, rather like alcohol. Those ideas exploded once the war was over. Looking back, they were happy days. . . .

Japanese traditional culture was promoted very strongly during the war, and so there were many opportunities then for me to be exposed to the traditional arts, from theatre to painting. During those war years, when directors weren't really allowed to say anything, we used to get together to construct *haiku* poems to relieve our frustration. It's funny to look back at it, but in fact that was very helpful too. After the war, when we were free to do anything, I sat down one day to write *haiku* again, and found that I couldn't. *Haiku* can only be constructed through concentrated effort, and it was a great help to me to learn this the hard way. I think that the only way to make a successful film is to apply the same kind of very concentrated interest in one thing.

Kurosawa on Kurosawa

INTERVIEW WITH DONALD RICHIE

K UROSAWA: I remember the first time I said *cut*—it was as though it was not my own voice at all. From the second time on it was me all right. When I think of this first picture I remember most that I had a good time making it. And at this period it was hard to have a good time making films because it was wartime and you weren't allowed to say anything worth saying. Back then everyone thought that the real Japanese-style film should be as simple as possible. I disagreed and got away with disagreeing—that much I could say. Still, I was anything but sure of myself. I remember doing a scene with the heroine, Yukiko Todoroki, and we decided together how it should be done. I remember when I saw an advertisement for the novel this film *[Sanshiro Sugata]* was based on, I intuitively thought it would be right for me. When it came out I went to the producer's house and asked him to buy the rights. He did so and two days later every major studio was wanting it. It was ideal for an entertainment film and that was about all we were allowed to make back in 1943. . . .

It was from here on [1948] that the critics started calling me a "journalistic" director, meaning that I interested myself in "topical themes." Actually, I have always thought of films as a kind of journalism, if journalism means a series of happenings, usually contemporary, which can be shaped into a film. At the same time I know that a timely subject does not make an interesting film, if that is all the film has. One ought to make a film in such a way that the original idea, no matter where it comes from, remains the most important thing; and the feeling that one had at that moment of having the idea is important. Timely then, in my sense, is the opposite of sensational.

Excerpted and reprinted from *Sight and Sound* 33, no. 3 (Summer 1964): 108–13, by permission.

Something Like an Autobiography: Epilogue

AKIRA KUROSAWA

THROUGH *RASHOMON* I was compelled to discover yet another unfortunate aspect of the human personality. This occurred when *Rashomon* was shown on television for the first time a few years ago. The broadcast was accompanied by an interview with the president of Daiei. I couldn't believe my ears.

This man, after showing so much distaste for the project at the outset of production, after complaining that the finished film was "incomprehensible," and after demoting the company executive and the producer who had facilitated its making, was now proudly taking full and exclusive credit for its success! He boasted about how for the first time in cinema history the camera had been boldly pointed directly at the sun. Never in his entire discourse did he mention my name or the name of the cinematographer whose achievement this was, Miyagawa Kazuo.

Watching the television interview, I had the feeling I was back in *Rashomon* all over again. It was as if the pathetic self-delusions of the ego, those failings I had attempted to portray in the film, were being shown in real life. People indeed have immense difficulty in talking about themselves as they really are. I was reminded once again that the human animal suffers from the trait of instinctive self-aggrandizement.

And yet I am in no position to criticize that company president. I have come this far in writing something resembling an autobiography, but I doubt that I have managed to achieve real honesty about myself in its pages. I suspect that I have left out my uglier traits and more or less beautified the rest. In any case, I find myself incapable of continuing to put pen to paper in good faith. *Rashomon* became the gateway for my entry into the international film world, and yet as an autobiographer it is impossible for me to pass through the Rashomon gate and on to the rest of my life. Perhaps someday I will be able to do so.

But it may be just as well to stop. I am a maker of films; films are my true medium. I think that to learn what became of me after *Rashomon* the most reasonable procedure would be to look for me in the characters in the films I made after *Rashomon*. Although human beings are incapable of talking about themselves with total honesty, it is much harder to avoid the truth while pretending to be other people. They often reveal much about themselves in a very straightforward way. I am certain that I did. There is nothing that says more about its creator than the work itself.

Reprinted from *Something Like an Autobiography,* trans. Audie E. Bock (New York: Vintage, 1982), 188–89. Copyright © 1982 by Akira Kurosawa. Reprinted by permission of Alfred A. Knopf, Inc.

Akira Kurosawa Talks about *Throne of Blood*

INTERVIEW WITH TADAO SATO

SATO: Why did you think of filming Shakespeare's *Macbeth?*

KUROSAWA: Well, in the age of civil wars in Japan, there are plenty of incidents like those portrayed in *Macbeth,* aren't there? They are called *gekokujo.* [Note by Sato: *Gekokujo* means that a retainer murders his lord and deprives him of his power. The age of civil wars for about 100 years starting from 1460 is named such, and during that age the trend of *gekokujo* prevailed here and there in Japan.] Therefore, the story of *Macbeth* appealed very much to me, and it was easy for me to adapt.

SATO: What did you intend to represent by *Macbeth?*

KUROSAWA: In *Macbeth,* the images of men who lived through the age of the weak falling prey to the strong are concentrated. There, human beings are described with strong intensity. In this sense, I think there is something in it which is common with all other works of mine.

SATO: Will you explain for me into what sort of Japanese speech you have changed the English speech?

KUROSAWA: In some degree, into stylized prose of the present-day Japanese. As it is difficult to understand if it is completely stylized, I preferred to adopt a median solution. Where I used some verse-style, I have referred to the speech of the Noh songs. [Note by Sato: The Noh song means the epic poem used for a script of the Noh.]

SATO: In *Throne of Blood* [or *Kumonosu-jo,* "The Castle of the Spider's Web"], the influence of the Noh is evidently seen. Did you make your adaptation with the style of the Noh in mind from the beginning?

KUROSAWA: As to the witch in the wood, I was, during the adaptation, planning to replace it with the equivalent to the hag that appears in the Noh named *Kurozuka.* The hag is a monster that at times eats a human being. The reason was that I thought if we were to search for the image which resembles the witch of the West, nothing exists in Japan other than that. The other parts, however, I went on devising on the stage of interpretation.

SATO: What sort of influence is given by the Noh play?

KUROSAWA: In general, the drama of the West makes up its character out of the psychology of men or circumstances; the Noh is different. The Noh, first of all, has the mask, and while staring at it, the starer grows to become the man whom the mask represents. The performance also has a style, and while devoting himself to it faithfully, he is possessed by something. Therefore,

---

Excerpted from a typescript contained in the Film Study Center, The Museum of Modern Art, New York. Translated by Goro Iiri. Published by permission of Tadao Sato.

showing each of the players the photograph of the mask of the Noh that is becoming to the respective role, I told him that the mask was his own part. To Toshiro Mifune who played the part of Taketoki Washizu [Macbeth], I showed the mask named Heida. This was the mask of a warrior. In the scene in which Mifune is persuaded by his wife to kill his lord, he revealed to me just the same life-like expression as the mask did. To Isuzu Yamada who acted the role of Asaji [Lady Macbeth] I showed the mask named Shakumi. This was the mask of a beauty already not young and represented an image of a woman immediately before she got into the state of craziness. The actress who wears this mask, when she gets angry, changes her mask for the one whose eyes are golden-colored. This mask represents the state possessed by an unearthly feeling of tenacity and Lady Macbeth gets into the same state. To the warrior who was murdered by Macbeth and later comes out as an apparition, I considered the mask of the apparition of a nobleman of the name of Chujo as becoming. The witch in the wood was represented by the mask named Yamamba.

SATO: I think the Noh is an extremely motionless performance, and yet you are widely known to be fond of extremely vehement motion. Why do you like the Noh, Mr. Kurosawa?

KUROSAWA: It is a general misunderstanding to think that the Noh is static and is a performance with little motion. The Noh also has terribly violent motions that resemble those of an acrobat. They are so intense that we wonder with surprise how man can move so violently. The player who is capable of such an action performs it quietly, hiding the movements. There co-exist both quietness and vehemence. Speed means how filled a certain period of time is. The Noh has speed in such a sense.

SATO: In respect to camera work, to what points did you apply yourself?

KUROSAWA: The camera work was very difficult because there were plenty of full shots, and the shooting was carried out as I gave strict directions about the poses of the characters. If the characters are in a certain position, the balance of the picture is broken, so when there are two persons, if one shoulder gets off the picture, it is all over.

SATO: I feel the influence of the traditional art of Japan upon the composition, but . . .

KUROSAWA: As I had once been a painter, I have seen plenty of the old pictures of Japan. The way of leaving a large space white and drawing persons and things only on a part of the space is peculiar to Japanese art, isn't it? The influence of such pictures has deeply penetrated into us, and without our special consciousness it comes out spontaneously in our choice of composition.

SATO: Did you make your set conscious of the Noh? I think the very room in which Macbeth murders the king well resembles the Noh stage. Yet as it was in the age of civil wars (which is the setting for this film) that the Noh originated, everything might have become a common style of itself.

KUROSAWA: That's right. In reality, the castles of those days were of such a style. When I investigated into the way of planning the castles of those days, some of them made use of a forest which was grown as if it had been a maze. Therefore, the forest was named "the wood of spiders' hair." It means the wood that catches up the invaders as if it were a spider's web. The title of "The Castle of the Spider's Web" [*Kumonosu-jo*] was chosen by me from this.

Akira Kurosawa

INTERVIEW WITH *CINEMA*

CINEMA: A comparison has frequently been drawn between your Samurai pictures, *Seven Samurai, Yojimbo, Sanjuro,* and others, and the Western films of our country. Have you consciously borrowed or learned anything from the latter?

KUROSAWA: Good Westerns are unquestionably liked by all people, regardless of nationality. As human beings are weak, they wish to dream of the good people and great heroes who lived in olden times. Western dramas have been filmed over and over again for a very long time, have been kneeded, pounded, and polished, and in the process have evolved a kind of "grammar" of cinema. And I have learned from this grammar.

Cinema: We have heard that you want to make a Western. Is this true? If so, what is planned?

KUROSAWA: I am a Japanese. I do not think I can make a Western picture.

Cinema: Can you define your style? What cinematic approaches do you most often use that might constitute a recognizable style?

KUROSAWA: Nothing could be more difficult for me than to define my own style. I simply make a picture as I wish it to be or as nearly as it is within my power to do so. I have never thought of defining my style. If I tried such a thing, I would be caught within my own trap. . . .

Cinema: Your use of sound (not speaking now of dialogue) seems to be another distinguishing feature of your films. Can you discuss the integration of sound with picture?

KUROSAWA: Since the silent film gave way to the talkie, sound appears to have overshadowed image. At the same time, the flood of sound has made sound itself meaningless. In motion pictures both image and sound must be treated with special care. In my view, a motion picture stands or falls on the effective combination of these two factors. Truly cinematic sound is neither merely accompanying sound (easy and explanatory) nor the natural sounds captured at the time of simultaneous recording. In other words cinematic sound is that which does not simply add to, but multiplies, two or three times, the effect of the image.

Excerpted and reprinted from "Akira Kurosawa," trans. Yoshio Kamii, *Cinema* (Los Angeles) 1, no. 5 (August-September 1963): 27–28.

The Emperor: Interview with Akira Kurosawa

INTERVIEW WITH YOSHIO SHIRAI, HAYAO SHIBATA, AND KOICHI YAMADA

CAHIERS: One can divide your films schematically into two categories: *gendai-geki* (modern film stories) and *jidai-geki* (historical film stories). Does this distinction relate to precise intentions in regard to the formulation of the scenario and to the filming itself?

KUROSAWA: For myself, I do not perceive any difference. After a modern film story, I desire to make a historical film story, or vice versa. For example, after making *Ikiru* I wanted to change style: this genre of human inquiry demanded a great concentration of spirit and left me exhausted. I desired, quite naturally, to make a lighter, more lively film, a simple and detached film . . . and I made *Seven Samurai*. At present, I am about to complete *Red Beard*. I have dedicated myself to it for two years, my eye fixed on great problems of misery and suffering, and truly I have no more courage to immerse myself in such problems right away. All this has distressed me. I have need of gentleness and mirth. I think this is normal. . . . The only advantage of historical film stories, with the exception of *Throne of Blood*, comes from their greater potential for spectacle, such as adventure, which is an essential element in cinema. I would not say that this element is indispensable, but it creates great appeal in cinema. Moreover, it belongs to the birth of cinema. There are, of course, a thousand concepts of the adventure film. . . . There are all sorts of adventures. For myself, if I may say so, adventure is spectacle in the historical film story, while adventure in a modern film story is more often of a metaphysical, moral, and social nature. . . . What interests me is the interior or exterior drama of a person and how to represent the person through this drama. . . . To describe a person effectively a social or political context is necessary. I also think that one should not coarsely show events of the present day. The public will be shocked if it is plunged coarsely into contemporary reality. One can only make the public accept such reality through indirect means: the story of a person in the world. I would make the same remark regarding your classification: it is somewhat schematic. They are different genres, but the subject always determines the form. There are subjects that one can treat more readily in the form of *jidai-geki*.

Excerpted and reprinted from "'L'Empereur': entretien avec Kurosawa Akira," *Cahiers du Cinéma*, no. 182 (septembre 1966): 34–42, 74–78, by permission. Translation by James Goodwin.

Cahiers: Like *Rashomon,* which some call a "modern" film that has a "historical" context.

KUROSAWA: Yes. Me, I live in modern society. Thus it is normal that my "historical" films contain "modern" dimensions.

Cahiers: You have filmed *The Idiot,* written by Dostoevsky, and *The Lower Depths,* written by Gorky. It seems that you are deeply attached to Russian literature.

KUROSAWA: Yes, I greatly admire Russian literature. I admire Dostoevsky and Tolstoy—particularly *War and Peace,* which I still reread. Tolstoy, above all in *War and Peace,* is the only writer to attain a literature so extraordinarily visual and an almost cosmic vision. Tolstoy is thus a wager lost in advance. It is impossible to create images more alive or more forceful than his. As for Dostoevsky, it is difficult for me to speak of him. He is even more singular. He is on the whole—how should I say—more psychological than visual. At the same time that he deepens characters and action through psychology, this author strives for representation that is rigorously objective. It is an objectivity that is total, even fatal, that attempts to present everything nakedly. But this can still be put into images. For this reason I was led to adapt Dostoevsky to the screen, but the effort was a veritable battle that left me exhausted. . . . I think *[The Idiot]* is wonderful. I rank it among the masterworks of Dostoevsky. At the end of the novel, Rogozhin murders Nastasya and goes mad, and the other suitor, Prince Myshkin, becomes an "idiot" again—it is this cinematographic passage, if I might call it that, that led Hideo Kobayashi to write insightfully: "This novel was written through observation of this room [in which the above scene is set], it was written through living in this very room." The scene is to my thinking the most beautiful, the most agonizing, the most profound, and finally the most hallucinating in the history of literature. However, there is an important problem: how to interpret this novel. How can one comprehend the work of Dostoevsky? In effect, each critic and each artist has given his own interpretation. I have given one myself and I translated into images the truth most compelling to me. I have been reproached for making a difficult and heavy film. Myself, I think I have simply stated a very simple truth.

Making Films for All the People

INTERVIEW WITH KYOKO HIRANO

KUROSAWA: I believe that the world would not change even if I made a direct statement: do this and do that. Moreover, the world will not change unless we steadily change human nature itself and our very way of thinking. We have to exorcise the essential evil in human nature, rather than presenting concrete solutions to problems or directly depicting social problems. Therefore, my films might have become more philosophical.

Cineaste: Did you think this way when you were young?

KUROSAWA: No. I did not think so when I was young and this is why I was making such films. I have realized, however, that it does not work. The world would not change. This is not a matter of simply moving things from right to left. I have been tackling problems which transcend specific periods. I am confident that I am saying what I should say in my films. However, I don't think that the messages of my films are very obvious. Rather, they are the end products of my reflection. I am not trying to teach or convey a particular message, because the audience does not like it. They are sensitive to such things and shrink from them. People go to see films to enjoy themselves. I think that I have made them aware of problems without having to learn about them consciously. . . .

Cineaste: Were you subjected to any political pressures when your films dealt more directly with political problems?

KUROSAWA: At the end of *Ikiru,* for example, after the funeral, everything goes bureaucratic again at the protagonist's office. The vice president of the film company told me that we had criticized bureaucracy enough before that scene and we did not need that last scene. I answered. "You are welcome to cut this scene out: but in that case, please cut all the scenes from this film as well." The company was at a loss, so they finally told me that the film would be all right as it was.

The film companies have tried to suppress such potentially problematic parts when I try to make straightforward statements, although I have not succumbed to such pressures. You mentioned that I have not made films about contemporary themes. I suspect that if I chose contemporary problems as my subjects, no film company would dare to distribute such films. If no company would distribute such films. I would have no reason to make them.

In the last scene of *The Bad Sleep Well,* everyone in the audience must have deduced that it must be the then premier Kishi who is the ultimate

Excerpted and reprinted from *Cineaste* 14, no. 4 (1986): 23–25, by permission.

source of corruption and who is talking at the other end of the telephone. This is why the company has never rereleased the film, although everybody has been anxious to see it again. Francis Ford Coppola said that it is his favorite film. The company would not have distributed it if this unidentified character had been identified. I intended to be obvious, although the film executives had not been able to understand it when they had read the script. That is why they approved the script and invested their money. Film executives are the people who understand films least. . . .

Reading and writing should become habitual: otherwise, it is difficult. Nowadays, young assistant directors do not write screenplays, claiming that they are too busy. I used to write all the time. On location, a chief assistant director's work was extremely hard and busy, so I used to write at midnight, in bed. I could easily sell such screenplays, and make more than my assistant director's salary. It meant that I could drink more. Therefore, I wrote, and I drank, then, when I got broke, I wrote again. My friends were waiting for me to write screenplays and make money for drinking. When we went to drink, we talked about films all the time. Some of these talks became part of the next projects. Even now, when we drink together with actors and crew after the day's work at locations, we talk about our work, and sometimes these are the most important talks we have.

[*Kagemusha*]

INTERVIEW WITH TONY RAYNS

K UROSAWA: At the beginning, something very ambiguous comes into my mind as an idea; I let it mature by itself, and it goes into several specific directions. Then I go away somewhere to immerse myself in writing the scenario. It's less a matter of working within a defined structure than of letting myself be moved by the characters I've chosen to work with. I always try to start with the first scene. I myself don't know what direction it will take from there; I leave everything to the natural development of the characters. Even if my collaborator suggests that we should do something specific the next day, it never works out as foreseen. The spontaneous development of the characters is the most interesting part of the writing process for me.

In the case of *Kagemusha,* I was working on an adaptation of *King Lear* (which production costs have so far prevented me from turning into a film) and I was researching the Sengoku Jidai period (the clan wars of the late 16th century). I grew very interested in the Battle of Nagashino, which remains a question mark in history. No one has satisfactorily explained why all the *taisho* of the Takeda Clan should have died, while not one *taisho* of the Oda or Tokugawa Clans did. I started to consider ways of tackling this interesting question. It occurred to me that Takeda Shingen was known to have used many kagemusha (doubles), and I thought that by approaching the historical enigma through the eyes of one such kagemusha I might keep the subject to manageable proportions. Once I'd hit on the idea of making the kagemusha a petty thief, I had to consider how this man could become so immersed in the character of Shingen that he would actually "become" him. I decided that it must be because of the strength of Shingen's own character. Then I reflected that the *taisho* who died in battle must also have been charmed or enchanted by Shingen. In effect, they committed suicide at Nagashino—they martyred themselves for Shingen. They must have been in love with him, if you will.

Excerpted and reprinted from "Tokyo Stories: Kurosawa," *Sight and Sound* 50, no. 3 (Summer 1981): 170–74, by permission.

Kurosawa Directs a Cinematic *Lear*

INTERVIEW WITH PETER GRILLI

KUROSAWA: What has always troubled me about *King Lear* is that Shakespeare gives his characters no past. We are plunged directly into the agonies of their present dilemmas without knowing how they came to this point. How did Lear acquire the power that, as an old man, he abuses with such disastrous effects? Without knowing his past, I have never really understood the ferocity of his daughters' response to Lear's feeble attempts to shed his royal power. In *Ran* I have tried to give Lear a history. I try to make clear that his power must rest upon a lifetime of bloodthirsty savagery. Forced to confront the consequences of his misdeeds, he is driven mad. But only by confronting his evil head-on can he transcend it and begin to struggle again toward virtue.

I started out to make a film about Motonari Mori, the 16th-century warlord whose three sons are admired in Japan as paragons of filial virtue. What might their story be like, I wondered, if the sons had not been so good? It was only after I was well into writing the script about these imaginary unfilial sons of the Mori clan that the similarities to *Lear* occurred to me. Since my story is set in medieval Japan, the protagonist's children had to be men; to divide a realm among daughters would have been unthinkable....

I push. Some directors seem to "pull" performances out of actors, but I'm always pushing them, nudging them to try new or different things. We rehearse a scene or bit of action over and over again, and with each rehearsal something new jumps forward and they get better and better. Rehearsing is like making a sculpture of papier-mâché; each repetition lays on a new sheet of paper, so that in the end the performance has a shape completely different from when we started. I make actors rehearse in full costume and makeup whenever possible, and we rehearse on the set.... In costume, the work has an onstage tension that vanishes whenever we try rehearsing out of costume.

Excerpted and reprinted from *The New York Times*, 15 December 1985, II, 1, 17. Copyright © 1985 by the New York Times Company. Reprinted by permission.

Kurosawa: An Audience with the Emperor

INTERVIEW WITH JOHN POWERS

KUROSAWA: The role of Kyoami [in *Ran*] is something quite similar to a Shakespearean fool, but there's an actual historical basis for it. Even Japanese don't know much about the culture of the period, but if you read in Japanese medieval history you find that the warlords of the period had people in their entourage of very low birth. Depending on their particular skills, they would dance, tell jokes, entertain. But their main function was to be a conversationalist. Through them, the warlord would learn about what the people he governed were really thinking. And since they were not of samurai class—you will notice that Kyoami doesn't wear a sword—they were exempted from the majority of the rules of etiquette. So Kyoami can say anything he wants. . . .

In the time of the samurai, when the warriors were away at battle most of the time and the women were hiding out in the castle, the "fool" was something like a page who waited on them and with whom they had sexual relations. They were treated with great affection. My feeling about the relationship between Hidetora and Kyoami was that they probably had that relationship in the past when Hidetora was a younger man out on the battlefield a lot of the time. That's one of the reasons Peter was cast for that role, because he is an entertainer—a transvestite entertainer. . . .

Many, *many* years ago (I can't remember exactly when), the then head of the Cinémathèque Française, Henri Langlois, took me aside and told me that I *had* to make films in color. He showed me Eisenstein's *Ivan the Terrible* and said, "Look, Eisenstein was doing this many years ago and getting very good results. *You* must try." But I felt at the time that the technology of color films wasn't good enough for what I wanted to do, and that's why I kept making black-and-white films. But I was inspired by what Langlois said —and I *did* want to try—so I made *Dodeskaden* as a kind of color experiment, and since then everything I have done has been in color. . . .

In the case of *Ran* and *Kagemusha*, I did paintings that elaborated the visual concept before the actual filming began. But it's very, very important to me *not* to film the movie exactly the way it's written or exactly the way I have it worked out ahead of time. It takes all the fun out of it. Because you're dealing with actors and circumstances of nature, a lot of things can change, and it's important to be able to take advantage of those things at the

Translated by Audie Bock. Excerpted and reprinted from *L. A. Weekly,* (4 April 1986): 45–47, by permission.

moment they occur. That's what makes me happy about filmmaking: to get something different and better than what I conceived at the earlier stage.

Even in the writing stage, I think a lot of directors conceive of their characters and sort of set them out there to carry the drama like puppets. The director pushes them this way and pushes them that way, and they do what they're programmed to do. But when I conceive of the character, it's very important to have that character develop his own life. When he does, then I feel *I'm* being led around like a puppet by the character. That's where my interest in film comes from.

Notes on Filmmaking

AKIRA KUROSAWA

THERE IS something that might be called cinematic beauty. It can only be expressed in a film, and it must be present in a film for that film to be a moving work. When it is very well expressed, one experiences a particularly deep emotion while watching that film. I believe it is this quality that draws people to come and see a film, and that it is the hope of attaining this quality that inspires the filmmaker to make his film in the first place. In other words, I believe that the essence of the cinema lies in cinematic beauty.

Although the continuity for a film is all worked out in advance, that sequence may not necessarily be the most interesting way to shoot the picture. Things can happen without warning that produce a startling effect. When these can be incorporated in the film without upsetting the balance, the whole becomes much more interesting. This process is similar to that of a pot being fired in a kiln. Ashes and other particles can fall onto the melted glaze during the firing and cause unpredictable but beautiful results. Similarly unplanned but interesting effects arise in the course of directing a movie, so I call them "kiln changes."

A good structure for a screenplay is that of the symphony, with its three or four movements and differing tempos. Or one can use the Noh play with its three-part structure: jo (introduction), ha (destruction), and kyu (haste). If you devote yourself fully to Noh and gain something good from this, it will emerge naturally in your films. The Noh is a truly unique art form that exists nowhere else in the world. I think the Kabuki, which imitates it, is a sterile flower. But in a screenplay, I think the symphonic structure is the easiest for people of today to understand.

I've forgotten who it was that said creation is memory. My own experiences and the various things I have read remain in my memory and become the basis upon which I create something new. I couldn't do it out of nothing. For this reason, since the time I was a young man I have always kept a notebook handy when I read a book. I write down my reactions and what particularly moves me. I have stacks and stacks of these college notebooks, and when I go off to write a script, these are what I read. Somewhere they

Excerpted and reprinted from *Something Like an Autobiography,* trans. Audie E. Bock (New York: Vintage, 1982), 191–98. Copyright © 1982 by Akira Kurosawa. Reprinted by permission of Alfred A. Knopf, Inc.

always provide me with a point of breakthrough. Even for single lines of dialogue I have taken hints from these notebooks. So what I want to say is, don't read books while lying down in bed.

During the shooting of a scene the director's eye has to catch even the minutest detail. But this does not mean glaring concentratedly at the set. While the cameras are rolling, I rarely look directly at the actors, but focus my gaze somewhere else. By doing this I sense instantly when something isn't right. Watching something does not mean fixing your gaze on it, but being aware of it in a natural way. I believe this is what the medieval Noh playwright and theorist Zeami meant by "watching with a detached gaze."

I am often accused of being too exacting with sets and properties, of having things made, just for the sake of authenticity, that will never appear on camera. Even if I don't request this, my crew does it for me anyway. The first Japanese director to demand authentic sets and props was Mizoguchi Kenji, and the sets in his films are truly superb. I learned a great deal about filmmaking from him, and the making of sets is among the most important. The quality of the set influences the quality of the actors' performances. If the plan of a house and the design of the rooms are done properly, the actors can move about in them naturally. If I have to tell an actor, "Don't think about where this room is in relation to the rest of the house," that natural ease cannot be achieved. For this reason, I have the sets made exactly like the real thing. It restricts the shooting, but encourages that feeling of authenticity.

I changed my thinking about musical accompaniment from the time Hayasaka Fumio began working with me as composer of my film scores. Up until that time film music was nothing more than accompaniment—for a sad scene there was always sad music. This is the way most people use music, and it is ineffective. But from *Drunken Angel* onward, I have used light music for some key sad scenes, and my way of using music has differed from the norm—I don't put it in where most people do. Working with Hayasaka, I began to think in terms of the counterpoint of sound and image as opposed to the union of sound and image.

FILM CRITICS ON KUROSAWA

Kurosawa's Fathers

TADAO SATO

IN 1942 the National Board of Information selected Kurosawa's script *All Is Quiet (Shizuka Nari)* as the winning entry for its annual award given to scenarios with nationalistic themes. While never made into a film, it is interesting to examine it since it reveals several characteristics of his later films, particularly, the close father-son relationship.

The hero, Keisuke Kikuchi, is a thirty-three-year-old chemist at a research institute working on processing soybean products. His father is a patriotic professor of Japanese architecture, who is especially interested in the connection between the aesthetics of the Nara temple of Horyuji and the spirit of the Japanese people. Both father and son are completely immersed in their respective pursuits.

On the day that Keisuke's conscription notice arrives, the whole family hides the tension behind a veil of calmness. The father comes home with a bottle of wine to celebrate the occasion. When Keisuke returns, father and son chat amiably as if nothing has happened. Because they are resigned to the inevitable both men remain composed, not showing the slightest surprise, for this, indeed, is the spirit of the Japanese people.

The only matter that disturbs Keisuke is not finding an appropriate replacement at the institute. For Keisuke, such a man should not only consider chemical research his duty but also his very life: "A man who is so impassioned with even such a mundane subject as soybeans that he is willing to sacrifice his life for it." He finally decides on Igarashi, a colleague who has published a treatise that embraced his own theory. The latter, however, as a result of idle gossip, is suspicious of Keisuke's motives and the two enter into a heated debate. Consequently, Keisuke spends his last night before entering the army arguing with Igarashi, after which they become close friends since they are able to confirm each other's fervor concerning the processing of soybean products.

Keisuke's love for his sister's friend, Reiko, may also have weighed on his mind, but during the war the following doctrine prevailed: Thou shalt not indulge in personal feelings. However, his mother and sister arrange a morning farewell meeting between them, cut short because of his late night with Igarashi. Reiko, therefore, resorts to playing the martial airs of Chopin's *Polonaise* to encourage him. In comment, the young Kurosawa wrote, "One

---

can only wonder where such a brave spirit can have lain hidden in the heart of this shy, young lady."

Keisuke is seen off by his stoic mother, his tearful sister, Yoko, and Reiko, whose face is drained of color. He turns a street corner and does not look back. At around the same time, his father is giving a lecture at the university. "Those buildings idly placed here and there have no national character," he says. "They are not works of architecture, but ghostly apparitions. They are merely boxes to put people in." In contrast, the five-storied pagoda in Horyuji is an expression of the ideals of Prince Shotoku. "For more than 1,300 years, this pagoda has given silent testimony to the beauty inherent in the spirit of the Japanese people. It presents us with a classical example of the superior qualities of the Japanese. Due to its strength, it is silent to the bitter end." The students applaud.

Kurosawa, following the rules of the war-time government, managed to avoid a show of fanaticism and presented this family drama in a light, humorous vein. However, his insistence on his characters repressing all their fears about the conscription results in some unnaturalness, rendering the work superficial and mediocre. However, its portrait of the father and the love between him and his son is central to all the major works of Kurosawa.

Dr. Kikuchi, through excellence in his profession, has become a man of elevated character, always able to remain calm in a crisis. Accordingly, the son becomes devoted to his own profession and tries to be exactly like his father, aware that he is trying a little too hard.

This ideal father-son relationship of militaristic Japan appears in several other war-time films. The father in the home was a microcosm of the emperor in the nation: as the emperor was the embodiment of virtue, so each father should be a small model of virtue. This was hardly the case in reality, as often mediocre fathers took advantage of this heaven-sent authority to play the tyrant at home, alienating their children.

This ideal, thought to embody feudalistic thinking, changed swiftly after the war, when several films were made in response to the call to overthrow paternal authoritarianism. Yet Kurosawa continued to portray noble fathers, or father-substitutes, even after the war. In his first film *Sanshiro Sugata* (1943), the judo master Shogoro Yano (Denjiro Okochi) is even more unashamedly idealized than Dr. Kikuchi. By mastering the secrets of his martial art, he is able to face any crisis with tranquility. His disciple Sanshiro lives with him in the hope of both mastering the art of judo and being morally influenced by him. Theirs is like an ideal father-son relationship where the young man is modeling himself after the old man. In Kurosawa's first film after the war, *No Regrets for Our Youth*, Denjiro Okochi plays a liberal college professor, who, on the basis of excellence in his profession, remains unperturbed in times of trouble. Although oppressed by an increasingly fascist government, he never wavers in his convictions and, after resigning his university post, lives his life in retirement. His daughter (Setsuko

Hara) is so influenced by her father that she marries a leader of the antiwar movement and is persecuted after his death.

Kurosawa returns to the fictive father-son relationship, i.e., teacher-disciple, in *Drunken Angel.* At first it is hard to detect any higher goal in the relationship between the hard-drinking, middle-aged doctor (Takashi Shimura) and the young hoodlum (Toshiro Mifune) he is treating for tuberculosis. As a young man the doctor himself had "erred" and so he feels sorry for the young hoodlum and tries to take him under his wing in spite of resistance and threats of violence. Through his fear of death, the young man eventually succumbs to the good intentions of the doctor and begins to feel respect for him. Since they are both battling for his life, their relationship approaches that of a teacher and disciple. However, at this juncture the old gangleader returns to find that the young man has forsaken him, and in the ensuing fight the young man forfeits his life. The doctor and the young hoodlum fail in their effort to maintain a teacher-disciple relationship because while the doctor is an upright man with an honest occupation, the young man is not. Kurosawa's attitude is that human beings should refine their characters through their occupations before they can give or even receive moral training. If this process is accomplished in an orderly fashion, there is joy and happiness in Kurosawa's works. However, in the above case, Kurosawa's drama turns into tragedy.

In this respect, both *The Quiet Duel* and *Stray Dog* can be classified among Kurosawa's "joyful" dramas. In the former, the father is not given a very important role, but he and his son are both hard-working, dedicated doctors. In *Stray Dog* the fictive father-son relationship appears in the paternal affection the cool, calm veteran cop feels toward his impetuous, reckless charge. The training he gives him transcends simple guidance to include character-building. This is especially evident when the young cop finds out that the suspect he has been tracking is a former soldier like himself, and he becomes maudlin and sentimental, wondering if he would also have turned to crime in the same circumstances. The veteran invites him to his house for dinner and, over a few beers, reassures him that he and the suspect are so different in character that they are like two different species, thus renewing the rookie's determination to continue.

Ikiru, on the other hand, can be regarded as a tragedy because the father is unable to tell his selfish son that he has cancer. Before *Ikiru,* Kurosawa portrayed people who were noble because of their devotion to their occupation. Excellence therein brought forth personal charisma, respect from their children, and/or the adoration of a worthy disciple. The main character in *Ikiru,* however, is only a mediocre official who had been rubber-stamping documents for years. No one respects him, and even his son only sees him as someone who will leave a retirement pension when he dies. For Kurosawa, this kind of man has to exert himself to the utmost in his occupation before he can really feel alive as a human being once again. A warm, touching relationship with his son is something that could have followed later if the son was not such a distasteful philistine, with whom strong ties were not necessary.

Ikiru is one of the high points in Kurosawa's career because he abandons one of his favorite conceptions—the beauty of trust between father and son, teacher and disciple—because it cannot survive in the face of bitter postwar realities and, as such, was able to create scores of incomparable images brimming with truth.

For Kurosawa the real culprit in society is none other than the dissolution of this trust as the younger generation becomes shallow and flippant. In *Ikiru,* however, he does not simply lament this condition and leave it, for what he detests most is not bringing the moral to its conclusion. In *Ikiru* his moral conclusion was that if modern youth rejects the beauty of the trust between father and son, one should cast them aside without regrets, with the consequence that work becomes the sole purpose of life.

Before cutting off his son, however, the father recalls how much he had loved him in a beautiful, emotion-packed sequence of flashbacks. He is with his grade-school son in the limousine following the hearse of his wife, and when it goes around a corner, his son cries out, "Mother has gone away!" Then he remembers turning down his brother's suggestion that he remarry, for fear of the effect on his son. There is also the time at the hospital when he bolsters his son's spirits at an impending appendectomy; and finally when he was in the stands rooting for him at a junior high school baseball game, his feelings rose and fell with his son's play.

In this sequence Kurosawa expresses the concept that a beautiful relationship between a parent and child is the most secure form of social order. Tragedy enters the picture when this is lost and a rupture occurs. The father's cancer is not *Ikiru's* tragedy, only the trigger that forces him to realize that in reality there is no trust between his son and himself—a fact he has avoided facing previously.

When this trust is missing, human beings have to bind society with something that has a more universal meaning, e.g., work for the public welfare or common good. This is Kurosawa's tragic but profound theme. When something one loves above all else turns out to be an illusion, salvation is sought elsewhere, without rejecting this feeling of loss and in a high state of spiritual tension. At this juncture is born the nobility of tragedy.

[Heroism and Humanism]

AUDIE BOCK

T HE EDUCATION of the hero, a difficult progression toward spiritual enlightenment, would later become the theme of many of Kurosawa's films. He would take it up in the Sugata format, as the personal struggle under tutelage of a wise older mentor in *Stray Dog, Sanjuro,* two of the relationships in *Seven Samurai,* extreme one-to-one form in *Red Beard,* and finally in *Dersu Uzala. The Most Beautiful, No Regrets for Our Youth, Ikiru,* and *Record of a Living Being* would present the hero in a solitary search for enlightenment without any single teacher. And conversely, the protagonist who rejects the option of setting out on this spiritual ascent ends by rushing headlong toward his doom, like the gangster of *Drunken Angel,* the greedy warlord in *Throne of Blood,* and the impetuous patriarch of another Shakespeare adaptation, the as yet unfilmed script "Ran" (Turmoil), based on *King Lear.* Kurosawa's existential humanism emerges in this education process because self-evaluation and searching for the right path almost invariably prove to entail movement toward active compassion. Kurosawa's own description of his goal in this approach is somewhat evasive, and yet at the same time more comprehensive. While calling himself a sentimentalist and insisting that a film must be both positive and constructive, he has denied attempting to make social films, and stresses that "what interests me is the drama, interior or exterior, of one man, and portraying this man through that drama."

In *Sanshiro Sugata* Kurosawa employs this spiritual drama to create one of the most memorable images of the film. The unruly Sugata is being disciplined by his master, who tells him to remain submerged in the garden pond looking at the moon until he understands. Here Kurosawa introduces a catalytic image to the pond scene from the novel: meditating on his errors, Sugata turns to see a pure white lotus in full bloom a few feet away from him. Its unexpected beauty overwhelms his stubbornness, and he leaps from the pond having found humility. A parallel to this device appears nine years later in *Ikiru,* where the discouraged bureaucrat suddenly recognizes the toy rabbit as the symbol of bringing joy to children. After he is dead and the playground is built in the slum, the toy rabbit reappears during his wake, just as Sugata's lotus recurs—less subtly—during his final battle as reminder of his enlightenment. Critics who seek to read a Zen interpretation into these humble objects' operation on the minds of the protagonists can amply justify their case, but in *Ikiru* the symbols are far more rationally integrated into the dramatic construction, perhaps too rationally for those who value a feeling of improvisation in film.

The personal struggle theme carries through *The Most Beautiful,* which underscores a far more strident support-the-war-effort message. But the heroine emerges as a real person despite the propaganda, because she is seeking her own identity through the socio-political situation in which she finds herself. Her rejection of the discouragement of influential people around her, her insistence on making her own contribution and meeting her own severe standards would be further developed in Kurosawa's most attractive postwar heroine, the determined idealist of *No Regrets for Our Youth.*

In *The Men Who Tread on the Tiger's Tail* Kurosawa attempted something completely different. From the serious period hero of *Sanshiro Sugata* and the serious contemporary heroine of *The Most Beautiful,* he turned to a serious classical Kabuki drama and added a comic hero, the humble porter played by Kenichi Enomoto. Such near sacrilege had never been dared before, and the film is so funny and unpropagandistic that it was not released. This foray into the comic form, which he completely overlayed on a classical suspense play, was an important step, revealing Kurosawa's innovative propensities from the earliest stages of his career. Later he would speak of *Yojimbo* and *Sanjuro* as his "first postwar comedies," although *The Men Who Tread on the Tiger's Tail* itself became a postwar film—released at last in 1952 when the U.S. Occupation ban on period films was lifted. It proved at that time to be quite competitively well made despite the wartime production limitations.

These three earliest films, all made during a time of low production standards and high propaganda demands, show that Kurosawa was more than, in the words of Kajiro Yamamoto, "ready . . . when his chance came." His themes are already clear, his technique expert and his approach to genre experimental. There is in fact no major break between wartime and postwar in Kurosawa's concerns: he shows his drama of individuals and technical virtuosity from the outset. As a result, Kurosawa has not felt the need to repudiate his wartime works, as have some of the famous Communist directors such as Tadashi Imai and Satsuo Yamamoto, saying they had no choice but to make the most abject propaganda. Other directors such as Yasujiro Ozu simply avoided making films at all after 1942, when material and ideological restraints became intolerably severe, but Kurosawa persisted in the search for his own cinematic expression. . . .

In discussing the impetus for his first postwar film, Kurosawa said: "I believed at that time that for Japan to recover it was important to place a high value on the self," and he added, "I still believe this." Accordingly, he created a heroine in *No Regrets for Our Youth* who remains an uncompromising idealist despite social and political opposition as well as physical exhaustion. Like the heroine of *The Most Beautiful* before her and the hero of *Ikiru* after her, she places the highest demands on herself, setting an example that is often misunderstood by those around her and seen as eccentric or self-destructive.

The most moving sequence of the film, like that of *The Most Beautiful*, shows this character in highly tense visual terms, almost without dialogue. Just as the optical instruments factory girl works all night, thinking of the needs of the soldiers at the front, to make up for a lost lens, the delicate city woman Yukie (Setsuko Hara), followed by her mother-in-law to work in daylight for the first time, labors in the mud until the whole rice paddy is planted. Covered with dirt, she collapses in exhaustion on arriving home. Having seen the extended montage of their toil and the first joy on the women's faces at its completion, we experience total empathy with their frustration, sorrow, and rage at the sight of their field the next day, trampled by persecuting villagers and bristling with placards accusing them of being spies and traitors. Without hesitation, Yukie begins removing the signs to start over, and her silent determination carries her mother-in-law, and finally her father-in-law, along in her fight against prejudice.

Silent determination in the face of bitter opposition would be the inspiring quality of the dying bureaucrat in *Ikiru* as well. Repeated images of Watanabe (Takashi Shimura), head bowed, standing immovable before embarrassed city officials and swaggering gangsters with his park project proposal become the *leitmotif* of the second half of the film. We see him alone, staggering with the pain of his fatal cancer, and responding to the gangsters with a quiet gruesome smile that makes them turn away in terror at the realization that murder threats mean nothing to him. His baffled subordinates, like Yukie's in-laws and the factory girl's colleagues, are swept along without really comprehending this exemplary figure, recognizing his accomplishment only after his death.

Kurosawa has said that in *No Regrets for Our Youth* he was able to say something for the first time, and that the critical response at the time was unfavorable simply because the protagonist was female. Yet from *Sanshiro Sugata*, through *The Most Beautiful, No Regrets for Our Youth,* and finally *Ikiru,* his ideas show a clear progression of emphasis on the individual finding self-definition, self-assertion, and finally a form of accomplishment that serves humanity. The choice of situations—Meiji Period martial arts competition, work for the war effort, persecution of Communists, and bureaucratic stagnation—and of young and old, male and female protagonists from varying social backgrounds, reveals a dramatic focus that is bound neither by politics, age, nor sex, but by existential challenge to the individual.

[Review of
The Men Who Tread on the Tiger's Tail]

JOHN McCARTEN

The Men Who Tread on the Tiger's Tail, a Japanese film, is a peculiar but interesting mélange of Kabuki solemnity and Oriental variations on Mack Sennett comedy. Derived from one of Japan's most famous classical dramas, the movie follows the original story pretty faithfully, I am told, and frequently, in the Kabuki manner, employs song to interpret the doings of the characters. The plot concerns the adventures of Yoshitsune, a twelfth-century nobleman of the Genji clan, who, during a civil war, has a feud with his brother, the shogun, and is compelled to flee the latter's jurisdiction. He is accompanied by half a dozen devoted and belligerent retainers, and the big problem of the fugitives, who are disguised as monks, is to get past a roadblock on their path to the north and freedom.

Before they reach the barrier, they hire a porter, a youth not too well in the head but sufficiently alert to discover that the monks are not true-blue ecclesiastics and to discern in particular the regal qualities of Yoshitsune, which anyone with half an eye could see. Yoshitsune is thereupon redisguised as a bearer, and the band, still accompanied by the porter, sets off again to try its luck at the shogun's barrier. At this point, the leader of Yoshitsune's guardians, a warrior called Benkei, encourages all hands to substitute craft for violence, and proves his point when he hoodwinks a provincial magistrate into believing that they are indeed holy men by pretending to read from a blank scroll a prospectus for the reconstruction of a temple, and by lining out several recondite prayers. In passing, he takes a stick to Yoshitsune, to make certain that the lord's false identity will not be discovered, and winds up having a high old time with his companions on some *sake* the magistrate has sent them. Then the entourage moves on, leaving the porter, who has passed out in the course of the festivities, sleeping peacefully under a rich cloak that they have given him.

It is largely the personality of this porter that has caused *The Men Who Tread on the Tiger's Tail* to have a most vicissitudinous history. The picture came into being some fifteen years ago, when the Kabuki theatres in Japan were shut down because legitimate drama was considered too restricted to help in the broad war effort. The big wheels in the military government having decided that films would be a fine medium for spreading an enthusiasm

Reprinted from *The New Yorker,* 16 January 1960, 97-98. Reprinted by permission; © 1960, 1988 The New Yorker Magazine, Inc.

for Japanese culture, Akira Kurosawa, who later directed *Rashomon,* was presently ordered to make a movie of *The Men Who Tread on the Tiger's Tail.* Mr. Kurosawa did as he was told, but introduced the porter, a decidedly non-Kabuki type, into the proceedings. Speaking in the language of a common modern man baffled by pomp, and conducting himself with a deplorable lack of dignity, the porter became a mocking image of the ordinary fellow plunked down in the midst of vanished traditional types, whose ways he could not understand and could only mimic. When Mr. Kurosawa's version of the Kabuki drama was revealed in 1945, it was promptly suppressed, on the ground that it attacked the feudalism dear to the samurai heart. Mr. Kurosawa was saved from further difficulty with his bosses by the end of the war, but once again the film was banned, this time because the American Occupation authorities considered it *pro*-feudal. It finally was released in Japan in 1953, and made a big hit.

The outstanding actors in *The Men Who Tread on the Tiger's Tail* are Denjiro Okochi, who plays the ingenious Benkei, and Kenichi Enomoto, who plays the low-comedy porter. Mr. Okochi is every inch the traditional Kabuki performer, and Mr. Enomoto is every inch the clown. At times, Mr. Enomoto, who is a kind of Japanese Joe E. Brown, gets so broadly comic that he's hard to put up with. But maybe Mr. Kurosawa let him loose so that the parody would be clearly understood.

Working with Fumio Hayasaka

MASAAKI TSUZUKI

K UROSAWA MET Hayasaka when he himself was at the peak of fullness and his most prolific. It was a time when he finally began to meet people like himself and was afire with the desire to try various things in his films. The two met for the first time on *Drunken Angel,* and it was from that time until Hayasaka's death eight years later that, tied by deep friendship, they would share together the pains and frustrations of being artists.

Hayasaka had already made his name as a film music composer. After the war, he received the Mainichi Film Concours first annual Film Music Award for *An Enemy of the People (Minshu no Teki,* 1946). He received the second annual Film Music Award for *Actress (Joyu,* 1947).

For that alone, Kurosawa was especially happy when the two became a combination. The production notes [by Kurosawa] for *Drunken Angel* contain the following statement:

About Music

Music is Hayasaka. It was his very first friend. When we spoke at conference time we hit it off terribly well. We matched so perfectly that when he talked about the music in the movies we had seen we both agreed that the best effect was in the murder scene in the Soviet film *The Sniper.*

We mainly talked about the oppositional handling of music and performance, but also about how when music is accompaniment the density of the wave-like ups and downs of a performance is lost. In other words, the key to film music lies less in riding on the rhythm of the performance, but rather is hidden in the difficulty of appropriately distancing one from the other. This is what we settled our opinions on.

And then on this job, with the intention of experimenting, we boldly decided to try out various new things. I hope that for film music and for this film as well it will be a good gamble. Although I thought about it, I couldn't feel that I had been anything but easy on film music up until now. I don't have any unusually finicky thoughts yet, but this time I want to try to use music with a definite intention.

Here we find the first mention of the "oppositional handling of music and performance" that they tested in *Drunken Angel.* Film music from that point on would trace the image explanatorily and depict a feeling from beginning

Translated by Michael Baskett for this volume from Tsuzuki Masaaki, *Kurosawa Akira: Sono Ningen no Kenkyu* [Akira Kurosawa: A Study of the Man] (Tokyo: Maruju Company/Internal Publishing, 1976), 1: 290-99, courtesy of the publisher.

to end. But Kurosawa, ever insistent on realism, could not be satisfied with this ornamental music. He needed a new challenge, a new logic in order to search out a reality thicker than that of real life. That is where he tried his "juxtapositional" experiments. About this novel departure, Kurosawa said the following. "What I really was interested in with *Drunken Angel* was joining a sad image with 'The Cuckoo Waltz.' Up until then, you could probably say that adding to the image multiplied the film. However, even though I say multiplication, if there were no experimentation it would all be worthless."

About this Hayasaka wrote the following:

> Near the end of *Drunken Angel* when Mifune hopelessly walks around the marketplace all the way until the bar scene, you can detect this unusual effect in the technique of using "The Cuckoo Waltz." At first it seems the music is poorly matched with the image. However, without looking at the intention deep within, you can't say you have a real appreciation for film.
>
> This treatment came from one of Kurosawa's real-life experiences. He said one day he had an indescribably unpleasant feeling as he walked through a Shinjuku traffic jam. Then he heard "The Cuckoo Waltz." The psychological mixture was said to have left quite an impression on his mind. Then at a certain inn in Atami where he wrote the script for *Stray Dog,* he heard "La Paloma" while he was writing the cheap hotel scene. That gave him the conviction to handle that scene with juxtapositional treatment.
>
> I anticipated that using "La Paloma" would be dangerous, but without giving in he strongly insisted that since it was something he experienced while writing the script it would be all right. And the result gives a shuddering effect. This type of sensitivity to the events in one's life, the spirit of criticism, and the use of a melody that anyone of the masses would know is a bold technique that deviates from the norm. You have to say he has extraordinary ability and courage.

So why does Kurosawa, who is always searching for reality in the image, use film music? Isn't it a large liability to the effect of reality? In one's everyday life there is hardly any intervention by music. For that reason alone it is extremely dangerous to put in music casually. What made Kurosawa value the musical effects of experience in daily life probably lies in that reason. Using experience as the base, Kurosawa then thought about film music. It was at that moment that "juxtapositional" music treatment was born. By adding to the image with film music, even music without any special meaning in itself, a greater effect is achieved.

In an article entitled "Kurosawa's Film Music Sense," Hayasaka wrote the following:

> As a principle, at the base of Akira Kurosawa's film music thought, film music is different from pure music. Film music differs from pure music, and the music used there, rather than being absolute music, arouses something

through uniting with the image, through association, and another meaning is bestowed to the music itself.

According to common sense image A and music B are things one would predict could never be harmonized, but a bold addition, through an act of multiplication, gives birth to a third dimension of expression, C, at that point. When music is used consciously the content, with more expressive ability than what the music alone has, is born through this type of method. The point where music and image are joined is not one of beauty, but probably one frighteningly psychological.

I don't know why it is, but for one image there is only one matching music. Kurosawa has the intuition to discover this internal unity. Therefore, in the films I've done with him, he is the musical director, and I am the composer, and nothing more.

Sometimes, however, aligning the image with the rhythmical tempo gives rise to a dense mood, and you can take the method that the human psychological analysis that the image has been following is strengthened by the music. But in principle, it is nothing but a hindrance that lies in the way of film music's strong point, handled juxtapositionally.

Kurosawa and Hayasaka used this juxtapositional treatment boldly and succeeded with *Drunken Angel* and *Stray Dog*. Since then the music has not simply traced the image, but through the joining of image and sound, this multiplication—a new expression of film music—was born. Of course, there was the newness of the contents of what they tried to depict, and the birth of this new expression of film music. It is this new spirit that demands new expression.

In film music, something that deserves special mention would certainly be the music of *Seven Samurai*. Its music is so deeply loved that nearly anyone can hum it even now. With popular appeal like that, others aren't even allowed to follow. With plainness, with simple clarity, it is entertaining, sad, beautiful, and heroic music.

Hayasaka explained his aim for the music of *Seven Samurai* as follows:

The reason *Seven Samurai*'s music was comparatively well received was because it was extremely simple and clear, I think. That is to say, the first music draft I wrote was in very complicated form. However, as I played it, I felt the intricacy wouldn't get through to the audience. I wondered what to do. Then I tried to abandon the difficult format and take it down to the bare bones as it were. Therefore the harmony, which was already written, was all taken out and all that was left was the melody. As much as possible I returned to a simplified form. That sort of thing I was able to do relatively easily.

This was how the simple, strong melody that nearly anyone could hum was born. *Seven Samurai* is a great work that runs over three hours, and contains many characters and scenes. And throughout it all runs the music. For that reason alone, the music motif was broken into several themes. Let me give you a few of the major ones here.

(1) The bandits' theme used drums and bowstrings to express violence.

(2) The samurai theme was a brave, march-like arrangement. This one flows throughout the entire film, sometimes heroically, other times sadly or beautifully.

(3) The farmers' theme is hummed in a chorus. This conveys the sense of fear and suffering at the coming of the bandits.

(4) The lovers' theme is played at Shino and Katsushiro's first meeting, their rendezvous, and during their passionate love in the hut on the eve before the battle. It flows lyrically, overtly, and sadly. Kurosawa calls it the most "Hayasaka-like number."

(5) The farming theme is played during the cutting and threshing of the wheat. The music is fast tempo, to match the farmers' spirit while engaged in the labor of cutting wheat. It is also a labor song the farmers sing while enjoying the twenty days of peace while threshing the grain.

(6) The rice-planting theme. According to Kurosawa's instruction, Hayasaka said, "This song was mixed with words from many dialects and old Japanese folk songs." After overcoming days of fear and suffering, it sounds victorious to the farmers, but to the remaining samurai it can only sound sad.

I gave just six main themes, but there is more music other than this in it. It is like opera, a world of only sound that he has been able to master. This is one of the things that comes with being a composer, but there seems to have been great suffering as well.

Hayasaka said, "While composing the melody for *Seven Samurai*, I wrote for 60 days and produced 300 pages of draft."

Great enthusiasm. At the time his ill condition was quite advanced and he was a gravely sick man, but on sheer spirit alone he accomplished it.

About this composer there is one interesting episode. Kurosawa recounts:

> I went to his house to hear the samurai theme. At that time Hayasaka had already written nearly twenty drafts in preparation. Then, one-by-one he played them for me on the piano. None of them struck my fancy and as I cocked my head and grew quiet, he stood up and said "I've got this one as well," and he took a crumpled page out of the waste basket. He smoothed out the music paper, stretched it out, put it on the piano's music stand and then he played me this melody. When I heard it I jumped up and screamed "This is it!" without thinking. Then, when I said "This! This! This is as heroic as the samurai and as sad and beautiful," Hayasaka faced the piano again and began to play different variations. Then the samurai theme was decided. In different scenes this theme was developed variously and used a lot.

Finding tenacity in Hayasaka's works is unusual. Looking at the fiery Hayasaka there seems to be something in the music that wasn't in his personality. If this were not the case, he could not have given us such a beautifully alive work. For him to have put in that much effort was also unusual.

According to music critic Kuniharu Akiyama: "The five-line music notebook he wrote in over and over again for *Seven Samurai* still exists today. In it what could be called unusual efforts for film music are made. He repeated from five to ten various leitmotivs and then finally completed the intricate theme that captivated him."

This was how the immortal and great melody was made.

Before *Seven Samurai,* Kurosawa was making *Ikiru.* At the time of *Seven Samurai* the two men's opinions were in accord and Hayasaka was able to work quickly, but in *Ikiru,* things did not go that way. *Ikiru* was a modern-day story and a bitter drama. As a grave drama, looking into how people should live their lives, the music had to be touching but not sentimental. The hero must face the reality of his own short remaining life span not with sentimentality but with realism. That is where Kurosawa and Hayasaka's opinions differed sharply.

In a letter about composing for *Ikiru* that Hayasaka sent to fellow composer Ichiro Saito, he writes in detail about the facts surrounding an incident that is quite interesting:

> I happily read your letter. Thank you for looking over *Ikiru.* I have really struggled on this. And while Kurosawa's orders are always difficult and strict this time I've literally lost weight over it. One by one I have worked on various Kurosawa productions. And because film sound and music is still in a creative stage, I know a lot of experimentation is needed. Today I realized that the desire to experiment is an important thing. Although I'm still not ready or good enough, I still want to do something, and feel I can do it if I try.
>
> About *Ikiru,* there is one more thing I want to say. It concerns the point where the wake scene and the recollection scene meet. The recollection scene is 13-14 spools. I dubbed them all, but after I saw the final rushes, I took out all of the music that I had put in.
>
> You might ask why I did this. By putting in the music the scene actually flows too much. Why does the sense of flowing too much seem to be at odds with good sense? Well although in many cases music is put in to help the flow, in Kurosawa's films that won't work. You can't make things flow with the use of music. Sweetening the acting or strengthening the audience's reception is also no good. That is why there were 14 spools taken and I made it all background music. It takes a bit of courage, like the handling of the latter half of *Ikiru* where the painful memories are experienced.
>
> For two to three days I was so down-hearted I had to stay at home. Then Kurosawa came to *comfort* me and I finally returned to normal.

In just one character, in one phrase of this letter, sincerity shines through. Expressing oneself without the fear of failure, using for reference the same inner knowledge that the two composers have, he is able to write openly. Kurosawa has spoken about the content of this letter:

> What I remember is in the hero's wake scene, where memories of the hero

when he was alive pop up; I talked over that recollection scene with Hayasaka and decided on the melody and he intended to put music to all of it. I had him write a score. However, when I went to put it in, the pictures and sounds didn't move together the way I thought they should. Finally I decided to take all of the music out. I thought I better tell Hayasaka, so I went to his house and Hayasaka with his head hanging down was just sitting there without saying a word. I took half a day to cheer him up, saying it wasn't his fault but probably mine.

You can almost touch the strong sense of self in Hayasaka's works. In Kurosawa's opinion he was a person who would listen with an open mind and vast patience. That is where he and Kurosawa shared a strong relationship of trust. In this way contact deepened between two men in the lonely world of art.

Not simply a friend in art, but a good life's companion as well. The idea for *Record of a Living Being* came out of that friendship. One day the sickly and weak Hayasaka said, "With this illness threatening my life, I can't work." At that time, around 1955, there was experimental nuclear testing and the ashes of death were falling on Japanese islands. Kurosawa received a strong shock from Hayasaka's words and that triggered the making of *Record of a Living Being*. However, in the midst of its filming Hayasaka died and Kurosawa fell into deep depression.

Detectives and Doctors

BARBARA WOLF

Kurosawa Akira's international reputation is based almost entirely on such period films as *Rashomon, Seven Samurai,* and *Yojimbo.* These passionate, expressionistic films, exotic in setting but universal in theme, strike the foreigner as having a special uniqueness. In comparison, Kurosawa's modern dress films seem rather ordinary. His doctors, clerks, detectives and criminals look and behave so much like characters in Western films that their differences seem unnecessarily annoying. Compared to his historical heroes, Kurosawa's moderns appear oddly diminished, as diminished as Sweeney beside Agamemnon. And compared to his broad historical canvasses, his modern settings seem cramped and desolate, wastelands of the spirit. Still, these films have a peculiar intensity of their own. At sudden revelatory moments, they seem to confront the viewer with his own image and experience.

Most of Kurosawa's contemporary films are either detective or medical dramas. By modifying that description only a little, by saying instead stories about sickness or crime, it becomes possible to include them all. *Drunken Angel* and *The Quiet Duel* are explicitly about doctors. But *Ikiru* is also about disease, although the cancer-ridden hero is beyond medical help. And *Record of a Living Being* is about the danger of disease, in this case, radiation sickness. *Stray Dog* and *High and Low* are both detective stories; but *Scandal* and *The Bad Sleep Well* are also about crime: slander and murder. And boundaries begin to blur when we observe how often Kurosawa links the themes of crime and illness. The TB patient in *Drunken Angel* is a gangster. The kidnaper in *High and Low* is an intern. A little less obviously, the doctor in *Drunken Angel* is an alcoholic and the doctor in *The Quiet Duel* has syphilis. These last examples typify the ironic confusion of values which marks all these films. The young detective in *Stray Dog* identifies himself with the criminal he is pursuing: both are veterans of the recent war, and the criminal's official police description fits the detective in every particular. In the penultimate scene of the film, struggling in the mud over the policeman's gun, they become completely indistinguishable. In the penultimate scene of *Drunken Angel,* when the reformed gangster is killed by his former rival, they are so besplattered with house paint that they too cannot be told apart. In *High and Low,* it is implied that the victim himself had brought on

Reprinted from *Japan Quarterly* 19, no. 1 (January-March 1972): 83–87, by permission of *Japan Quarterly.*

the crime, by living in a mansion overlooking a slum, an affront to the eyes of the poor. And in the final scene, when the kidnaper and his ruined victim confront each other in the prison, the glass wall which separates one from the other also reflects one upon the other, so that the expressions of each are mirrored upon the other's face. These superimpositions are no mere camera trick, but the expression of a likeness approaching identity. In all these films, made over fifteen years, characters catch likeness, catch crime as well as disease from one another.

I think it can also be said that all these films are about people who need to save or be saved. The doctors, of course, supposedly want to save their patients, and their patients want to save themselves. However, it seldom works out that simply. In *Drunken Angel,* for example, the gangster patient is considerably less eager to achieve a cure than the doctor is. In order to save his patient's life, the doctor would first have to make him give up his dangerous and unhealthy way of life, which is the reason why the gangster resists. And the doctor is intent on saving his patient in order to redeem his own wasted life. The policemen also consider themselves in the salvation business. In *Stray Dog* there is an undercurrent of conflict between the veteran detective and the novice over whom they are supposed to be saving. The veteran thinks of himself as a guardian of society, which he must protect from victimization by the criminal. But the young detective sympathizes with the criminal as the victim of society, and expends more of his compassion on him than on those he robs and kills. The characters are often misled by a false self-image into becoming the very thing they most detest. In *The Bad Sleep Well,* the man intent on avenging the murder of his father becomes a murderer himself. The clinic intern in *High and Low* thinks of kidnaping for ransom as a kind of judgment against the exploiting rich in the name of the poor. But he is himself a doctor who kills instead of cures and uses overdoses of life-saving drugs to commit his murders.

The constant recurrence of these ironies from film to film constitutes a thematic pattern. Kurosawa uses sickness and crime much as Thomas Mann had done: metaphorically. Sometimes they are employed to symbolize the destructive forces inherent in nature and man. More often and more exactly, they are used to symbolize what the artist conceives as the special decadence of the modern world, especially the postwar Japanese world. In Kurosawa's films, as in Mann's novels, physical illness is sometimes directly attributed to the effects of leading the wrong sort of life. Even before examining him, the doctor in *Drunken Angel* warns the burly gangster that he expects to find TB: "Your way of life breeds it," he explains. In *Ikiru,* the insidious destruction of the clerk's body by cancer is equated with the ruin of his mind, soul and senses by a lifetime spent, as the narrator tells us, on shuffling papers and keeping his chair warm. The doctors in such films, at least those who really want to cure, must reach their patients' souls before they can treat their bodies. And so must the policemen. Before the young detective can get information from the murderer's girl in *Stray Dog,* he has first to persuade her that it would be *right* for her to inform on her lover. The scene is an interesting one. Like the kidnaper in *High and Low* who blames the rich man for tempting him, the killer's girl blames everything on the shop owner who displayed an expensive evening gown. Embittered because he could not buy it for her, her lover became a thief. The policeman feels her logic deeply and can find no reply. But the girl's mother breaks in, demanding whether a dress is a thing worth stealing and killing for. The policeman's doubts are resolved, but the girl, although shaken, remains defiant. The policeman then insists that she put on the gown, to prove to them how greatly she values it, and her defenses crumble. She is overcome with shame, bursts into tears, tears off the gown and gives the detective his information. In *Drunken Angel,* too, the gangster's redemption is signaled by just such an emotional crisis and breakdown, followed by a shift of allegiance from his gang to his doctor. In each case, the character has undergone a kind of conversion at the hands of a priest-like agent, a conversion which amounts to a rebirth, which sets his heart at ease and even changes his bearing and expression. The gangster puts off his swagger: the girl's hard, suspicious face becomes gentle and open. In *Ikiru,* the doomed civil service clerk must awaken and convert himself. Beyond the help of doctors or policemen, and not religious, he must be his own priest. Or rather, the agent which both breaks and revivifies his spirit is the very cancer which is killing his body.

The film in which all these themes are given their most explicit and complete expression is *Red Beard,* which oddly enough is not set in modern times. In an interview made soon after *Red Beard*'s release in 1965, Donald Richie observed that the film seemed to be the ultimate statement of everything which Kurosawa had always been struggling to express. Kurosawa agreed, adding that his statement was complete and that he could no longer make films of that kind. For the next five years, in fact, Kurosawa made no films at all and, when he finally did get back to work in 1970, it was to produce *Dodeskaden,* lighter in mood but identical in theme to everything that had come before. Apparently *Red Beard* still remains his ultimate, if not quite his final, word.

Red Beard has had an uneven career, perhaps because it is the most uneven of Kurosawa's major films. In Japan it proved to be the director's greatest critical success and also one of the greatest money-makers in Japanese film history. Abroad, it floundered badly, receiving mixed notices and few revivals. Dwight Macdonald asked "Is this what Kurosawa's famed humanism finally comes down to? Dr. Gillespie and Dr. Kildare?" Apparently, the film had something to say to the Japanese which was not communicated to many foreigners.

Until *Red Beard,* Kurosawa had usually dealt with two apparently different sets of themes. There were the modern films with their continual

reworking of the ideas of sickness, crime, and rebirth; and the costume dramas, which dealt with much broader, more obviously humanistic themes:
studies of the nature of man and the nature of good and evil. Except for
Ikiru, the modern films rarely had quite the grandeur, the objectivity, the
philosophic breadth and scope of the historical ones, although several had
a striking power and immediacy of their own.

Kurosawa seems always to have looked upon man and modern man as
almost distinct species, modern man being sick and criminal in a very special
way. His criticism of modern life is taken, I believe, from a traditionalist
rather than a revolutionary standpoint, and it is also important to remember
that most of his modern dress films deal specifically with the depressive
atmosphere and morale of a nation in defeat. The Westernization of postwar
Japan repelled him, unquestionably, but even more so, the mood of moral
and cultural defeatism that went with it. In all his films, Kurosawa shows
himself to be selectively committed to the premodern Japanese system of
ethics and aesthetics; and that ethics and aesthetics are so linked in his mind
is itself a very Japanese way of looking at things. It is also true that he has
always been intensely critical of many traditional Japanese ways; authoritarianism and militarism seem to lure and repel him at the same time. He is at
once egalitarian and élitist. But the acceptance of modern ways seems to
him a leap from bad to worse, and the rich ambivalence which he brings to
his studies of the past is missing from his vision of the present. The images
by which he describes the modern scene: the dance halls, the bars, the
industrial slums, the smoking factories, the blaring music and roaring mer-
ciless traffic, the sex shows, the billboards, drug dens, the sad insensitive
faces, littered streets, and boring offices: these images and the scenes built
around them bespeak an overwhelming disgust, pity and contempt. The past
may have been brutal, full of injustice, exploitation and tyranny; but at least
it fostered better taste, handsomer scenery and a breed of men with more
dignity, purpose and mental and physical health than the modern world can
show. Where once there was the peasant, ignorant and oppressed but at
least intimate with nature and his comrades, now there is only the anonymous office drudge. Where stood the samurai, a cruel fighting man but disciplined by his breeding and his code of honor, there is now only the vulgar,
ignorant gangster. The priest and sage have given way to the doctor and
policeman, themselves unsure of their values and often as much in need of
cure or policing as those they are responsible for, and surrounded on all
sides by monsters of selfishness and greed. This vision, this sense of contrast between past and present, is familiar enough to the modern West, especially in the works of such writers as Yeats. It is one of the many modern
forms of Romanticism, and such Romanticism is even stronger in Japan than
elsewhere. It is in fact an indigenous and not a borrowed theme. Such concepts compelled Mishima's life and death. In the gentler Kurosawa they
found gentler expression. As he envisioned it, in feudal times salvation and

purpose could be achieved in whatever place one happened to be born into, because each class had its useful function, its value, its joys as well as its sorrows. In modern times, these conditions do not exist. The factory girl in *Ikiru* radiates joy and goodness, but she was miraculously born that way: she was neither taught nor can she teach. Those few characters who struggle toward becoming what she so easily and simply is, do so with overwhelming difficulty. In modern society, as Kurosawa sees it, redemption and salvation are private, personal events. Society itself is all but devoid of values, except for the wreck of those which it has inherited from the past, and which it continues to reject, ignorant of their worth. Kurosawa may have arrived at his vision of the modern world by a route which few Western intellectuals have taken, and yet his vision is one which any Western intellectual would instantly recognize.

If *Red Beard* does represent Kurosawa's ultimate vision and revision, it is because it expresses a reconciliation of the present with the past, an abatement of his bitterness against the modern world. In *Red Beard* he applies to the past the same metaphors of sickness, guilt and redemption which were previously reserved for the modern scene. Manners may have been more gracious, but the underlying realities were the same. In every age, the same laws of life apply, especially the Buddhist law of karma, the concept that acts breed consequences after their own likeness. The transformation of this breeding of like by like can be transformed from the physical to the spiritual plane, much as energy and matter are understood to be interchangeable in physics. Illness breeds evil which breeds more illness. Good breeds health, which breeds more good. An evil society breeds sickness, moral and physical, which a good doctor may treat, and sometimes cure, by the power of his goodness. But the world has accumulated so much evil that even the best doctor must fail much of the time, since he struggles not merely against physical illness but spiritual evil as well. The hope he represents is that the good he does must necessarily breed good consequences.

It is this pervasive metaphysic which must have made *Red Beard* seem so strange, so sentimental, to the West. The social despair and the stoic Existentialism of *Ikiru* seemed all too familiar and made it acceptable, despite its optimistic elements. But although *Red Beard* offers plenty of despair and even something resembling Existentialism, its pervasive mood and theme are gaily optimistic. Optimism, in the West, has become associated with sentimentality; but the Japanese have retained sufficient optimism (or sentimentality) to be able to take the likes of *Red Beard* in their stride. *Red Beard* is set in a time when there were no antibiotics, no heart-lung machines, no anesthetics, when a doctor had no tools but his own will to cure. The leading character runs an underfinanced government clinic in a slum, and most of his patients have already accumulated the effects of so much evil that they are incurable. The doctor can only ease their dying or patch them up temporarily. He rations his time, concentrating on the youngest patients and those few older ones who really want to live. Above all, he concentrates on his intern, a vain and resentful young man assigned to the clinic against his will. Since a good doctor cures and a bad one kills, and since this intern has years of practice before him, *his* reform is the doctor's most urgent business. Redeeming him, he saves not only one individual but also aids by proxy all the intern's future patients.

Perhaps Kurosawa finally had concluded that the evils of modern society are basically the same ones which have always existed: greed, selfishness, wrath, sensuality, fear: all of them, according to Buddhist ethics, the fruit of egoism. And that the way of cure must be that of the Bodhisattva: the influence of a humble, selfless life devoted to service. Kurosawa has said that he has made all his films for one audience, young Japanese in their teens and twenties, in order to remind them of their heritage. Apparently, Kurosawa conceives of himself more as a moral teacher than an artist. Still, he *is* an artist, and a particularly great and honest one. His works transcend not only their time and place but also their deliberate purpose. It is not necessary to share his values to be stirred by his art. Yet his values, his opinions, do matter. Kurosawa has the reputation of being the most Western of Japanese directors, yet he is certainly also very Japanese. And it seems to me that his works are best understood in the context of the ethics from which they take their life and purpose.

Kurosawa's Detective-Story Parables

NORMAN SILVERSTEIN

K UROSAWA AKIRA'S detective-story films have as their model neither the
intruder into nice families nor the syndicate of criminals, as do American counterparts in the genre. In *Stray Dog* (1949) and *High and Low*
(1963), his apparent subject is the art of detection, as in Sherlock Holmes
stories, but the real subject is unmotivated goodness, like Bogart's in *The
Maltese Falcon.* Both Kurosawa films are morally instructive.

In *Stray Dog,* Kurosawa's detective, played by Toshiro Mifune with Bogart's powers, is a good man who *wills* himself to do good. The film begins
with a shot of a mongrel breathing hard, but the sound track produces, not
the dog's sounds, but the rumbling of a train in motion. Since the chief setting is the railroad and the antagonist a "stray" veteran of World War II, the
train's rumbling and the dog's breathing introduce both the film's setting
and its chief symbol. The protagonist, also a veteran, has become a detective.
While he is riding the train in the rush-hour, his gun is stolen. The detective
is ready to resign from the force. With the help of older men on the force, he
learns two lessons of life: first, that the "stray dog" who has stolen his gun is
likely to become a "mad dog," desperate enough to kill many; and, secondly,
that the detective's ill fortune may be turned into good fortune. That the
stray dog becomes a mad dog is one element of the parable. Like the detec-
tive-hero, the gun-robber has been struggling for existence in postwar Japan,
both men having had their knapsacks stolen on their return to Japan. The
stray dog has hardened into evil. In the end, Satan-like, he becomes a creature of despair, causing evil out of his will-less inability to do good. The
detective persists in good. In their final confrontation, the two grapple amid
flowers (a garden of Eden) in a Miltonic struggle between good and evil,
which, according to Milton, "first came into the world as twin progeny."
Donald Richie, in *The Japanese Film,* says of this struggle that the two are
indistinguishable—good and evil being covered by a primeval ooze. Unfortunately, he does not take the outcome of the struggle into consideration.
When both men become exhausted, the detective handcuffs the gun-robber.
Their similarity is only momentary. The good detective triumphs by an act of
will. The message, therefore, is that good Japanese can overcome the hard-
ships in their social lives by a will to do good.

A second lesson of *Stray Dog* applies both to the Japanese of 1949 and to
men generally. The detective who wants to resign in the face of the loss of

Reprinted from *Japan Quarterly* 12, no. 3 (July–September 1965): 351–54, by permission of
Japan Quarterly and the Estate of Eleanor S. Peiser.

his gun at first accepts despair. When he subsequently engages in the struggle for his honor, he performs the difficult task of making fortune reverse itself. By stalking a woman who knows where the gun is, by following the guns-for-hire criminal syndicate who loan out his gun, and by, at length, fulfilling his plan of finding and bringing to justice the original gun-robber, the hero enables the capture of a ring of criminals, not of his own enemy alone. The message for the Japanese of 1949 is that they too may force their destiny——a philosophy that is the opposite of fatalism. It is a message that absorbs best what Americans pretended to teach the Japanese in their occupation of that country. Armed with a philosophy of good works, men may turn bad fortune into good fortune.

Fourteen years later, in *High and Low,* Kurosawa restates the triumph of good over evil in a second detective-story parable. Based on *King's Ransom,* an American detective novel of the Eighty-Seventh Precinct series by Ed McBain, pseudonym of Evan Hunter who wrote *The Blackboard Jungle* and *A Summer House,* this Tohoscope (Cinemascope) film uses various devices that raise the film above the level of the melodrama and the sentimentality toward which the genre is prone.

In *King's Ransom,* an executive, faced with the dilemma of saving his fortune or someone else's son, refuses to pay a ransom. As Judith Crist reviews the original:

> Well, much to the distress of McBain's humane cops, the American tycoon refuses [to pay the ransom]. His wife leaves him, taking their son; the cops scorn him—but he cannot, as a self-made man, destroy himself. Finally, with a suitcase stuffed with newspapers instead of money, he goes off to the rendezvous. Simultaneously, however, the wife of one of the kidnapers has a change of heart and she turns informer. The tycoon helps in the capture of the master criminal, the child is saved, the goodhearted criminals escape, and we suspect that the errant wife will be wooed back.

Out of these materials, with the easy optimism of their solution, Kurosawa has made a parable that educates men in how to live.

In Kurosawa's story, an intern tries to kidnap the son of a shoe manufacturer but demands the same ransom of 30 million yen for the chauffeur's son whom he has taken by mistake. For the first hour of the film, Kurosawa restricts the setting to the rich man's house on a hill in Yokohama, the *high* of the title. In order to gain control of National Shoes, the self-made capitalist has mortgaged his possessions. His noble purpose is not naked power, but rather the God-like role of controlling what base capitalists would pervert: he rejects their planned obsolescence for increased shoe consumption. After the kidnaping, the executive faced with the alternative of saving the chauffeur's boy or maintaining his money and his social position chooses the former course. The setting then moves to the payoff, to the boy's return, and to the kidnapper who represents the *low* of the title.

After the payoff, the police, who have been docile, undertake recovery in the mass police action common to such films. "Now," says the lovable bull-like detective, "let us become bloodhounds." When the police wander in the slum-valley below the house on the hill, one of them, looking up, says, "The kidnaper is right. That house makes me sore." Kurosawa shows the house on the hill, cuts to the cramped, ugly houses in the valley beside a stream in which the hill house is reflected, plays on the sound track Schubert's "The Trout," and leads us along with the kidnaper to his room.

The story is not new. And the suspense of Joseph Hayes' *The Desperate Hours* and of "B" detective films is here repeated. The genre is lowbrow, but Kurosawa's elevation of the theme is strong. The kidnaper is not made psychopathic. Instead, like Dostoevsky's Raskolnikoff, he is smitten with *angst*, the despair, partly social, that comes when one finds that life is hell. Satan-like, the kidnaper has set out to make a fortunate man unfortunate. After receiving a death sentence, the kidnaper requests to see, not a priest, but the good man whom he has undertaken to torment. In a confrontation of good and evil, high and low, the tycoon asks, "Why must you hate?" In torment, the kidnaper trembles, weeps, and shakes furiously. He explains that from the Hell below, the house on the hill looked like Heaven. In a final image, an iron curtain falls between them: good on one side, evil on the other—the inescapable duality of choice that confronts each man.

Like other Christian artists, Kurosawa sees the triumph of unity and therefore of good and of God in the moral war among men. He tells in detective-story form a parable of the ultimate as well as the daily triumph of good over evil. The victory is hard fought and far from hollow. Kurosawa's good man does not grow tired. Vigilant in his goodness, he struggles for his triumph.

The screen pullulates with small delights. The technical device known as the *wipe*—as of a windshield wiper—by which a director punctuates a scene and makes a transition to a next scene, is brilliantly used when Kurosawa wipes a scene in the hill house with a speeding train from which the ransom will be paid. After the payoff—two cases containing ransom shoved through a seven-inch opening in the train's bathroom window—the tycoon washes his hands as if after defecation. The moral evil has made him feel his body to be dirty. At the capture, a radio ironically plays "good night" music, the song being "There's No Tomorrow." In another bit of sound montage, Kurosawa creates cosmic implications for his parable. He uses three electronic beeps as he shows a panorama of Yokohama—sounds that function in the film like Chekhov's famous "sound of a harp string breaking," a cosmic omen in *The Cherry Orchard*.

Between 1949 and 1963 Japan has undergone material prosperity and heightened westernization—evident in the *mise en scène* of the two films. The goal of Kurosawa's hope in 1949 was political and religious. He taught free Japanese the responsibility of their actions—the essential message of the democratic occupation of Japan. He also believed in Christian right reason such as he found it in Dostoevsky and in his own Christian faith. However adverse the circumstances of postwar life, he seemed to say, a man will forge his own destiny. In 1963, with *High and Low,* he could reinforce this belief in man's free will. While Fellini, Antonioni, and Bergman—his compeers—demand only a hesitant faith in right action, Kurosawa insists on the simple duality of good and evil. For example, Bergman's Christian trilogy is more complex. The *angst* of the tired good before an uncomprehending God leaves the good with only the forms of worship: doubting parsons preach on. Kurosawa's parables show men the joy of goodness that controls fortune. In times of simpler folk, Jesus spoke in terms of sheep-herders and fishermen about how men should live. Using the more complex imagery of modern fiction, Kurosawa uses the detective story to urge democracy and to restate a Dostoevskian faith in man.

Rashomon

STANLEY KAUFFMANN

L ITTLE IS emptier in art criticism than the global pronouncement. Whenever we see the assertion that "X is the best in the world," we have a right to suspect enthusiastic ignorance. From time to time, we get a sharp reminder about our limited knowledge of an art, in world terms, and few such reminders have been sharper than the showing of *Rashomon* at the Venice Film Festival in 1951.

Up to then, although the Japanese film industry had been enormously active, with high annual production figures, it might as well have been situated on the moon as far as the West was concerned. World War II was not a prime reason for the gap; relatively few Japanese films had been seen in Europe and America before 1939. When *Rashomon* opened in New York in 1951, it was the first Japanese film to be shown there in fourteen years. The barrier to import was financial, not political—the same barrier that obstructs the import of foreign literature.

The cultural shock that followed from the Venice Festival showing was a smaller mirror image of the shock felt in Japan a century earlier when Commodore Perry dropped in. Then the Japanese had learned of a technological civilization about which they knew very little; now the West learned of a highly developed film art about which they knew even less. It would, alas, be untrue to say that the import situation is greatly improved. It is not: the money barriers still intervene because Japanese films have not been very profitable in the United States. But at least we now have a much clearer idea of what we are missing, and maybe in that knowledge lies some hope.

The first Japanese director to be known in the West was Akira Kurosawa, who made *Rashomon.* This was lucky, because Kurosawa is not merely a good director, he is one of film's great masters. Moreover, his career tells us something, prototypically, about the Japanese film world. He was born in Tokyo in 1910, the son of an ex-army officer who was teaching physical education. Kurosawa, unattracted to either of his father's professions, studied painting at the Doshusha School of Western Painting. (Note its name.) In 1936 he saw an advertisement by a film studio looking for assistant directors; applicants were asked to send in an essay on the basic defects of Japanese films and how to remedy them. He replied, and—along with five hundred others—he was invited to try out further, with a screen treatment and

Reprinted from *Living Images* (New York: Harper and Row, 1975), 316-24. Copyright 1975 by Stanley Kauffmann, reprinted by permission.

an oral examination. He was hired, and became an assistant to a director named Kajiro Yamamoto.

This assignment was momentous in Kurosawa's career. In that invaluable book *The Japanese Film* by Joseph L. Anderson and Donald Richie, there is a chart that shows the apostolic succession of Japanese directors—who trained whom after being trained by someone else. The system of Japanese film training very early took on some of the tradition-conscious quality of Japanese culture generally. From Yamamoto, Kurosawa learned, among other things, a high regard for the script. (He has often quoted Yamamoto's remark: "To understand motion pictures fully, one must be able to write a script.") Besides his work as assistant, he also worked on screenplays. In 1941 Yamamoto made a film called *Horses,* of which he said later, "When we were making *Horses,* [Kurosawa] was still called my assistant, but he was much more than that, he was more like my other self." In 1943 Kurosawa was given his first solo directing assignment, and by 1950 he had made eleven films. Some of them, shown in the U.S. after *Rashomon,* are very much more than apprentice works, but it is this twelfth picture of his that proclaims his mastery.

The script, by Kurosawa and Shinobu Hashimoto, is based on two short stories about medieval Japan by a twentieth-century author, Ryunosuke Akutagawa, who died at thirty-five in 1927 and is so well esteemed that a literary prize has been established in his name. He is best known for his short stories, and those stories, says C. J. Dunn, have a modernity and universality of approach that "make them readily appreciated by Western readers." (Remember Kurosawa's painting school.)

From the first Akutagawa story, "Rashomon," the film takes little more than a setting—the place where the film begins, to which it returns, and where it closes—along with a mood of desolation caused by the waste of civil war. Rashomon was the name of the largest gate in Kyoto, the ancient capital of Japan; it was built in the eighth century, and by the twelfth century, the time of the film, it was already in disrepair. In this great but dilapidated gate three men—a woodcutter, a priest, and a man called simply a commoner—huddle together out of a pouring rain and recount various versions of a murder that took place recently in the vicinity.

The second story, "In a Grove," is the source of the murder narrative. There are some central facts: a samurai and his wife were traveling through a forest and were waylaid by a notorious bandit who tied up the husband and ravished the wife; the husband was killed, and his body was found by the woodcutter.

But there are four versions of the events surrounding these central facts, and we see each version as it is recounted. The first is that of the bandit who was captured soon after and told his story to a police magistrate. The bandit says that he tricked the samurai, bound him, and assaulted the wife who quickly became compliant. Afterward, at the wife's insistence, he released the husband so that they could fight, and killed the samurai in a long hazardous duel.

Then the priest gives the version he heard the wife give the magistrate. She says that, after the rape, the bandit left. She saw the hate in her husband's eyes, because she had not resisted sufficiently, and in a frenzy of grief and shame, she (apparently) killed him, then ran away.

The third version, also recounted by the priest, is that of the dead husband, who spoke through a medium. The husband says that, after the seduction, the wife urged the bandit to murder him and take her along. The bandit declined, released the husband, and left. Alone, the husband killed himself with a dagger. Later, after his death, he felt someone take the dagger away.

The woodcutter then says this can't be true—no dagger was there, he was killed by a sword. Under the commoner's pressure, the woodcutter then revises his story of discovering the samurai's body—and gives us a fourth version. He says that he came along just after the ravishing and watched from behind a bush. The wife was crying, the bandit was pleading with her to go away with him. She said that the men would have to decide whom she was to go with. She cut her husband free with the dagger, but he was at first unwilling to fight for this woman he now despised. She taunted them into fighting—a brawl that was a parody of the noble duel recounted earlier by the bandit. The husband was killed. The woman fled. Somewhat dazed, the bandit limped off with his sword and the samurai's.

The "true" version is never established. At the end of the film the three men in the Rashomon gate are in various states: depression about human beings (the woodcutter), cynical glee (the commoner), desperate hope (the priest). Suddenly they hear a baby crying in a corner of the huge gate, an abandoned infant. The commoner tries to steal the baby's garments, and when the woodcutter stops him, the commoner turns on him fiercely, calls him a hypocrite, and accuses him of stealing the samurai's expensive dagger, which was not found at the scene of the crime. The woodcutter does not explicitly admit it, but he offers to take the infant home, into his already large family, perhaps as a penance for his lie and his (presumable) theft, perhaps as a token of his hope for human hope. This final sequence with the infant has been much criticized for its patness and sudden surge of uplift, but one can argue that Kurosawa felt that the very arbitrariness of this incident would make the central story's necessary ambiguity resonate more strongly.

Why should this film have had such a strong impact? Surely not because of the script alone. It is a good enough Pirandellian teaser with somber overtones, but—on paper—it is little more than one more statement of a familiar idea, the contradictory nature of truth, the impossibility of absolutes. On film, because of its cinematic qualities that grow out of the script but surpass it, *Rashomon* becomes a work of greater size.

One general reason for the film's impact is its cultural accessibility. Many Japanese directors, including at least one who is on Kurosawa's creative plane, Yasujiro Ozu, are more difficult to approach, more "Japanese." Kurosawa has always resisted being labeled a Westerner in any sense that makes him seem unsympathetic to his own culture, but he has always asserted that "the Western and the Japanese live side by side in my mind naturally, without the least sense of conflict." His fine-arts training and his response to Akutagawa, of all Japanese authors, support this thesis. Also, as he has said many times, he greatly admires American directors, especially John Ford, William Wyler, and Frank Capra. So, at Venice in 1951, those who might have expected this film to be couched in the esthetics of Noh or kabuki—which Kurosawa has indeed used elsewhere—found instead a work that was intrinsically Japanese yet certainly not remote in style or dynamics.

But of course there are other values in *Rashomon* that give it stature, much larger and deeper than Kurosawa's cosmopolitanism. Chief among these, I think, are three particular beauties.

First, the acting. As the woodcutter, Takashi Shimura runs through the film like a quiet stream of human concern—human enough to be himself found out in wrongdoing. Shimura, who was trained in the theater, had already played in eight pictures for Kurosawa and later gave (very different) wonderful performances for this director in *The Seven Samurai* and *Ikiru.* The samurai's wife, Machiko Kyo, who began her career as a dancer, is a famous star of Japanese film. The four versions of the murder story provide, in effect, four women to play, each of whom she draws precisely. But the outstanding performance, partly because it is in the most colorful role, is that of Toshiro Mifune as the bandit.

Mifune, now the best-known Japanese actor in the world, began in films in 1946 after five years in the Japanese army. He made four Kurosawa films before *Rashomon* and made many subsequent ones, including versions of Dostoevsky's *The Idiot,* Shakespeare's *Macbeth,* and Gorki's *The Lower Depths.* He has said of Kurosawa, "I have never as an actor done anything that I am proud of other than with him." Kurosawa has told the story that, while the company was waiting to start on Rashomon, they ran off some travelogue films to pass the time, including one about Africa. In it there was a lion roaming around. "I noticed it and told Mifune that that was just what I wanted him to be." Mifune succeeded. He gives one of the most purely feral performances on film—animalistic in both the bestial and the elemental senses, a man concentrated wholly on physical satisfactions and with a fierce power to satisfy them.

The second important aspect of this film is the use of blocks, or plaques, of visual texture. Each of the three main locations of the story has a distinct visual "feel": the gate, the courtyard of the police station where the witnesses testify, and the forest where the stories take place. The gate scenes are drenched in rain. Until the very last moments, each of these gate scenes is seen- and heard-through torrents, frequently emphasized by being shot from ground level so that we see the rain pounding the earth. The fall of the rain is often matched by a vertical view of the scene from above.

In the testimony scenes the witnesses kneel before us, motionless. (We never see the magistrate, who "is" the camera.) In contrast to the gate scenes, these courtyard scenes are sunlit, and the composition is horizontal. Three great parallel bands stretch across the screen: one of shadow, close to us, in which the testifying witness kneels; one of sunlight behind it, in which the preceding witness kneel; and the top of the low courtyard wall behind them. The camera rarely moves in these scenes. Kurosawa creates a tension between the violent stories being recounted and the serenity of the picture.

The third plaque of texture, the forest, is dappled with sunlight and filled with movement—horizontal as the characters move forward, vertical as the camera frequently looks up at the sun.

These three distinctive textures are, first, aids to our understanding of a complex narrative: we know immediately where we are at every moment. They also provide a contrapuntal texture: the somber setting for the conversation of the troubled woodcutter and the priest and the cynical commoner; the quiet place of recollection; the kinetically lighted and composed setting for the rape and murder.

The last major esthetic component of *Rashomon* is the quality of the motion in those forest scenes. Kurosawa has said:

> I make use of two or three cameras almost all the time. I cut the film freely and splice together the pieces which have caught the action most forcefully, as if flying from one piece to another.

He has made this use of motion in motion pictures uniquely his own, and never more "forcefully" than in the forest scenes of Rashomon. In the forest, where there is danger to people and, more important, danger to truth, the camera hovers, darts, glides, and swoops, like a skimming bird.

The very opening of the first forest sequence sets the style. Near the end of the gate scene with which the film begins, we are looking down from high above at the men crouched below out of the rain. We cut to a close-up of Shimura's face as he begins to tell his story. Then there is a sharp cut to the bright sun, seen through tree branches as the camera travels forward—a cut accompanied by the sudden entrance of strong rhythmic music. The sequence that follows is dazzling—dazzling both in the virtuosity of the shooting and editing and in the way that these skills are used for mood and point. The next shot is of the woodcutter's ax, on his shoulder, gleaming in the sun as he strides along. Then the camera precedes him as he walks toward us, follows him, and in one especially beautiful moment, arcs across toward him as he strides toward us, crosses in front of him as he approaches, then follows him from the other side. More than underscoring the burst of sunlight and movement into the film, this camera motion sets a tone of comment, of near-teasing, implying, "Stride on, stride on. An ordinary day's work, you think, woodcutter? Stride on. And see." He does see. He and the camera's ballet around him halt suddenly when he spies a woman's hat hanging on a bush. He and the camera resume—and stop again when he spies a man's hat and some other objects. Again he and his observer resume —and this time he halts in horror. We see his face through the upright, death-rigid arms of the slain samurai. The camera, fulfilling its implied promise, looks through those arms at the woodcutter's face.

This marvelously intricate and graceful dance of the camera continues through all the versions of the forest story. In a sense we are always aware of it; it would be overly reticent if we were not. The language of a good poem is enjoyable at the same time that the poem moves to something for which the language is only the visible sign. Kurosawa is always sure to make his camera movement, wonderful in itself, inseparable from what it treats. For instance, the bandit and the samurai fight twice, once in the bandit's story, once in the woodcutter's. In the first, both men fence brilliantly. The second fight is a frantic brawl in which both men look foolish. In both encounters the camera leaps around them like an imp, heightening the fever, but the camera rhythms and perspectives match the quality of the fight in each case.

Now since all this camera movement is silken smooth, at the furthest remove from sickening hand-held improvisation, every smallest action of the players and of Kurosawa's camera had to be planned in detail. Tracks had to be built on which the cameras could dolly. These sequences were obviously shot outdoors, in a real forest, so every inch of the camera's traverse had to be prepared, sometimes in a way that allowed a camera to come around and look back—without a break—at the place it had just left, without revealing the tracks on which it had traveled. These technical details of preparation would not be our concern except for what underlies them: a realization of how thoroughly Kurosawa had to know in advance what he was doing and why. A film director does not have the freedom of inspiration, in sequences of this kind, that a theater director or choreographer has. Long-range design is of the essence here; and the quicksilver insight of these designs—their feeling of spontaneous flight—is extraordinary.

That Venice festival audience must have had a bit of a shock when the music began in that first forest scene. Many have noted its strong resemblance to Ravel's *Bolero*. Not by accident. Kurosawa told his composer, Fumio Hayasaka, to "write something like Ravel's *Bolero*." Apparently the Ravel piece was not then well-known in Japan and had not become something of the self-parody that it now is to Western ears. Western music can be heard in many Kurosawa films. In the films set in the present, it is often used to show the alteration of Japanese culture. Here Kurosawa apparently thought he was appropriating a helpful Western vitality for *Rashomon*. But whatever the effect of that music was or is on Japanese ears, it is still bothersome to ours. Kurosawa is big enough to bear a blemish. If we can forgive Dickens for naming one of his female characters Rosa Bud, we can forgive Kurosawa for his Ravel imitation.

Earlier I noted that *Rashomon*, the film, is a far larger work than its good-enough script. This is a commonplace about any satisfying film, of course, even about some unsatisfying ones, but it has a special pertinence in this case. Kurosawa's vision, his steely yet sympathetic sense of drama, his power to make the screen teem with riches yet without any heavy-breathing lushness, his overwhelming faculties of rhythmic control that translate emotion into motion, all these produce a question in us. We ask: Can such a subtle and complex artist really have bothered to make a film about—as has been said—"The unknowability of truth"? Would that trite theme have been enough for such a man? Finally, the very quality of Kurosawa's art opens up this banal version of relativism to reveal the element that generates the relativism: the element of ego, of self. Finally, *Rashomon* deals with the preservation of self, an idea that—in this film—outlasts earthly life. That idea is not the sanctity of each individual as a political concept, not the value of each soul as a religious concept, but stark, fundamental *amour-propre*. The bandit wants to preserve and defend his ego, the wife hers, and the husband, dead and out of his body, wants the same. Even the woodcutter, who has little *amour-propre* to protect, is forced to tell a more complete version of his story in self-defense.

Ego underlies all, the film says at last. What is good and what is horrible in our lives, in the way we affect other lives, grows from ego: not merely the biological impulse to stay alive but to have that life with some degree of pride.

In the Christian lexicon, pride is the first deadly sin; but in our daily lives, Christian or not, Westerner or Easterner, we know that this sin is at least reliable. We can depend on it for motive power. All of us acknowledge that we ought to be moved primarily by love; all of us know that we are moved primarily by self. *Rashomon* is, essentially, a ruthlessly honest film. Exquisitely made, electrically exciting, it reaches down—by means of these qualities—to a quiet, giant truth nestled in everyone of us. Ultimately what the film leaves with us is candor and consolation: if we can't be saints, at least we can be understandingly human.

Rashomon

ANDRÉ BAZIN

T HE QUALITY, originality, and importance of a work like *Rashomon* are
deeply disconcerting for criticism. Indeed it throws the viewer into an
absolutely Oriental aesthetic universe. It does this, though, through a cinematic technique (photography and editing) which implies a solid and already
ancient assimilation of the whole evolution of Western film, so that it completely enters a radically foreign system. Indian films are slow; Egyptian films
are elementary and don't count. A series of psychological filters seems to
come between us and the story they tell. These filters are not the same as
material awkwardness but determine certain characteristics of the technique:
shot length, slowness of the acting, simplicity in editing, lack of ellipse, and
so forth. But one is certainly less alienated by the *technical* aspects of
Rashomon than by those of a Soviet film, for example. I tend to think that
this phenomenon on the cinematic level is merely the result of Japan's particular evolution in the last fifty years (coinciding with the invention of filmmaking). We hear that the first Japanese films date from 1902. Our surprise
in seeing *Rashomon* stems from the distant echoes of the Western world
when faced with the 1905 Russian defeat and, more recently, Pearl Harbor.
I mean to say that we are surprised by the Japanese ability to assimilate the
technology of Western civilization and still retain an Oriental metaphysics,
ethics, and psychology.

Be that as it may, the artfulness of the staging and directing in *Rashomon*
implies not only technological *means* of the same caliber as those of Hollywood, for example, but total possession of the expressive resources of film.
Editing, depth of field, framing, and camera movement serve the story with
equal freedom and mastery.

And yet this story is specifically Japanese in subject matter if not in structure. The action takes place in the Middle Ages. A rich traveler and his wife are
traveling through a forest when a thief ambushes them. He subdues the man,
ties him to a tree, rapes his wife before his eyes, and then kills him. A woodcutter witnesses all this. But during the trial of the thief, captured a few days
later, the three survivors of the scene—the thief, the woman, and the woodcutter—each tell a different version of the event. The film presents us with
three successive versions, or rather four. With astounding boldness, the filmmaker also presents us with a version of the murder as told through a witch

speaking in the dead man's voice. But nothing leads us to believe that the dead man's tale is more accurate than that of the others. This apparently "Pirandellian" action also has a moral purpose: it serves to illustrate not so much the impossibility of knowing the truth through the human conscience as believing in the goodness of man. In each of these versions, one of the protagonists in the drama reveals an evil side. We can suppose that this radical phenomenon is fairly sincere once we know that *Rashomon*'s plot is based on a novel by Ryunosuke Akutagawa, who committed suicide in 1927.

I spoke of a mastery on a par with that of the most developed Western films. I did not say "identical." It so happens that certain aspects of the film are purely Japanese: first of all the action, as we have seen. Can we imagine an American or European script based on such an audacious situation as a wife being raped before her husband's eyes? Needless to say, no one is bothered by this boldness any more than by the obscenity of Phaedra's origins in *La Fille de Minos et de Pasiphaé: Minos' and Pasiphae's Daughter.*

The film is especially Japanese in the acting style. The influence of Noh theater is quite obvious. Yet the true problem, which only a specialist could resolve, would be how and in what way were the traditions of Japanese theatrical acting adapted to cinematic realism. But if the acting is always perceived as excessive, it is never exaggerated nor is it symbolic. In other words, the acting style is in the tragic vein (in which it evokes the masque) and yet it does not abandon psychological realism. It could not be more different from the exaggerated acting, reinforced by makeup, of the silent expressionist cinema. The actor is at the same time tragic and natural, perfectly integrated with the real set in which he performs. The basic problem of the tragic style, which Western films could only resolve infrequently and uncertainly *(Nosferatu,* 1923; *The Passion of Joan of Arc; Les Dames du Bois de Boulogne,* 1944; *Hamlet)* is not in question here. It is resolved immediately.

In the same way there is no break or dissonance between the acting style and the cutting. If it were possible to justify that filmology is the concern of philologists and logicians, such a film would be a solid argument for it. Is film as a language SELF-encompassing as is human reason? We canot say that here the filmmaker is copying Western films or even that he is inspired by them. It would seem, rather, that he attains the same result through fundamental unity and universality of screen vocabulary, grammar, and style. A traveling shot is a traveling shot, be it Japanese, French, or American. But there is a certain rhythm, speed, and harmony between frame and camera movement. The traveling shots in *Rashomon* are therefore no more imported than the acting. There is an even more significant example relative to the use of sound: the tale of death is told through the words of a witch during a dance of possession. The oracle speaks with the dead man's voice, although strongly off-key and high-pitched. As could be expected, the effect is hallucinating. Such an original idea—Western films quickly lost interest in the expressionism of sound—implies a mastery of technology that is only equaled by the freedom with which it is used.

   How does it happen that all these reasons for admiring this film do not, however, result in an unqualified approval? *Rashomon* implies the past and future existence of a solidly established production with skilled technicians, perfectly trained actors, a national cinematic talent—in short, a situation much more comparable to that of England or France than to Mexico. Beneath our admiration and astonishment for such a work lies an uneasy feeling that we are perhaps being deceived. *Rashomon,* in its own way, is a serial film. Wouldn't we have the same feeling when seeing a good American film for the first time? At the one hundredth viewing we would discover that language is, in the last analysis, only language, and that a great film is something more. In a word, I suspect that hidden by the originality (relative to our ignorance) of *Rashomon,* there is a certain banality of perfection that limits my pleasure. This reservation is also a compliment. I have heard that Japan produces better films. I willingly believe it and would not be too surprised to learn that Akira Kurosawa is the Julian Duvivier of Japanese films.

Kurosawa's Women

JOAN MELLEN

I n *RASHOMON* woman is perceived as castrating female taunting competing males for not being "real men." "A woman can be won only by strength, by the strength of the swords you are wearing," she screeches near the end of the film. And it is with this view of her character that Kurosawa leaves us. He has given no grounds for belief in Masago's own story, the only one in which she does not respond passionately to the bandit. And even in that story, she is a murderess. Her punishment is presented implicitly as a just reward for her having assumed the role of docile wife under blatantly false pretenses.

After *Rashomon,* Kurosawa seemed to have abandoned his interest in the potential of women, as if repelled by Masago, that half-demon of his own creation. His response is parallel to that of the culture itself. Women are rendered powerless and subordinate and hence reduced, like Masago, to manipulation or deceit for influence and survival. Then the image of the feline woman is reified by male perpetrators into a stereotype. It is a classic example of the self-fulfilling prophecy and the prototype of all social victimization, unmediated in the Japanese film by the presence of women directors, with the exception of a few minor directorial efforts by the actress Kinuyo Tanaka. And once, of course, the stereotype is elevated to a symbol in the arts, presented as an image of truth, the impact of this perpetuated myth in turn conditions the view women have of themselves. It is indeed a vicious circle, as yet unbroken in Japan by profound social change.

Kurosawa has made two adaptations from Russian literary works, *The Idiot (Hakuchi,* 1951) and *The Lower Depths (Donzoko,* 1957). In both, the women fall into one of two summary categories. The sensual woman is portrayed as the castrating bitch and the "good" girl is devoid of any capacity for pleasure. Thus, in his version of Dostoevsky's *The Idiot,* Kurosawa's Nastasya, called Taeko Nasu (and played by Setsuko Hara), the woman whom Mishkin wishes to save, is reduced to the stereotype of the female who destroys men. Her destructiveness is so devastating that it pains Kameda (Mishkin) even to look at her. Further, her frenzied outbursts, which Kurosawa accepts from the Russian original to reinforce his sense of her "badness," are so out of keeping in a Japanese context that she causes embarrassment instead of serving as a suitable object for the hero's compassion.

Reprinted from *The Waves at Genji's Door: Japan Through Its Cinema* (New York: Pantheon, 1976), 50–54, by permission of the author.

Kurosawa's equally close adaptation of Gorky's *The Lower Depths* finds the two women who love the thief Sutekichi (Toshiro Mifune) again expressing the two sides of Masago; together they capture Kurosawa's now fixed sense of woman. The landlord's vicious wife, Osugi (Isuzu Yamada), is manipulative and malicious as a woman scorned. Sutekichi prefers Osugi's sister, Okayo (Kyoko Kagawa), who embodies woman as angel, sweetly obliging and therefore weak and unable to survive on her own. "Some day I'll end up like this," she says, observing the coughing old woman dying in pain and freezing under her thin blankets. It is a direct echo of Gorky's Natasha, who laments, "Some day I will end up like that—in a basement— forgotten by everybody."

By the end of the film, Osugi has beaten up her sister many times and engineered, as well, Sutekichi's murder of her old, usurious husband. In Gorky's original she says, "I beat her so hard, I cry, myself, out of pity for her." Okayo, in panic, irrationally denounces both Osugi and the innocent Sutekichi: "They killed him [the landlord] and now they're going to kill me." She is too callow to perceive the sincerity of Sutekichi's love. In a hysterical fray, evil triumphs. Okayo disappears, and it isn't known if she is alive or dead. Osugi is in prison, as is Sutekichi. All has come to nought. The knowing whore, Osen, echoing the secret feeling of all oppressed women, exclaims, "I wish every man was banished from the town." Okayo is good and Osugi, evil, but both bring chaos and further disarray to a world already burdened by endemic poverty and disillusionment. Neither woman is worth a man's love.

In his great period films Kurosawa upholds without irony or distance the accepted feudal and samurai view of woman as possession and object. The only important female character in his otherwise brilliant *Seven Samurai* is the peasant girl, Shino, who seduces the youngest of the samurai, the innocent Katsushiro. The irony is that her father, out of fear that the samurai defending the village might rape her, forcibly cuts her hair so the samurai would not realize she is a woman. It is she who is the brazen seducer.

Yet only because he is not yet an adult, not yet a mature samurai, does Katsushiro hesitate even for a moment, at the film's end, before leaving Shino behind. He will join the leader, Kambei, on the further adventures that will lead indubitably to their extinction. A samurai, even a disciple-samurai like Katsushiro, could no more allow love for a woman to be the central emotion of his life than he could become a peasant.

Sanjuro (*Tsubaki Sanjuro*, 1962), the sequel to *Yojimbo*, introduces a woman who is indeed a match for the *ronin* hero, and one of the rare women in the later Kurosawa films to possess an intellect. But she is merely a peripheral character, and Kurosawa gives her no name. We know her only as Mutsuta's wife. She is also a woman of late middle age, having long passed the time when she could use her sexuality against men.

Kurosawa's last period film, *Red Beard* (*Akahige*, 1965), is a love story between two men: the doctor, Kyojio Niide—Red Beard—(Toshiro Mifune), and his young disciple, Noboru Yasumoto (Yuzo Kayama). As in the deepest of love relationships, one learns from, and is profoundly changed by, the other. Red Beard, in winning Yasumoto over to serve the people with his talents as a doctor, gives him a meaning in life. The spiritual union between these two men is expressed even in the use of the music. The central motif from Brahms properly belongs to the great man, Niide. When Yasumoto begins to imitate him, and when he has learned from him how "to live," the sound track allows him this motif as well. It is a tribute to both, and an expression of intimate harmony between the two men before which the idea of mere sexual congress with a woman pales. Yasumoto marries finally, but it is clear that his new little bride, a shallow creature, cannot offer, even remotely, emotional or moral competition to the great teacher.

With *Red Beard,* women in Kurosawa have become not only unreal and incapable of kindness, but totally bereft of autonomy, whether physical, intellectual, or emotional. It is through men that understanding is reached. Women at their best may only imitate the truths men discover, as when Miss Watanabe had to behave like a *bushi,* a warrior, during the war. It takes men, and in hard times as our own, supermen such as doctor Niide, to teach us how to live.

Like the younger Shinoda and Imamura and so many of Japan's film directors, Kurosawa has been appalled by the lack of direction afflicting Japanese culture. From *Red Beard* on, he turns to basic and simple human virtues as the only response to an irremediable society: kindness towards one another, indulgence of human frailties, dedication to helping people, but now without the hope implicit in an early film like *Ikiru* that society can be changed if we care enough. When Red Beard says "there are no cures, really," he speaks not merely of the state of medicine in late Tokugawa Japan, but of social remedy in Kurosawa's time.

Kurosawa's *oeuvre* embodies the central angst, the defining crisis and experience of Japanese society and culture. As in Oshima, the true war is now being waged within the Japanese psyche. Obsolete feudal responses, however frantically the Japanese cling to them, are no longer effective, yet new values and a correspondingly more humane mode of behavior have not yet come into being. Kurosawa's work is set at moments of transition, when old ways pass before the new has coherently emerged. For the human being confronted by the chaos inherent in the disintegration of a once fixed and secure code of values and set of social responses, the absence of any clear, supportable, or understandable alternative brings a form of hysteria and madness. This is the mood which suffuses *Red Beard* perhaps more despairingly than it did earlier films like *Record of a Living Being* (*Ikimono no Kiroku,* 1955), set more literally amidst the postwar ruins.

In Kurosawa's late work, men and women alike are perceived as victims. Sexuality represents, now more than ever, a distortion of the humane, a point of view which, in *No Regrets for Our Youth*, seemed directly attributable to the frenzy and stress of the wartime setting. Yet, on closer examination, all the settings in Kurosawa are, in their deepest sense, "wartime." For Kurosawa has always accepted the *bushido* dichotomy—the choice between duty and love. "To live" is the central theme of *Ikiru*—which is the Japanese for that phrase. But it is, as well, the motif of *No Regrets for Our Youth* and it expresses in many of Kurosawa's films the necessity to choose between love between man and woman and love of humanity. To act meaningfully obliges one to reject the former. In *Ikiru* the old bureaucrat, Watanabe, had to be freed from a relationship with a young woman before he could begin to build the playground for slum children which became the redeeming act of his life. Only in experiencing the emptiness of seeking love from another individual could he make the choice that rendered his life worth living. And by making the young woman so much younger, and thereby unsuitable, Kurosawa rendered love and work incompatible.

The world Kurosawa has come to love is, finally, one in which women have become superfluous. The Soviet-sponsored *Dersu Uzala* (1975) is, like *Red Beard,* a love story between two men. In an allegorical encounter between the passing of a pure way of life and the "civilized" inauthenticity of the culture to come, the explorer, Arseniev, discovers the Soviet Asian hunter, Dersu Uzala, who still lives within nature. Dersu becomes Arseniev's guide through Siberia, teaching him what remains meaningful in life. Dersu is a human being who has since become lost to us, who died out with the advent of industry, technology, and the urbanization of the planet. Kurosawa must turn to the beginning of the twentieth century, and an exploration of remote Siberia where most of the film was shot, to locate a man capable of authentic communion with his natural environment. Finally, the theme of *Dersu Uzala* becomes the landscape itself, with Kurosawa seeming to have lost interest almost entirely in man and his plight.

Kurosawa's Heroes

DENNIS GILES

T HE TITLES of the film are joined to an X-ray negative of a cancerous stomach. The word *Ikiru* is a verb, meaning "to live." Yet the first image is an image of death.

The scene which follows the X-ray exposes the life of the hero as a tedious routine. He is a bureaucrat, sitting at a desk piled with paperwork. He methodically stamps these papers, ignoring the complaints of a group of citizens at the front desk who demand the drainage of a pool of contaminated water. The narrator informs us that Watanabe is a living corpse: "actually he has been dead for the past twenty-five years." There follows a series of "wipes" in which one image is pushed laterally off the screen by the following image. Yet the successive images do not progress. They all detail the same event: the citizens' committee appears at various city desks and offices—Public Works, Parks, Sanitation, Health, Anti-Epidemics, Pest Control—and at each is referred to still another office. No clerk will take responsibility—the citizens are brushed off by this bureaucracy as effectively as they are wiped away by the push of the succeeding shot. Finally gaining an audience with the Deputy Mayor, the petitioners are referred once more to the Citizens' Section where Watanabe "works." The clerk again directs them to go to Public Works! This bureaucracy refers only to itself. At no point does it engage, or even recognize, the social world with which it was designed to cope.

Watanabe is not yet a hero. The narrator admits that he "is not very interesting, yet." Kurosawa finds his protagonist enmeshed in the everyday world of his concern, a repetitive world which he takes for granted. Like Heidegger, like Sartre, Kurosawa begins his study of human possibility by considering man in his most ordinary manifestation—*in situation* within the banalities of normal existence. The protagonist is defined by what he does, by his job. As we will see in other films, Kurosawa's man is constituted by his objectified actions in relation to the world, and not by his intentions. In *Ikiru*, however, Watanabe's doings, so far, can scarcely be termed actions, since they have no goal other than movement itself and they evade any grasping of the material world outside the bureaucracy. The hero has not yet awakened to the exterior world, nor has he begun the double movement "outside" his customary reality to the "inside" of his isolate, death-bound self.

At present, Watanabe is inactive, "like a corpse," says the narrator. "He's busy—oh, very busy." But, "he's just passing the time, wasting it, rather." Once, however, "he had some life in him. He even tried to work." Watanabe

First appeared in *Arion, A Journal of Humanities and the Classics,* New Series 2, no. 2 (1975): 270–99. Excerpted and reprinted by permission of Linda L. Giles.

has somehow fallen prey to the world. This protagonist's existence was once linear, purposeful, but now he is head of the Citizens' Section—a petty chieftain in a circular structure of evasion. Yet the very fact that Watanabe once worked, that he has fallen from activity into this corpse-like state, informs us that the self is not in essence a state or permanent stamp but is at least fluid enough to fall. The steady-state self is not yet heroic insofar as it is merged with a world which is ultimately static in its repetitive movement. Watanabe can recover his fluidity only if he is shocked out of the round of daily existence by an event which shatters his habitual self and renders it linear—projected towards a future. For Kurosawa, as for Hegel, the spirit "attains its truth only when it finds itself in the midst of being utterly rent apart" (*Phenomenology of Spirit*). Death is the event which tears apart the static self and dissolves its accustomed world. The spectacle of his cancer—the X-ray—is for Watanabe the equivalent of Sartre's nausea, or Jaspers' shipwreck—the event which discloses the self as nothing but possibility. The event of death is the advent of a temporal self.

The second scene of *Ikiru* finds Watanabe waiting in a doctor's office. A garrulous patient graphically details the symptoms of cancer.

> The doctors always tell you it's ulcers, that an operation's unnecessary. They tell you to go on and eat anything—and when you hear that, you know you've got a year left, at the most. Your stomach always feels heavy, and it hurts; you belch a lot and you're always thirsty; either you're constipated or else you have diarrhea, and in either case your stool is always black. And you won't be able to eat meat, or anything you really like, then you'll vomit up something you ate a week ago; and when that happens you have about three months left to live.

Watanabe goes in to confront the doctor, asking point-blank if it's cancer. "Not at all. It's just a light case of ulcers." He can eat anything he likes, "so long as it's digestible."

If the doctor's stratagem were successful, Watanabe would never awaken from the stupor of his daily routine. But despite the "kind" lie Watanabe knows it is cancer. Evasion is no longer possible.

Outside the doctor's office, Watanabe moves in a daze. The street is crowded with traffic. He walks oblivious, his isolation emphasized by an absolutely silent soundtrack. He attempts to cross the street; a truck bears down on him. At the last moment, the deafening sound bursts on. Watanabe sees the truck, is suddenly immersed in a roaring, buzzing world. He retreats to the curb to stare dully at the endless swarming of *their* world—a world that is no longer his *own*.

What has happened here? No less an event than the sudden disclosure of a private self which has nothing in common with the familiar Watanabe of the bureaucracy. The hero, in one shocking leap, has passed from the general proposition "men die" to the terrifying certainty that "I am to die." The public Watanabe has been shattered by the knowledge that his death is purely his own, cannot be shared by his fellows. No one else can die for him. A barrier now separates him from all other men; his everyday world seems but a phantom. An isolate self—and the possibility of self-determination—is born at the very moment the world-bound self knows that it is soon to be nothing, no one. Watanabe's brutal discovery of death as "my" death has stripped his existence of its habitual public cover and revealed him as nothing *but* death. The mortal self which is disclosed is thus essentially negative. But in its very negativity lies freedom. Watanabe must die, is constrained to die, but is simultaneously freed to give his suddenly empty existence a content. At this moment of the film, however, Watanabe is still in shock, blinded and deafened by the dread of certain death. He does not yet see the freedom to which he is released.

The story, thus far, recalls Tolstoy's *The Death of Ivan Ilych* in its paradoxical insistence that only through dying can one begin really to live. In each, the hero is born through the negation of his customary realities. As Plato insists in his cave analogy, the individual must be forced to freedom—he will not turn to see the truth of his own accord.

Plato's everyman is chained to a parapet, watching the shadows of objects on the cave wall, as though fastened to a theatre-seat, watching an endless movie which he believes to be real. His situation is analogous to that of Watanabe, who knows the outside world—its stagnant pools—only through the "stories" of the complaining citizens. He disregards these myths, turns back to the "real" task of stamping papers.

Then, says Plato, "suppose one [of the prisoners] were set free and forced suddenly to stand up, turn his head, and walk with his eyes lifted to the light; all these movements would be painful, and he would be too dazzled to make out the objects whose shadows he had been used to seeing." To see the light of his death is a most unpleasant experience for Watanabe. It kills the habitual world before he can adjust to the reality of the discovered world. He is blinded, "dazzled" (and in this case deafened), and yearns to turn back to the familiar world even as that world is discredited. A dim, habitual instinct of self-preservation moves Watanabe out of the path of the truck, even though events have rendered this instinct meaningless. Having lost his everyday world, he cannot yet comprehend the new one. At this moment of passage, Watanabe is shipwrecked in uncharted seas. He feels himself sinking; he panics, grabs wildly for anything solid, familiar, but all these things have vanished. He is utterly alone—and dying fast. Is it any wonder that Watanabe's expression during most of *Ikiru* is one of sheer misery? It will take time for him to see anything but his pain. He knows only that he is negated, dying; he has not yet begun to live.

The hero of *Ikiru,* suddenly mortal, is now awake, but miserably so. He is free, but free to do what? To give a content to his freedom, Watanabe must, like Plato's man, climb through various levels of reality until he reaches the "truth." But here the Platonic analogy breaks down, for Kurosawa's reality is considerably different from Plato's *eidos*. The point for Kurosawa, as for Marx, is not to contemplate the world but to change it. The world of men and materials is the only real world to Kurosawa. The hero must return to this social/physical world in order to work within it and upon it. One who turns his back on the existing world to contemplate an ideal is no hero, but only a visionary. At this point in the plot, Watanabe has withdrawn from his customary world, or rather, it has withdrawn its reality. His mode of being has become quite subjective; he is alone with himself. To retreat into subjectivity is for Kurosawa to recover the self previously lost in the public world, and this necessitates a corresponding devaluation of that world. Once Watanabe has withdrawn from it he is able to see its disease from his new-found distance and can determine a strategy for acting upon it. The withdrawal prepares the return. The two movements are inseparably paired in Kurosawa's conception of heroism. Simply being cut loose from the habitual world, discovering its "fictitious" character, is not real freedom. It is rather a freedom without objective content, i.e., without projects.

The first stage of Watanabe's death-bound life is still an attempted evasion. He declines to go to the office, withdraws fifty thousand yen from the bank, and tries to forget death through liquor. On one of his lonely drinking bouts, Watanabe meets a third-rate writer, and when questioned, reveals the fact of his cancer. In this conversation, he reveals the pathetic truth that he doesn't really know how to enjoy himself. The writer offers to guide him to "good times."

> Let's find that life you've thrown away. Tonight I'll be your Mephistopheles, but a good one, who won't ask to be paid.

There follows a night of hedonism. Watanabe drinks, dances, sings, buys a new hat, watches a strip-tease. But on the way home, he must stop the car to vomit. The disease ceaselessly asserts itself.

In the next stage of his withdrawal Watanabe meets a young girl. She works at his office, is bored with the job. She refuses to adopt social masks, is direct in her speech and actions. Toyo confesses she knows Watanabe by a nickname—"The Mummy." Although Watanabe's relatives prefer to believe he has taken a mistress, his interest in Toyo is not primarily sexual. "The Mummy" wants not her body, but rather her soul. The girl becomes irritated by his endless attentions. She demands an explanation. Why is he always following her? What does he want? He tries to explain. She is so "full of life... young and healthy... I'm envious of that." Through watching her eat, drink, and live, Watanabe is living vicariously. But Toyo feels, with some justice, that she is but a victim/host to a parasitical Watanabe. He drains her; she lives his suffering as much as he lives her healthiness. Her sympathy becomes mingled with horror. The relationship is an unnatural one; she wants to end it, even if it means leaving Watanabe once more with his death—the mummy who cannot live. Watanabe pleads with her to push him to life:

WATANABE: I don't know what to do. I don't know how to do it...
   please, if you can, show me how to be like you...

TOYO: But all I do is work and eat—that's all.

WATANABE: Really?

TOYO: Really. That and make toys like this one.

She shows him a toy rabbit. She winds it up. The rabbit hops. Suddenly a decision is born. Watanabe's eyes light up; he even smiles. Toyo shrinks back in fear of this maniac. He picks up the rabbit and rushes down the stairs, leaving her alone.

The next scene finds two bureaucrats entering the office in the midst of discussing who will succeed Watanabe as Chief. They stop, transfixed at the sight of Watanabe's new hat on the coatrack. He interrupts their amazed silence, tears off the notice on the citizen's petition which says, "Forward to Public Works." "Take care of this," he says. "Call me a car." In amazement, the bureaucrats follow their chief—the late mummy—into battle. The first movement of the film is finished by this call to action.

The remainder of *Ikiru* details Watanabe's active heroism through a series of flashbacks "narrated" by the puzzled mourners at the hero's funeral. Through dogged insistence, Watanabe has coerced the bureaucracy into building a playground on the scene of the open sewer. He has built the playground in spite of the bureaucracy and yet through it. He has rendered a broken tool temporarily functional, forcibly turning it around to face the material world it so long ignored. The self-referential circle has been straightened in accordance to Watanabe's new-found linear existence.

The mourners understand that something extraordinary has happened, but it seems to them to be a freak occurrence in an otherwise placid existence. Was the playground caused by Watanabe? What nonsense, they say. The park was built "despite" his interference. Watanabe interfered with the normal workings of the official machine. He was a troublemaker, some of them decide, well intentioned, but ... maybe he was insane, or merely stupid?

As they drink, Watanabe's office-mates continue to discuss his strange behavior—each memory visualized by a flashback. They marvel at his persistent disregard for bureaucratic channels. As the saki is consumed, Watanabe's stature rises in a babble of talk. Emotions run high—the chief has become a martyr! The wake ends with a drunken orgy of accusations, self-recrimination, and hysterical vows to "turn over a new leaf," to "work for the public good."

Comes the dawn, and the bureaucrats are back at their accustomed task; the resolve of the night before is only a memory. Sewage water has overflowed in Kizaki-cho. The complaining citizens are referred to the Public Works Section. One man starts to protest. He rises from his chair, then thinks better of it. He slowly sits down again as the camera also descends, until the whole screen is filled with the immense piles of paper on his desk.

The last scene is ambiguous. The man who began to protest stops on his way home to gaze at the park Watanabe has built, his face somber but ultimately unreadable. This is the end of *Ikiru*. There is a possibility that Watanabe's heroism will be relayed to a second bureaucrat, but such an event is far from assured. It seems more likely that the hero will have no heir and that the bureaucratic inertia will reassert itself. Indeed, it has already done so. A "survivor" has been shaken by the heroic example, but is not yet ready to negate his habitual existence. He is unwilling to act—unable to "live."

"I want to *do* something," cries Watanabe to the girl from his office. He speaks out of his cancer, from a self he now sees as negative, in need of an act by which he can regain control over his own existence. He is caught wide-awake in the deathflow, knows himself to be merely treading water on his way to the abyss. To *do* something is imperative to the dying bureaucrat. But what? And how? He knows only doing nothing, has done nothing all his life, yet only now knows it to be precisely nothing.

To do nothing is, for Kurosawa, to perform all the movements of the daily routine which confirm the *status quo,* i.e., most of the "acts" of life. The movement is circular, repetitive. One does not stop to think the "why" of these movements; the habitual man is moved at every moment by the expectations of the world that he will continue to repeat himself. Kurosawa's world *is* this endless round of habits. In *Ikiru* it is given concrete form by the futile cycle of the petitioners through the various offices of the bureaucracy. Society seems but a worm of autonomous segments which blindly devours its own tail, growing fat on its cannibalism. The Citizens' Section does not remember that the petition referred to them by the Deputy Mayor was formerly disgorged by their office—they merely pass it on.

Normal life in the rural society of *The Seven Samurai* is as circular as the bureaucratic wheel. Each year the farmers labor in their fields to grow food for the winter. And each autumn the bandits descend from the hills to rob the harvest.

> You can't bargain with them. You reason with them now [summer], give them something, and they'll be here in the autumn just the same.

The hired samurai break the cycle of growth-harvest-plunder by killing the predators. These masterless samurai no longer have a stake in the given world—they are unemployed *ronin,* whose profession is rapidly becoming obsolete through the introduction of fire-arms and the break-up of the feudal hegemony. They perceive the inevitable extinction of their class, and are thus freed from the traditional samurai task of defending the static power of their feudal lord. Into the repetitive circle of rural existence come these suddenly temporal beings—"wild" agents from outside the round. Their interruption of the cycle is more spectacular by far than Watanabe's translation of a piece of paper into a playground. Yet each act renders the a-temporal world productive, historical, in accordance with the hero's perception of his personal existence as a linear movement toward nothing but death.

The hero who understands that death is in every case "my own," is able to regard the world in terms of ends. He moves in a straight line toward death in contrast to those who flee in the face of mortality, who defer it to sometime later or someone else. In this everyday life there is no effective terminus, since everything can be deferred to a receding tomorrow. One feels at home in this world of endless re-statement. Its movement can always be predicted; one always knows one's place in the pattern. Enmeshed in redundancy, existence is rendered static, becoming only what it *was.* This world is effectively a-temporal. Habitual man, having fallen prey to the repetitive world in which he is distracted, preoccupied, assumes that what *could be* is only what *is.* "To be" is a state, not an activity. Unaware, with any real consciousness, that his life must end, this man is a stranger to ends. He acts only insofar as he acts again, i.e., re-acts. But because the hero knows the goal of his life to be death, he is able to project a goal to each of his movements. Insofar as they are terminal, these movements become acts-projects which constitute the self. The hero is "already" dead, so he can risk dying by every act.

The stability of normal existence—guaranteed by the time-honored procedures of Watanabe's bureaucracy—is disclosed to the death-bound hero as a fiction upheld only by the *belief* of the world-bound that self and world are indeed static. The hero who sees life as a movement *toward,* loses faith, as it were, in the givens of the circular world. He sees it from the new-found distance of the dying self to be no longer in agreement with his linear existence. The world, for Watanabe, is suddenly "other." By his awareness of death the hero has separated a private self from a public world, thus de-realizing the world, converting it into *mythos,* a mere ideology of stability. In order to act in it and upon it, the hero must believe that the world is not, in essence, this repetition of givens. His action destroys the fiction of the world's stability, proves that bandits are not "fated" like weather conditions, that open sewers need not be a permanent condition of life. It is thus an act of negation. The hero creates through first destroying the habitual world and uncovering, beneath a world moving toward death. One can thus assert that the Kurosawa hero institutes death in the world, and with it, the possibility of action.

Seven Samurai

ANDRÉ BAZIN

IT IS quite fashionable these days to be finicky when speaking of Japanese films, as well as to insinuate that their exoticism seduces the naïve among us, and that the Japanese critics are not wrong. Let us duly note in reporting the ratings given to Japanese films by Japanese critics, published in the outstanding issue of *Cinéma 55* (no. 6, June-July), that *Rashomon* was rated fifth in 1950; *Tales of Genji* seventh in 1951; *Okasan* seventh, and *Life of Oharu* ninth in 1952. *Ugetsu* was third in 1953 as was *The Seven Samurai* in 1954. It is thus worth noting that these titles were far behind many others that are totally unknown to us.

Should this decrease our enjoyment of these films in any way? Their exoticism and strangeness probably play a role in our admiration. I know for a fact that Americans rated all Pagnol's films on the same level, whether good or bad. But first of all they are only half-wrong. Seen from that distance, from the wrong end of the opera glass, Pagnol looks like Pagnol. In the second place, European critics are now seeing more Japanese films than a big Hollywood director has seen French films. I have seen over two dozen. Of course, that is not very many, but is perhaps enough to permit me to discriminate among them.

For five years I have been waiting for my admiration for Akira Kurosawa to wane, finally to expose my alleged naïveté of the preceding year, but each film festival strengthens the feeling that I am in the presence of everything that constitutes good cinema: the union of a highly developed civilization with a great theatrical tradition and a great tradition of plastic art.

The Seven Samurai might not be the very best Japanese production. There is undoubtedly more reason to prefer the tender lyricism and subtly musical poetry of a Mizoguchi (director of *The Life of Oharu* and *Ugetsu Monogatari*, both 1952). Like *Rashomon, The Seven Samurai* exhibits a too facile assimilation of certain elements of Western aesthetics and their splendid blend with Japanese tradition. There is in this case a narrative structure of diabolical cleverness. Its progression is arranged with an intelligence which is all the more disconcerting because it respects the romantic approach and the progressive blossoming of a narrative that requires much time and labor.

Reprinted from André Bazin, *The Cinema of Cruelty*, trans. Sabine d'Estree (New York: Seaver Books, 1982), 196–99. Copyright © 1975 by Editions Flammarion. English translation copyright © 1982 by Seaver Books. Reprinted by permission of Seaver Books.

All dubbings considered, *The Seven Samurai* is a kind of Japanese Western worthy of comparison to the most glorious examples of that genre produced in America, notably those of John Ford. However, mentioning this only gives an approximate idea of a film whose ambition and complexity go far beyond the dramatic framework of the Western. Not that *The Seven Samurai* is a complicated story in the sense that *Rashomon* is—on the contrary, the plot is as simple as can be. But this universal simplicity is enhanced by the delicacy of details, their historical realism, and their human truth.

To summarize the plot in a few words: a village, plundered every year by a gang of bandits, recruits seven samurai to protect it against the next attack. The forty bandits are destroyed one after another, even though they are armed with weapons that were almost unknown in sixteenth-century Japan. Four samurai are killed, but the villagers can once again plant their rice in peace. The beauty and cleverness of this story arise from a certain harmony between the simplicity of the plot and the wealth of details that slowly delineate it. Obviously this kind of narrative reminds one of Ford's *Stagecoach* (1939) and *Lost Patrol* (1934) but with a more romantic complexity and more volume and variety in the fresco.

As we see, these points of reference are very "Western." The same holds true for the content of the extremely Japanese images, where the depth of field is obviously reminiscent of the effects obtained by the much-lamented Gregg Toland. In conclusion I can't do better than quote Kurosawa's own declaration of faith: "An action film can only be an action film. But what a wonderful thing if it can at the same time claim to depict humanity! This has always been my dream since the time I was an assistant. For the last ten years I have been wanting to reconsider historical drama from this new point of view."

The Circumstance of the East,
the Fate of the West

BERT CARDULLO

I must categorize the films of the world into three distinct types. European films are based upon human psychology, American films upon action and the struggles of human beings, and Japanese films upon circumstance. *Japanese films are interested in what surrounds the human being.*

—MASAHIRO SHINODA[1]

KUROSAWA'S *The Seven Samurai* (1954) is such a film, one which portrays the power of circumstance over its characters' lives. The major "circumstance" in the film is this: with the invention of the gun and the development of the horse as an instrument of warfare, the samurai have been rendered obsolete as the warrior or fighter figures in Japanese society (Sengoku Period, 1467–1568). Whereas it is the samurai swordsmen who once would have raided the peasant village for rice and women, it is now the gun-toting bandits on horseback who do so. This places the peasants in a unique position: they can hire the samurai to defend them for the price of a meal (three meals a day, actually). But it also places them in a precarious position: the samurai will teach them to defend themselves, too, something the peasants have never done before. "Circumstance" has forced a new role on them. They are farmers by nature, fighters by chance (and necessity). "Circumstance" forces dignified samurai to go about in shabby clothing and even chop wood for a meal; it forces them to work for the very class of people they once had the most contempt for. "Circumstance" gives the gun to anyone who can pay for it (unlike the sword, which takes a master to wield it, the gun can be mastered—especially at close range—by almost anyone), and thus turns the petty thief into the roving, deadly, greedy bandit, part of a larger robber band or "army." "Circumstance" then dictates that three guns—all the bandits have—are not enough against the expertise of the samurai combined with the numbers of the peasants. The day will come when all the bandits have guns, and that day will spell the end of the samurai for good and the rise of the military, and later the "police," to protect the people.

The "force of circumstance" is clearly at work throughout *The Seven Samurai.* But the film is hardly a treatise on man's helplessness before circumstance, his dwarfing by it. The art of the film, for me, is in man's playing out his destiny before circumstance, at the same time circumstance seems to

Reprinted from *Literature/Film Quarterly* 13, no. 2 (1985): 112–17, by permission.

engulf him. The farmers fight and die for their freedom. The samurai defend the farmers no differently than they would defend themselves: nobly and fiercely. The bandits fight to the last man, against in the end unbeatable odds, apparently forgetting that their initial objective in storming the village was to seize the farmers' crops: it is their own honor and fighting ability that have become the question. We see the ironies in the situation, but the farmers, the samurai, and the bandits do not, or they do only in passing. They *act,* and in action are ennobled. That, perhaps, is the sense in which this is truly an "action" or "epic" film: action does not occur for its own sake, or for the sake of mere spectacle; instead, it ennobles. The different protagonists act, no matter what they think or do not think. If they are aware of "circumstance," they forget it, and, again, *act.* The concentration is thus always on the human struggle more than on the existential dilemma. What matters is the present and the human more than the historical and the circumstantial. In this sense, the human transcends the circumstantial: those dead at the hands of circumstance are not mourned (farmers, samurai)[2] or rejoiced over (bandits) at the end of the film; the living go on living—the farmers plant rice, the surviving samurai move on, *unhailed*—the dead are dead (the final shot of the burial mounds).

The point must be made again, for the sake of contrast: *The Seven Samurai* is a film about circumstance, or about man and his relationship, at his best, to circumstance; it is not a film about fate. In tragedy, man acts, often stupidly if inevitably, and then reflects on his actions, wisely. In the work of circumstance, man acts wisely in the face of the stupidity and unpredictability of circumstance. Tragedy focuses, in a way, unnaturally on man and his deeds. It presumes the authenticity and absolute rule of "fate," and then sets man happily against it, or against himself (in whom fate may reside). The work of circumstance focuses, more naturally, on the vagaries of circumstance and man's often instinctive response to them. The foolishness is in the universe; the wiseness, if not the temperance or caution, is in man. Man assumes a more modest position and, in my estimation, comes off the better for it. Circumstance is the real enemy, the real force lurking at all times in the background of our lives. "Fate" is the straw man in tragedy: one senses, often, that it has been created or invented merely for the display of man's vanity, his self-obsession. "Fate" seems dominant in tragedy, but man outside fate is the real star ("Look at me!"). "Fate" is something man has invented to *explain away* his own obsessions and inadequacies. Circumstance is real or tangible; man is most often defeated by it. At his best, he meets it (the adverse kind, that is) on equal ground, and if he does not triumph, he does not lose, either. He distinguishes himself in the fight. That is all, and that is enough. Of the three groups of characters in *The Seven Samurai*—the farmers, the samurai, and the bandits—this can be said with almost tactile sureness.

The work of circumstance is interested in what surrounds the human being, and how he reacts to it, under stress. Tragedy is interested in what is immutable (it thinks) in each human being, and the world, and how this leads to man's (noble) destruction. It is interested, in short, in man above all else, and in all, his flaw. Circumstance places man more squarely in the world; "fate" pushes him back into himself. The one art looks out, the other in. It is the difference between East and West, self and other. Appropriately, tragedy focuses on one character; the work of circumstance, on several or many. *The Seven Samurai* is not about the seven samurai themselves, it is about the characteristics of samurai—courage, honor, dignity—that circumstance conspires to bring out in others. Remember, for example, that it is the farmers who first decide to fight the bandits; only then do they think to hire samurai to help them.

One small example, distinguishing between Western tragedy and the Eastern "work of circumstance": Near the end of the film, circumstance presents the young woman Shino with a difficult choice. By now she is in love with the samurai initiate Katsushiro; she must go with him, a man of a higher class, or stay behind in her native village. She chooses to stay behind. Even though she loves Katsushiro, it is a wise choice. She will forget him in time —indeed, she seems to forget him immediately—and marry a man of her own class. She will suffer momentarily, prosper in the long run. Shino suppresses self for "other," for her relationship to her family, village, and the world she has known since birth.

What would have happened in a tragedy, given a similar situation? This would have been the basis *for the entire film*. Shino would have been irresistibly drawn to Katsushiro and would have planned to run off with him. Her parents would have disapproved of the relationship (if they had known about it; it is kept secret from them until the end). Shino's love for Katsushiro would have been true, but doomed by its own very intensity, and the intensity of Katsushiro's love as well, and the lovers' consequent willingness to go to any lengths to marry. Shino and Katsushiro would both end up committing suicide, and only in this way, in sorrow, would their families, separated by class, be joined. We are in the world of *Romeo and Juliet,* where foolish, if sincere and inevitable, action on the part of the protagonists leads to the wisdom of reconciliation between their long-feuding families. Romeo and Juliet choose self-fulfillment before duty to family, and pay for it with their lives. To a Westerner, it is a noble sacrifice; to one such as Kurosawa, a senseless one—senseless, because it is the very intensity, if not obsessiveness, of Romeo's love for Juliet that causes him to kill himself upon finding her "dead." Even as Romeo was irresistibly drawn to Juliet, despite the serious feud between their families, so too is he compelled to commit suicide without investigating the circumstances of her "death." Romeo does not sacrifice himself for Juliet; he sacrifices himself to his own ideal of romantic love. His suicide is, in other words, paradoxically a form of self-endorsement: if he can't have Juliet, then no one can have him. He places himself before the other members of his family and community, and it is this absorption with himself, this retreat into self, that makes him commit suicide when he finds Juliet's body. He is finally all alone, with no reference outside himself with Juliet "dead," and therefore he fancies suicide the only way to remain "alone" without suffering. He cannot think of anyone but himself, and that is what kills him: he exhausts his powers of reason and measure.

Clearly, I am not trying to say that characters in Japanese films do not commit suicide or otherwise come to ruin. Think only of Shinoda's own *Double Suicide* (1969) and his recent *Ballad of Orin* (1978). But there is a great deal of difference between lovers' deliberately *choosing* suicide as a means of escape from society's strictures—killing themselves, in a sense, so as not to rend the fabric of society, or because they cannot fathom society's harsh workings—and Romeo's (or Juliet's) killing himself in a hysterical moment of grief, because he thinks his Juliet dead. Romeo and Juliet's suicide is an *accident.* It would never have happened but for the intervention of Friar Laurence. It is a "tragic" accident, in the sense that it was inevitable that Juliet, in her consuming love, would go to such extremes to be with Romeo, and in the sense that her family will not relent in its feud with the Montagues; but is an accident nonetheless. Keep in mind that the reason for Juliet's taking the potion in the first place is to appear dead *to her family,* so that she will be buried and then freed from her tomb by Friar Laurence, to run away with Romeo. She rejects her family and city, that is, for Romeo.[3]

Shakespeare, then, devotes a whole play to the actions of Romeo and Juliet. Kurosawa makes the relationship of his Shino and Katsushiro a small part of a work devoted to illustrating commitment to "other" before self and to depicting sure and noble action in the face of unfavorable circumstance. Shino is one of many in *The Seven Samurai* who choose duty to "other" before self, and I think observers of the film have largely missed this aspect of it. Some of the samurai, for instance, at first resist the idea of joining up with Kambei to defend the village for two basic reasons: there is not enough monetary reward in it, and there is no honor in defending farmers. But they come around, primarily because of their attraction to Kambei, their desire to ally with him as *samurai,* to help his cause. The individual, vagrant samurai cohere into a single-minded fighting unit. The young Katsushiro himself becomes Kambei's disciple, against Kambei's wishes at first. He suppresses self, that is, for devotion to a master. And the few farmers outside the village proper want to save themselves, not the village as a whole, but they, too, after some coercion by the samurai, forget self and fight for "other." The same goes for the bandits. Every one of them sacrifices self to "other": every one of them is killed in the battle with samurai and farmers. No one runs, for fear of death at the hands of his chief (the chief says, pointing to a dead bandit, "Remember! Every coward here will get the same treatment"); no one runs, despite one bandit's remark, "The whole thing is back to front. Now we're burnt out and hungrier than they are."[4]

Circumstance unites man: the farmers with one another, just so the samurai, just so the bandits. It "unites" man further: it turns farmer into near samurai-like in his courage and pride in fighting to the end; it makes the samurai farmer-like in his desire to keep the rice crop from the bandits (it is this crop that the samurai, too, now shares, whereas once he had been bandit-like in its seizing).

Tragedy divides and isolates man. The knowledge that its protagonists derive from suffering is not common knowledge; it is knowledge that can only be had from profound suffering. So the message of tragedy is that man will suffer again. The calm at the end of tragedy is the calm before another storm. Man is steady and united in his facing circumstance: it draws him outside himself, and gives him an experience common to many. He is unsettled and alone in the face of tragedy, or his own fate. This is the message of tragedy, but beneath it is buried a more important message, hinted at earlier in this essay: that it is precisely this excessive emphasis on the individual in the West, and in the tragic literature of the West, that condemns man to further suffering. It is the total fascination and absorption with self, in other words, in art as in life, that leads to continued self-destruction. "Fate" in literature or film becomes almost beside the point. Individual deeds leading to isolation and suffering become almost beside the point. The point is that when man lacks a reference outside himself, when he is devoted to nothing but self-fulfillment and self-glorification, he will suffer, grandly. He will break down. Tragic heroes in the West are, then, condemned to defeat before they ever step onto the page, the screen, or the stage. The very way of life, or world view, that has produced them, condemns them. This is not "fate" as it is applied to individuals in works of art ("It was Oedipus' peculiar fate to . . . etc.," for example). It is *life* as applied to Western man generally.

Notes

1. Joan Mellen, *Voices from the Japanese Cinema* (New York: Liveright, 1975), 242.

2. There is one ceremonial burial (of Heihachi, a samurai) earlier in the film, but, significantly, the "struggle" interrupts it: the bandits appear en masse on the horizon.

3. While the characters in such a Western film as *Elvira Madigan* (1967) appear at first deliberately to choose suicide (actually, he shoots her, then himself) as a means of escape from society's strictures, they are actually the victims of director Bo Widerberg's own absorption with himself and his devices. Widerberg wanted his two lovers to end their predicament by killing themselves, probably because he felt this was the most romantic way to end his romantic story (recall, too, that we hear the shots, but we do not see the unromantic dead bodies). Either that or he knew they would, because the Elvira Madigan story, at least in its outline, is true (and I think it is), and this is why he chose it. But he does not for one moment convince us that there is no way out for the army officer and his mistress: it is almost as if they commit suicide for want of something better to do, or out of fear that life outside the bounds of bourgeois society will not be good enough for them. If indeed for the latter reason (although this is not developed in the film), then so much for their concern not to injure the fabric of society or their inability to accept society's harsh workings. Just *what* to fill in the outline of the Elvira Madigan story with, just what really happened, no one can know. What I am concerned with here is how Widerberg, as a Western artist, treated or responded to the few facts that came down to him: self-indulgently.

4. Akira Kurosawa, *The Seven Samurai*, trans. Donald Richie (New York: Simon and Schuster, 1970), 193–94.

[Kurosawa and the Samurai Genre]

ALAIN SILVER

T HE FATALISM over the role of samurai, *ronin,* and bandit alike which Kuro- sawa evinces in *Rashomon, Seven Samurai,* and *Throne of Blood* is a specific one, directed at individuals or small groups rather than large social units. While these films may suggest that the fate of the various individuals is grounded in a kind of social determinism, that Washizu, Tajomaru, and the seven *ronin* are equally victims of the feudal system, the actual drama with which the audience is asked to involve itself is focused on personal rather than institutional conflicts (i.e., Tajomaru versus the samurai; the *ronin* and farmers versus the bandits; Washizu versus first his wife then Miki and those loyal to the murdered Lord). In short, Kurosawa does not compel the viewer, as Kobayashi and other directors may, to regard institutions as the villainous figures or even as major antagonists.

In Kenji Mizoguchi's *Tales of the Taira Clan,* the young clansman Kiy- omori Taira is incarnated by Raizo Ichikawa. Ichikawa's image, as a then youthful star coupled with the particulars of costuming and make-up, render the ambitious, high-ranking samurai whom he portrays easy to empathise with simply because he has an attractive aspect. While Mizoguchi's sympa- thies may not lie with either of the factions that participated in the Taira/ Minamoto wars or in the conflict between the Tairas and the clergy as described in *Tales of the Taira Clan,* the viewer is clearly directed by the film's formal values to identify with Kiyomori and his cause. For eventually, Mizoguchi's mutely-tinted frames and stately-moving camera make the ener- getic figure of Kiyomori the film's incontestable centre visually as well as narratively. In the course of that formal detailing, the historical reality of the twelfth century itself is transformed, and Kiyomori's struggle is characterised so as to appear that he supports democratic ideals or the advancement of the general (clan) cause as opposed to the clergy's elitism. This effect is not cited to question the prerogative of the film-maker to distort the past or to use it as a ground for a dramatisation of ideological conflicts which it did not actually contain (in this case, a fictional encounter between ostensibly democratic and oligarchic factions). Rather, *Tales of the Taira Clan* is one of the last (in time) illustrations of an essentially pre-War *genre* typing at work in the samurai film. Kiyomori is not alienated by the institutions or feudalism itself but by the monastic attempt to subvert those constructs to their own purposes. The iconoclasm which Kiyomori demonstrates in "defiling" the

sacred Buddhist palanquins with his arrows is not aimed, literally or figura-
tively, at the whole structure of government but only at a symbol of special
interests which, he feels, imperil that structure.

In Kurosawa's *Yojimbo* and *Sanjuro,* the sardonic *ronin* (called Sanjuro
Kuwabatake and Sanjuro Tsubaki respectively—the surname changes but
the character remains the same) is incarnated by Toshiro Mifune. The costuming and make-up—soiled kimono, unkempt hair, unshaven face—do
not immediately encourage the spectator to identify; but the fact that
Yojimbo opens with this character alone in the shot restricts the audience's
choice considerably. More significantly, an expository title even before he
appears places the narrative stress squarely on historical events: "The time is
1860. The emergence of a middle-class was brought about by an end to the
power of the Tokugawa dynasty." The generic invocation is bi-focal. The central character is defined in terms of audience expectation (he is, despite his
physical unattractiveness, alone in the frame and the star of the film); the
narrative core, in terms of historical reality. Finally, the notion of predes-
tined action is brought into play when the unidentified swordsman pauses
at a fork in the road and throws a stick to decide which path he will follow.

Unlike Kiyomori, this figure has neither a history nor a cause. He is decen-
tred to the extent that he fashions his surname from whatever he happens to
be gazing at when asked to identify himself ("Sanjuro" means "thirty";
"Kuwabatake" means "mulberry fields"; and "Tsubaki" means "camellias").
Lacking allegiances, he does not, like Kiyomori, have any inbred enemies or
any reason to seek quarrels. Instead, conflict finds him; for the arbitrary
choice of path in *Yojimbo* leads him to a town disrupted by warring gangs,
and the hut in which he seeks shelter before *Sanjuro* even begins turns out
to be the meeting place for a group of rebellious young samurai. What identity "Sanjuro" does possess consequently derives entirely from *genre* typing-
—not the typing of a figure such as Kiyomori, which depends, as do other
forms of fiction, on a reading (exposition) of character rather than context,
but one which develops from an *interplay* of character and environment,
of figure and ground. Because the ground is inscribed first in *Yojimbo*
(through the opening title) the figure is distinguished against it. In other
words, because Sanjuro is to be a re-actant rather than an actant in the
unfolding narrative, the historical context *must* be invoked first so that the
hero without a name or a past may be defined in relation to it.

What Kurosawa also makes clear from the first—in the stark image of the
isolated figure on a windswept road, arms tucked protectively inside his
sleeves, or in the grim verbal aside when he is greeted at the edge of town by
a dog with a human hand in its jaws ("The smell of blood brings the hungry
dogs")—is that his main character is strongly alienated. As man and animal
cross paths there is an identification of one with the other—the swordsman
is typed as a "stray dog." But becoming a *yojimbo* ("bodyguard") in no way
re-integrates him. In a sense, the *ronin* spends the entirety of *Yojimbo*

perched mentally on the watchtower which he climbs to scoff at the tremulous gangmen facing off in the street below. The immediacy of his contempt for others is carried through the film not because of his sardonic dialogue with the other characters, but because it is a symptom of the role of indifference into which he has retreated and which, for his own peace of mind, cannot be violated. The sincerity of this role is never resolved; but clearly Sanjuro is not a Zen-man. His angry threat to the family he assists in *Yojimbo,* that he will kill them if they cry because he detests pathos, or his parting words to his would-be disciples in *Sanjuro* ("Don't follow me, or I'll kill you") reveal his own emotional insecurity. If he is a fallen romantic, he is still not a complete fatalist. As he tells the ambitious peasant's son whom he sees fleeing his home at the film's beginning and whose life he spares near its end: "A long life eating mush is best." But Sanjuro is caught between the lack of awareness which would allow him to be content eating mush and the Buddhist conviction to disengage himself mentally, which might make him equally content to eat mush. He kills the rival master at the conclusion of *Sanjuro* knowing that the duel has lost all "real" or political meaning but unable and, to some degree, unwilling to avoid it. He cannot follow the Zen-like advice which he gives the young samurai, explaining that a skilled rival is "exactly like me: a drawn sword. But the lady is right; really good swords stay in their scabbards."

What differentiates such an ending generically from that of *Seven Samurai* is that the central character in *Yojimbo* and *Sanjuro* enters the film not only alienated but—much more so than Kambei in the earlier motion picture—already aware of that alienation and likewise of his inability to resolve it. As a consequence, the principal dramatic statements of both films—given that the viewer, standing outside the film's *genre* structures, possesses an added level of awareness—must be grimly ironic. The beaten figure smuggled out of town in a coffin in *Yojimbo* must return to settle the score, half out of indifference to escaping and half out of the unstated fear that what minimal identity he does have—through action, through swordsmanship—will disappear unless he returns. What becomes the pervasive irony of the entire *genre* is that the hero cannot find satisfaction in that action or any action. Where Tajomaru did not perceive the complex fabric of personal and social exchange which restricted his freedom of choice and action, and where Kambei saw that fabric but resigned himself to surviving and assisting others even without fulfillment, Sanjuro cuts through it with his sharp wit and his sword only to find that he is still entangled in it and no freer.

What this means iconically is that a symbol like the gun which fells the four *ronin* in *Seven Samurai* and which liberates the central figure in a film such as *The Ambitious* is parried indifferently by the *ronin* in *Yojimbo.* The most pessimistic reading of this *genre* action might conclude that the alienated figure must overcome his opponents and survive—and to some extent the audience does expect just that—because death would be a genuine release. If his *genre* identity is primarily a social one, then death permanently annihilates the awareness of social ills, which potentially he could communicate to others. This is the question which Kobayashi and others take up; but for Kurosawa, the last statement, however stylised, remains more direct. The *ronin* says "So long, old man" to the innkeeper and walks away in *Yojimbo,* his back to the camera and flattened against the empty street by a long lens. In *Sanjuro,* the closing image reduces the whole conflict of the narrative into an abstract one of lines of force: the young samurai stand backlit against bright windows and another long lens reduces the title figure to little more than an intermittent shadow which moves through the foreground of the frame.

Akira Kurosawa and the Atomic Age

JAMES GOODWIN

WITHIN A year after the end of World War II, Akira Kurosawa began to write and direct a succession of *gendai-mono,* or contemporary story films, that address social issues rising out of Japan's defeat, reconstruction, and the Allied Occupation. The *gendai-mono* he released over the ensuing six years—*One Wonderful Sunday (Subarashiki Nichiyobi,* 1947), *Drunken Angel (Yoidore Tenshi,* 1948), *The Quiet Duel (Shizukanaru Ketto,* 1949), *Stray Dog (Nora Inu,* 1949), *Scandal (Shubun,* 1950), *The Idiot (Hakuchi,* 1951), and *Ikiru (Ikiru,* 1952)—engage concerns such as the continued physical and psychological effects of wartime traumas, postwar corruption, urban decay, and the impotence of civil bureaucracy. Kurosawa has explained his motive in creating these films as one of investigative journalism—not to achieve any topical or sensational effect, but rather to explore the forces that underlie contemporary experience.

One issue left unexamined in these films, however, is the immediate cause of Japan's defeat in 1945, the American deployment of atomic bombs against Hiroshima on August 6 and against Nagasaki on August 9. Kurosawa first directly engaged the implications of these world-historical events with the film *Record of a Living Being (Ikimono no Kiroku,* 1955) and he has returned to it recently in *Dreams (Yume,* 1990) and *Rhapsody in August (Hachigatsu no Kyoshikyoku,* 1991). Two *jidai-geki,* or period dramas, of the 1950s reflect Kurosawa's responses to the unprecedented destructiveness with which the atomic age begins. The twelfth-century setting of *Rashomon (Rashomon,* 1950) is depicted as an era of ruin in Japan's cities and of social chaos. The narrative frame to dramatized events in *Throne of Blood (Kumonosu-jo,* 1957) is set in a period after cataclysmic destruction to a center of Japanese life and political power. For the duration of the prologue and epilogue to *Throne of Blood,* an expanse of barren plains and opaque fogs evokes a historical ground zero in Japan's feudal past.

Kurosawa has explained that the storyline to *Record of a Living Being* was deliberately conceived around a "social problem." Through such narrative treatment, he adds, "I can make a question better understandable to my audience."[1] During the seven years after defeat, however, few hard questions had been raised in Japan's mass media over the social, political, medical, and psychological effects of atomic war against the country. The first Japanese film to record atomic devastation was taken by a documentary crew

---

This essay was written specifically for this volume and is published here for the first time by permission of the author.

from Nippon Eigasha (Japan Film Corporation), which shot footage in Hiroshima and Nagasaki in September and October 1945. While their work on location was in progress, one cameraman was arrested by American military police in October. Within two days, General Headquarters of the occupying army prohibited Japanese from filming the bomb sites. U.S. Strategic Bombing Survey staff confiscated the documentary footage and retained it in order to make damage assessments. After the Survey team judged the film evidence to be valuable as military intelligence, it issued a special order permitting the Nippon Eigasha crew to complete location work in January and February 1946. Occupation authorities promptly impounded the exposed footage and shipped it to the United States. Members of the production crew secretly withheld ten reels of film, but these were not shown to a Japanese audience until 1952.[2]

Cultural historian Tadao Sato describes one effect of sanctions over the Japanese popular media against documentary images or critical realism in the representation of the atomic attacks: "In the Occupation years [1945–1952] it was strictly prohibited to criticize America's role in the tragedy, and the only way the subject could be broached in film was sentimentally."[3] In Sato's estimation, Kurosawa's 1955 film on the subject stands as a unique achievement: "In the history of cinema, few, if any, films have presented the crisis in human relations as well as *Record of a Living Being.*"[4] Sato cites as one principal innovation the film's treatment of the atomic bomb "for the first time as a psychological force devastating human life from within, rather than simply as an outer force of destruction."[5] Joan Mellen considers *Record of a Living Being* to be "the finest Japanese film on atomic war" and identifies its protagonist as "the typical Kurosawa hero, too great a man not to insist on doing something about his fate."[6]

To understand the originality and insight Kurosawa achieves through his cinematic investigation into social psychology in *Record of a Living Being,* consideration must be given to major events that mark the atomic age in its first decade. Developments in atomic energy over these years came through the construction of exponentially more destructive weapons. On 1 July 1946, less than a year after the attacks on Hiroshima and Nagasaki, the United States tested a larger atomic bomb at the Bikini atoll in the Pacific Ocean. Another American atom bomb test was conducted on 17 May 1948. The Soviet Union announced in September 1949 its development of an atomic bomb. On 30 November 1950, five months after the start of war in Korea, President Harry Truman threatened to use atomic weapons. Great Britain conducted its first test of an atomic bomb in October 1952. The United States tested its first hydrogen bomb the following month on the Eniwetok atoll in the Pacific. The Soviet Union tested a hydrogen bomb in August 1953. On 1 March 1954 an American hydrogen bomb test at Bikini atoll burned and contaminated with radioactive ash both Micronesian islanders and the crew members aboard the Japanese fishing vessel *Fukuryu Maru*

No. 5 (*Lucky Dragon No. 5*). One of the crewmen, Aikichi Kuboyama, died on September 23 from these injuries.

The Japan-United States Security Treaty signed in September 1951 gave the United States the right to maintain its military forces in Japan. American global strategy in the Cold War era made Japan pivotal to a nuclear "umbrella" protecting Western interests in Asia. The accelerating rate of destructive potential continued beyond this first decade of the atomic era, marked next by Great Britain's first test on 15 May 1957 of a hydrogen bomb, conducted on Christmas Island in the Indian Ocean.

In his book *The Fate of the Earth*, Jonathan Schell reflects on the legacy left by the dawn of the atomic age. The experience of Japanese caught in the Hiroshima and Nagasaki bombs is "of much more than historical interest. It is a picture of what our whole world is always poised to become—a backdrop of scarcely imaginable horror lying just behind the surface of our normal life, and capable of breaking through into that normal life at any second." The destructive force of the bomb against Hiroshima was twelve kilotons, that against Nagasaki twenty-two kilotons. Within a decade, the standard of measurement for nuclear destruction had risen from the kiloton to the megaton, an increase of a thousandfold. Schell observes of the fifteen-megaton bomb tested at Bikini atoll in March 1954 that "to the amazement of the designers of the test, fallout began to descend on Marshall Islanders and on American servicemen manning weather stations on atolls at supposedly safe distances from the explosion. It was not until this test that the world was alerted to the real magnitude—or, at any rate, to the magnitude as it is understood so far—of the peril from nuclear fallout."[7]

Under the Allied Occupation government, a news press code and other legislative measures prohibited Japanese public access to or distribution of information on the consequences of the Hiroshima and Nagasaki bombings. An Atomic Bomb Casualty Commission (ABCC) was established by the United States in 1946 and its facilities were based in Hiroshima and Nagasaki. The Commission diagnosed and recorded the conditions of surviving bomb victims, but it provided no treatment for them. The ABCC was exempt from Japan's national Medical Treatment Law, which required responsible care for every patient under medical attention. Public debate over the terms of Japan's nuclear defeat began in earnest after the end of Allied Occupation (28 April 1952). Through the publication of *Devil's Heritage (Ma no Isan,* 1953), a book whose fictional plot provides a frame for much factual description and historical narration, Hiroyuki Agawa reported the medical effects of radiation from the atomic bomb dropped on 6 August 1945 for the first time to a general audience in Japan.[8] The charge is made in *Devil's Heritage* that in being examined but not treated at the ABCC Japanese bomb victims were made to serve the Americans as human guinea pigs. The motives of the Commission, according to Agawa's book, were to conduct medical research for

Cold War purposes in formulating an *American* civilian defense strategy in the event of an atomic attack on the United States.

Survivor is not a term commonly used by Japanese to refer to those who lived through the Hiroshima and Nagasaki bombings because in its emphasis on the living it might convey insensitivity toward the dead victims. The term commonly used instead is *hibakusha* ("explosion-affected persons"), a more neutral reference. One of the *hibakusha* portrayed by John Hersey in *Hiroshima* is the Reverend Kiyoshi Tanimoto, pastor of the city's Methodist Church in 1945. Reverend Tanimoto was two miles from the bomb's hypocenter at the time of explosion. Within a month, he began to manifest symptoms of a new medical syndrome of the atomic age, radiation sickness. Nonetheless, Reverend Tanimoto was able to lead a productive life over the next four decades. Much of his work involved fund-raising and the arrangement of medical treatment for fellow *hibakusha*. In 1948 he toured the United States for this purpose, delivering the lecture "The Faith That Grew Out of the Ashes." Such acts of altruism seem somewhat compromised, however, by the minister's historical myopia and political appeasement. Invited to deliver an opening prayer to a session of the United States Senate in 1950, Reverend Tanimoto gave the following benediction: "Our Heavenly Father, we thank Thee for the great blessing Thou has granted America in enabling her to build in this last decade the greatest civilization in human history.... We thank Thee, God, that Japan has been permitted to be one of the fortunate recipients of American generosity. We thank Thee that our people have been given the gift of freedom, enabling them to rise from the ashes of ruin and be reborn."[9]

Conditions of historical amnesia and political narcissism characterize American popular consciousness through the first decade of the atomic age. One prominent instance is evident in *The Family of Man,* the photographic exhibition prepared by Edward Steichen and his staff for the Museum of Modern Art in New York and displayed there in 1955.[10] Under the sponsorship of the United States Information Agency, exhibitions of *The Family of Man* were mounted in several foreign countries, including Japan. One major section to the exhibition, accompanied by the excerpt from Deuteronomy (14:29), "Bless thee in all the work of thy hand which thou doest," features the universality of human work, in all its variety. The section opens with images of manual labor by men and continues with those of domestic work by women. It concludes with photographs of managerial, scientific, and engineering endeavors. Five photographs in the last group are mounted against a design that suggests an abstract of the structure of the atom. Two inscriptions amplify this photographic montage:

> This is the fire that will help the generations to come, if they use it in a sacred manner. But if they do not use it well, the fire will have the power to do them great harm.
>
> —Sioux Indian

Nuclear weapons and atomic electric power are symbolic of the atomic age: On one side, frustration and world destruction: on the other, creativity and a common ground for peace and cooperation.

—U.S. Atomic Energy Commission

While the two texts allude to a potential cataclysm in the future, the exhibition contains no image of the devastation of Hiroshima and Nagasaki in 1945, or of the greater destructive forces of hydrogen bombs tested in 1952 and 1954. Meaningful reference to history or political reality is in this fashion elided from *The Family of Man* exhibition. A pious, inarguable sentiment is offered in their place.

At the time he was completing *Seven Samurai* (*Shichinin no Samurai*, 1954), and with the nuclear weapons tests in the Pacific prominent in his thoughts, Kurosawa discussed with Fumio Hayasaka ideas for his next film. Hayasaka, a close collaborator and a film composer for Kurosawa, was terminally ill at the time. (Hayasaka would die before he could complete the music for *Record of a Living Being*.) In their conversations in 1954 about possible story ideas, Hayasaka reflected on the psychological paralysis and the social inaction that accompany an individual's fear of death. To develop the film story, Kurosawa initially sought to bring together events in the nuclear arms race with Hayasaka's personal reflections and with his own directorial interest in making a satire. His initial effort was blocked, however, by a realization: "I didn't know how to do a satire on something like the H-bomb."[11] After Kurosawa began collaboration on the story with Shinobu Hashimoto and Hideo Oguni, he recognized the impossibility of a directly satirical treatment.

In making *Record of a Living Being,* Kurosawa was acutely aware of the unreflective complacency with which a majority of the world's population met events that marked a new, nuclear age: "No one was thinking seriously of atomic extinction."[12] Indeed, of the fifteen films he had directed up to that point, *Record of a Living Being* would attract the smallest audience. In expectation of such complacency, Kurosawa had redirected the mode of his film story away from satire and toward absurdism. According to his *Something Like an Autobiography* (*Gama no Abura,* 1982), Kurosawa gained early in life a fundamental lesson in humanity in the aftermath of the huge Kanto earthquake of 1923, which he experienced at age thirteen. An event of incredible destructive force that left an estimated 70,000 dead in Tokyo, the earthquake was for Kurosawa ultimately more overwhelming in its psychological consequences for survivors than in loss of life or physical damage. He witnessed mass hysteria that led survivors to massacre Koreans residing in Tokyo. Such experience convinced him of the terrifying "ability of fear to drive people off the course of human behavior."[13]

The opening credits to *Record of a Living Being* are superimposed over images of dense pedestrian and vehicle traffic at busy Tokyo intersections. Seen at a distance and in great numbers, contemporary Japanese seem completely absorbed in workday routines and oblivious to the world-historical circumstances of the atomic age. The soundtrack score is a composition for jazz ensemble, over which plays a high-pitched, nervous tone that rises and falls in its intensity. The tone is deliberately evocative of the science fiction film genre of the 1950s. Concerns about the effects of atomic testing in the Pacific inaugurated a commercially successful series of Japanese monster movies the previous year. The first domestic production in this genre is *Godzilla* (*Gojira*, 1954), which features a prehistoric monster revived by a nuclear explosion in the Bikini atoll. *Godzilla* was directed by Ishiro Honda, who apprenticed with Kurosawa at the P.C.L. (Photo Chemical Laboratory) studio in the 1930s and who later assisted on *Stray Dog, Kagemusha* (*Kagemusha*, 1980), *Ran* (*Ran*, 1985), and *Rhapsody in August*.

Record of a Living Being unfolds as a family drama centered on the father Kiichi Nakajima and his rising anxiety about nuclear destruction. Nakajima is a shrewd and prosperous foundry owner who supports a large immediate family, two mistresses, and three children from his extramarital liaisons. His preoccupation with the dangers of nuclear weapons has a rational basis, given Cold War politics and the atmospheric testing conducted in the Pacific. The family, however, has brought Nakajima to the Tokyo Family Court with the intention of having him declared mentally incompetent to manage business and personal matters. Dr. Harada, a dentist and a mediator for the court, is an external observer of the entire matter. Harada's role is a variation on the medical and investigation motifs that Kurosawa scripted for earlier films on contemporary social issues, notably *Drunken Angel, The Quiet Duel, Stray Dog,* and *Ikiru.*

When Dr. Harada arrives at Family Court, Jiro, one of Nakajima's legitimate sons, mistakes the dentist for a relation connected to his father through one of the mistresses. This early comic incident is indicative of a heroic yet fallible side to the personality of Nakajima. In his dread of nuclear annihilation, Nakajima shows equal concern for all individuals who belong directly within his personal life. Focused on saving those with whom he has intimate ties, Nakajima is blind to the baseness of their motives and to their indifference toward his welfare. His son-in-law Yamazaki attempts to placate Nakajima with the assurance that "Your worry is the worry of all us Japanese," but such remarks are contradicted by the narrow self-interest that guides most family members. Nakajima's preoccupation, which at first appears selfless, will prove selfish, desperate, and destructive in his last attempt to save the family.

One member of the Family Court—the lawyer Hori—is visibly amused by Nakajima's situation when it is first presented. Harada also responds at first to the proceeding in a light spirit, but as the family's petition is read he becomes pensive. Driven to the action by her sons and daughters, Nakajima's wife Toyo has petitioned the court to declare her husband incompetent and to leave his personal and business matters in her custody. The ground for such action stipulated in the petition is Nakajima's state of mind once he became "fearful of atomic and hydrogen bombs and radiation there-from." With the court's recitation of this phrase, the transcript of the petition is superimposed over shot compositions of Nakajima and family members, who wait in the court's lobby. For the film viewer, the historical and politi-cal realities of the atomic age thus stand as a superscript to the family drama.

Tadao Sato attributes the dramatic power of *Record of a Living Being* to its portrayal of family conflict far more than to its treatment of atomic dan-gers. He considers the theme of nuclear threat to be subsumed by the domestic drama and to be posed through the question "Why is the powerful patriarch unable to convince his family of this terror?"[14] From Sato's per-spective the family, the traditional center of spiritual strength in Japanese culture, is destabilized through its dissension and is ultimately destroyed with the confinement of the father, its symbolic head, in a mental hospital. In *The Warrior's Camera,* Stephen Prince evaluates *Record of a Living Being* as a project in which Kurosawa attempts to apply the visual and narrative structures of heroic individualism to a global political issue. The magnitude of nuclear dangers clearly transcends the powers of an individual hero or the capacities of a family, no matter how united. Prince concludes that the film fails to integrate the two principal dimensions of its story material: "While the topic calls for a political analysis, this is deflected by a focus on the psychic cost of living in the shadow of the bomb. The film is split between its two voices, the social and the psychological."[15]

In *Record of a Living Being* the irreparable breach between the collec-tive and the individual and, equally, between the political and the psycho-logical is, in my estimation, key to its insights into contemporary experience. Jacques Derrida has speculated on the problematic status of reality in the nuclear age and of reference to reality through language in such circum-stances. While attacks with atomic weapons occurred in 1945, nuclear *war* thus far remains a threat, a possibility, a hypothesis, "a fable, that is, some-thing one can only talk about." Derrida formulates the problem of the ref-erent in relation to reality in the nuclear age as follows:

> One has to distinguish between this "reality" of the nuclear age and the fiction of war.... The "reality" of the nuclear age and the fable of nuclear war are per-haps distinct, but they are not two separate things. It is the war (in other words the fable) that triggers this fabulous war effort, this senseless capitalization of sophisticated weaponry, this speed race in search of speed, this crazy precipi-tation which, through techno-science, through all the techno-scientific inven-tiveness that it motivates, structures not only the army, diplomacy, politics, but the whole of the human *socius* today, everything that is named by the old words culture, civilization.[16]

Social reality in the nuclear age is thus constructed on the basis of a possible yet still imagined event that could result from the accelerating real potential for global destruction.

Such circumstances accelerate the processes in individual experience, already advanced in industrial and postindustrial societies, of dissociation in public life and atomization of the self. Nonetheless, the overriding concerns in consumer society with material well-being and stability in personal life provide a rationale that still binds individuals in a common social purpose. In *Record of a Living Being,* Nakajima is acutely conscious that in the atomic era reality and potentiality have merged. Nakajima finds himself in a position of social revolt by virtue of the intensity of his conviction that any sense of security in everyday life is a tenuous fiction. Kurosawa shapes the narrative as an intensive test of Nakajima's perceptions and convictions.

The first session of Family Court reveals that Nakajima's previous efforts to protect his family have included plans for a complete private shelter built underground. At present, his intention is to relocate his entire family, his mistresses, and their children to South America. After this first session, Dr. Harada evaluates Nakajima to be mentally competent and stable, but he admits "I really can't understand him." A man of science, Harada will try objectively to reach an understanding of Nakajima's extreme position. In time, the routines and norms of everyday life, not Nakajima's personality, will start to seem abnormal to Harada.

Persuaded that he has convinced the immediate members in his family to emigrate, Nakajima single-mindedly visits each illegitimate child and each mistress to announce their departure for South America. His first visit, with the grown son of a mistress who has died, typifies the resistance Nakajima meets in his mission. The young man intends to remain in Tokyo and he callously attempts to negotiate a cash settlement before his father leaves the country. During these scenes of Nakajima's visits to various locations within Tokyo, Kurosawa's shot compositions emphasize a great *density* of population through constant background activity in the adjacent streets and neighboring apartments. The eccentric personality of the film's protagonist is thus dramatized against a background of daily routines and social norms.

Events in the film story occur during summer months that are subject to extremes in weather. An intense heat wave is punctuated by sudden, blinding flashes of lightning and the sonic boom of thunderclaps. In a visit to his youngest mistress and their infant, Nakajima becomes distraught when a deafening scream from jets flying low overhead is followed by a sequence of violent lightning and thunder. In rapid succession, strong wind gusts raise thick clouds of dust and heavy rains fall. The sequence of atmospheric effects mimics an atomic bomb event, with the last two features suggesting the "ashes of death" and "black rain" that occurred in Hiroshima. In *Hiroshima Mon Amour* (1959), Marguerite Duras and Alain Resnais depict the entwined bodies of lovers, a Japanese man and a French woman, "covered successively with the ashes, the dew, of atomic death—and the sweat of love fulfilled."[17]

The rains depicted in *Record of a Living Being* hold no promise of purification or absolution, as they do in *Rashomon.* In the second session of Family Court, Harada expresses support for Nakajima's plan, but the dentist's efforts to persuade the family are futile. Nakajima declares to the court that he has no fear of hydrogen bombs as long as he can act to escape their range. Harada tries to convince the other two panel members of the ultimate rationality of Nakajima's intentions. But they decide in favor of the petition on pragmatic grounds, in order to protect the family business from any rash decisions the father may make. Nakajima is declared partly incompetent, and management of his affairs is transferred to his wife. Nakajima's determination to appeal the decision to a higher court delays its implementation.

Nakajima has proclaimed to the Family Court: "Men have to die. But I hate to be killed." In other words, Nakajima accepts his own mortality, but he will not resign himself to the new fatalism borne of the atomic age. In his heroism of resistance to nuclear annihilation, Nakajima embodies an existential, absurdist paradox. His lucidity is met with accusations that he is deranged. His isolation and reasoned dread are the source of profound insight into social reality and historical circumstances. One exception to his rejection by family members is the youngest mistress, who offers Nakajima what money she has managed to save in order for him to make a deposit on farmland in Brazil. His wife Toyo, who has acted according to the dictates of her children, ultimately pleads with the family on behalf of Nakajima's plan, but to no avail.

After the arrangements for emigration have been blocked by the court and the family, Harada encounters Nakajima on a streetcar. For the first time, Nakajima considers himself "deadlocked" by fear. Persisting in his convictions, and in desperation to take some action, Nakajima subsequently gathers his family, his mistresses, and their children and he humbles himself before them with a final plea. A reversal of the family's traditional obligations toward him, this act of humility fails. With its failure, Nakajima collapses. While he lies semiconscious, family members, legitimate and illegitimate alike, calculate their share of the estate. A close shot of Nakajima slowly regaining consciousness, and overhearing the discussion of inheritance, portrays his face through the insect netting that protects his sleeping mat. The mottled shading cast across his features evokes the ashes of death.

Nakajima's last, desperate efforts lead him to commit arson at his own foundry in order to "free" his family from their expectations of inheriting the business and to make the plan to emigrate finally viable. Ironically, the complete ruin of the foundry brought by his act of arson is the one event *within* the film story to bring real, material catastrophe. The foundry's workers are horrified by the arson and, in protesting the destruction of their livelihoods, they prompt Nakajima to consider for the first time the destructive social consequences of his preoccupation with the family's safety. He apologizes sincerely and vows to make possible the emigration of workers and their families. By this point, the threats of radiation sickness from weapon testing and of global nuclear war have contaminated Nakajima's thinking.

Jailed immediately after the arson, Nakajima shares a cell with two common criminals who ridicule his fears of nuclear catastrophe. They taunt Nakajima with the proposition that he will be safe only if he leaves the planet. In the end, a mental hospital provides Nakajima sanctuary from danger. Confined there, he is secure and confirmed in his convictions. Looking at the sun, Nakajima is convinced that he is watching the earth being consumed by the flames and radiation of a nuclear apocalypse. A perceptive individual's rational caution has escalated into a delusional state. The refusal of most people in Japanese society to take atomic danger seriously, even against the evidence of their own recent history, has led to Nakajima's "insanity." The ideology that has prevailed is the Cold War doublethink of a global security gained through mutually assured destructive capability on the part of the Soviet Union and Western powers. Nakajima's insightful concern achieves social expression only through his monological and monomaniacal persistence, which results in his exclusion from society.

Against the doublethink of the nuclear arms race, the only salvation possible for Nakajima is in the end an individual one. His resolution to the problematic potentiality of meaning in the nuclear age is complete dissociation from reality. Noël Burch explains the neglect and underrated status of *Record of a Living Being* as the result of the film's ideological challenge to established power: "Its message was in conflict with the interests of the ruling class and reflected popular aspirations, but the time had not come for this desperate expression of mass feeling to be recognized by the intelligentsia of Japan or of the capitalist West." Kurosawa's film prefigures what Burch identifies as the "Shoin complex" in Japanese independent cinema of the 1960s and early 1970s, notably in the work of director Nagisa Oshima.[18] In politicized art, the Shoin complex refers to a use of conditions of extremism, eccentricity, and madness for the expression of social revolt against capitalist norms.

Such conditions of expression in Kurosawa's cinema developed through the director's profound responses to the modes of human inquiry and to the worldviews he had discovered in the fiction of Feodor Dostoevsky.[19] Kurosawa is affiliated to Dostoevsky in the constant exploration, through narrative form, into the author's own ideas on human existence and into his characters' experience of the world. The mode of such inquiry in both Kurosawa and Dostoevsky is dialogic. That is, their fictions render the exploration into humanity and society through a constant interaction of meanings, meanings that are often in contradiction and competition with one another. While a character such as Nakajima may be shown to adopt a monologic position, the characterization is developed in a larger, dialogic context.

The experiences of Dr. Harada depicted in *Record of a Living Being* are manifestly dialogic in structure. In his role as mediator and judicial panelist, Harada is commissioned to inquire into the matter of Nakajima's sanity. This process, however, rapidly becomes one of self-inquiry, into the sanity of his own passive acceptance of the nuclear status quo. Harada's refrain in regard to Nakajima, "I really can't understand him," becomes progressively internalized and reflexive to the point where it is indicative of Harada's sense of division and disbelief toward himself.

Gilles Deleuze describes the Dostoevskian property in Kurosawa's cinema in this manner: "In the most pressing situations, [a Kurosawa film] feels the need to see the terms of a problem which is more profound than the situation, and even more pressing." As a consequence, the problem breached by the narrative exceeds any possibility of narrative resolution: Kurosawa "goes beyond the limits of knowledge, but also the conditions of action. He reaches a purely optical world, where the thing to be is a seer."[20] Deleuze delineates this optical dimension as a "breathing space or encompasser to contain a profound question."[21]

The sun into which Nakajima stares from his hospital window leaves open just such a space as *Record of a Living Being* draws toward its final scene. The brilliant radiation from solar fires stands as an image of a concept beyond the presence or purpose of the character. The concept exists without any objective correlative. Rather, it exists as an image of events and phenomena knowable only through their potentiality. The inchoate, blinding space of this image is a rendering of the dilemmas of the nuclear referent in the atomic age. The film as a whole renders the social and psychological legacies produced by this era as a condition of existential absurdity.

Sankichi Toge, a Hiroshima poet and *hibakusha,* expressed the existential legacy in these words:

> August 6, 1945:
> that midday midnight
> man burned the gods
> at the stake.

These lines are contained in "Flames," one of Toge's *Poems of the Atomic Bomb (Genbaku Shishu).*[22] A book first published in a mimeographed edition in 1951, *Poems of the Atomic Bomb* appeared in print for the first time in 1952 and has been reprinted more than forty times. Publications such as the Toge volume contributed to a growing protest and peace movement in Japan. The movement voiced opposition to the national government's security agreements with the West and to its neglect of *hibakusha.* A peace ceremony planned to mark the fifth anniversary of the bomb against Hiroshima was prohibited by Occupation authorities. Participants who gathered in Hiroshima on 6 August 1950 despite the ban were dispersed by armed police. The anniversary observations in Hiroshima on 6 August 1955 mark the birth of a mass peace movement in Japan. In that week five thousand delegates attended the first World Conference Against Atomic and Hydrogen Bombs. The following month Nihon Gensuikyo (the Japan Council Against Atomic and Hydrogen Bombs) was formed.

For over a decade, the Japanese national government made no special provision for the economic relief of *hibakusha*. Only after the radioactive contamination of the vessel *Fukuryu Maru No. 5* in 1954 did concerted official efforts for legislative action begin. The A-Bomb Victims Medical Care Law did not go into effect, however, until April 1957. This prolonged period of official neglect and denial is indicative of the widespread social stigma and marginalization suffered by *hibakusha*. The Hiroshima writer Yoko Ota describes a caste separation in the relations between nonvictims and victims: "From the first, the average person treated the injured, from whom he differed only in not being injured, almost as if they had always been dirty beggars. He was arrogant in words and attitude and treated them as inferiors." This observation is made in Ota's account *City of Corpses* (*Shikabane no Machi*), which was published in 1948 in a censored version and in its first full edition in 1950.[23] She further observes that the victims themselves conformed to this caste division in being servile, even though many were from the middle and prosperous classes.

In his novel *Black Rain* (*Kuroi Ame*, 1966) Masuji Ibuse compassionately examines *hibakusha* as they are further victimized by a society that reacts to them with suspicion and fear. Set in a village in the Hiroshima region some years after 1945, the local radiation victims remain subject to the narrow customs and superstitions of rural life. Destruction from the bomb continues to the body and the mind, with human consequences that are incalculable. In the city, the bomb left civil chaos, official corruption, and moral ruin in its wake. In village life, necessary activities and even some local festivals resume, but family life for *hibakusha* does not return to normal. In Shohei Imamura's film adaptation of the book—*Black Rain* (*Kuroi Ame*, 1988)—the dramatic focus is on Yasuko, who was twenty years old in 1945 and who remains unmarried because of fears about her radiation sickness.

Based on documents, interviews, and the diaries of victims, *Black Rain* also records unexplained changes to ecology in the bomb area. The devastation is accompanied by grotesque forms of growth. Ibuse's short story "The Crazy Iris" ("Kakitsubata," 1951) is set in the town of Fukuyama and its surrounding villages in the summer of 1945. Fukuyama is 100 miles to the east of Hiroshima; two days after the atomic attack, American planes dropped incendiary bombs and destroyed much of the town. A young woman, who had survived the Hiroshima bomb and returned to town, is driven mad by the air raid in Fukuyama. She drowns herself in a local pond, where a purple iris has blossomed out of season. After her body is recovered, an onlooker comments, "the iris blooming in the pond is crazy and belongs to a crazy age."[24]

With the episodes "Mount Fuji in Red" and "The Weeping Demon" in *Dreams,* Kurosawa takes the legacy of human and natural destruction to nightmarish extremes in imagining an apocalypse that ends the atomic era. The narrative momentum and continuity in *Dreams* as a whole is based on activi-

ties of searching, following, journeying, and wandering engaged in by the protagonist from childhood through adulthood. That action reaches a terminus
when nuclear reactors explode at the base of Mount Fuji, a traditional site of
Japan's cultural identity. In one scene of *Record of a Living Being* Mount Fuji
stands prominently in the background as Nakajima tries to negotiate the purchase of farmland in Brazil, in pursuit of his goal of expatriation.

After explosions destroy the nuclear reactors, the protagonist in *Dreams*
is caught in a terrified exodus of Japanese toward the island's coast. In the
panic, one person clearly voices the inevitable: "Japan is so small there's no
escape." In the next scene the dreamer, along with a few other refugees,
stands atop a coastal cliff, at land's end. Tens of thousands of people have
already leapt into the sea. The episode comes to a close with the dreamer
attempting to drive off a thick cloud of radioactive poison, emitted in gases
that nuclear scientists have colored for purposes of identification and safety.
One refugee curses the absurdity of such "precautions" and hurtles from the
cliff.

In the story "Summer Flowers" ("Natsu no Hana," 1947), which Tamiki
Hara completed within four months of his survival of the Hiroshima bomb,
the fires and windstorms created in the bomb's wake are associated with
damnation: "I don't remember clearly what color the surrounding air was.
But I think we must have been enveloped in the dreadfully gloomy faint
green light of the medieval paintings of Buddhist hell."[25] In *Devil's Heritage,*
Agawa regards the atomic bomb as a new principle of evil: "There was nothing to do but to regard the atomic bomb as an evil spirit which had appeared
in the world in the form of a scientific creation. America, in order to solve
one difficult problem, had in the end sought the aid of the evil spirit. But
what was even worse was explaining it as the so-called will of God."[26] The
first decade of the atomic age is said to compound such evil with the invention of cobalt and hydrogen nuclear weapons.

"The Weeping Demon" episode to *Dreams* imagines the global realm that
remains after the detonation of nuclear missiles. The dreamer encounters a
world that has mutated and its monstrosities are measured by film viewers
against the extraordinary beauty depicted in earlier episodes. Survivors who
were formerly businessmen and government officials have been transformed
into horned fiends. The horde of these demons, shrieking in pain and howl-
ing in aggression, is an antithesis to the procession of dancers at the wedding of foxes in the first episode. Dandelions have grown taller than a
human being and they appear as a grotesque distortion of the passionate
intensity of the sunflowers in the famous van Gogh canvas, seen in episode
five. After he learns that the fiends survive through cannibalism, the dreamer
is threatened by his demon guide and, in flight, he flails down a mountain
slope that is all ash and cinder. This terrain stands in complete contrast to
the romantic, impressionist landscapes that invite the child dreamer in
episode one and the artist dreamer in episode five.

In a critique of *Dreams,* Stephen Prince places the film within a revisionist project in Kurosawa's career that dates from *Dodeskaden (Dodeskaden,* 1970). With the rendering of a slum dreamworld in *Dodeskaden,* according to Prince, Kurosawa began a process of redefinition that has entailed an "intensifying renunciation of politics, of the possibility for social reform, and of the willful and impetuous commitment to social and cultural progress exemplified by his earlier film heroes."[27] Audie Bock believes that with *Dodeskaden* and *Dreams* Kurosawa has lapsed into blatant "message" movie-making and the result is two films that are undramatic, tiresome preachments.[28]

Without question, *Dreams* lacks the dialogic interaction among possible truths and courses of action that are contained in *Record of a Living Being.* Written alone and in a matter of weeks, the finished script to *Dreams* was thought by Steven Spielberg to be only a schematic treatment when he read it.[29] The script was not subject to the creative process of contention and reconceptualization that distinguishes Kurosawa's close collaboration over most of his film career with writers like Hideo Oguni and Shinobu Hashimoto and with composers like Fumio Hayasaka. The two episodes on nuclear destruction do not benefit from the debate among viewpoints and the admixture of dramatic modes found in the narrative and visuals to *Record of a Living Being.* The conditions of resignation, powerlessness, and empty rhetoric in *Dreams* can nevertheless be understood as aspects of an absurdist predicament in the atomic age.

With *Rhapsody in August,* Kurosawa considers what remains in contemporary Japan of the social and psychological conditions that had compelled his inquiries into Japan's defeat through his *gendai-mono* during the decade 1945–55. *Rhapsody in August* proceeds at a gradual, reiterative tempo that reflects the mental processes of its principal character Kane, the grandmother to a large family. The film's deliberate pace and uneventful narrative have caused much dissatisfaction among reviewers and critics.[30] In defense of these qualities, it should be emphasized that *Rhapsody in August,* released in the year Kurosawa reached eighty, depicts Kane through the sensibility of old age.

In conversation with the novelist Gabriel García Márquez, Kurosawa reflected on the film's approach to his country's atomic defeat:

> I have not filmed shockingly realistic scenes which would prove to be unbearable and yet would not explain in and of themselves the horror of the drama. What I would like to convey is the type of wounds the atomic bomb left in the heart of our people, and how they gradually began to heal. I remember the day of the bombing clearly, and even now I still can't believe that it could have happened in the real world. But the worst part is that the Japanese have already cast it into oblivion. . . . Even now [1991] there are still 2,700 patients at the Atomic Bomb hospital waiting to die from the after-effects of the radiation after forty-five years of agony. In other words, the atomic bomb is still killing Japanese.[31]

Asked by Márquez "Had Japan surrendered without the atomic bomb, would
it be the same Japan it is today?" Kurosawa answered that a form of historical
amnesia is part of the bomb's legacy: "The people who survived Nagasaki
don't want to remember their experience because the majority of them, in
order to survive, had to abandon their parents, their children, their brothers
and sisters. They still can't stop feeling guilty. Afterward, the U.S. forces that
occupied the country for six years influenced by various means the accelera-
tion of forgetfulness, and the Japanese government collaborated with them."[32]

Rhapsody in August is set in a village outside Nagasaki, separated from
the city by low mountains. Kane has continued to live in this farming community after the death of her husband, killed in the city by the 1945 bomb.
As the forty-fifth anniversary of that event approaches, she receives an
extended visit from her four grandchildren—three adolescents and one
younger boy. The children prove to be receptive and responsive to the family's history, in which the atomic bomb is integral. For middle-aged family
members, who stay with Kane later, such history has long been displaced
by their preoccupations with work, status, and material comfort. Circumstances change with the arrival of a Japanese-American relation named Clark.
To their surprise, Clark asks to visit the bomb site where his Japanese uncle,
Kane's husband, lost his life. In paying their respects, the adult members
are brought back to family history, and thus to world history.

In *Rhapsody in August* Kurosawa seeks to establish the contemporary
meaning of the past without recourse to narrative and cinematic devices of
the diary form, retrospective voice-over, or flashback such as Imamura uses
in the film *Black Rain*. The memories of those who lived through the bomb
are largely unspoken in Kurosawa's film. When Kane is visited in her home
by another widow, the two remain in prolonged, respectful silence. This
past remains tangibly present only in a few physical vestiges of the devastation, such as a half-standing playground apparatus that was melted into a
twisted, misshapen figure by the bomb blast. The playground is the site
where Kane's husband died. While Clark and family members are at the site,
a group of *hibakusha* come to tend a plot of flowers that encircles the dam-
aged climbing apparatus.

Addressing the subject in an interview given in 1991, Kurosawa considers the 1945 atomic explosion an event that cannot be represented directly:

> It is absolutely unfilmable. That state of destruction and of such terrible human
> anguish does not belong to the realm of the presentable. There is no way to
> express it, to film it, to reproduce it. These are events that provoke only one type
> of reaction: to avert one's eyes. It is better not to present them. It is better to have
> them imagined by the spectator since in the end one risks showing them in such
> a manner that people will turn away. . . . It is better to evoke and nurture the imag-
> ination; this is far more terrifying. I have not seen Imamura's motion picture, but
> I think it is impossible to film such events. Things reach a point where the people
> who experienced the events cannot even speak of them. They are unspeakable.[33]

The film's undramatic, reflective pace is indicative of the unspeakable and the unrepresentable in Japan's recent past.

Activity in Kane's life remains defined by the bomb. Her consideration of visiting the family in Hawaii is deferred until the annual memorial observances of August 9. Many villagers participate in the services for the bomb dead, conducted at the local shrine. Nagasaki has established an official memorial in the city, a plaza dedicated to world peace. The plaza is shown to be, however, an impersonal tourist attraction void of the experiential dimensions of events on 9 August 1945. *Rhapsody in August* demonstrates that for non-*hibakusha* in the atomic age denial, indifference, and historical amnesia are common impairments to consciousness.

The 1945 bomb blast in Nagasaki is rendered in *Rhapsody in August* through an image retained in Kane's thoughts. Standing in the spot where it was conceived, she explains the image to the grandchildren, and it is visualized on screen. Seen from her home in the village, a crimson mushroom cloud rose from the rift in the mountains; within the cloud a massive eye appeared to blink open. The eye image is a subject that one of Kane's brothers drew obsessively after the bomb blast. Its symbolism suggests the awakening of perception and consciousness to a new age. Katsuzo Oda, who was exposed to the atomic bomb as an adolescent, recounts a similar perceptual experience in his story "Human Ashes" ("Ningen no Hai," 1966). The flash of the bomb was so unexpected, massive, and unique that he did not *see* it in any normal sense of the word: "The phenomenon that occurred at that instant registered on my eyeballs, but I had no way of knowing what it was. And whatever it was, it came and went with extraordinary speed. At first I thought it was something I dreamed."[34]

Kurosawa's commentary on the nature of his subject matter in *Rhapsody in August*—"These are events that provoke only one type of reaction: to avert one's eyes"—stands in contradiction to artistic aims he maintained in the *gendai-mono* of 1945–55. In that period, Kurosawa sought to achieve the qualities of human complexity and insight that he so greatly admired in the fiction of Dostoevsky. Dostoevsky, Kurosawa has stated, is the author "who writes most honestly about human existence" and he possesses "the kind of gentleness that makes you want to avert your eyes when you see something really dreadful, really tragic. He has this power of compassion. And then he refuses to turn his eyes away; he, too, looks; he, too, suffers."[35] Through a similar willingness to face the profound paradoxes in human existence Kurosawa created the dark, absurdist undertones to *Record of a Living Being*.

In these senses of the term, *Rhapsody in August* leaves the human gaze largely averted. The film's image of a cosmic, atomic eye in effect transposes the agency of consciousness from humanity to an abstract realm. Kurosawa intended a similar effect for the epic battle scene in *Ran:* "In eliminating the sounds from the scene of battle I wanted to indicate that the perspective was that of the heavens: the heavens watch such unthinkable and bloody battles and become literally mute."[36] The last sequence in *Rhapsody in August* bears some visual resemblance to the closing tableau of *Ran,* but it does not share the earlier film's indictment of the unheroic history of human power.

In the final images of *Ran* the blind Tsurumaru, a survivor of political terror and chaos, is unattended as he moves gropingly at the edge of a precipice. With only a reed cane as his guide, Tsurumaru haltingly steps forward. When the cane tip reaches into thin air, Tsurumaru is startled and he drops the scroll of Buddha Amida, which was intended to secure him from harm. Now his only two comforts in life—the scroll and a flute that was left behind—are lost. The image of Tsurumaru's precarious position is a summation of what humanity has become, having brought itself to the brink of extinction. The prospect of nonexistence, now manifest, has been the dialogic subtext throughout *Ran.* Tsurumaru's predicament is the culmination of the film's tragic absurdity.

In *Rhapsody in August* Kane, on the night prior to her family's planned departure, reacts to an atomic explosion that she imagines has just occurred. Like Nakajima in *Record of a Living Being,* Kane is startled into this reaction by a rapid succession of blinding lightning flashes, rolling and explosive thunder, and sudden winds. She tries to protect children from the imagined blast and radiation by covering them with bedding. Concerned for her emotional stability, the family remains with Kane, but she disappears from the house the next day. Kane wanders a country road, where she is overtaken by heavy rain and strong winds that have arisen abruptly, unannounced by lightning or thunder. Running alone on the road, Kane outdistances the family members who race toward her.

Kane's sole protection against the elements is a light umbrella, which is everted by the gale winds. At this moment storm sounds are displaced from the soundtrack by a children's choral version of "The Wild Rose" ("Nobara"), a Franz Schubert song that had been recited by her grandchildren in an earlier scene. Its verses "the wild rose blooming beautifully, its color lovely, ... fragrant, crimson" recall the previous, startling image of an ant column rising up a thorny rose stem to a red blossom. They also recall, ironically, Kane's vision of the Nagasaki bomb as a blossoming, crimson cloud. The telephoto camera perspective collapses both depth of field and the space around Kane, and the pace of her movement is slackened through slow motion, so that she finally appears to be moving in place. With the accompaniment of the choral song, the image becomes lightly comic. *Rhapsody in August* thus culminates without the undercurrents of existential and tragicomic absurdity that give *Record of a Living Being* such unsettling insights into human experience in the atomic age.

Notes

1. Donald Richie, *The Films of Akira Kurosawa*, rev. ed. (Berkeley: University of California Press, 1984), 113.

2. The Committee for the Compilation of Materials on Damage Caused by the Atomic Bombs in Hiroshima and Nagasaki, *Hiroshima and Nagasaki: The Physical, Medical, and Social Effects of the Atomic Bombings*, trans. Eisei Ishikawa and David L. Swain (New York: Basic Books, 1981), 509–10, 584–85. An informative discussion of Occupation censorship and of Japanese documentary and fiction films on the atomic bomb is provided in Kyoko Hirano, *Mr. Smith Goes to Washington: Japanese Cinema under the American Occupation, 1945–1952* (Washington, D.C.: Smithsonian Institution Press, 1992), 1–9, 34–46, 59–66.

3. Tadao Sato, *Currents in Japanese Cinema*, trans. Gregory Barrett (Tokyo: Kodansha International, 1982), 197.

4. Ibid., 120.

5. Ibid., 199.

6. Joan Mellen, *The Waves at Genji's Door: Japan Through Its Cinema* (New York: Pantheon, 1976), 202, 204.

7. Jonathan Schell, *The Fate of the Earth* (New York: Knopf, 1982), 46, 74–75.

8. Hiroyuki Agawa, *Devil's Heritage*, trans. John M. Maki (Tokyo: Hokuseido Press, 1957).

9. John Hersey, *Hiroshima*, enl. ed. (New York: Knopf, 1985), 181.

10. My analysis is based on the best-selling book that contains the exhibition's complete contents: Edward Steichen, curator, *The Family of Man* (New York: Museum of Modern Art, 1955). The quotations cited appear on 79, 82.

11. Andrew Sarris, ed., *Interviews with Film Directors* (New York: Avon, 1967), 301.

12. Ibid., 302.

13. Akira Kurosawa, *Something Like an Autobiography*, trans. Audie E. Bock (New York: Vintage, 1983), 51.

14. Sato, *Currents in Japanese Cinema*, 129.

15. Stephen Prince, *The Warrior's Camera: The Cinema of Akira Kurosawa* (Princeton: Princeton University Press, 1991), 160.

16. Jacques Derrida, "No Apocalypse, Not Now: (full speed ahead, seven missiles, seven missives)," trans. Catherine Porter and Philip Lewis, *Diacritics* 14, no. 2 (Summer 1984): 23. In *Discourse and Reference in the Nuclear Age* (Norman: University of Oklahoma Press, 1988), J. Fisher Solomon provides a thorough commentary and counterargument on Derrida's "nuclear criticism."

17. Marguerite Duras and Alain Resnais, *Hiroshima Mon Amour*, trans. Richard Seaver (New York: Grove, 1961), 8.

18. Noël Burch, *To the Distant Observer: Form and Meaning in the Japanese Cinema*, rev. and ed. Annette Michelson (Berkeley: University of California Press, 1979), 306–7; for his discussion of the Shoin complex, see 330–31.

19. In *Akira Kurosawa and Intertextual Cinema* (Baltimore: Johns Hopkins University Press, 1994), I discuss at length the legacy in Kurosawa's cinema of themes and structures of expression prominent in Dostoevsky's work.

20. Gilles Deleuze, *Cinema 2: The Time-Image*, trans. Hugh Tomlinson and Robert Galeta (Minneapolis: University of Minnesota Press, 1989), 128, 176.

21. Ibid., 15.

22. A translation of *Poems of the Atomic Age* is included in Richard H. Minear, ed. and trans., *Hiroshima: Three Witnesses* (Princeton: Princeton University Press, 1990), which is the source for the quotation.

23. Minear, *Hiroshima,* 217. A full translation of *City of Corpses* is contained in the Minear book.

24. Masuji Ibuse, "The Crazy Iris," trans. Ivan Morris, in *The Crazy Iris and Other Stories of the Atomic Aftermath,* ed. Kenzaburo Oe (New York: Grove, 1985), 35.

25. Minear, *Hiroshima,* 51. A full translation of the story collection *Summer Flowers* is contained in the Minear book.

26. Agawa, *Devil's Heritage,* 222.

27. Stephen Prince, "Memory and Nostalgia in Kurosawa's Dream World," *Post Script* 11, no. 1 (Fall 1991): 31.

28. Audie Bock, "The Moralistic Cinema of Kurosawa," in *Kurosawa: Perceptions on Life, An Anthology of Essays,* ed. Kevin K. W. Chang (Honolulu: Honolulu Academy of Arts, 1991): 16–23. A similar assessment is made in Linda Ehrlich, "Kurosawa's Fragile Heroes: Another Look at the *Tateyaku,*" in the Chang volume, 34–45.

29. Jim Bailey, "The Edge of Dreamland," *Los Angeles Times Calendar,* 26 August 1990, 3, 92.

30. See Bock, "Moralistic Cinema of Kurosawa," 22–23; François Chevassu, "*Rhapsodie en août:* La pesanteur et la grâce," *La Revue du Cinéma,* no. 472 (juin 1991): 21–22; Jonathan Romney, *Sight and Sound,* n.s., 1, no. 9 (January 1992): 43.

31. "The Conversation: Kurosawa and García Márquez," *Los Angeles Times Calendar,* 23 June 1991, 28.

32. Ibid., 29.

33. Thierry Jousse, "Entretien avec Akira Kurosawa," trans. Catherine Cadou, *Cahiers du Cinéma,* no. 445 (juin 1991): 12; the translation from French is mine.

34. Katsuzo Oda, "Human Ashes," trans. Burton Watson, in *The Crazy Iris and other Stories,* 68.

35. Richie, *Films of Kurosawa,* 81.

36. "Propos d'Akira Kurosawa," *Revue du Cinéma,* no. 408 (septembre 1985): 69; the translation from French is mine.

At the Rasho gate the priest (Minoru Chiaki), the commoner (Kichijiro Ueda), and the woodcutter (Takashi Shimura) reflect on the meaning of events in the forest, in *Rashomon*.

In *Ikiru*, the writer (Yunosuke Ito) places a new hat on Watanabe (Takashi Shimura) during their nighttown odyssey.

Toho

The foundry owner Nakajima (Toshiro Mifune), in *Record of a Living Being*, confronts Dr. Harada (Takashi Shimura), a mediator for the family court.

Asaji (Isuzu Yamada) and Washizu (Toshiro Mifune) in the "forbidden," bloodstained chamber of North Castle, in *Throne of Blood*.

Toho

Three inhabitants of *The Lower Depths*—Tatsu (Haruo Tanaka), Otaki (Nijiko Kiyokawa), and Osen (Akemi Negishi)—come to the aid of Okayo (Kijoko Kagawa), the landlady's sister.

Toho

The businessman Gondo (Toshiro Mifune), with back to camera, confronts the kidnapper Takeuchi (Tsutomu Yamazaki) in *High and Low*.

Kurosawa Films

In *Red Beard,* the medical intern Yasumoto (Yuzo Kayama) responds
to his mentor, Dr. Niide (Toshiro Mifune), known as Red Beard.

The fool Kyoami (Peter) accompanies his fallen master, the warlord
Hidetora (Tatsuya Nakadai), in *Ran.*

Greenwich Film / Herald Ace / Nippon Herald

The samurai Kikuchiyo (Toshiro Mifune) and Kyuzo (Seiji Miyaguchi) in the climactic battle of *Seven Samurai*.

Tobo

[*The Lower Depths* and *Throne of Blood*]

NOËL BURCH

KUROSAWA'S SOCIAL concerns are reflected in all his *gendai-geki* and most of his *jidai-geki*.[1] *The Lower Depths* (*Donzoko*, 1957) might actually be called his one *Meiji-mono* except for the curiously symbiotic relationship between nineteenth-century Japanese and Russian culture already materialized in *The Idiot*. The helpless pessimism and ludicrous outbursts of Gorki's *lumpen* outcasts make them close kin to the cantankerous iron-master. This film also involves a new and important avatar of Kurosawa's basic geometry. In a thorough exploitation of the possibilities of a deceptively simple set, he lays out successive camera set-ups according to ruthlessly mechanical patterns. Moreover, in both indoor and outdoor sequences, he creates a remarkable instance of specifically Japanese centripetal composition. This is intimately associated with a principle of "booby-trapped space" *(espace piégé),* whereby at any time a curtain or a door may draw back, or a face emerge from the shadows in an unexpected corner of the screen. The effect is one in which the free-floating gaze required by the centripetal composition is suddenly focused on some new and unexpected point of interest, thereby further emphasizing the centripetal potentiality of the image. The film's geometry is completed by systematically sharp contrasts between relatively long takes and brief flurries of "rough-hewn" editing. Indeed, every cut in the film seems made with a rusty ax, so brutal are the reversals and other strategies, including precisely these cuts from wide-angle shots to the first in a given series of briefer and closer shots. Most remarkable of these wide-angle shots is a long, single take backyard scene, already mentioned as a singular suspension of the film's stylistic unity and which acts as a formal and diegetic "breathing space." The characters sit about warmed by a pale ray of sunlight, exchanging fantasies, while the discreetly moving camera proposes variations on a theme, as it were: a succession of different compositions all foregrounding a diagonal wooden prop. In some respects, and despite the willfulness of its spatial organization, this film is less of a model than others, since, as with *The Idiot,* the original narrative structure does not lend itself to the strict construction of *Living (Ikiru)* or *Cobweb Castle (Throne of Blood).* In some respects, however, it deserves to be explored in far greater depth than is possible here. For this is Kurosawa's most richly

---

pragmatic dramaturgy, considered independently of any "geometry." Or rather, the geometry itself is "spontaneous," nascent, incompletely rationalized, as it were.

Cobweb Castle (*Kumo-no-su jo,* 1957),[2] made earlier in the same fruitful year that produced *The Lower Depths,* is indisputably Kurosawa's finest achievement, largely because it carries furthest the rationalization process of his geometry.

As most readers know, this film is an adaptation of Shakespeare's *Macbeth,* structurally faithful to the point of respecting the play's division into acts; the spoken word is, however, sparingly used. Furthermore, in a way evocative of the two adaptations from the Russian, the film plays upon essential similarities between the European and Japanese "middle ages."

In connection with the early films, I have already referred to an opposition between extreme violence or pathos and moments of static, restrained tension which is, in fact, to be found in nearly all of Kurosawa's films. *Cobweb Castle* is entirely founded upon this principle. The film's overall plan involves two regularly alternating types of scene. Those of the first type are characterized by violent agitation, repeated rather than developed. They are, in one way or another, peripheral to that central zone of the classical diegesis which we call plot-line, and to its hardest core, "character building," tending on the contrary to be theatrical signs for elided action. Examples are: the dashing messengers, whose agitation stands for an "off-stage" battle; the headlong ride through the storm-swept forest, which signifies the invisible gathering of occult forces; the confused gallopings which signify rather than depict the battle that is to follow the "king's" murder; the portentous panic of Miki's horse, which *prefigures* the off-screen murder of his master; the ominous invasion of the throne-room by a flock of birds, presumably fleeing the advancing forest. Contrasting with these are similarly protracted tensely static, dramatic moments: the scene with the "witch" following that first mad ride; Asaji ("Lady Macbeth") waiting for her husband Washizu to return after murdering his lord; the funeral procession endlessly advancing towards the castle gates, a scene in which time and space are dilated with blatant artificiality; and the long introduction to the ghost scene, as described below. The dance-like scene in which Asaji waits for the first murder to be accomplished also incorporates a trait otherwise reserved to the scenes of agitation—the evocation of an off-screen event—while as we shall see, the opposition between the two types is dialectically resolved in the final sequence.

This dramatically "full" stasis and this "empty" agitation are also interrelated in a sequence early in the film which shows Washizu's and Miki's blind wanderings through the mist-shrouded forest after their encounter with the witch. Twelve times the horsemen advance towards the camera, turn and ride away, in twelve shots that are materially separate but identical, apparently, in the space they frame—grey, misty, almost entirely abstract. Not until the last shot, in fact, do we realize that this was supposed to have been a forest. This aspect of the scene is strongly reminiscent of the strategies of the oriental theater in general, with its conventional representation of (for example) long journeys within the avowedly limited here-and-now of scenic space. Kurosawa, however, on the basis of what is, in fact, a coded figure ("durational montage,"[3] the model for all of the scenes of de-centred agitation in the film) builds one of the most sustained variation structures in narrative cinema, combining in never-repeated order three or four well-defined stages chosen from the range provided by each and all of the principal parameters of the action: the distance from the camera at which the approaching horses pause, the duration of their turn and the radius of the arc described, their distance from the camera when the shot begins and ends. At times they ride into view out of the mist or disappear into it; at others, the shot begins when they are already in sight, or it ends before they have vanished. From the eighth to the eleventh shot, a shift occurs, the process grows increasingly complex, the riders reverse direction as they ride laterally to the invisibly panning camera, become separated as one rides out of the shot, then join up again, ride out together leaving an empty shot, re-enter unexpectedly in close-up, etc. (these four shots may in fact be regarded as a series of variations of the "second order"). The last shot, which shows a landscape emerging from the rising mist, provides a final return to the original motif: the horsemen ride towards the camera as in the beginning, but at a perceptibly slower pace than the steady trot which has marked the rest of the sequence, then pull up in medium shot. "At last we are out of that forest," says Washizu, speaking the first words of a sequence in which the only sounds have been the hooves and whinnying of the horses, and an unobtrusive, very simple, sustained line of woodwind music. The sequence is actually brought to its close by a thirteenth shot of the two men sitting near the edges of the frame, their battle pennants flying in the wind, calmly, amicably discussing the witch's prediction—but already separated, symbolically, by the castle, the seat of power which they will dispute, looming in the distance, squarely between them. This shot is also a striking instance of a "geometrical" strategy which determines the imagery of most of the film: a rigorous *symmetry* of shot-composition associated at times with a temporal symmetry, in the organization of the set-up/editing relationship *(découpage)*. This is exemplified by the remarkable banquet sequence.

It begins with a shot of an ageing courtier singing and dancing in the centre of a large dining-hall between two rows of courtiers sitting face to face along opposite walls. Washizu and Asaji, each seated on a low dais, preside from the far end. (The "near" end of the hall will appear only towards the end of the sequence, with the entrance of the assassin, which will of course further singularize that dramatic moment.) The camera pans with the moving dancer through three well-defined and symmetrically framed stations: first, he is flanked in the background by two anonymous guests, then by the two empty mats still awaiting Miki ("Banquo") and his son, and finally by

Asaji and Washizu. We cut to an absolutely centred, frontal, medium shot of Washizu. He looks to his left, and there is a close-up of the empty mats. We cut back to Washizu who looks away from the mats again, and the principle of symmetry is respected also in these repeated and opposite eye movements around the pivotal cutaway. The same eye movement is repeated a few shots later with Asaji (whose shot matches, in both senses, with an identically symmetrical shot of Washizu called forth by her glance at him, and followed by her turning back to face the camera). We cut back to the dancer in a shot identical to the symmetrical frame in which we last saw him (Washizu and Asaji in background): Washizu suddenly calls in anger for the performance to end, having detected in the words of the singer a parallel with his own history. The startled performer kneels, then scurries back to his seat on the left side of the hall, followed in a panning movement which is the symmetrical complement (or continuation) of the sequence's first shot. He takes his place, bowing to his lord. The next shot is perfectly symmetrical to this last frame; it shows the opposite row of guests—but with the two empty mats at the far end offering a disquieting flaw in the symmetry. After a repeat of the earlier three-shot figure (ABA), in which Washizu again looks at the empty mats, we come to the first apparition of the ghost, shown in a long, single shot, completely symmetrical in its *construction* rather than its framing. The first composition shows Washizu from the absent Miki's "viewpoint," with the empty mat in the lower foreground. The camera tracks slowly towards Washizu, who now looks for the third time towards the empty mats (the camera) and jumps up in terror. The camera draws quickly back to the starting position (end of first period of symmetry); the whitened figure of Miki is sitting on the mat reserved for him. Terrorized, Washizu staggers away to the left, passing before Asaji, who rises and tries to reassure the guests ("He's always this way when he's been drinking!"). The camera pans with him until Miki is out of shot; then, as he calms down and returns to his seat, the camera, panning back, fails to find the ghost. Actually, however, as a supreme refinement, the ghost's presence or absence remains ambiguous for a moment, since the slightly higher angle of the camera on its return makes Miki's mat invisible, even when Washizu has reached his dais. Only when the warlord finally squats down again, does the camera tilt imperceptibly so that the frame is exactly as at the beginning, with the empty mat in the lower foreground—and the second period of symmetry is seen here to absorb the first. The following shots introduce a new, wider angle. The entire right-hand row of guests is seen, together with both Asaji and Washizu seated at the end. The medium shot of Washizu reappears, followed by a shot symmetrical to the penultimate one (the left-hand row in its entirety, again with Asaji and Washizu in the background). A servant rises at the near end of the row—and his movement, on the following cut, which brings back the correspondingly symmetrical shot seen previously, is perfectly matched with that of his opposite number as he rises to serve the right-hand row. This extravagant visual sleight of hand may be regarded as the central point of symmetry within the sequence, since it comes between the ghost's two apparitions. We now return to a series of shots which very nearly repeat the beginning of the sequence: Washizu looks at the two empty mats, close-up of Miki's, etc. This time, however, when Washizu reacts (in a fixed frame) to the second apparition, we see it in reverse angle to his terrified gaze. This is the first appearance of the classical form of the reverse angle in this scene (it is used only sparingly in the film as a whole). The next shot, as Washizu again leaves his dais and staggers across the hall with drawn sword, involves another long pan and tracking shot, similar to the previous one but extended, pivoting much further to the left for its final composition, showing the empty mat from an angle symmetrical with that of the earlier final composition and, like that one, tilting slightly downwards to include the mat as Washizu slashes at the empty air above it. Following Asaji's dismissal of the guests, the confrontation between the couple is filmed in two symmetrical reverse shots. The final image, in which Washizu murders the assassin who has returned with only the one head (Miki's son having escaped him), is a wide, perfectly symmetrical frame in which the two figures are like puppets in the centre of a stage, performing some bloodless execution ritual. This is the first element of violence actually to appear on the screen: it is so distanced, however, that it hardly modifies the de-centering of violence which characterizes all but the last few moments of the film.

It is also interesting to note the part played by changes in the "role" of the camera in the sequence just described. The camera, especially in the two long tracking shots, alternately sees the scene "with" Washizu, "with" the witnesses and even "through Miki's eyes." Most of these role changes, moreover, take place within the continuity of the shot, and are perceived "belatedly." We suddenly realize, for example, that we have been looking at the space occupied by Miki's ghost when we thought it was still off-camera; we realize, in other words, that the camera no longer sees the scene from Washizu's viewpoint but from that of the witnesses—and that this shift took place some seconds before. This lends significant ambiguity to the subsequent disappearance of the ghost from Washizu's subjective vision, which is signalled only by a gradual calming down of the hallucinated man.[4]

The entire film, as I have said, is structured by a dichotomous principle of tension and relaxation, though only here is it applied from shot to shot rather than from scene to scene. The resolution of this dichotomy, as I have suggested, is delivered in the final sequence, when, after the motionless mass of soldiers has listened in complete silence to Washizu's harangue, he suddenly finds himself pursued about the ramparts of his own castle by the unerring rain of whistling arrows shot by his own archers. This bravura passage is usually recognized by Western critics as such, but nothing more; it is seen as grotesque *and* gratuitous or brilliant *but* gratuitous. On the contrary, it is the very keystone of the film's formal structure. Here at last that tense, horizontal alternation between scenes of de-centered frenzy and dramatic but static scenes is resolved into a vertical orgasm of on-screen violence. While the hieratic symmetry is swept away by this holocaust, it is reasserted in the epilogue, a near-repeat of the opening sequence: the foggy landscape, the chanting chorus, Washizu's tomb.

Notes

1. They are least apparent, perhaps, in *Three Bad Men in a Hidden Fortress* and *Sanjuro of the Camellias*.
2. Shown in England and the United States as *Throne of Blood*.
3. As Christian Metz has dubbed it.
4. For a more comprehensive examination of this notion of the "roles" of the camera, see my remarks on Dreyer's *Vampyr* in Richard Roud, ed., *Cinema: A Critical Dictionary,* 2 vols. (New York: Viking, 1980).

[The Making of *Throne of Blood*]

YOSHIO SHIRAI

KUROSAWA ALWAYS uses three cameras on the set [of *Throne of Blood*]. One is a telescopic camera for closeups of Mifune's Washizu. Another is also telescopic and it is used primarily for the movements of the people around Washizu and for medium closeups. The third is for long shots of the entire scene. Of course it is in a completely different place. This way, by doing all this at once, you can film a scene in three different ways.

The multiple camera method first became a vital condition for the advancement of realism in Kurosawa's films with the final battle scene in *Seven Samurai*. Putting in the Noh stylization, and depicting people's movements in a monumentally formal way, a tense realism like that of a newsreel can be achieved from the cameras following them from three directions relentlessly.

First, placing the cameras so that they are not in the screen's line of vision is a tricky thing. Then, getting enough effective lighting to give visibility to the dark mood is also difficult. Deciding the actors' positions also takes countless tries. Kurosawa himself thoroughly checks each of the three cameras, and decides the angles. Because they are telescopic lenses, the cameras are set apart from each other, and the one used for long shots is set up far in the distance.

Coming and going time and again, he checks on them like a demon. That alone is mentally tiring, but it's hard physical labor too.

Assistant directors jump to commands as if they were death threats, lighting men run around in a frenzy, prop men come and go, and in the midst of it all Kurosawa's voice can be heard over a mike scolding, "You idiot! You! The third warrior there. To the left! Left! Assistant director! Set the vassals in the right place. Not that way! Do it just like I instructed you to! Faster! Do it faster!"

The actors begin their performance and the lights and cameras are set in the midst of this warlike commotion. Mifune speaks his lines to someone and the crowd around him mumbles. The director doesn't like it. Kurosawa, now fed up, bounds over to the distant camera. While watching the movements, one time, two times, three times, he oversees the three cameras. Movements get stiffer.

Translated by Michael Baskett for this volume from Shirai Yoshio, "Kurosawa Akira: Sono Ningen, No. 1," [Akira Kurosawa: The Man, No. 1] in *Sekai no Eiga Sakka—Kurosawa Akira* [Film Directors of the World—Akira Kurosawa], ed. Kotoda Chieko (Tokyo: Kinema Jumpo Sha, 1970), 40–48, by permission.

Again, "No good" is heard. The lights are changed and people's movements change slightly. A carefully and minutely planned scene, in accordance with his own image, filmed with the realism one would feel in glancing at a newsreel—it is this decisive moment that he is aiming for and this is very difficult to achieve.

Finally, right before shooting, the assistant director yells out in a loud voice, "Test! Here we go!" Then Kurosawa's voice over the mike echoes, "Ready... Action!" Once, twice. Trying for your best, all of one's movements strictly condense, and as a member of the cast, deep within me to the point of pain, I understand. Finally the voice says, "All right, this is a take." Dry ice is broken up and dropped into water kept hot since morning. Heavy white smoke billows and begins to crawl over the ground. The smoke effectively flows, and a number of people watch over it attentively while spreading it with large fans and pieces of cardboard. A few hundred people swallow their breath when a sharp voice shatters the silence and says, "Ready... Action!" The cameras roll, the smoke begins to flow, Mifune gives his lines and others respond. When one scene is filmed in one shot, one's anxiety grows over the long take.

This activity in the midst of the unusual silence continues. Then everyone anticipates, as if in prayer, and the tense scene's movements near their end. Kurosawa calls "CUT!" and without a pause says, "The general's movements are no good. Once more!" Suddenly the quiet set becomes like a child's toy box turned upside down, quickly everything becomes frenzied. Lights are fixed, props and costumes are rearranged, and it starts all over. New boiling water is put into the oil cans, and new dry ice pieces wrapped in paper are readied. Placing dry ice in hot water produces smoke that lasts only for about five minutes. Once a take is over, all the good smoke is already gone. . . .

Kurosawa on location is a terrible perfectionist, a tyrant, and, seen from my perspective, always fearfully isolated. No matter how many times it's done, the filming isn't good enough, the assistant director's tension grows, and the actors, staff, and everyone else on the open set lower their voices and talk, the cameramen sweat a cold sweat, and in the middle of all this is Kurosawa trying to visualize on screen his image, while tirelessly giving instructions, working like a demon and shouting and yelling at everyone.

The Hidden Fortress:
Kurosawa's Comic Mode

VERNON YOUNG

O N A vast arid plateau with a horizon of forest clump and mountain peak, two all-but-naked clowns of God take their stumbling progress: vagrant peasants, two remnants among a million scattered in the wake of feudal warfare. Exhausted and embittered by their failure to find either glory or bread, unnerved by their own puny hearts and enfeebled wills, they abuse fortune and, with what monkey-spiteful courage they have left, each other— while the slow-tracking camera at their backs makes eavesdroppers of us all. Their impotent scrapping is interrupted by a Something that freezes them with fear; they break off to stare in *our* direction. Abruptly, a hunted figure lurches into the wide-frame view from the right, twisting his painted and sweating face backward at his pursuers. Another instant, as his legs give way while he fumbles with his sole weapon, a bow, they overtake him—a band of mounted warriors which sweeps over and past the victim, spearing him *en route.* The miserable pair now clutch each other in belated need while the horsemen race by, yielding to their own impetus before wheeling to canter back again. Scarcely halting to take in the presence of the terrified couple or the doubled-up samurai, they disdainfully ride away, lances at rest and pennons fluttering. The dust settles over the plain, emptied once more of visible life save those two shuddering monkey-men and the fallen samurai—fallen but not at rest: crumpled up, rather like a roasted beetle, one defensive bow-arm still half extended, trembling faintly in the last spasm before rigor mortis.... At this precise moment, a huge cloud-shadow moves over the landscape, like a delayed and barely sensed ripple over one's scalp.

Such is the opening scene of Akira Kurosawa's latest *samurai*-film, in Tohoscope, *Kakushi Toride no San-Akunin,* premiered in San Francisco as *The Hidden Fortress* (called *The Wild Flight* in Sweden, where I saw it). With no time to wonder where we are, in what century—or on which planet!— we are sucked into the event like gulls into a cyclone. And the whole film has this air of wild cogent invention, of visual shock and of abrupt outrage. Grandiose, raw, implausible (yet conventional in a sense), *The Hidden Fortress* recapitulates and enlarges, in more than "aspect-ratio" terms, virtually every feature of the so-called entertainment film, as we know it, from the Fairbanks genre to *Treasure of the Sierra Madre,* while incorporating

Reprinted by permission from *The Hudson Review* 14, no. 2 (Summer 1961): 270–75. Copyright © 1961 by The Hudson Review, Inc.

stylistic vestiges of the older Soviet masters and from a host of *samurai-films*. On wide-screen, Kurosawa re-affirms his already manifest command of the witness point and of its collaborative art, editing, as he cuts brilliantly from latitudinal compositions to those aligned diagonally, uses depth of field and, as it were, distended surface, and concentrates one's obedient eye no less on two or three figures within engulfing space than on a compactly seething mass in the torch-lighted gloom of an earthworks prison. (The latter shots, by the way, are not reminiscent of any other film sequence I can recall, but they do suggest the monstrous episodes depicting the Chinese coolies packed into the hold of the *Nan-Shan*—in Conrad's *Typhoon.*) No doubt the following scene when these captives erupt from their hole in the ground like angry bees, then swarm down a flight of steps to freedom, was inspired by Eisenstein's Odessa climax—but with no such dialectical purpose and in reverse order: Kurosawa's mass moves *downward;* the Shogunate guards, facing them from below, and nowise as disciplined as the Czar's whitecoats, after emptying one lethal volley into the descending mob, break and run as before a lava flow. (After a dissolve, there's a single impressive shot of the steps, cleared of all but a dozen rag-naked sprawled bodies, glistening like outcroppings of the masonry.)

Kurosawa's modes of action are seemingly inexhaustible, his bravura editing tireless. As a time transition, to indicate rapidly that the two scaramouches have been followed all day by Rokurota, who guards the royal gold they've stumbled onto, he projects two successive frames of their heads against a *daylight* sky, then *cuts directly* into a night background. Better than anyone now working in film, perhaps, he knows when to *hold* his camera position and exploit wide-screen, not simply as a theater tableau but as a magnitude wherein movement is never absent and space is viable. He frames compelling laterals of horsemen with pennants crossing a distant bridge, from both ends and with variant pace, catches a line of premonitory banners coming up over the brow of plateau like hawks to the kill, takes traveling shots of a panting race through underbrush or of a horseback pursuit at blurring speed (which goes back to Ermler's *Peasants,* notably, and might have been Kurosawa's source for the same effect in his *Rashomon*). He involves those sons of Thersites, the two peasants, in marvellous excursions of fatigue, cupidity, false courage, fright, sly desperation, and giggling lust, each a gem of grotesquerie and broken rhythm, enforced by Masaru Sato, whose accompanying score is a fantasia of staccato whistles, hardware squeals and groans, skipping flute melodies. Throughout the action, mainly unified by the trek of four characters bearing gold concealed in bundles of firewood, Kurosawa's sense of the exact faltering gasp and shift of weight, the side-steps of momentum and recovery, is infallible. Which makes more astonishing the information that he once envied Toyoda for that director's *physiological* emphasis. All the evidence we have defines Kurosawa as perhaps the *most physical* director in the history of the movies!

This, alone, may be thought of as a drawback if we're expecting another multi-level masterpiece of the *Rashomon* order. In *Seven Samurai,* which I don't see as the outstanding achievement critical opinion would make it, the exclusively kinetic emphasis vitiated, or just replaced, an implied interior drama (relating to the hero) never conveyed. However, I'm prepared to acknowledge that I've overstated the force of such an implication—in this case. But not in *Ikiru,* where Kurosawa's rage for excess was a seriously distracting indulgence. The moral crisis of a dying man, who in his last pitiful months achieves the selfless life (even as he recognizes how little of the self he has ever asserted), should have emerged as uncluttered as the chiming of a clock-tower (if not without overtones) or as De Sica's *Umberto D.* But Kurosawa couldn't resist the impulse, especially in the Tokyo-at-night scenes (which *are* apocalyptic) and in the Shavian epilogue, to prove again his inordinate virtuosity. In retrospect I will see only that little man, dead in the swing in the empty playground: all else remaining to my mind's eye will be a profusion of effects—as if the little man had been abandoned not only by the impinging and heedless world but also by Kurosawa; as if, in fact, like a cat with a broken mouse, Kurosawa had quickly dropped him upon being diverted by other stimulants to his feral eye, an analogy to which I shall return.

The Hidden Fortress, a less ambitious venture, to be sure, is more consistently adhered to. Like *Seven Samurai* or, from what report insists, the feudal-Japan *Macbeth (Throne of Blood)* of Kurosawa, this film is relentlessly exterior: a tall tale—*jidai-geki,* if I know how to read my Anderson and Richie—wherein our two vagrant fools, Matashichi and Tahei, are prodded into being the muleback saviours of a princess-in-flight by her loyal ex-general, Rokurota. This superman, emblematically dignified and infinitely resourceful, engineers the strategy which saves all four, despite the truant efforts of the pair to cheat him and escape. At the adventure's end he rewards them with a single plate of gold which, depending on whether their innate avarice or their rudimentary wisdom gets the upper hand, will allow them to live munificently ever after. As a morality of the proto-human utilized by a disciplined elite, the story is no doubt open to complaint from those who consider themselves too sophisticated for delight in such fables. I wonder if dissenters on these grounds are willing to ask themselves honestly if the latest capers of Elia Kazan, John Ford, or Stanley Kramer are any more worldly or if, to take hats-in-the-air examples, *A Place in the Sun* or *Look Back in Anger* say anything more pregnant about man's management of his destiny? It is fashionable and probably right—for us in our time and place—to assume that a work of art which gets beneath the skin and bone of its subject is superior to one which doesn't. Yet we may be withholding deserved praise by laboring the distinction too strictly and in un-historical terms. *The Hidden Fortress* is definitive of its kind and not to be identified with the latest western or ben-hurern: it honors the flow of events and quietly predicates an ethic.

I saw the film in a three-week period during which I also saw three European movies unsurpassed by any shown this season: Bernhard Wicki's *The Bridge,* Truffaut's *The 400 Blows,* and Bergman's crowning masterpiece, *Jungfrukallan (The Virgin Spring).* These, the last-named two especially, come from depths of compassion, from articulated sensibility and power which place them, for psychological man, beyond relevant comparison with any external-adventure film, no matter how vividly related. Even with this acknowledgement, I find they did not, by contrast, *reduce* the Kurosawa film, as they would have any meretricious item of a similar category. And I believe that film criticism almost everywhere has failed a discrimination when relegating the better *samurai*-film. Conceivably the just distinction here is not between Art and Entertainment, a falsely puritan terminology anyway, but between tragic and comic modes, in that broad reading urged by Susanne Langer's summary of dramatic forms (see *Feeling and Form,* chapters 18 and 19). Tragedy is equated with guilt and expiation, comedy with vanity and exposure. "Tragedy is the image of fate, as comedy is of fortune... comedy is essentially contingent, episodic, and ethnic; it expresses the continuous balance of sheer vitality that belongs to society and is exemplified briefly in each individual." For my present inference, *ethnic* is a key word here. There are assumptions in the Kurosawa approach we do well to note, since they underlie the singular depiction of personality which, as much as any visual pyrotechnics, gives *The Hidden Fortress* its character. "The continuous balance of sheer vitality" is here "exemplified briefly" within an elemental social scheme, innocent of our concept, Humanism.

Donald Richie has alleged that when Kurosawa was filming *Rashomon* he sent his actors to circuses and jungle films to observe the behaviour of wild animals. It seems probable that the practise has become chronic: certainly, in *The Hidden Fortress,* Toshiro Mifune (Rokurota) is as much a soft-padding genial tiger as in *Rashomon* he was a lion, *rampant guardant;* Misa Uehara's Princess is patently, even stereotypically, of the domestic-cat family, alternately arch-backed and kittenish—and it's evident I've been unable to describe the peasant couple without recourse to the lower primates! After watching *them* for half an hour you'd not be too surprised by a following-shot fifty feet above the ground, implacably recording their hand-over-hand passage through the tree-tops! And yet they're monkeys by default: they lack the creatures' coordination, while displaying the bad temper, the amoral cunning, the susceptibility to the lure of the moment. (A parenthesis should be expended on the performers, Minoru Chiaki and Kamatari Fujiwara: their self-effacing talent for being wretched, ludicrous, or loathsome is exercised beyond all conventional boundaries of naturalism.) These analogies are of the essence. Watch Toshiro Mifune, then listen to Henri Bergson:

> Even reflexion itself, the secret of man's strength, might look like weakness, for
> it is the source of indecision, whereas the reaction of an animal, when it is

truly instinctive, is instantaneous and unfailing. Even the fact that it lacks the power of speech has served the animal by surrounding it with a halo of mystery. Its silence, moreover, can pass for contempt, as though it had something better to do than to converse with us.

And in *The Hidden Fortress* both Rokurota and the Princess *simulate* speechlessness when it serves their purpose!

I'm but half-way to my point. Kurosawa's instructions to his actors most intrigue me by what they reveal of *his* faculty of observation. Does not Kurosawa view his actors as if he, himself, were a wild animal?—a wild animal who happened to have a flair for cinematography? No fanciful supposition, merely: an animal, more so than Bergson's enlightened man, observes in other animals only their governing qualities. To him, man is simply another species of animal, with habits he is unable to "analyze." Had he a degree of aesthetic consciousness, might he not see men as Kurosawa sees them, from the outside and principally—i.e., as *animals in motion?* To this end, I believe, Kurosawa, no matter what he claims about wanting to be honored for making films of *contemporary* Japan, is inevitably attracted by the feudal setting, wherein social man was more broadly, essentially, ethnically differentiated. And it is just this regressive, if you like, purity of vision which sustains the dramatic tensions of his comedy. When the imperious Princess cries or the stoical Rokurota smiles or the bondsmen cooperate reasonably, an inhibition of impulses has been temporarily released, and the surprise engendered is a basic element—dramatic relief. (Our own puritan heroes and heroines—in Westerns, noticeably—who sulk for seven reels before the fadeout embrace, represent a like instinct for dramatic procrastination. Unfortunately, since they're without style in the interim, they are more often boring than tantalizing—their vacuity is not redeemed aesthetically by compensating mannerisms.)

A cliché is reborn as a perennial mode when vitality confounds a formula. The impassive samurai or loyal retainer unmoved by the sex appeal of the bare-legged (here) Princess he is defending, is a staple of the Japanese period-film. As such, Kurosawa makes no attempt to disguise it. He intensifies it. At one juncture all hope for the fugitive seems lost, in which eventuality death before dishonor, for the Princess above all, is an imperative. Before preparing a final desperate strategy, Rokurota offers her the weapon with which she may have to destroy herself—in a resolute straight-arm gesture. As he does so, their eyes meet and his expression, in a single closeup, is as nakedly complete as any half-dozen reaction shots could ever be: a wordless suffusion of his face with the emotions he has until then suppressed, in which the whole meaning and mettle of the man is made explicit. The human soul has entered the landscape where before there was a type, less human than zoological, a personable creature equipped with prepotent powers of endurance and specialized prowess who has otherwise belied the warmth his rarely flashing smile suggested. (No such moment of truth relieved the gymkhana of *Seven Samurai.*) The story recovers, so to speak, from this subjective intrusion and terminates in its no-doubt generic fashion, at the precedent level of dispassionate continuity. But by such touches—in this instance a momentarily piercing recognition of the nobility which crouches in the cage of the heart—Kurosawa restores to man the quality that individualizes him, and reaffirms the actual as a vital ingredient of the unbelievable.

Narrating the Human Condition: *High and Low* and Story-Telling in Kurosawa's Cinema

DAVID DESSER

ABOUT HALFWAY into *High and Low* (*Tengoku to Jigoku,* 1963), Kurosawa's thriller about a kidnapping and extortion scheme adapted from Ed McBain's *King's Ransom,* there is a scene that lasts only about a minute or so. It features Inspector Tokura operating an 8mm projector and discussing the footage the police shot of the delivery of the ransom money from the rushing bullet train. To the gathered family, the inspector explains what they (and we) are seeing on this screen within the screen. In Japanese, Tokura's activity would be called *eiga setsumei,* or "film explanation," while Tokura himself would be termed, at least in this role, an *eiga setsumeisha.* As it happens, *eiga setsumeisha* is one of the terms applied in the first decades of the Japanese cinema to what is more properly called the role of the *katsuben*—nothing other than the traditional narrator in the so-called silent Japanese cinema.[1]

Here is how J. L. Anderson describes the *katsuben,* from his definitive article on this unique Japanese institution: "The *katsuben* gave a vocal performance which involved dialogue, narration, an interpretation of content, and incidental comments while the movie was being shown."[2] While the motion picture was a foreign invention, which itself inspired much curiosity for its own sake, the experience of a *katsuben* performance at a motion picture a few years after the introduction of film technology to Japan enabled the cinema to be recuperated into elements of Japanese tradition. As Anderson has it, "Unlike spectators in other countries, the Japanese did not come to view motion pictures as a new, different, modern, mass produced, machine-driven, autonomous entertainment. What they experienced with the *katsuben* at the movies was 1) *an extension of an indigenous narrative practice* [called] *commingled media,* and 2) *a modern variation of vocal story telling traditions.*"[3] One such vocal narrative tradition is called *etoki,* which has been described by Barbara Ruch as a performance in which "painting, story, chanter, and even the sounding of musical instruments... combine to create a total audio-visual experience rare, if not unique, in the pre-modern history of world literature."[4] Another, seemingly direct, link to the *katsuben* performance is the variation of *etoki* called *utsushie* (projected pictures):

This essay was written specifically for this volume and is published here for the first time by permission of the author.

> In *utsushie,* separate pictures of major characters in a story were painted with transparent colors on glass slides and back-projected onto a paper screen. Each character . . . had its own separate projector which was hand-held by an operator who moved the projected image across the screen to give movement to the character. Slides changed as the attitude of a character changed. . . . Two stationary projectors at the extreme left and right sides of the screen showed scenic elements.[5]

Yet another link to the *katsuben,* which which survived after the *katsuben*'s decline, is the *kamishibai* (paper play), a modern form of *etoki.* "In *kami-shibai,* the performer showed successive pictures painted on fifteen to thirty sheets of cardboard as he read aloud a text written on the reverse side." For Anderson, the *kamishibai* is "a direct precursor of the television cartoons and comic books of today's Japan."[6] Similarly, for Anderson, the *renzoku terebi shosetsu* (continuing television novel) represents yet another variation, if not of *katsuben* necessarily, then at least of a commingled media where characters, scenery, and narration intermix in the telling of a story. Anderson claims that "voice-over narration not only recaps previous episodes but every so often talks about things that are happening right now on the tube. I don't have to look at the television drama. I hear it."[7]

This sequence wherein Kurosawa seems to reproduce almost precisely the performance of *katsuben* cinema might not necessarily be an homage to his own brother, Heigo, who became a successful *katsuben* in the late 1920s and whom he fondly recalls in his autobiography.[8] Yet it is certain that Kurosawa, far from being merely aware of the *katsuben* cinema, has a special fondness for it in his heart. Just as Kurosawa's exposure to American formula films, which he recalls seeing with his father ("a lot of action serials and William S. Hart movies" [30]), obviously later worked their way into films like *The Hidden Fortress, Yojimbo,* and *Sanjuro,* so, too, his interest in storytelling was formed at an early age. In addition to the *katsuben* cinema, Kurosawa also fondly speaks of his father's excursions with the family "to listen to storytellers in the music halls around Kagurazaka" (37). Unfortunately, the English translation does little to help the Western reader with knowing exactly what Kurosawa means here—he is speaking about attending the *yose* (music hall) and being entertained by *rakugo.* Anderson sees the *rakugo* as being an important precursor to, and a significant contemporary with, the *katsuben.* Moreover, although Kurosawa does not mention it in his autobiography, *yose* evenings also frequently featured the storytelling art of *utsushie.*

These references to traditional Japanese storytelling practices, or to the early days of the Japanese film, are part of the larger pattern in which Kurosawa implicates a narrating presence in *High and Low.* As it happens, the use of a kind of *katsuben* conjoins with a form of *emaki-mono* (narrative picture scrolls) as the criminal in the scene preceding Inspector Tokura's *katsuben* performance is seen reading newspapers about the kidnapping. The words and images of the newspapers are unrolled like a scroll by Kurosawa's panning camera. And surely Shinichi's picture of the locale where the kidnappers took him is a form of *kamishibai.* It is part of the richness of Kurosawa's cinema, I suppose, that we may take these highlighted moments as either fond recurrences of a traditional art or modernist deconstructions of a powerful contemporary institution (the cinema).

The question of narrativity seems to me an ever-more interesting one to bring to bear on Kurosawa's cinema. David Bordwell defines narration as a process: "the activity of selecting, arranging, and rendering story material in order to achieve specific time-bound effects on a perceiver."[9] All story films, by definition, involve narration. But do all story films involve a narrator? David Bordwell is loath to think so. He wonders, "Even if no voice or body gets identified as a locus of narration, can we still speak of a narrator as being present in a film? In other words, must we go beyond the process of narration to locate an entity which is its source?" (61–62). For Bordwell the answer is no, or not necessarily: "Most films . . . do not provide anything like such a definable narrator, and there is no reason to expect they will" (62). Yet narrating presences in a variety of forms are one of the distinguishable elements of the Kurosawa canon. For instance, we find, that is we *hear,* narrators in Kurosawa's films in the form of voiceovers. *Stray Dog (Nora Inu,* 1949) and *Ikiru* (1952) begin with offscreen narration. Alternately, Kurosawa is extremely fond of utilizing characters as narrators, as storytellers, within his films. *Rashomon* (1950), of course, is notorious on this score, but the strategy also recurs in *Ikiru, Red Beard (Akahige,* 1965) and *Dodeskaden* (1970), among other films. Even beyond the literal presence of narrators we can still point to the presence of a narrator, a narrating agent outside the film. The narrating presences within these Kurosawa films must be understood in combination with Kurosawa's penchant for narrative experimentation across the body of his works. Thus we may link Kurosawa with what Bordwell calls an "art cinema" wherein "the overt self-consciousness of the narration is often paralleled by an extratextual emphasis on the filmmaker as source" (211). In *High and Low,* we have very little of characters who tell stories, and no voiceover narrator at all. Yet as I have indicated, narrational strategies derived from Japanese tradition abound, strategies which have the precise effect of foregrounding narration.

The interest one has in narrativity in Kurosawa's cinema, that is to say, its *significance,* revolves around related issues of authorship, tradition, modernism, and the value of Kurosawa's canon as moral lessons, as allegories of living in a complex, commingled, interdependent world. The notion of authorship applied to Kurosawa's cinema might prove a useful way of understanding the variety of narrational strategies he utilizes, just as an acknowledgment of these strategies provides a richer understanding of the status of Kurosawa as auteur.

The notion of authorship, of the auteur director, brings with it the idea of a unity across a (relatively) large and (possibly) varied body of works. The auteur director was identified, constructed, exactly out of the body of his films through the recognition of a recurring set of themes, characters, motifs, and certain stylistic practices and proclivities. It does not take, perhaps, a fierce French cinéaste forever sitting in the Cinémathèque, to recognize the authorial characteristics of the films of Ozu Yasujiro or Mizoguchi Kenji. But then Japan has, to a large extent, been a director's cinema. Directors in Japan are, to be sure, constrained by commercial considerations, a problem of Kurosawa since the middle 1960s when his films became too expensive for the dwindling Japanese domestic audience to make profitable, a situation which has turned around only in recent years as Kurosawa has produced films like *Dreams* (*Yume,* 1990) with far lower budgets than the jidai-geki like *Kagemusha* (1980) and *Ran* (1985). The director in Japan is also constrained by genre, as much, if not more of a factor in Japan than in even the Hollywood industry. The director is also constrained by tradition, the traditions of filmic creation and the far older aesthetic systems which continue to exert some force in Japan. The very system in which the director arose even through the 1970s—the assistant director system—imposed a clear work style and approach on a director. Nevertheless, the director in Japan is given control over his films in an overt manner often (though even in the studio era, not always) denied his/her American counterpart. Kurosawa was both constrained by a studio system in his early days, and even by an ideological system as he came of age during the Pacific War. Further, he achieved directorial maturity under yet another system of constraints: the American occupation. His career may thus be understood as a genuine struggle between a system of constraints and the realization of a personal vision.

The question of Kurosawa's authorship also frequently revolves around encapsulations of a "world view." Audie Bock, in *Japanese Film Directors,* maintains that Kurosawa's "ideas show a clear progression of emphasis on the individual finding self-definition, self-assertion, and finally a form of accomplishment that serves humanity."[10] Tadao Sato, in *Currents in Japanese Cinema,* finds that for Kurosawa "the meaning of life is not dictated by the nation but is something each individual should discover for himself through suffering."[11] For Donald Richie, in *The Films of Akira Kurosawa,* Kurosawa's cinema is remarkably consistent: "Though Kurosawa's films appear to be of infinite variety, there is at the same time a unity, a completely responsible and ultimately serious attitude toward life that makes them, despite their seeming differences, all of a piece."[12] I have characterized Kurosawa as being interested in the existential question of how to live, and claim that he has explored this concern through a focus on the possibility of heroism in a corrupt world. Kurosawa's characters are typically faced with moral/ethical choices, and they must opt for the proper course of action.[13] Stephen Prince, in *The Warrior's Camera,* takes his lead from this notion and expresses Kurosawa's overarching concern as "the familiar Kurosawa lesson of the responsibility of each for all."[14] If these assertions, and others one could point to, are correct, then virtually any individual Kurosawa film, and the vast majority of them all, should reveal these characteristic beliefs and ideals.

Attempts have been made over the last decade and a half to undercut the auteur idea(l). Under the varieties of ideological criticisms, like semiotics, structuralism, Marxism, feminism, and psychoanalysis, authorship has been revealed as a romantic notion of the lone individual struggling to achieve his (that pronoun is deliberately chosen) unique vision. In this deconstructive turn, authorship becomes a theoretical impossibility, for a film text is really (take your pick): a language or symbolic system at work over which the individual has no control; a series of mythic ideals which have been naturalized to the point that the film creator is unaware of their existence; an economic system whose ideology is structured into the very terms and devices of cinematic language; a masculinist/Oedipal desire to control and own, and to put women in their (symbolic) place; a system of linguistic and symbolic structures which in fact create the individual who can then only reproduce them. To a large extent these have been useful correctives to an overly romantic, if not simplistic, view of how films especially, but other cultural products too, are produced.[15] Nevertheless, auteurism continues to exert a powerful critical force. It is possible, however, to modify our notions of auteurism away from sweeping statements of worldviews or thematic consistencies (though these are still, I would insist, useful and important). Instead, we could approach authorship more literally by invoking the issue of narration precisely to give us a speaker, an author, who informs us of something to teach us something.

Beyond the question of authorship, however, we may find in Kurosawa's invocations of narrating presences the kind of adherence to Japanese tradition that a critic like Noël Burch (*To the Distant Observer*) acclaims as the true significance of Japanese cinema—that in its use of traditional Japanese aesthetics, the Japanese cinema at its best provides both a formal model and a metaphysical program at variance with the logocentric, individualistic West. Thus the recurrence of narrators in Kurosawa's cinema is not simply an authorial characteristic but a deliberate foregrounding of cinematic storytelling that is at variance with the "invisible" or "transparent" strategies dominant cinema has arrived at to repress the mechanisms of filmmaking in order to disguise the ideological components which underwrite them. This is to say, the traditional practices we may point to in Kurosawa's films, from *katsuben*-like voiceovers at the start of *Stray Dog* or *Ikiru,* to the range of commingled narrative modes implicated in *High and Low,* make Kurosawa's cinema a profoundly "modernist" one.

I began my exploration of narration in Kurosawa's cinema in my article on *Ikiru* in *Reframing Japanese Cinema.* There, I link the process of narration, the question of the film's narrativity, to *Rashomon,* which foregrounds not only point-of-view, as is well known, but also the idea and act of narration. Let us be clear on this point: films like *Rashomon, Ikiru,* and *High and*

Low (along with others in Kurosawa's canon) foreground, make explicit, the process of narration that is unreeling. I use the example of Hitchcock's *Psycho* in my article on *Ikiru* to demonstrate another instance where a narrative choice has been made; that is, at the start of Hitchcock's film the camera seeks out the hotel room which contains Marion Crane. But Hitchcock's camera, his narrating agent, might have made another choice of subject. Of course, what we most remember about *Psycho* as a text is the way in which its story shifts. The narrative of the film experiences a major rupture, but the process of narrating it is all of a piece. Put simply, from the story of Marion Crane who steals money from her boss, *Psycho* shockingly becomes the story of Norman Bates. That is, Marion's narrative suddenly comes to a halt; this is *Psycho*'s major trick. In contrast, the stories, the narratives, of *Rashomon* and *Ikiru* do not shift. The basic story of *Rashomon* remains maddeningly the same amongst all four narrators; and while Watanabe, like Marion Crane, suddenly dies long before the film is over, the story of Watanabe's rebellion from bureaucratic malaise does not shift when his character dies. On the other hand, in Kurosawa's version of McBain's novel, we seem to find Hitchcock's strategy reproduced: we have a story which comes to a halt halfway through the film when the kidnapped boy is returned.

But Kurosawa's attention, his story, has never been about the return of the kidnapped boy. In a sense, the kidnapping of the boy is itself a turn away from a different story, the story of Gondo's attempted takeover. Thus the kidnapping becomes the reproduction of the *Psycho*-strategy (and the kidnapper is a bit of a psycho himself to be sure). The kidnapping may be seen as the interruption of an earlier story which is then free to continue when it is solved. As it happens, however, the return to the story of Gondo's corporate ambitions is not attempted; the seeds of that story came to an end when Gondo paid the ransom. He knew he would be fired from his job and lose his possessions. Richie is quite right, therefore, in stating that neither the kidnapper nor Gondo's dilemma is on Kurosawa's mind. But is it the search, capture, and confrontation with which he is concerned, or is it, rather, the *process* of the search, capture, and confrontation; with the telling rather than the results? That is, is *High and Low* a story about storytelling, about narration?

Stephen Prince describes the structure of *High and Low* as utilizing "a highly formalized narrative design that shifts among multiple voices, permitting an analytical, not merely descriptive, inquiry." Like *Ikiru, High and Low* adopts a shifting level "of perspective in place of a single context or vantage point of perception" (188). Analytical inquiry and a shift among multiple voices implies the presence of a narrator who undertakes the analysis or permits the multiplicity of voices to be heard. The idea that *High and Low* is centrally concerned with storytelling, with implicating a directorial presence speaking the action, is noted by Donald Richie when he writes of how the film is concerned with *looking:* "The references to seeing in this

film are many and varied; . . . devices for seeing—still pictures, motion pictures, drawings, are constantly used; . . . a kind of paranoia is felt—someone
is always *watching*" (167; emphasis in original). That Kurosawa references
seeing may be true, but the venerable Mr. Richie has got it slightly wrong:
Still pictures, motion pictures, and drawings, after all, are not devices for
seeing. The binoculars of the police, the glasses that many of the characters
wear, and the mirrors in homes or cars are indeed, as Richie notices (167),
nearly ubiquitous in the film, and these are indeed devices for seeing. But
movies are devices for showing and telling; not for looking but having
looked, not for seeing but having seen—and having seen relating one's
vision to others. It seems more apt to say about *High and Low* that someone
is always *showing.*

Stephen Prince is somewhat closer to the mark when he calls Kurosawa's
use of "technologies of perception" a self-reflective attention to images and
vision (196, 198). But "self-reflective" implies a cinematic modernism that
Kurosawa is not entirely willing to reproduce. He is no Godard, no Oshima
or Yoshida. We must be careful in claiming that Kurosawa may be fit into
the mode of art cinema narration, and thereby placing him alongside other
cinematic modernists of the primarily European or Japanese New Wave
model. He is still very much a classicist. However, there is a classical tradition
at work here, precisely the tradition of commingled narrative media, that
moves beyond the Hollywood cinema, one which it might be tempting to
call a "modernist" technique. But to do so would be a disservice to the way
in which Kurosawa reproduces this aspect of Japanese tradition, which,
while it might be modernist by Western standards is nevertheless a part of a
unique cultural context. The opening sequence of *Stray Dog* may highlight
how a narrating presence works to link Kurosawa's cinema to traditional
practices, yet how this particular use of tradition becomes problematic in
the very modern medium of the motion picture.

The narrating presence in *Stray Dog* is relatively unimportant, for the off-
screen voiceover narration is used only at the film's start and then drops out
altogether (unlike *Ikiru,* where although the offscreen narrator is not a dominant storytelling strategy, it does recur on a few separate occasions: at the
start, a short while later, then a short while before Watanabe's death, and
finally two-thirds of the way through to announce the hero's death). If we
link this narrator in *Stray Dog* to the *katsuben,* as, for instance Donald
Richie does when he says that the narrator opens the film in *benshi*-like fashion "to tell us what we are seeing as we are seeing it" (63) it is important to
remember that the *katsuben* functioned in Japanese cinema precisely
because "Japanese story films were not autonomous."[16] Or, to put it another
way, as Komatsu Hiroshi does in an article on Japanese cinema before World
War I, early Japanese films "do not narrate for themselves."[17] At issue in the
Japanese cinema after World War I was the question of autonomy for the
cinematic image; the "Westernization" of Japanese cinema inevitably

revolved around the dissolution of the *katsuben* as much, if not more, than in the elimination of *onnagata* (male actors of female roles). Thus we may say that because Kurosawa's cinema in a modern one, its images, its story-telling capacities, are autonomous in its combination of visual and aural material. Therefore, the narration is *redundant.*

The narrator offers the first instance of speech in the film, whose "one very hot day" clearly invokes a "once upon a time motif" (a point to which I will return). The visuals and dialogue of the film proper then reveal Detective Murakami (Toshiro Mifune) having already lost his pistol to a pickpocket. The voiceover now (whose aural quality is different for some reason than in its first utterance, as if now it were heard over a radio or loudspeaker) tells us what we have just learned. Similarly, in the flashback to the robbery, the voiceover tells us what we are about to see, and then explains to us what we can clearly see for ourselves. At one point, the voiceover even describes for us what we can clearly *hear* for ourselves ("a baby wails"). The information given to us by the narrator is either clearly implied (the heat, for instance, by the sand stirred up by Murakami's foot-steps, or the tread marks of truck tires left in the hot tar) or overtly stated by the dialogue (Murakami tells his fellow officers at the shooting range that he is tired, and we believe him). Not only is the information delivered by the voiceover redundant, but one can argue that the entire flashback sequence at the opening is similarly redundant, merely showing us what someone has already said. Except to provide an early glimpse of the pick-pocket, otherwise not seen until the film's famous climactic struggle in the dirt, the flashback seems as redundant, as overdetermined, as the narrator.

For Richie, this use of a *benshi*-like narrator is a mistake, "a glaring mis-calculation," in fact (63). Another mistake for him is what he calls "the end-less montage sequence of Mifune disguised and searching in Asakusa and Ueno for his gun" (63). It is a mistake for Richie simply because the sequence is too long. This same sequence for Prince halts the narrative com-pletely in order for Kurosawa to explore "the purely visual properties of wipes, dissolves, superimpositions, and shots articulating movement from the right, left, diagonally, and horizontally" (91). He also notes that the sequence is shot silently, except for environmental sources of music. In a footnote he references Kyoko Hirano's contention that a rice-planting sequence in *No Regrets for Our Youth* is done in a silent film-style montage, thus repeating a strategy he had earlier employed.

We might understand this lengthy, "audacious" in Prince's term (309), sequence as the flip side of the *katsuben*-style opening. For it is the case that neither *No Regrets for Our Youth* nor *Stray Dog* could be characterized as having a silent film-style montage sequence, at least not in the *Japanese* silent cinema, which, of course, was never silent as the *katsuben* ensured, and which was not, as we have indicated above, an autonomous storytelling medium. Thus Kurosawa's invocations of a strategy drawn from outside the

Japanese (silent) cinema have the effect of foregrounding another narrational tradition, precisely the sort of experimental attitude toward narrativity I am claiming characterizes Kurosawa. These experiments in narrativity may be derived from Japanese tradition, but are also owed to ongoing experimentation in international cinema (the films of Fritz Lang, for instance, foreground technologies of perception similar to some of the means found in *High and Low*).[18] It is only true, as Richie claims (63), that after *Ikiru* Kurosawa "gave up narration completely" if we understand narration in the very limited sense of offscreen voiceover narration.

We might say, then, that for Kurosawa the invocations of narrative modes characteristic of traditional Japanese storytelling practices intersect with a modern, international film culture. This is to say, that for Kurosawa, storytelling strategies partially revolve around the question of a range of options, a question, that is, of choice. This matches what is a recurring thematic concern of Kurosawa: protagonists who must question how to live when confronted with moral and ethical choices. The woodcutter in *Rashomon* must choose to remain optimistic in the face of a world rendered meaningless by relativity; the public employee in *Ikiru* must choose to work for the social good in a world rendered meaningless by bureaucracy; the warriors in *Seven Samurai* must choose to defend the farmers in a world where might seems to make right; the bodyguard in *Yojimbo* is seemingly confronted by the choice of two warring factions, although he amusingly makes a third choice; the bodyguard in *Sanjuro* similarly is faced with choosing sides. In *High and Low*, Kurosawa's protagonist, Gondo Kingo, is faced with one of the most difficult choices in all of the director's canon: to realize his life-long dream or pay an exorbitant ransom for a child who is not his. Gondo's dream, moreover, is not simply his wish to run his own shoe company. Rather, he wants to make quality, durable shoes in contrast to the cheap, disposable goods being foisted on the average consumer. Thus he has something like the public good in mind when he hopes to make his financial coup. Further, if he pays the ransom not only will he lose the opportunity to take over the company, but he will definitely lose his job and most of his property (which does, in fact, occur). Thus the question revolves around his personal ruination vs. the life of someone else's child. This choice made by the main character in the narrative is also mirrored by the choices made by the director in both what he will tell, and how he will tell it.

In bringing *High and Low* to the screen, Kurosawa eliminates a sub-plot of McBain's novel: King's assistant's sexual dalliance with a neighbor. More drastically, Kurosawa eliminates the basic structure of McBain's novel, which moves between events at the King household and events among the kidnappers, especially a relationship between the kidnappers and the kidnapped boy. Kurosawa, in slightly and drastically altering the story, has chosen what to tell. Donald Richie recognizes this aspect of the issues raised by *High and Low*. He states, "Kurosawa plainly shows what *he* thinks is important. It is not the kidnapping itself (done off screen) nor the fate of the small victim (the return is purposely done in extremely long shot as though to rob it of all emotion), nor is it Mifune's moral dilemma. It is the search, the capture, and the confrontation. The form would indicate this—or else why have the boy returned half way through the film?" (164; emphasis in original).[19] Yet more important, however, are precisely the varieties of narrational strategies Kurosawa employs, the means by which he chose to tell his story.

The homages to *katsuben, kamishibai,* and *emaki-mono* should not obscure the very real command Kurosawa has over the cinema as an autonomous storytelling medium. He is very much a cinematic classicist, a director who understands the language of cinema and uses the possibilities of the medium to speak for him, to speak the story. Thus while we may find these homages, these subtle recollections of traditional storytelling practices, Kurosawa also implicates a narrating presence through more standard, albeit well-chosen, cinematic means. A common device, although handled especially brilliantly in this film, is to allow framing to symbolize thematic elements. For instance, Richie points out that "the background for the credit titles is scenes of Yokohama taken from high up." He relates this to the idea of Heaven *(Tengoku)* vs. the Hell *(Jigoku)* of the later portion (163–64). Yet it also implies omniscience, a god-like view. This high-up vantage point reproduces the opening of *Psycho,* as well as, although without the humor, the opening of another Hitchcock film, *The Birds* (1963). The high angle shots which open Hitchcock's horrific comedy play with the idea of omniscience, of course, while foreshadowing the events to come. Thus the shots under the credits here serve the symbolic function of Heaven and Hell/High and Low, while they also foreground the question of narrative point of view.

Framing is used to symbolize conflict in the film's first scene, which, like many sequences in this film, relies strongly on the long-take with constant reframings. At the start, we find Gondo alone in the frame. He crosses left to turn on the room lights. His assistant, Kawanishi, enters from the left and the two of them cross the space Gondo has just traversed. Now, however, we see Gondo's partners in the room. Gondo takes a seat opposite them, and Kurosawa's framing highlights the conflict that is developing by showing the three of them together in shots which alternate with Gondo alone in the frame.

Framing strategies and story moments can be used as reflective of larger issues, as foreshadowing, and as forging links between separate sequences. For instance, the introduction of the two boys, Jun and Shinichi, is handled in such a way as to foreshadow story events, to compare childhood play with adult actions, and to make a connection visually between the boys and the kidnapper later. As Kawanishi bids goodbye to Gondo's partners following an intense argument, Kurosawa introduces Jun and Shinichi from the background as the company executives drive away. Kurosawa then cuts to a shot of Kawanishi in the mid-ground as the boys cross left to right behind him. Kawanishi moves right and Kurosawa cuts on his motion to watch the boys enter a room from the left of the frame, still moving left to right. Jun is shown wearing a cowboy hat, six-guns and shooting off a toy repeating rifle. Their entry and actions may be taken as symbolic—they reproduce Gondo's own violence and ruthlessness. This is supported by Mrs. Gondo, who says about Jun, "He takes after you. He likes violent games." It may be a foreshadowing of the violence to come, especially as Jun, in this first sequence with the boys, is shooting Shinichi, who will shortly be the kidnapping victim. The idea of foreshadowing is strengthened shortly thereafter when Shinichi enters the room dressed as Jun was earlier and is mistaken for him by Mrs. Gondo. Shinichi, of course, will be mistaken for Jun by the kidnapper. Finally, the framing strategy used to introduce the two boys is formally recalled by the sequence in which the kidnapper is first shown. Two police stand in mid-ground of a shot, and then exit right. The camera tilts down to reveal Gondo's house reflected in a sump. The reflection of someone entering from the right catches the camera's eye, which then follows the figure.

Framing also implicates directorial attitudes and helps guide, or even manipulate, audience response. The shots taken in the Gondo household detailing Gondo's moral dilemma are extraordinary for their formal complexity and thematic weight. Stephen Prince perceptively reads Kurosawa's framing strategies within the household in the film's first part as reflective of Kurosawa's insightful social analyses. Gondo, Prince notes, is continually implicated

> within the institutional spaces of family, corporation, and police, all of whom have representatives within the room.... Kurosawa manipulates the positions of Gondo, the police, Kawanishi, and the chauffeur, among others, to stress both the density of the social fabric and its relational nature.... The cameras capture social process itself, defining Gondo's reduced range of options as a function of the social construction of his position within the narrative and its visual construction within the frame. The individual is clearly shown to be embedded within a network of institutional roles and expectations. The individual hero has explicitly become an interactionist self. (191, 193)

Surely we must note Gondo's moral dilemma highlighted in a particularly powerful way when Kurosawa uses the cinemascope frame to focus on Aoki (Shinichi's father) and Gondo at opposite sides of the screen as the businessman agonizes over whether to pay the ransom.

Another particular aspect of Kurosawa's framing in this film is also striking. And that is the way in which Gondo is rarely alone, not just in the room, but in the frame, following the kidnapper's demand that he pay the ransom to save Shinichi, his chauffeur's son. By insinuating others into the frame with Gondo, Kurosawa may indeed transform his hero from the loner of Western mythology (hence, perhaps, the particular costuming of Jun and Shinichi as sheriff and outlaw?) into an interactionist self more in keeping with Japanese society, but he also provides notations for the audience. Kurosawa's storytelling strategy guides viewers toward desired responses. For instance, when Aoki pitifully asks Gondo to save his son, we see Aoki in the background, Gondo in the foreground, *and three policemen placed between them.* Far from isolating the two central protagonists of this dramatically intense moment, Kurosawa implicates a kind of audience between them. In fact, this particular moment is part of one of the film's most densely layered takes, a shot some three minutes long (an extremely long take, especially for Kurosawa, whose editing strategies and dynamism seem to be his forte). This lengthy take is sustained by constant reframings, from a tight close-up of Gondo on the telephone to the kidnapper, to a wider shot encompassing Gondo, the police, Mrs. Gondo, Kawanishi, and Aoki, to a two-shot of Gondo and Aoki, to a final shot in which Gondo and Aoki face each while we see Inspector Tokura in the foreground left.

This strategy of placing others in the frame is something like a chorus which comments on the action, but it is more particularly an audience surrogate. A kind of chorus can be found constantly in *Throne of Blood;* in fact a choral chant opens the film. Throughout the film Kurosawa also occasionally focuses on ordinary soldiers who provide a commentary on Washizu's declining fortunes. With its direct borrowing from the Noh theatre, the chorus in *Throne of Blood* is rather easy to assimilate. We may even see the three protagonists of the frame story of *Rashomon* as a chorus— their reactions and responses reproduce and guide the audience's response to the varying tales. In *High and Low,* this choral group response is rather ubiquitous. Thus we see the police watching as Gondo and his wife argue about the ransom demands; when Gondo agrees to pay we not only find the police in the frame, but they are in medium close-up while Gondo is in the background!

Another narrational strategy that serves to foreground storytelling within the cinematic medium is the way in which Kurosawa handles the first taped phone call from the kidnapper. Gondo answers the telephone when it rings, and we see and hear him begin to speak. After his initial contact with the kidnapper, Kurosawa uses a wipe as a transitional device to indicate the passing of time. (The wipe was a very outdated device by 1963.) We then see Gondo and the police gathered around the tape machine, and again hear Gondo begin to speak to the kidnapper. This time, however, we hear the entire conversation. Why handle this sequence in this manner? After all, the rest of the phone calls from the kidnapper are handled more conventionally, i.e., Gondo answers the phone and the entire scene plays out. One answer may be that the use of the tape player provides more dramatic possibilities. Instead of being confined to the phone, Gondo is free to move about the frame, and in so doing, Kurosawa's framing can dramatize the developing moral dilemma. Thus there are two shots of Gondo and Aoki isolated at opposite ends of the frame, Gondo standing at the extreme left, Aoki at extreme right. Another aspect to handling it this way is that it highlights the filmmaking process itself by focusing on a device used to record things. That is to say, it foregrounds storytelling. By the same token, storytelling is foregrounded in the recitation by the various policemen at the station house who report on their activities, which are then illustrated, as it were, by a flashback as their voiceovers continue. *Katsuben* cinema again?

I would like to make the claim that by foregrounding narration both through references to traditional Japanese storytelling modes and through a classical use of cinematic techniques, Kurosawa ensures that the audience not only recognizes that a story is being told to them, but is being told to them for some purpose by someone. It does not matter who that someone is precisely. We do not take value from the story due to the value, *a priori,* of the storyteller—at least, that is to say, of the storyteller as a real person available to us beyond the text. Of course, it is either a function or a by-product of the auteur theory that having established the presence of an author in past works, an author's subsequent works do, indeed, take on value based on this constructed or discovered author. Thus we look forward to the next film by Martin Scorsese to see what he has to say and how he chooses to say it. The foregrounding of the author has also by now been quite literalized: *Fellini Satyricon* or *Fellini's Roma* give title to two of Federico Fellini's films; in the United States, Kurosawa's latest film was entitled *Akira Kurosawa's Dreams.* In the case of *Yume,* one wonders how the dreams would have played to audiences had they not been identified as belonging to Kurosawa. For here it is important to note that in the Japanese version of the film (i.e., with no subtitles) the individual dream sequences are not named as they are in the American release version. Each dream is introduced by a title card, which is the same for each section: *Kono yume o mita* (I had this dream). The particularities of the Japanese language are important to recall in this context, for the subject of that sentence ("I") is only implied. Literally we may take this intertitle to read "A dream was had" (more literally, "A dream was seen," from the verb *miru*—to see, cf. the silent-film homage, *Yume Miru Yoni Nemuritai.* "To Sleep So As to Dream"). Thus we may justifiably claim that we do have an offscreen narrator, precisely the one who had these dreams, who we may identify as Kurosawa. Through a textual narrator, overt or covert, an audience becomes cognizant of the process of narration and must interact with the text in a dynamic way, become an active listener, discern the narrator's point. Thus *High and Low* is not simply about a process (the search, the capture, and the confrontation as Richie has it), or a meditation on narration for its own sake, but is about a moral dilemma, a dramatization, a narration, of the myriad choices we each must make in order to live: Once upon a time, this happened.

A focus on narration as a process within Kurosawa's cinema enables us to gain new perspective on this director still frequently described as "Japan's most Western director," still frequently aligned with Hollywood-style filmmaking.[20] This new perspective, it is hoped, aligns him with elements of traditional or distinctively Japanese modes of storytelling. This perspective is engaged not for the sake of isolating Japanese vs. Western elements, or thereby reifying one at the expense of the other. Japan itself is, after all, both a traditional and a modern culture, both East and West, a place where tradition and innovation co-exist in usually fascinating relation. Rather, by recalling some specifically and uniquely Japanese modes of storytelling we bring greater complexity to Kurosawa's cinema—it is not simply Hollywood style; or "art film" style; or, for that matter, traditionally Japanese in style. It is a fascinating amalgam of choices, options, traditions, and innovations in its own right, much like the country which gave rise to it.

Notes

1. The term *benshi* is still perhaps more popular in the West to name the live narrator/explainer who invariably accompanied all commercial film presentations in Japan, even into the sound era. Following the lead of J. L. Anderson, however, the term *katsuben* is preferred. See Anderson, "Spoken Silents in the Japanese Cinema; or, Talking to Pictures: Essaying the *Katsuben,* Contexturalizing the Texts," in *Reframing Japanese Cinema: Authorship, Genre, History,* ed. Arthur Nolletti, Jr. and David Desser (Bloomington: Indiana University Press, 1992), 259–311.

2. Anderson, "Spoken Silents," 260–61.

3. Ibid., 261; emphasis in original.

4. Quoted in ibid., 263.

5. Ibid., 267.

6. Ibid., 293.

7. Ibid., 294. I am not familiar with the *renzoku terebi shosetsu* as a performance, so to speak. However, Anderson's example requires further research, lest a technological innovation be mistaken for a peculiar performance practice. I am speaking of the utilization of Japanese television's stereo capabilities to aid the blind in enjoying programming. Watching Japanese television, one may be struck by the broadcast, for instance, of the soundtrack of a foreign motion picture over two channels: on the main channel one hears the Japanese dubbed dialogue; on the secondary channel, the original language is broadcast. The stereo capabilities may be utilized further by listening to both channels simultaneously. Thus I was confused one evening when the main channel of a Japanese drama had Japanese dialogue; the sub-channel had the same dialogue in Japanese but with a narrator describing what was apparent visually—not reproducing or recapping the dialogue, but discussing the setting and the emotional or physical attributes of the characters. When puzzled by this seeming reproduction of the *katsuben* (albeit one unseen), I was told that this was programming for the blind. What Anderson describes above sounds suspiciously like it might be a technological device rather than a narrative strategy. We must make further inquiries.

8. Akira Kurosawa, *Something Like an Autobiography,* trans. Audie E. Bock (New York: Vintage, 1983), 74–75; hereafter cited in the text.

9. David Bordwell, *Narration in the Fiction Film* (Madison: University of Wisconsin Press, 1985), xi; hereafter cited in the text.

10. Audie Bock, *Japanese Film Directors* (San Francisco: Kodansha International, 1985), 168.

11. Tadao Sato, *Currents in Japanese Cinema,* trans. Gregory Barrett (Tokyo: Kodansha International, 1982), 116.

12. Donald Richie, *The Films of Akira Kurosawa,* rev. ed. (Berkeley: University of California Press, 1984), 229; hereafter cited in the text.

13. David Desser, *The Samurai Films of Akira Kurosawa* (Ann Arbor, Mich.: UMI Research Press, 1983), 77; and David Desser, "*Ikiru:* Narration as a Moral Act," in *Reframing Japanese Cinema.*

14. Stephen Prince, *The Warrior's Camera: The Cinema of Akira Kurosawa* (Princeton, N. J.: Princeton University Press, 1991), 190; hereafter cited in the text.

15. In point of fact, a salient movement away from auteurism has been to ignore conditions of production completely and focus on issues of reception, on the audience instead of the creator.

16. Anderson, "Spoken Silents," 270.

17. Komatsu Hiroshi, "Some Characteristics of Japanese Cinema Before World War I," in *Reframing Japanese Cinema,* 240.

18. I would like to thank Darrell William Davis for invoking Lang in this context.

19. One should be careful about making sweeping statements about the effect a certain film technique has *a priori,* even in this specific instance. It seems to me not true that the fate of the small victim is of little concern to Kurosawa; his use of a long shot to show the boy's return does not necessarily indicate a lack of importance. The camera's physical distance from a subject does not necessarily reflect an audience's corresponding emotional distance. Many instances of a long shot in a scene of great emotional impact may be found in Mizoguchi's cinema, for instance. The idea that the audience is distanced from emotional contact via such a technique is belied by the very intense responses such scenes always engender. To aid what in fact is a fairly moving scene (where Gondo welcomes the boy into his arms), Kurosawa uses a fanfare on the soundtrack, which always indicates a dramatic highpoint in this film, and he utilizes his strategy of the audience surrogate—here, one of the policemen turns his head away from the action and sheds tears of joy.

20. I myself am guilty, if that is the right word, of aligning Kurosawa with the West, both in terms of what I claim is his basic humanism and individualism, and for his basic use of character-driven stories of heroes who must make existential choices. Even his techniques, at their essence, are recuperable to the Classical Hollywood style, I have claimed. And if I still stand by this claim, the focus of this essay remains an attempt to re-place Kurosawa within a traditional Japanese context as well.

Images of Son and Superhero in Kurosawa's *Red Beard*

KEIKO McDONALD

*R*ED BEARD (*Akahige,* 1965), which is often cited as the most humanistic of Kurosawa's films, has not enjoyed the critical attention that has been given to Kurosawa's earlier major works, *Rashomon* (1950) and *Seven Samurai (Shichinin no Samurai,* 1954). Donald Richie's study is the only comprehensive work about this film to date. In his study Richie discusses various aspects of the film including the story, the process of production, characterization, and Kurosawa's treatment of such important filmic constituents as symbols, musical motif, and flashback.[1] In *Kurosawa Akira no Sekai (The World of Akira Kurosawa),* Tadao Sato makes a brief yet insightful comparison of the medical doctor in *Red Beard* with one in *Drunken Angel (Yoidore Tenshi,* 1947). This suggests further comparisons, which may improve our understanding of character type as a crucial constituent of the film.[2]

Akira Kurosawa makes the following comments on the film:

> In this movie I only wanted to express the anger manifested in Red Beard's (Dr. Kyojio Niide's) cry, "Did anybody enforce the order that we must not leave human beings ignorant and poor?" And I thought that I had been able to express this anger straightforwardly. I considered this work as the final completion of my works, and I often asked myself what I should direct after this film.[3]

The entire corpus of Kurosawa's filmic works explores his moral and social concerns. His films begin with an acute awareness of a fragmented world, of which the half-ruined gate in *Rashomon* and a dog with a human hand in its mouth in *Yojimbo* are two good examples. Yet man's choices of action in so morally and politically bleak a world are central to his films. As Donald Richie points out, Kurosawa's films present compassion or altruism as offering at least some potential for the betterment of society.

Red Beard begins in true Kurosawa fashion. It is set in a world seemingly governed by forces beyond man's control: the economic destitution of the late Tokugawa period. The story concerns the various stages that a young intern, Noboru Yasumoto, must pass through before he is finally awakened to the greatness of humanism embodied by his chief, Red Beard. The fragmented nature of the world is unfolded gradually rather than presented all

Reprinted from *Cinema East: A Critical Study of Major Japanese Films* (Rutherford, N.J.: Fairleigh Dickinson University Press, 1983), 71–87, by permission of the author and Associated University Presses.

at once as in some of Kurosawa's other films. As Yasumoto's perceptions of his surroundings change and enlarge, the seamy aspects of society become more real and immediate.

At the beginning of the film, Kurosawa presents the patients' ward in Red Beard's clinic as a microcosm of the lowest social strata. Yasumoto, returning from Kyushu after three years' study of Dutch medicine, hopes to be assigned to the Shogun's medical staff. Instead, he finds himself assigned to the public clinic run by Red Beard on a tight budget in shocking circumstances. He is appalled by the poverty-stricken patients who are packed into the dingy quarters of the clinic. We in the audience, who have a much wider perspective than the young intern, already realize that this ward is symbolic of the sickness of society, the worst symptom of which is poverty. With this premise, Kurosawa already posits the central problem of the film, "How can one act in the face of a hostile social environment?"

To explore this central problem, Kurosawa delineates a struggle between two clear-cut value systems: the humanistic confrontation with social evil, a dedication to the public good; and a selfish turning away from social evils, which Kurosawa presents as a bondage to personal aims and understandings.

Kurosawa employs two character types to represent these opposing value systems. Red Beard is the superhero, a man who transcends the prevailing sociopolitical system; a man capable of humanitarian action. He is not only a medical doctor, trying to comfort or cure the poor invalid, but also a psychologist, with some understanding of the emotional sufferings of the poor. Kurosawa invests him with positive human traits: flexibility, fortitude, sense of justice, insight, wisdom, and both physical and spiritual strength. To his young intern, Red Beard (Dr. Niide) is an ideal, and more; he is a father figure. Since curing sick patients serves as an apt metaphor for curing a sick society in this film, Red Beard can be the representative of anyone who is concerned about humanity. As Red Beard's antithesis, Kurosawa creates the son image in Yasumoto. This young rebel, who at first challenges Red Beard's authority, embodies inflexibility, impatience, self-conceit, and immaturity. Significantly, this dichotomy of character types gradually dissolves as the *son,* in his gradual awakening to the *father's* intrinsic qualities, begins to wish to emulate the father image.

Kurosawa often talks about the rhythmic continuity of his scenario, and as the basis for continuity he alludes either to the *Jo-ha-kyu* pattern of a *Noh* play (Introduction, Development, and Recapitulation at the ratio of 1:3:1) or the symphonic structure.[4] The *Jo-ha-kyu* pattern seems to be more appropriate in this film because it can easily be divided into three parts. The narrative progression of the film is just as straightforward as Kurosawa's character types. The introductory part involves Yasumoto's arrival at Red Beard's clinic and his disgust with his situation and his superior. The second part, the focal point of the film's action, with the turning point at Red Beard's opportune rescue of Yasumoto's life, covers the young man's conversion. It is symbolized by Yasumoto's decision finally to put on the clinic uniform, which he has repeatedly refused to wear. It is in this part of the film that Yasumoto comes to appreciate Red Beard's personality and also to understand the evils of social inequity. The final part of the film, the recapitulatory part and the shortest of the three parts, consists of Yasumoto's affirmation of the importance of humanism. His spiritual learning process has been completed; not only does he demonstrate flexibility in forgiving his ex-fiancée for betraying him but he also shows his dedication by giving up his aspiration to the Shogunate medical staff. In the fusion of the father and son images, this part of the film affirms the potential of humanitarianism for bettering the world.

The first part opens with a shot of the roof tiles of the house in the vicinity of the Koishikawa Public Clinic run by Red Beard. It is raining. A street vendor's voice is intermittently broken by the sound of the wind. Thus, initially establishing gloom as the predominant mood of the film, Kurosawa introduces Yasumoto, an inexperienced, self-centered youth. We see him walking toward the gate of the clinic away from the camera; he stops when he is greeted by Tsugawa, a member of the medical staff. Throughout the film Kurosawa presents this gate as a pivotal point expressive of the various stages of Yasumoto's learning process. At this initial stage, the gate to Yasumoto is just a shabby gate of a public clinic, a place he considers beneath his dignity.

Through Tsugawa, Yasumoto comes to form a false preconception of Red Beard. From this first misconception, Yasumoto begins to mold a negative image of Red Beard as he becomes more acquainted with him. At the gate of the clinic Tsugawa tells Yasumoto that he has been waiting for him so that he can be released from his job. Yasumoto, in dismay, replies that he has simply been advised to go to the clinic to see it. He also proudly says that he has spent three years in Nagasaki studying medicine.

From what little of Yasumoto has been shown us by Kurosawa, we have already learned a lot about him. Yasumoto is somewhat exotically attired as if he were showing off an elite status gained from studying in Nagasaki. His manner, arrogant and conceited, clearly corresponds to his appearance. As the cinematic action progresses, he becomes more and more self-centered. During his stay in Nagasaki in Kyushu, his teacher, Amano, promised him a position on the Shogunate medical staff. Thus, thinking that he is simply visiting the clinic, Yasumoto exhibits a crude curiosity at the shabby place as if he did not belong there at all. Tsugawa explains to Yasumoto that the medical doctors there are underpaid and constantly put to hard labor by their chief, Red Beard. The camera follows Tsugawa and Yasumoto as they go through the corridor of the outpatient clinic. Yasumoto, with a frown, says blatantly, "What is this smell?" Tsugawa answers: "It is the smell of poverty.... This place is frequented by outpatients. Every afternoon, they can receive free medical treatment.... These people look as if they would be better off dying than living. . . ." Then, the camera shifts to a crowd of the young, the old, the male and the female—all poorly dressed and crowding into the room. Both visually and verbally, Kurosawa has already presented poverty as the great social evil. He has also made it known to us that Yasumoto must learn to see it as an aspect of social injustice if he is to grow spiritually.

Tsugawa and Yasumoto continue down the long corridor of the ward. In this introductory part, Kurosawa frequently presents Yasumoto walking down the long, dimly lit corridor to foreshadow the long learning process that he will undergo before he finds both his guide and his goal in Red Beard. At this learning stage, Yasumoto responds to poverty as a complete outsider; his response simply remains on a visual level. Thus, he says coldly "Don't you have *tatami* mats around here?" Tsugawa replies that no room in the clinic has *tatami* mats. One of the patients in the ward, pulling his white kimono sleeve, complains that he, much less a female patient, cannot die in such a shabby uniform.

Later, Yasumoto learns that the missing *tatami* and patients' uniforms are part of Red Beard's reforms. Yasumoto believes Tsugawa when he says: "Red Beard is a dictator here. He is very enthusiastic about medical treatment and is indeed an excellent doctor. He enjoys great trust among the feudal lords and rich merchants. However, he is so obstinate, despotic, and extreme. Lately, he has also been acting stuck up." Unable to judge the legitimacy of his informant's description, Yasumoto comes to see his new boss as the very epitome of inflexibility and despotism. But he is doing Red Beard an injustice, as Sakichi, one of the dying patients explains; a *tatami* room is hygienically unsound as it accumulates moisture and dust. Simple white clothes easily show stains so that it is easy to tell when they are clean and hence to keep them more sanitary than colored clothes.

After their tour of the kitchen and staff members' room, Yasumoto has his first meeting with Red Beard. Tsugawa informs Red Beard that he has brought Yasumoto in. We do not see Red Beard but hear his *commanding* voice ordering them to enter. This simple mode of representation signifies that Yasumoto's first impression of Red Beard is formed without his seeing the man. When Tsugawa opens the door, Kurosawa cuts to both Yasumoto and Tsugawa looking at a middle-aged man in a hospital uniform sitting at a desk. All three of them are shown with their backs to the camera. This take magnificently portrays Yasumoto's complete discord with this strange environment, emphasizing the very cold light reflected upon the old *shoji* door and the furniture, and Red Beard's showing his back to the newcomer. Yasumoto's preconceptions about Red Beard are reinforced during this short meeting. Red Beard gruffly introduces himself: "I'm Red Beard." He stares at Yasumoto very intensely, and as if commanding him, he tells Yasumoto that he will start work as an intern at the clinic immediately. Ignoring Yasumoto's objections, Red Beard orders him to hand in all the notes he took during his study at Nagasaki. To the flabbergasted Yasumoto,

Red Beard simply says that there is nothing more to discuss. Red Beard then goes back to his desk, showing complete indifference to the two visitors.

As Yasumoto reveals later in a speech to Mori, another doctor at the clinic, his values are entirely conventional; he is a social climber. Thus, Yasumoto arrogantly shows disgust with his assignment to the dingy clinic. Mori quietly tells Yasumoto that the town magistrate, who supervises the clinic, has officially appointed him to the staff at Red Beard's request. At this stage Yasumoto's conceit is so strong that he cannot believe that Red Beard wants his notes from Nagasaki for the public good. Instead, he thinks that his boss wants to use them for his own advantage. Furthermore, influenced by his negative impression of Red Beard, Yasumoto refuses to believe that Red Beard treats even those he likes with something like indifference, even when Mori tells him so. Yasumoto's fleeting view of Red Beard has been less "telling" than ours. Kurosawa shows us clearly a keen insight into other people in Red Beard's glittering eyes but also a humanistic concern for others beneath his superficially rude manners.

The rest of the cinematic action in this introductory part portrays the impetuous son's open challenge to the tolerant father. Thus, Yasumoto first must repudiate Red Beard's values to assert his own until he is brought to see the light. Yasumoto's challenge manifests itself in his violation of a number of Red Beard's hospital rules. First, he enters the off-limit area. Kurosawa employs a quick follow shot as Yasumoto passes through the corridor, then through the herb nursery on his way to the forbidden building. This follow shot again emphasizes Yasumoto's long learning process.

In the later scene wherein Red Beard, Mori, and Tsugawa are seated at the dinner table, Yasumoto refuses to eat. Red Beard does not scold him at all. Yasumoto's challenge to Red Beard becomes more violent when he refuses to yield up his notes from Nagasaki. Yasumoto claims that while he learned advanced Dutch medicine he contrived his own methods of diagnosis and medical treatment, and that what he acquired is all his, not anybody else's. Red Beard loudly responds that medicine belongs to the pubic, not to any specific person. As early as this stage, we already witness the confrontation of two value systems represented by Red Beard and Yasumoto, respectively: dedication to medicine versus the exploitation of medicine. Yasumoto, wrapped up in his own world, continues to show his defiance. Against clinic regulations, he orders the kitchen maid to go and buy sake for him.

Thus, Yasumoto's challenge to Red Beard is not only an independent youth's defiance of authority but also a raving against the world, which he thinks is not giving him his due. He has assumed that social advancement would come easily to him for his learning but not for his professional experience.

Yasumoto's lack of insight into human motives is also manifested in his inflexibility. He flatly refuses to see Masae, the younger sister of Chigusa, his ex-fiancée, who betrayed him and married somebody else while he was in Nagasaki. Moreover, he simply idles his time away in the clinic, disregarding Mori's advice that his childish attitude is not worthy of sympathy. Significantly, in the final analysis, Tsugawa, who is anxious to leave the clinic for better employment, is what Yasumoto would have become had he not undergone his gradual learning process. Concomitantly, Mori, who is devoted to Red Beard, setting him up as a model, is what Yasumoto might have become had he had a poorer education and a more submissive attitude.

Yasumoto's confrontation with his crushed ego and his subsequent witness to Red Beard's sincere concern for him mark the culmination of the cinematic action of the introductory part. Proud of his acquisition of new medical knowledge in Nagasaki, Yasumoto thinks that he is capable of treating the deranged girl when she escapes from her confinement into his room. Taking at face value her confession that she is not a mad person and that she had to kill her servant for a legitimate reason, Yasumoto encourages her to confess everything to him. While the two sit still, the camera, which has been active so far, becomes almost stationary, externalizing Yasumoto's first professional enthusiasm with the patient, whom he thinks he can cure. This stationary camera position, which has created tension, is ironic; the wind on the sound track during the girl's confession creates a sinister atmosphere, foreshadowing Yasumoto's approaching danger of entrapment in her snare. While the camera is still immobile, Yasumoto approaches the girl closely to show his eagerness. Telling him that she was a helpless victim of rape, she circles around him and then leans against him. Next, the vertical alignment of the two, which the slightly high-angled camera has hitherto emphasized, changes suddenly into a horizontal alignment as she lies down on him and tries to stab him with her sharp hair ornament. This abrupt compositional change, enhanced by a sudden change in the girl's voice, indicates the collapse of Yasumoto's overconfidence in his medical knowledge. It is Red Beard who comes to his rescue just in time.

The following shot presents Yasumoto lying in bed with a white bandage around his neck, which was slightly cut by the girl. The camera cuts to Red Beard's silhouette moving back and forth along the wall. The moving silhouette, more effectively than Red Beard's face in a close-up, conveys his deep concern for Yasumoto, which the youth has not yet come to appreciate. Red Beard now enters Yasumoto's room. Witnessing Yasumoto's embarrassment, Red Beard quickly consoles him, saying that all men have a weakness for a pretty woman. Upon hearing this, Yasumoto cannot stop his tears. Red Beard tries to take a tissue out of his kimono to give to Yasumoto so that he can wipe his tears, but on second thought he blows his nose with it. A close-up of Red Beard blowing his nose—an amusing gesture to hide his sentimental orientation—indicates his good nature, which is not so frequently shown outwardly or dramatically throughout the film. This episode marks the beginning of the change in Yasumoto's impression of Red Beard.

The second part of the film, the expository part, unfolds Yasumoto's technical and spiritual development, through which he becomes awakened to his moral and professional responsibilities. The first stage of Yasumoto's learning process is his attendance at an operation, wherein he finds his hitherto inflated ego again fatally crushed. When Red Beard asks him to diagnose the patient's illness, he concludes that it is a case of stomach cancer. Red Beard disagrees, telling him that Yasumoto's own notes from Nagasaki show that it is liver cancer. Asked by Yasumoto if there is any cure for this illness, Red Beard answers that there is no way of curing any type of disease. Here Red Beard acts as a mouthpiece for one of Kurosawa's strongest convictions: that poverty and ignorance are the real sources of disease. Red Beard says: "All we can do to compensate for the present poor stage of our medical technology is to fight against poverty and ignorance.... Everybody says that poverty and ignorance are simply social issues.... But have politicians done anything to cure poverty and ignorance? Is there any law that says we must not abandon human beings to poverty and ignorance?"

We have now fully acknowledged that Red Beard is gifted with both medical acumen and empathy for his patients, and that he channels these assets into his actions on behalf of social justice. In the process of becoming, Yasumoto must pass through a series of encounters with clinic patients, who epitomize the sufferings inherent in society. To emphasize Yasumoto's growing sensitivity to his patients, Kurosawa pervasively uses techniques that are easily accessible to the general audience: point-of-view shots, loud music, and flashback. For example, in one scene, three children are brought to the clinic by their mother and are served rice balls in the kitchen. But they are ashamed to show their hunger in the maid's presence, as if this were their childlike defiance of their poverty. As soon as she leaves, they pounce on the food. At this moment Yasumoto passes by the kitchen. They suddenly put the rice balls back on the plate. A medium shot of the children, taken along Yasumoto's line of sight, articulates his impression of these poor children; they gaze at him scared and timid, and huddle together as if fraternity were their sole means of protection. This marks the beginning of his realization of how poverty can deform a child's personality as surely as a disease can deform its body.

Another example is found in the scene of Okuni's confession of her father's (Rokusuke's) gloomy past, through which Yasumoto is awakened to a degree of suffering and misery that his own class is unlikely ever to experience. When Okuni asks Red Beard whether her father died peacefully, Red Beard tells her that her father died a peaceful death. To highlight Yasumoto's perception of Red Beard's insight into his patients, Kurosawa presents (in the intern's recollection) a very quick flashback of Rokusuke's profile on his deathbed while loud music is heard on the sound track. Rokusuke's face, which looked ugly and appalling earlier, no longer looks so to Yasumoto. He realizes that the old man's face expresses the dignity of a man who has silently ended his misery. While the music roars, we recall Mori's earlier remark about his boss: "Dr. Niide can diagnose the patient's body and his mind simultaneously.... For example, in Rokusuke's dead silence, he detected terrible unhappiness.... That's why he said that his death was solemn."

Yasumoto passes through another stage in his learning process when he witnesses the death of Sahachi, who has always been good to the other patients. Kurosawa again resorts to a series of flashbacks to mark Yasumoto's involvement in the patient's suffering. In the flashback, Sahachi is presented as a good, healthy youth, who married Onaka from a poor farmer family. During their happy marriage, a great earthquake devastated Edo, and Onaka suddenly disappeared. A few years later, Sahachi encountered her with somebody else's baby in her arms and learned the truth of her dissimulation; she was afraid of enjoying a happy marriage and thought that a girl like her from a poor family did not deserve to be happy. She saw the devastation of the earthquake—shaking windows, smoke, fissures, and fires—captured by low-key photography in the flashback—as an omen. Sahachi's healthy smiling face at the height of his happiness in the flashback contrasts with his sorrowful, skinny, aged face, and this contrast clearly demonstrates the effects of socioeconomic forces crudely operating in individual lives. Furthermore, the snow-covered farmyard where Sahachi courted Onaka is in stark contrast to the dingy room in the ramshackle house where he is now dying. Again this articulates the innocence of love betrayed by economic determinism.

As Sahachi dies, Yasumoto learns about compassion among the poor for the first time. Deeply concerned about Sahachi's condition, the inhabitants of the slum gather at this house where he was carried from the clinic according to his wish. The pouring rain outside and the torn *shoji* door in the background add a desolate texture to the scene corresponding to their gloom, and the onlookers show genuine sorrow over Sahachi's approaching death. In one scene, the *shoji* is slightly askew, as the house was tilted by a landslide that took place shortly after Sahachi's return. This shot, however, achieves Kurosawa's desired effect in conveying a sense of social inequity victimizing the poor as a feature of Yasumoto's awareness.

The point at which Yasumoto begins to grow is symbolically marked by his decision to wear the clinic uniform. The uniform is the emblem of public service, as evidenced by Sahachi's remarks that when the poor, who cannot afford a doctor, see a person wearing the uniform on the street, they rush to him for help.

Kurosawa frequently terminates a stage of Yasumoto's learning process with a didactic monologue by Red Beard, which makes it easier for the audience to comprehend the nature of the young intern's learning process. One of the earlier examples is Red Beard's comment on corrupt officials after his and Yasumoto's visit to Lord Matsudaira, whom he has charged an exorbitant medical fee. Yasumoto discovers Red Beard's flexibility; Red Beard tells him that his unlawful conduct is simply a means of helping the poor. Thus, Red Beard emphasizes the politically bleak society in which the transcendence of the existing corrupt system is the sole means by which one can avoid victimization by that corrupt system:

> I don't like officials. They publicly impose all sorts of unlawful and cruel things upon people in the name of the public authority. . . . I am not going to close my eyes to their inhuman ways. . . . Crime for crime. . . . An eye for an eye. . . . As human beings they are the worst and most ignorant. . . . I hate them.

Another example occurs at the end of the brothel scene involving Red Beard's decision to take Otoyo, a brothel chambermaid, back to the clinic. A monologue leads both Yasumoto and the audience to realize that social injustice paralyzes the poor:

> The madam, who molests this child, is a hideous hag. . . . But this is indeed a miserable aspect of the social institution. That old lady is also weak and cannot live unless she torments those weaker than herself. . . . But why do children like this girl have to suffer? She is physically ill, but her mind is much worse. . . . It is infected as if it had been burned. . . .

The middle section of the second part involves Yasumoto's subsequent treatment of his first patient. Through it, he, unlike the observer, actually experiences social evil molding little children's personalities. Yasumoto changes: the son image gradually alters and assumes certain traits of the father image. This section is accompanied by a reading of Yasumoto's *karte* (notes) describing Otoyo's progressive recovery. Point-of-view shots again pervade it, and Yasumoto's consciousness of Otoyo's eyes becomes dominant, indicating his empathy for the patient. At the initial stage of treatment, the patient resists. From Yasumoto's point of view, Kurosawa films Otoyo's face with glittering eyes. Yasumoto's narration on the sound track expresses his dismay at her hardened feelings: "When I am gazed at by Otoyo, I do not know what to do, for her eyes are full of suspicion, a strange arrogance, and mistrust of others." On the third day of treatment, Yasumoto suddenly finds her out of bed and scrubbing the floor. Again to emphasize Yasumoto's awareness of her eyes, Kurosawa presents Otoyo in a different setting. Low-key photography evokes a desolate atmosphere in the narrow corridor. Otoyo's suspicion-filled eyes loom from darkness, clearly showing her resistance and fear.

In the subsequent scene, Yasumoto not only has developed compassion and fortitude but also finds his efforts rewarded. In response to his remark that not only Red Beard but he, too, wants to cure her crippled heart, Otoyo suddenly breaks the bowl of gruel he is about to serve her, and asks him if he still wants to cure her. Here, we encounter Yasumoto's first, almost melodramatic display of compassion. He starts picking up the broken fragments of the bowl, saying sobbingly: "You, poor child.... You're a good child by nature."

The following scene starts with Otoyo's disappearance from the clinic. Yasumoto's search for her brings him to a bridge where he finds Otoyo begging. He follows and stops her when she comes out of a shop with something in her hands. Otoyo, surprised, drops her purchase; she has just bought a new bowl to replace the one she has broken. The shattered bowl —a symbol of destruction—ironically conveys a sense of solidarity growing between Yasumoto and his patient. A close-up of Otoyo's face from her perspective, emphasizing the tears of which she has never before been capable, reveals her awakening to human love.

A later conversation between Red Beard and Yasumoto indicates a further stage of the young intern's conversion. When Red Beard returns the notes and charts he borrowed from Yasumoto, Yasumoto, crestfallen, admits the selfishness of his having previously refused them. Thereupon, Kurosawa presents Yasumoto's long confession, making it too easy for the audience to grasp the young intern's regret of the values to which he has hitherto adhered:

> I was no good in every respect.... I was so conceited and so arrogant.... Why on earth did I rave about my unhappiness when I was not happy?... Rokusuke and Sahachi died quietly without any complaining though they were so unfortunate.... Look at Otoyo.... I am happy to be ashamed of it.
>
> I am such a despicable fellow.... While I blamed Chigusa, I was so easily seduced by that mad woman.... I was bragging of my training in Nagasaki so much that I made fun of this clinic.... Nay, I even despised and hated you.... I am such a despicable fellow—arrogant and impudent....

As a result of his strenuous effort in treating Otoyo, Yasumoto is attacked by a high fever. While he is asleep in bed, Kurosawa presents a memorable scene that communicates the extent of Yasumoto's conversion. It is snowing outside his room. Only the lattice windowpanes covered with the snow are light while the rest of his room is dark. Otoyo reaches out to the snow through the lattice window and picks up some of it to wet a towel to put to Yasumoto's fevered head. Her gesture—reaching out to the pure snow— symbolically conveys a sudden surge of her suppressed affection for him and thus marks the reward of his fortitude and compassion. When Yasumoto recovers, we now see the result of his changed image of Red Beard. He frankly tells Otoyo about Red Beard's greatness, emphasizing his role as his model and guide.

Before his learning process can be complete, Yasumoto also must deal with Otoyo's attachment to him and its consequences. It is again Red Beard who, with his sagacious knowledge of human psychology, explains to Yasumoto the complexity of human relationships.

Thus far, we have been shown many stages of Yasumoto's conversion in clear-cut ways, even to the extent that we feel that we have had enough. However, in order to make doubly sure of Yasumoto's immediate sense of poverty ingrained in the lowest social strata, Kurosawa adds one more episode. An entire family, who have attempted to poison themselves, is brought into the clinic. Chobo is the only survivor. What keeps this episode from becoming boring is Kurosawa's investment of ordinary reality with a supernatural quality. A strange cry, "Chobo," rings on the sound track whereupon Yasumoto goes to the kitchen, from which the cry was heard. He sees the clinic's kitchen maids, who are in deep sympathy with Chobo's plight, shouting down a deep well to pray for his recovery, since they believe that "all wells lead to the bottom of the earth and that the departing soul may be called back."[5] The camera pans down the well. It is a deep well, and at the bottom the silvery ripples on the surface are captured. The overall effect of the camera work and the filmic composition is a strangely sinister atmosphere; the fearful aura of death associated with the public clinic. It is in this nocturnal atmosphere that Yasumoto confirms that genuine compassion exists among the poor. Again as in other Kurosawa films such as *Drunken Angel* (1948), *Rashomon* (1950), and *Dodeskaden* (1971), compassion appears in this film as the ethical fortification of the poor, without which the world of poverty would be absolutely unendurable.

However, Kurosawa implies in this film that to change society for the better, individual compassion must be channeled into the daring and devoted public action embodied in Red Beard. In order to become the father image, Yasumoto first had to become himself, that is, to discover himself. His self-discovery has been achieved as a result of his contact with poverty wherein he realized the complexity of human motives, the evil of society, and the good of Red Beard's humanistic values. The second part of the film ends with a succession of shots of Yasumoto; he walks out to the yard after learning that Chobo will be saved. It is now dawn and the air is cool. Yasumoto inhales deeply, and his gesture indicates the end of his journey in search of himself and the beginning of his independent commitment to the public cause.

The final section, which is the shortest of the three, concludes the film in a happy mood. Yasumoto is now entirely different from what he was at the beginning of his quest. He has begun to assume the nature of his father image, Red Beard, as witnessed by Mori's remark: "These days you even talk like your boss." Yasumoto's quest not only results in the spiritual gratification of serving as a doctor for a humanitarian cause but also yields the more traditional satisfaction of acquiring a bride, Masae—the standard reward for the romantic hero. Through his series of confrontations with interactive human motives, Yasumoto has developed compassion. We now witness him forgiving Chigusa for having betrayed him. In this concluding part, the geographic location shifts from the dark, gloomy clinic to the bright, elegant home of Yasumoto's parents, where his wedding takes place. Red Beard opens the white *shoji* door of the room. Thereupon, Kurosawa introduces the traditional images of the early spring. Plum blossoms are in bloom in the yard, and a nightingale sings on the sound track. This scene is a relief for us, especially after we have been accustomed to the claustrophobic interior of the clinic often captured by low-key photography. It is a clear index of Yasumoto's initiation into a new life after his groping for his moral roots.

Yasumoto is now firmly determined to follow in his father image's footsteps. At the wedding ceremony he openly declines the offer to serve on the Shogun's medical staff and decides to stay at the clinic. The final scene presents the fusion of the father and the son images in a joyous mood, as Yasumoto and Red Beard walk together to the gate of the clinic. In the earlier scene involving Yasumoto's first visit to the clinic, this gate looked gloomy and disreputable against the background of the desolate wind. But now it looks like the emblem of pride and dignity, externalizing Yasumoto's spiritual regeneration. Red Beard walks to the gate, and Yasumoto follows him. The shot predicts that Yasumoto will keep pursuing the virtues for which Red Beard stands.

In *Nihon Eiga Shisoshi (The History of Intellectual Currents in Japanese Cinema),* Sato indicates his dissatisfaction with the clear-cut good-evil allegory in *Red Beard,* declaring that other Kurosawa films go beyond this simplicity in their exploration of eroticism and violence as "a symbol of man's spasmodic, deep-rooted desire for freedom."[6] However, if Kurosawa's intention in *Red Beard* is the Horatian doctrine of *"dulce et utile,"* rather than the production of a serious film, his creation of the two character types clearly achieves his desired effect; the film is really amusing and also accessible to the masses in his portrayal of the superhero type and his son image. At the same time the film is didactic in transmitting the importance of altruism channeled into meaningful professional action as a potential for a better society.[7]

Notes

1. Donald Richie, *The Films of Akira Kurosawa* (Berkeley: University of California Press, 1970), 171–83.

2. Tadao Sato, *Kurosawa Akira no Sekai (The World of Akira Kurosawa)* (Tokyo: Sanichi Shobo, 1969), 250–53. Comparing Dr. Sanada with Red Beard, Sato strongly admires the spirit of protest embodied in Dr. Sanada. Though he is denied a high position as a doctor and the wealth it would bring and is not physically strong, he makes strenuous but vain efforts to make wicked gangsters human. Sato claims that whereas Red Beard's public dedication and fortitude are derived from his responsibility for farmers and townsmen as a samurai leader, Dr. Sanada's stem mainly from the Japanese struggle amid the aftermath of Japan's defeat in World War II.

3. Chieko Kotoda, ed., *Sekai no Eiga Sakka: Kurosawa Akira (Film Directors of the World: Akira Kurosawa)* (Tokyo: Kinema Jumpo, 1970), 3:138.

4. Akira Kurosawa, *Akuma no Yo ni Saishin ni: Tenshi no Yo ni Daitan ni (Be Careful as the Devil: Daring as an Angel)* (Tokyo: Toho, 1975), 115.

5. Richie, *The Films of Akira Kurosawa,* 179.

6. Tadao Sato, *Nihon Elga Shisoshi* (Tokyo: Sanichi Shobo, 1970), 324.

7. Sato states that Utopia, for Kurosawa, is a society wherein human beings, freed from the bondage of social and political organizations, are united in such affection as is found among parents and their children, friends, or teachers and their disciples. A protagonist Kurosawa frequently chooses is a scientist as in *Being Quiet (Shizuka Nari)* and *The Snow (Yuki)*; a sportsman as in *Sanshiro Sugata*; or a medical doctor as in *Drunken Angel (Yoidore Tenshi), The Quiet Duel (Shizukanaru Ketto),* and *Red Beard (Akahige).* He selects such a protagonist because in these professions, individuals, to a certain extent, pursue what they want to do, without obeying orders. See Sato, *Kurosawa Akira no Sekai,* 243–44.

Dodeskaden

PHILIP STRICK

A KUROSAWA film without its scowling superhuman seems a contradiction in terms, but *Dodeskaden,* Kurosawa's first production for the new company he shares with Ichikawa, Kobayashi, and Kinoshita, deals with a shanty-town society in which leadership is unknown. The chaos that once was kept in check by Mifune's glare is now the dominant environment, an all-too-tangible thicket of rubbish that encloses a mob of wretches with nothing but their small store of courage to keep them going. Kurosawa examines these tiny sparks of heroism through a collection of intermittent biographies: the young tram-driver daily going the rounds in his invisible vehicle, the exhausted girl struggling to keep house for her drunken stepfather, the sepulchral zombie with a face of inexpressible sorrow who padlocks his shack as if to protect a fortune, the ageing tramp who entertains his son with elaborate descriptions of a palatial house being built for them both, and the lame little businessman with a nervous tic that periodically halts him in his tracks for a programme of appalling convulsions. Emphasising the classicism of this narrative structure is the crowd of nattering women at the local pump, whose contorted expressions, mirroring every mood from horror to prurience, follow the pattern set by a long line of Kurosawa's peasant commentators.

Rubbish dumps are much overworked symbols, and it is accordingly with some misgivings that one ventures into Kurosawa's garbage world. Despite his own previous expedition into the lower depths, however, Kurosawa comes upon the territory as if it had never been charted before, with an inventive and engaging enthusiasm accounted for, perhaps, by the fact that this is his first colour film (discounting a plume of smoke in *High and Low*). That his use of colour is naturalistic for much of the time makes his departure into surrealistic shades for points of crisis all the more effective. As delirium overtakes a couple of sufferers from food-poisoning, there is an oppressive glare of reds and greens through the skeletal mounds of refuse, themselves become theatrically insubstantial in the height of fever. Such a departure from strict naturalism in the application of color is of course nothing new to Japanese cinema, but it adds a genuinely disturbing dimension to Kurosawa's parable; that the fantastic should be added to his study of fantasies, further embroidered by the livid emerald and blue faces of his suf-

Reprinted from *Sight and Sound* 40, no. 1 (Winter 1970–1971): 18, by permission.

ferers, seems an indulgence both acceptable and, by the time it has reached its most extreme form, curiously logical.

At the other end of the spectrum, Kurosawa turns colour into comedy with the running joke of the two drunks who can only identify their houses and their wives by the prevailing hues of the decor. The settings of *Dodeskaden,* for all their simplicity, are indeed the most striking that Kurosawa has used; colour seems to have brought out the more strongly his feeling for contrasting textures, while he has some remarkable long-shots in which tiny figures are isolated against the sweep of a long low barrier marking the boundary of the slums. His unworried intermingling of lurid studio shots with the daylight locations beside Tokyo Bay implies a confidence in his audience that is appropriately reminiscent of John Ford's similar challenge in *Seven Women*. Like the dagger in *Rashomon* or the bridge in *High and Low,* Kurosawa's symbols have always enjoyed several layers of interpretation, but *Dodeskaden* is possibly his first film in which the surfaces are so brittle and the inferences so deep.

The Chorus aside, each of the units in the film provides a different perspective on the complexities of loyalty. The interdependence of the tram-driver and his mother, both staunchly preserving the illusion of his vital duties and each secretly worrying about the other's well-being, is illustrated in more extreme form by the tramp with his endless house-building tales sweetly and tolerantly endured by the small boy who forages for them, falls ill and dies, and is buried in a tiny white carton. In both cases we are involved in their fantasies: we hear the tram-car, and we see the bizarre architecture of the house. By contrast, a more delicate, Ozu-like manner is used for the tale of the girl who tries to kill a delivery-boy rather than reveal that her drone-like guardian has raped her. The most tragic sequences, in which Kurosawa once again celebrates Dostoevsky, reveal the betrayal of the man with the haunted face by his now repentant wife and her desolate discovery that the shock proved fatal.

Slightly outside the pattern is the community's elder statesman, a gentle cousin of the omniscient Mifune, who acts as father confessor to the neighbourhood miscreants and floors them by taking their exploits seriously. Visited by a burglar, he is at pains to hand over all the money in the house; a would-be suicide is cured by the prompt gift of poison, while a lout swinging his sword at passers-by in the rain is stunningly silenced by the old man's sympathetic offer to change places with him. The role would fit Kurosawa himself, in that it places the other characters' dreams in their context; more importantly, it is a role which, like the closing shot of the film in which colours play across innumerable paintings of crowded tram-cars, recognises its own impotence when confronted by a daily infinity of pathetic masquerades.

Kagemusha

MARSHA KINDER

*K*AGEMUSHA *(The Shadow Warrior)*, Akira Kurosawa's six-million-dollar epic on sixteenth-century Japan, is being widely acclaimed for its historical accuracy, dazzling visual beauty, and exciting battle scenes. From some accounts one would expect an ordinary genre film, only more expensively mounted, more expertly crafted, and on a more colossal scale. Yet not since Jancsó's *The Red and the White* has there been a period war film that is so conceptually bold. The film focuses not on action as one would expect, but on the process of signification—the crucial role played by the selection and interpretation of signs in shaping the course of history and in creating a work of art.

The opening sequence introduces, not only the main characters and situation through dramatic exposition, but also the semiotic subtext through its brilliant *mise en scène.* Positioned in the center of the screen and facing the camera. Shingen Takeda, the Lord of Kai, sits on a raised platform under an insignia, presumably a symbol of his clan. His position both in the room and in the frame signifies his importance. Although two other men are present, both dressed exactly like Shingen, only the Lord casts a shadow. The signified, surrounded by four signifiers: a symbolic insignia, an indexical shadow, and two human icons who function as doubles. (Charles Peirce distinguishes three categories of signs: *indexical,* a sign in which meaning is based on an existential bond between the signifier and the signified; *iconic,* a sign that represents its object mainly by physical resemblance; and *symbolic,* a sign that is arbitrary and coded.)

The human doubles in this scene are more ambiguous than the other signs. We learn from the dialogue that one is Shingen's younger brother Nobukado, who is indexically bound by blood and who has been functioning as the Lord's double in battle; we see that he is also iconically linked by physical resemblance and that he too sits on the dais on the right side of Shingen, also facing the camera. The alternate double is Kagemusha, a thief, who is now being presented to Lord Shingen by Nobukado as an interpretant, or replacement for both of them; he humbly sits across from the brothers on the floor with his back to the camera. Within the narrative, Kagemusha is the icon who, after the death of Shingen, emerges as the film's protagonist, fulfilling the Lord's goals, deceiving his enemies, and unifying

Reprinted from *Film Quarterly* 34, no. 2 (Winter 1980-1981): 44–48 by permission. Copyright © 1980 by the Regents of the University of California.

the clan. The plot affirms that the hero is an icon and that this is the primary source of his power both in the context of human history and in any dramatic narrative. From a more self-reflexive perspective on the film, we realize that the roles of Lord Shingen and Kagemusha are both being represented by the same actor, Tatsuya Nakadai, which establishes an indexical bond between them: we might even wonder whether an additional stand-in is being used in this scene for one of Nakadai's roles. Conversely, the alleged brother Nobukado, who is played by Tsutomu Yamazaki and whose blood relationship is a fiction within the text, is merely an icon. This scene demonstrates that the filmmaker, whose medium combines all three categories of signification, is able to play with his signs—selecting, coding, and manipulating the interpretations of his viewers. This gives him an extraordinary power—one that is analogous to the power of an historical leader like Lord Shingen, who also understands these processes of signification in directing human events.

This focus on signification is maintained throughout the film and developed with great richness and variation on both the visual and audio tracks, and through the unusual development of the narrative. In the sequence following the titles, our eyes and ears are directed toward an anonymous messenger, who moves like an arrow from exterior shots to interiors, noisily rushing through silent halls filled with sleeping soldiers, who follow his vigorous movements like a passive audience. The tracking shot accentuates his purposeful motion; both he and the camera urgently seek out the leaders of the clan, who will interpret the news. Instead of opening with the siege of the enemy castle, Kurosawa devotes his first action footage to the process of delivering and decoding a message. This narrative strategy signals that in *Kagemusha* this process will be the primary focus of the action.

This same emphasis also occurs in the death of Lord Shingen. From dramatic exposition we learn that the Takeda clan is laying siege to an enemy castle; the outcome of both the battle and the sequence at first seems to focus on whether the castle will fall. The dialogue informs us that each night someone within the castle plays a flute with great artistry, signifying the power to maintain spirit and control in the face of danger. Assuming that his opponent also knows how to manipulate signs, Shingen comes to believe that if the flute is played again tonight, the castle will not fall. Just as Shingen has his army listen for the flute, Kurosawa directs his audience to focus on the sound track. After a few anxious moments we hear the expected melody, confirming that the castle will not fall, but then we also hear the unexpected—a gunshot ringing out in the darkness. This sign shifts the attention of both the combatants and the audience to the most significant question in the film—is Lord Shingen dead or wounded? The direction in how to listen to the sound track is not limited to this one scene, for throughout the film Kurosawa relies very heavily on audio signs, not only for their traditional functions of accentuating physical gestures and creating emotional tonalities, but also to advance the narrative line and resolve dramatic conflicts.

After being introduced by a sound, the question of Shingen's condition is answered by conflicting visual signs. We see him on horseback, parading before his troops—a sight that heartens his men, and confuses and frightens his enemies. We in the audience soon surmise that this is the debut performance of the Shadow Warrior, an interpretation which may lead us to conclude (prematurely) that the real Lord is dead. In fact, the figure is still Tatsuya Nakadai, who is neither dead nor wounded. We are reminded of the illusion and artifice both in the story and the medium by the dazzling *mise en scène*. We see the Shadow Warrior, garbed in historically accurate costume, posed against an expressionistic red sky that looks like a rear-projection or painted backdrop. In another shot, a line of samurai with spears pass ceremoniously before a setting sun in the background, creating a human shutter that beams dramatic spokes of light toward the dark silhouette of the Lord in the foreground, as if he were the center of the cosmos. These dramatic visual effects remind us that film is a medium of light and shadow, creating an illusion of motion out of still images.

These illusory scenes are followed by visual demonstrations of Shingen's wounds and eventual death, yet these scenes rely heavily on rhetorical ellipses and cultural codes. As if in a courtroom, we are presented with a scene that indicates precisely how the sniper arranged to shoot Shingen in the dark. At the supposed moment of death, we see the Lord, sallow faced and feeble, rising from his sedan chair and then collapsing: a doctor reads his pulse, drops his hand, and we conclude the Lord is dead. Just as the medical profession has coded the signs of life, the cinematic medium has coded the signs of death. Later we see a large majestic vase being carried in a small boat across a placid lake shrouded in mist. This action is observed both by the generals of the Takeda Clan and by enemy spies, a fact which focuses our attention on interpretation. When the boat re-emerges from the mist, we see that it is empty and conclude with the other observers that the urn carrying Shingen's body has been thrown into the lake. To subvert this reading of the signs, the generals issue a public proclamation reinterpreting the event as a clan ritual. Despite the fact that we have never seen Shingen's corpse, we reject this explanation as a deceptive move to mislead the rival clans. Yet the generals have been no more deceptive or manipulative than Kurosawa, who demonstrates how minimal signs can be the basis of certainty about historical matters of life and death. Were there any fewer ellipses in the signs concerning the deaths of John F. Kennedy, Malcolm X. Martin Luther King, Jesus Christ, or any other iconic hero from the past? Will we ever know for certain who killed Kennedy or what really happened in Vietnam, or in any other war? We experienced these historical events through verbal and visual signs that were filtered through our cultural institutions and mass media. *Kagemusha* suggests that all historical accounts, including a samurai saga, are based on the reading of signs.

This idea is developed in the climactic battle sequence, which Kurosawa handles in an extremely bold way. Despite the fact that this is the most expensive Japanese epic ever made, he shows amazing restraint in depicting actual violence, particularly in contrast to his earlier period pieces. Although some of his previous samurai films, such as *Yojimbo* and *Throne of Blood,* also emphasize the reading of signs and alternate between action and interpretation, they still contain many graphic scenes of violence.[1] For the first time in *Kagemusha.* Kurosawa seems to be exploring how little can be shown of a battle while still having it signify what happens with great emotional impact.[2] His choices are stylized and effective; they evoke the Japanese aesthetic of minimalism and understatement. The single resonant image as in haiku. The single physical gesture punctuated by stillness as in Kabuki theater. Before the battle, we are explicitly told that the Takeda generals must know what the moves of the enemy mean, but by the time they interpret the signs it may be too late to act. We are also told the enemy's strategy—to first shoot the horses since traditionally the Takeda Clan have not been able to fight on foot. We also learn that the Takeda Clan intend to change their strategy—for the first time Lord Shingen or his icon will *not* be seated behind them, like a mountain, embodying their traditional stability: for the first time they will be led by his son who will take the offense. This advanced information provides a context that shapes, not only the way each side reads the moves of its opponents, but also the way the audience watches and interprets the minimal signs of battle. The camera pans across a line of soldiers firing sequentially through slatted beams, evoking the earlier scene at the debut of the Shadow Warrior. As we hear the violent sounds of war, we scan the faces of the generals and of the thief Kagemusha who are observing the battle, reading defeat in their grimaces and in their eyes. When we actually see the battlefield, the war is over. We perceive only the bloody aftermath—the corpses twisted into contorted postures, the twitching hooves of dying horses. The final image is of Kagemusha being mortally wounded and running toward the lake where Lord Shingen was earlier buried; the corpse of the Shadow Warrior floats on the water, drifting toward the banner of the Takeda Clan. The icon and the symbol are united and manifest on the surface, while the original lies latent in the depths below.

It is significant that the final image is of Kagemusha. Although we had earlier been told, "When the original is dead, the double has no meaning," the Shadow Warrior has been permanently transformed by his identification with Shingen. The Lord has become part of his living memory, altering his values, consciousness, and behavior, and appearing as a vivid image in his dreams. This transformation is dramatized quite wittily in one scene where Kagemusha sits before an audience who is aware of his disguise, imitating Shingen's gesture of stroking his mustache, winking at his acting coach

Nobukado, and evoking tears and looks of astonishment in his admiring observers. We in the film audience simultaneously judge his performance; but since we are aware of the double deception, we realize that Nakadai is merely impersonating himself. The self-reflexiveness of his performance is underscored by the inclusion of a brief inset theater scene and by the line that accompanies the discovery of his true identity. "The play is over!"

Just as Freud suggested that jokes frequently are based on the same latent content as child's play, fantasies, and dreams, we find that one of the few jokes in *Kagemusha* reveals the same semiotic subtext. Before the Shadow Warrior first arrives at the Lord's castle where his performance will receive its second major test, two attendants literally try to clear the path of all signs of previous traffic, but keep marking the surface with their own footprints. The humor depends on the futility of trying to erase the signs of one's own identity and past experience—a premise that foreshadows the ultimate failure of Kagemusha's impersonation.

It is precisely when Kagemusha is forced to resume his persona as thief that Shingen's influence on him receives its harshest test. We see that the Shadow Warrior has internalized the role: he has grown to love the heir; has come to feel a fierce loyalty to the clan, even though its members now reject him; and no longer wants to renounce his identification with the Lord. In the climatic battle that follows, he is even willing to sacrifice his life. The Shadow has become a man of substance; the iconic bond has grown indexical. Kagemusha dies serving his Lord, and in this sense Shingen's spirit is still alive within him, giving his final action meaning. From this perspective, the entire film could be read as religious allegory, which would lead us to assign new significance to certain details—e.g., Kagemusha had been saved from crucifixion to embody the Lord; in an earlier battle when representing the symbolic role of the Mountain, he was told, "Stand still as if you were crucified."

Lord Shingen's life-after-death is evoked, not only in religious terms, but also on the more general level of human civilization. It is the creation and manipulation of signs that has allowed humans to transcend the mortality of the individual, to pass on what they know to the next generation, and to insure the survival of the species. Even after his death, Lord Shingen's will directs the destiny of the clan, for it is woven into the cultural tradition and is respected by the generals who support the power of his icon. While the clan shows respect for Nature, they always transform it into symbols. For example, the four main armies are named after natural forces that represent change (Fire and Wind) and stability (Forest and Mountain). Such a heavy reliance on signs leads to the valuing of learning over instinct, culture over nature—choices that distinguish humans from other animals. Carl Sagan speculates in *Dragons of Eden:* "Much of the history of life since the carboniferous Period can be described as the gradual (and certainly incomplete) dominance of brains over genes."[3] The film dramatizes this shift in dominance. Kagemusha is accepted as icon by everyone—with two exceptions. Only Lord Shingen's horse and his young grandson/heir instinctively know he's an impostor. The horse remains committed to his instincts and ultimately reveals the deception, but the child is programmed to reinterpret his intuition: he concludes that he no longer fears his grandfather, attributing the difference to his own human potential for learning and maturation. Shingen's enemies, the Lords of the two rival clans, exhibit the same tendencies. Both instinctively "feel" Shingen is dead, yet they reinterpret this feeling as their own strong desire for his death. In other words, they see it as a wish fulfillment, as if they were interpreting a dream. When one of the Lords finally learns that Shingen has been dead for three years, he performs a strange ritualistic dance, chanting "Life is a dream, a vision." As in the case of the grandson, their interpretation is not wrong; it is merely partial. Like dreams, these intuitive signs in humans are overdetermined. The evolutionary development in mammals of dreaming sleep helped to further the dominance of brains over genes. As the dreaming mechanisms grew increasingly complex in humans, the brain developed new ways of processing sensory images from the past and generating new combinations of signs for directing the future.

Both the human power of interpreting signs and the surviving influence of Lord Shingen are vividly demonstrated in Kagemusha's nightmare. It occurs shortly after Shingen's death and while Kagemusha is still resisting his role as double. In the dream we see Kagemusha against a vivid multicolored sky, walking through stylized waves whose substance is dust rather than water. Suddenly Lord Shingen materializes, and Kagemusha rushes back and forth in desperation. The final image is a close-up of Kagemusha's feet submerged in water. When he awakens from the nightmare, he says: "I was surrounded by thousands of enemies." Although we did not see any enemies in the dream, we conclude that he sensed their presence and that's why he was running. At this point in the film, we might see the nightmare as a reflection of his debut performance as Shadow Warrior, in which he was surrounded by soldiers; the expressionistic visuals link the two sequences. Such an interpretation might lead us to conclude that Lord Shingen has now become Kagemusha's Shadow. By the time we reach the end of the film, we realize the dream was prophetic. Both the visual images and the verbal commentary foreshadow the climactic battle in which Kagemusha is surrounded by thousands of enemies, and in which he joins his Lord in a watery grave. The prophetic nature of the dream is also underlined by the mysterious rainbow that appears in the sky just before the battle. Not only does it evoke the multicolored sky in Kagemusha's nightmare, but the Takeda Clan generals explicitly interpret it as a sign of Lord Shingen's presence and as a warning against their offensive strategy. Just as the scene with the flute taught us how to listen to the sound track, this rainbow scene instructs us in how to interpret expressionistic colors and lighting effects throughout the rest of the film. It may lead us to reinterpret Lord Shingen's role in the night-mare—not merely as Kagemusha's Shadow or as a prophecy of the Shadow Warrior's coming death, but to indicate the survival of the Lord's spirit and his continuing influence over the way his clan interprets human experience. One instinctively feels, if only Kagemusha had understood the dream, per-haps he could have prevented the defeat of the Takeda Clan. But then we recall the words of the generals on the eve of battle: "By the time we inter-pret the moves of the enemy, it may be too late to act."

The same may be true of dreams. Yet unlike battles, dreams contain only the images of action, not the actions themselves. The same is true of both movies and history. *Kagemusha* emphasizes this distinction, for it is an his-torical reconstruction that foregrounds not even the *images of actions,* but the human process of interpreting them.

Notes

1   For a discussion of this pattern in *Throne of Blood,* see my article "*Throne of Blood*: a Morality Dance," *Literature/Film Quarterly* 5 (1977): 339–45.

2.   I realize I am taking a risk in making this claim since 20 minutes have been cut from the American version of the film and I have not seen the original.

3.   Carl Sagan, *Dragons of Eden* (New York: Ballantine, 1978), 49.

The Double and the Theme of Selflessness in *Kagemusha*

FRANCES M. MALPEZZI AND WILLIAM M. CLEMENTS

I N *Something Like an Autobiography,* which covers his childhood, youth, and early professional career, Japanese filmmaker Akira Kurosawa writes:

> I like unformed characters. This may be because, no matter how old I get, I am still unformed myself; in any case, it is in watching someone unformed enter the path to perfection that my fascination knows no bounds. For this reason, beginners often appear as main characters in my films. . . . Now, when I say I like unformed people, I don't mean I'm interested in someone who even if polished will not become a jewel. (129–130).

Though he is thinking particularly of characters in his first film, *Sanshiro Sugata* (1943), this statement relates to other Kurosawa characters. Most certainly it pertains to the nameless thief who serves as protagonist of *Kagemusha.* An action film set in the disintegrating feudal society of sixteenth-century Japan, *Kagemusha* centers thematically on character formation, for the protagonist's growth into a social role that has been defined for him provides the film's unifying focus. However, unlike many narratives of character formation, *Kagemusha* is not a tale of the awakening of individual identity. Instead, the thief's gradual dedication to a role that has been forced upon him ultimately destroys his individuality and replaces it with a wholehearted devotion to the social group.

Kagemusha opens on a council of the leaders of the Takeda clan, one of the rival factions struggling for political hegemony in Japan of the 1500s. Nobukado, younger brother of the clan leader Shingen, has conceived a plan for ensuring both ubiquity and immortality for his brother. He has located a petty thief, about to be crucified for his crimes, who bears a remarkable resemblance to Shingen. In fact, he is his exact double. Nobukado, another Shingen look-alike, has been doubling for his brother on occasions when it is efficacious for the clan leader to be in two places simultaneously. Shingen is intrigued by the thief's possibilities, for the criminal resembles him much more closely than his brother does. Moreover, the clan leader believes that his own presence is vital to the Takeda fortunes and would like a hedge against the disarray that might result should he die unexpectedly. His goals, to which he is willing to sacrifice even his own personal concerns, involve

Reprinted from *Literature/Film Quarterly* 17, no. 3 (1989): 202–6, by permission.

unification of Japan and an end to war and bloodshed. He shares this vision with his subordinates, and they view the thief as a potential tool for its realization. Shortly after encountering the thief, Shingen is wounded by a sniper while besieging an enemy's castle. He avers that if he lives, his immediate aim is to capture the city of Kyoto, but if he dies, his death must be concealed for three years while his troops consolidate their position. When the wound proves fatal, it becomes the thief's part to assume the clan leader's place, to submerge his own identity in the social role.

The film depicts the thief's assumption of the role as he struggles with self-doubts and with the tests he must pass to avoid exposure as an imposter. By treating the role of double from the thief's point of view, the film also provides a fresh perspective on what for Western viewers is a familiar narrative concept. Both ideas, that of character formation and that of the double, offer structures to Kurosawa upon which to develop what he perceives as the characteristic Japanese ethic—that of unselfishness. In his autobiography, Kurosawa remarks, "The Japanese see self-assertion as immoral and self-sacrifice as the sensible course to take in life"(146).

In John Millington Synge's *The Playboy of the Western World,* the protagonist, Christy Mahon, is mistakenly perceived as a heroic figure by the habitués of Michael Flaherty's pub in the west of Ireland. Really a meek, timid lad, Christy is far removed in character from the brawling, brawny figure he is assumed to be, at least at the beginning of the play. But before the action concludes, Christy becomes a heroic figure in reality, an athletic champion, a genuine playboy. He has grown into the role which others have defined for him. He has had "greatness thrust upon him." Like Christy, the thief in *Kagemusha* develops into an externally defined role. He too becomes great. But his greatness accords with the Japanese ethnic of unselfishness.

The thief's inner development, his journey toward the heroic and unselfish ideal, is more clearly delineated when it is seen in the context of three other characters in the film—Shingen, the clan leader; Nobukado, Shingen's brother; and Katsuyori, Shingen's son. Both Shingen and Nobukado as previous players of the thief's part have already characterized his role for him. Shingen as leader of the Takeda clan and Nobukado as his brother's double have sacrificed concerns of self to the part which they must play in the general clan welfare. The film's setting in a period of civil conflict, a bloody era of territorial consolidation in Japan, requires a special kind of selflessness. For example, Shingen has exiled and killed close relatives in order to reach his goals of national unity and cessation of warfare. For him, personal relationships become secondary to public responsibility. That his actions against his relations were not merely a move to attain personal power becomes clear from Shingen's willingness to entertain the idea of a double. His own personality is submerged in the social role, for he insists that the role and the goals which are associated with it must persist in an uninterrupted continuum even after his death.

Nobukado serves as a behavioral model for the thief; he has previously served as his lord's double and shares his values. Moreover, because he has been the double, he has insights into the difficulties of that role and compassion for the thief, recognizing, as the thief does not, both the problems of the role and the pain that will ensue with the inevitable cessation of the role. Reflecting on his own experience, Nobukado acknowledges that it is not easy to suppress one's self to become another. There were times he wanted to be himself and be free of the restraints of the role. But he recognizes the selfishness of that desire and quells it. For Nobukado the needs of society transcend those of the individual. Clearly he achieved oneness with the role he played, identity with his brother/lord; he asserts, "The shadow of a man can never desert that man." After his brother's death, after he no longer plays the role, he feels he is nothing. In repressing his own individuality, his need for freedom, his personal desires, Nobukado has sacrificed personal identity for his clan. He became his brother, internalized his goals, and assumed another identity for the social good. In relinquishing selfhood he exemplifies what Milton termed the "better fortitude/Of Patience and Heroic Martyrdom." We see, in him, the kind of hero the thief is on the way to becoming.

Katsuyori, on the other hand, is a foil for the thief. Because he consistently places self above the group, he eventually brings about the downfall of the Takeda Clan. Katsuyori so resents his father, so bristles at living in the shadow of the great man that we know he could never—like Nobukado and the thief—*be* his shadow. He wants to assert himself, to manifest *his* prowess, *his* greatness. In hiding Shingen's death, the clan leaders realize Katsuyori will be their biggest problem. Ambitious, envious, and petty, Katsuyori has never smiled since Shingen chose Katsuyori's son Takemaru as heir rather than him. As a victor in numerous battles, he feels the slight of being guardian and is revolted at having to call a thief his father. When the generals, respected warriors themselves, remind him they must also acknowledge a thief as their lord, they speak of the necessity of putting aside personal feelings because "we must all be united." The generals share Shingen's goals of unifying the country and ending bloodshed and are willing to put aside personal feelings and sacrifice their pride. Katsuyori is never able to accomplish this. After his father's death, he goes into battle on his own—without a clan conference and expressly against his father's dying words. Later when the thief as double is exposed, Katsuyori assumes control of the entire clan and again leads the men into battle. When the generals interpret a rainbow as a sign from his late father reminding him of his instructions not to attack, but to stay and guard the domain, Katsuyori disregards them and pridefully leads the troops into what Shingen before his death prophesied as their doom.

The thief's development in the film is toward the ideal of unselfishness and social responsibility manifested in Shingen and Nobukado, his predecessors in the clan leader role, and antithetically exemplified by Katsuyori, his successor as clan leader. At the beginning of *Kagemusha,* the thief is about to die because of crimes committed against society. As a petty thief, he has habitually placed the needs and desires of self before even the slightest social concerns. The only motive for his entertaining the idea of becoming Shingen's double at this point is his selfish desire to escape execution. He does not share—has not even considered—the social goals articulated by the clan leader and his associates.

The thief's sense of responsibility beyond that to self begins to emerge only after Shingen's death, but even then his commitment wavers. He learns of the clan leader's death while engaging in his accustomed pursuit, thievery. The thief breaks into an enormous lacquered urn, expecting to find treasure, only to discover Shingen's body awaiting burial. His cries of fright summon Nobukado and other leaders of the clan, who confront the thief with the fact that he must begin playing Shingen's part immediately. He categorically refuses to do so, his social sense still in abeyance before his selfish concerns. Apparently defeated, Nobukado releases the thief and plans to bury Shingen's body in a secrecy that will continue until the clan leaders decide how to break the news of the lord's death to the clan. They transport the burial urn to fog-enshrouded Lake Suwa, where Shingen had wanted to be buried. As they lower the urn into the lake, spies from enemy clans observe the proceedings from the shelter of a ruined building. The spies, though, are observed by the thief, for he has followed the funeral party to its destination. When the spies depart with their news, the thief rushes to Nobukado to warn him. When he realizes that the enemy clans will learn of Shingen's death anyway shortly, the thief understands that the only way for the ideals of Shingen to survive requires his assumption of the double role. The thief's confrontation of the inevitability of his own mortality has served as an initial turning point in his character formation. The dead face, that of the dead king whom he resembles so much, which stares at him from the broken urn is his own face. Donald Richie notes that "having seen the reality of death of the lord, he now begins to understand that he can really be Shingen" (209). His sense of relationship with the person who is submerged in Lake Suwa influences the thief to submerge his own individuality. That individuality submerged, his social responsibility can emerge.

A second turning point for the thief occurs during the first battle in which Katsuyori rashly leads his troops. Though he has acted arrogantly and not sought clan approval, though his abrogation of authority jeopardizes the fiction that Shingen lives, the clan leaders feel compelled to send troops to protect him. The thief, in the role of Shingen, stands behind Katsuyori and his men in battle. Instructed by Nobukado not to move, the thief becomes Shingen's spirit, the immovable mountain (a Takeda clan symbol represented on their banner by a Chinese character) whose obdurate strength, constancy, and towering presence inspire the men and frighten the enemy. Katsuyori is incensed at the thief's presence at *his* battle. Though he knows the figure is the thief, he feels as if Shingen's image continues to haunt him and preside over him as it had in life. He is angered at being treated as a child, at being dominated by the greater warrior, his father. As the thief functions in this scene, he has become Shingen. He remains steadfast through the horrors of the battle, even as his bodyguards are killed about him. And his presence creates the same impact for Katsuyori, for the troops, and for the enemy that Shingen's actual presence would have. After the enemy retreat, after the Takeda clan return home, we see the thief has a new confidence in himself, that he behaves "as if the late lord were inside of him." In fact, he is so at one with his role that he undertakes to ride Shingen's horse, a beast that would tolerate no rider other than the lord himself. When the thief is thrown and Shingen's mistresses rush to assist him and check for injuries, they realize he does not have the scar Shingen had received in battle long ago. The imposter is unmasked.

However, it is when the disguise is gone, when the externals of his role are stripped away, that the thief most conforms to that role. Once again in the clothes of a thief, driven from the premises, the thief most exemplifies the essential characteristics of his lord. Unlike the thief of old, he is unconcerned with the money a servant conveys from Nobukado. He is no longer motivated by selfish interests. As Marsha Kinder in her review of the film has argued:

> It is precisely when Kagemusha is forced to resume his persona as thief that Shingen's influence on him receives its harshest test. We see that the Shadow Warrior has internalized the role; he has grown to love the heir; has come to feel a fierce loyalty to the clan, even though its members now reject him; and no longer wants to renounce his identification with the Lord. In the climactic battle that follows, he is even willing to sacrifice his life. The Shadow has become a man of substance. (47)

In that battle we see the sharp contrast between Katsuyori and the thief. When the imposter is exposed, Katsuyori makes the most of his opportunity and seizes the leadership of the Takeda Clan, determined that once more he will attack the enemy in defiance of his father's dying command. Nobunaga, the leader of a rival clan, pronounces their doom: "Takeda will be no more. The mountain has moved." Through the assertion of his personal desires for glory and ambition, Katsuyori places his own needs above the clan's and brings a bloody end to the social group. The thief, on the other hand, having watched the massacre of the Takeda Clan, grabs a spear and runs through the dead toward the enemy until he is shot. Bleeding, he falls into the water and his corpse floats by a partially submerged Takeda banner. This image captures the submerging of his individual identity by his sense of social responsibility. The thief is one with the clan even if it means his death, and he joins Shingen in a watery grave: The two are gone in the "final apotheosis of impersonator into lord" (Richie, 209). We see in Katsuyori the destructive nature of selfishness and in the thief the heroic ideal of unselfishness.

C. F. Keppler argues, "Every second-self story, so far as the first self is concerned is to one degree or another a story of shaping, a *Bildungsroman*" (195). Such is Kurosawa's *Kagemusha,* a narrative of character formation; however, the end product is singularly different from what we might expect in a Western tradition. As Claire Rosenfield notes, "the novelist who consciously or unconsciously exploits psychological Doubles may either juxtapose or duplicate two characters; the one representing the socially acceptable or conventional personality, the other externalizing the free, uninhibited, often criminal self" (314). In many fictional treatments of the double, the reader descends into the conventional personality to discover there the potential for evil, the criminal self which lurks within. Rosenfield comments: "In Conrad's *The Secret Sharer* and *Heart of Darkness,* a bodily Double is present whose outlaw freedom is evidence for the narrator and the reader that even the most rational man possesses a dual nature, that no man is above the threat of the irrational" (319). But in Kurosawa's *Kagemusha* we look into the criminal self and see there the potential for good as the thief transcends his petty and personal desires and places the needs of the social group above his own. The figure of the second self is usually but not always evil, as Keppler shows in his analysis of that entity as saviour (99–129). And it is this less conventional model—at least from a Western perspective—which Kurosawa's film approximates. When we look into the thief's heart of darkness, we find planted there the seed that grows and blossoms into the ideal, the ethic of selflessness which Shingen has demonstrated.

This signals another important difference in Kurosawa's treatment of the double. In twentieth-century Western fiction, as Rosenfield notes, the double usually signifies "the constant menace of personal disintegration which apparently threatens us all" (331). And David Desser suggests, "Even the temporary loss of one's actual identity... is a major trauma to the Western hero" (117). *Kagemusha,* however, is not concerned with the disintegration of self, but with the integration of the whole, the unifying of the social body. Loss of personal identity is not a threat or a menace here, but an ideal. Desser avers, "The thief in Kurosawa's Japanese film becomes admirable precisely for this ability to deny his true self and redefine it" (117). The real threat to the Takeda Clan is in Katsuyori's assertion of his own identity, his unwillingness to remain in the shadow of his father. Those who give over their identities to their social role—Shingen, Nobukado, and eventually the thief—are heroic exemplars. After he learns of Shingen's death, his enemy Nobunaga mourns that leader with a ritualized song and dance in which he comments on the evanescence, the transience of human life: "Life is but a dream, a vision, an illusion. Life, once given, cannot last forever." The song seems to underscore Kurosawa's theme in this narrative of character formation which challenges the traditional Western use of the double: The mutable, ephemeral individual must subordinate himself to the larger social group. When selflessness was the ruling ethic in the Takeda clan, the clan, like their ruler, possessed the endurance of the immovable mountain. When selfishness, through Katsuyori, took hold, the mountain crumbled to dust.

Works Cited

Desser, David. *The Samurai Films of Akira Kurosawa.* Ann Arbor: UMI Research Press, 1983.

Keppler, C. F. *The Literature of the Second Self.* Tucson: University of Arizona Press, 1972.

Kinder, Marsha. "Kagemusha." *Film Quarterly* 34, no. 2 (Winter 1980–1981): 44–48.

Kurosawa, Akira. *Something Like an Autobiography.* Trans. Audie E. Bock. New York: Alfred A. Knopf, 1982.

Richie, Donald. *The Films of Akira Kurosawa.* Revised edition, Berkeley: University of California Press, 1984.

Rosenfield, Claire. "The Shadow Within: The Conscious and Unconscious Use of the Double." *Stories of the Double.* Ed. Albert J. Guerard. Philadelphia: J. B. Lippincott, 1967.

[*Ran*]

JAN KOTT

M ADNESS AWAITS everyone at the close of that cold night. "These four are
already mad," wrote Camus about *King Lear.* "One is mad by profession, another by choice, and two from the suffering they could not bear."
The jester is mad by profession; Edgar, in order to save his life; Lear escapes
into madness; and Kent alone tries to fend it off to the very last. In the middle of the third act the three exiles find their last refuge from a raging nature
in the abject hut where Edgar had hidden himself earlier. This is the key
scene for every interpretation of *Lear* but even more so for a theatrical or
cinematic vision of the play.

In both the theatrical and film versions of Peter Brook's *King Lear,* a
Beckett-like dialogue between cripples takes place on the sack bedding in
the mud hut, and it is here that the madmen judge Goneril and Regan,
personified by two overturned wooden stools. In Grigori Kozintsev's film
adaptation of *King Lear,* some fifteen years ago, the abandoned hovel
where the exiled old man who was once king finds his last shelter teems
with human bodies. We see old men and women, cripples shaking their
stubby limbs, women nursing infants, and even a *yurodivy* ("God's fool"),
intoning unending litanies which mix with "poor Tom's" exorcisms. Sitting on rags, sacks, or the bare ground, they fill every corner, are packed
one on top of the other. In Kozintsev's dramaturgy, the exiles from the
royal court walk past "refugees" streaming into the steppe from razed set-
tlements and villages. In that enormous shack, the mad ruler and his subjects find themselves sharing a common Russian fate: poverty, degrada-
tion, and suffering.

In Kurosawa's *King Lear* it appears, for just an instant, that there is no
one in the abandoned hut when the former ruler, the Jester, and his last
servant finally reach it. But a strange figure glimmers in the darkness. By the
feeble light of a candle stub, the newcomers can make out hair falling over
someone's eyes. He turns out to be a blind man. Hidetora, the Japanese
Lear, recognizes the blind man as one whose life he did not take, but whose
eyes he put out. The blind man was allowed to keep only a flute and it is on
this flute that he now plays to Hidetora. Just as in those scenes in the kabuki

Reprinted from "The Edo Lear," trans. Lillian Vallee, *New York Review of Books,* 24 April
1986, 13–15. Reprinted with permission from *The New York Review of Books.* Copyright ©
1986 Nyrev, Inc. [Ed. note: In characterizing *Ran*'s historical setting, Kott has mistakenly
associated it with the Edo period (1603–1867) and he has identified the capital of the
shogunate as Kyoto (instead of Edo, now Tokyo). *Ran* is set in the Sengoku period of civil
wars (1467–1568), before the Edo era of rule.]

theater where the murderer returns to the scene of the crime, the flute wails over the orchestra, moans, rises in more and more penetrating tones, as if it were tearing not only at the ears but at the heart as well. The memory and reproach of the flute are unbearable. The Japanese Lear, exiled by the voice of the flute, flees the cottage and submits himself again to the storm and torrential rains.

When *Lear* is staged in the theater, the décor is always conventional, even in the most illusionistic scenic conception. In the film, the landscape is real, and of all the royal tragedies, *King Lear* is probably the one that most needs a real landscape. Yet the selection of landscape in *Lear* is, perhaps more than in any other play, simultaneously a selection of costume and historical time. In *King Lear* the question *where* is also the question *when.* What Mikhail Bakhtin called the chronotope, the unit of time and place, has a degree of concreteness different in film from that in theater. In Shakespeare's dramas, the other place—the other "historicity" outside Elizabethan England—gives, at the same time, the plays' other universality. And what is more, the place often supplies their other contemporary meanings.

Everyone, adapters as well as stage producers, has had to grapple with the historical setting of *King Lear.* The play has been transported to the time of Druids, with menhirs built on stage. There was even a production where Lear was ruler of the Aztecs. Peter Brook wanted to avoid a narrow historicity in both of his productions, the stage adaptation at Stratford in 1967 and the film version five years later. He placed his *Lear* somewhere in the epoch of William the Conqueror, but at the same time he veered away from historical verisimilitude. He dressed his actors in the simplest costumes: furs, boots, and long, voluminous robes. He wanted to suggest the severity and primacy of the Renaissance royal court while at the same time showing its sophistication and menace. Brook transported the film version into the cold landscape of Jutland. Kozintsev took his *Lear* into the Russian steppe—a Russian Orthodox priest presided at the wedding of the King of France and Cordelia.

Brook's Jutland and Kozintsev's broad Russian steppe were a way of introducing *Lear* into universal history. Kurosawa places the drama of *Lear* in sixteenth-century Japan. For the second time since *Throne of Blood,* his memorable adaptation of *Macbeth,* Kurosawa has discovered a new historical place for Shakespeare's royal dramas. In the Edo period, before the consolidation of the almost absolute power of the shogun in Kyoto, samurai clans, whose power depended on mercenary armies and the blind obedience of their vassals, devoted themselves to ravaging the land and killing one another. There are striking analogies between these wars and the Wars of the Roses in England or, perhaps even more, between the samurai wars and the fratricidal battles and unceasing betrayals of Scottish clans.

In Kurosawa's *Ran,* Hidetora, lord of a wooden fortress, has extended his rule to the limits of the horizon—all three castles, situated on distant hills and visible from the camp tent, now belong to him. In the twilight of his years, the cruel tyrant divides his kingdom. Among his sons, however, not his daughters.

Kurosawa's greatness lies in his capacity to reveal historical similarity and variance; to find a Shakespearean sense of doom in the other, remote, and apparently alien historical place. He trims the plot to the bone. Hidetora's three sons are all that remains of Lear's three daughters and Gloucester's two sons. Shakespeare added the second plot of Gloucester, Edgar, and Edmund to the old folk tale about three daughters (two vile and one noble). Kurosawa has cut and compressed it. In this Japanese condensation of plot and character, only the eldest son's wife, a substitute for Goneril and Regan, is left in the castle where Hidetora has murdered her entire family. In this samurai epic, it is her drive for vengeance that destroys Hidetora's clan and legacy.

In the first scene of *Ran,* the aged Hidetora dozes off before his tent in the noon sun. His youngest son cuts down three small trees and plants them next to his sleeping father to provide him with shade. This is how Cordelia's silent faithfulness is translated into the signs of another theater. In *Ran,* Goneril/Regan in one body grows to the dimensions of a new, forbidding Lady Macbeth, but her glassy, immobile, white face with uplifted brows is like the mask of the woman-vampire and woman-serpent in the Noh theater. In the only love scene, she becomes violent before she yields. Seizing a sword, she slashes at the face of Hidetora's second-born. He had murdered her husband, the eldest of the sons. Now he will become the instrument of her revenge. The long white sash of her kimono falls to the empty mat and slowly unwinds like a serpent. In the theater of kabuki, and in the Japanese custom which is still honored, the sash of the kimono thrown to the floor is a sign of sexual compliance. The concubine now demands the head of her lover's wife. A standard prop in Elizabethan theater was a head in a cage. In the kabuki a standard prop is a head wrapped in rags. In the Japanese *Lear,* the Goneril/Regan character unwraps just such a head. But it is not the head of her lover's wife, but the sculpted, stone head of an animal.

In Laurence Olivier's film version of *Richard III,* pages carry crowns, set on vermilion pillows, into the Coronation Hall. They trip on the stairs and the crowns, destined for the royal brothers, fall to the scarlet carpet. Twenty-five years have gone by and I remember only that one scene from the entire film. It has settled into my memory like Shakespeare's aphorisms, which are the essence of his dramas. In the language of film, that short scene with the falling crowns is also its essence. In Kozintsev's *Hamlet,* Ophelia is put into a rigid corset before she is led into the royal chambers. In Rome a few years ago I attended a large exhibit showing instruments of torture from the Middle Ages to our own century. I saw steel cages with spikes inside that were designed to dig into the flesh. Except for the spikes, Ophelia's corset was amazingly similar to that instrument of torture.

In the last scene of Kurosawa's *Throne of Blood,* Macbeth hangs from the walls bristling with arrows like an enormous dying porcupine. The farther the "other" setting in Shakespeare's dramas is from Elizabethan England, the less likely it is that the image will match the text. It stops being an illustration and becomes its essence and sign. In *Throne of Blood* and *Ran,* Shakespeare is moved not just into another cultural circle, but into another theater. And here lies Kurosawa's genius and the singularity of his Shakespeare. The theater he makes use of is, of course, classic Japanese theater: Noh and kabuki.

Noh is medieval theater and kabuki would be considered late Renaissance theater by our standards of chronology. But it is exactly here that we find amazing chronological surprises: the years around 1600, when Hamlet was first performed, mark the beginning of kabuki theater. But it is not chronology that is the most important. Of the two extreme choices at the disposal of a modern producer of Shakespeare's royal tragedies, that is, historicism and anachronism, faithfulness to history (but which history?) seems the most deceptive. The costume, of course, can be faithfully copied from a museum, but an actor—who is unfamiliar with the gestures of the ruler or the heir awaiting the falling crown—must know how to move in the trappings of another age. Even when the scene takes place in the bedchamber of the queen or concubine, the modern actor knows only the rudimentary sexual gestures that would have been used. Perhaps this is why modern film adaptations of *Macbeth* prefer to show Lady Macbeth in the nude.

It seems that the traditions of Japanese feudal culture have endured. The rituals of the conjugal bath, of flower arrangement, and of the tea ceremony are still rigidly observed. Of course they may simply be gestures and empty signs, but gestures and signs are the basic material of theater. Classic Japanese theater has preserved them, lent them an enduring form, and repeats them unchanged. The wife of Hidetora's eldest son and the concubine of his second-born bites at the hem of her kimono in an attack of furious weeping, just as the *bunraku* dolls and geishas in kabuki cry and bite the hems of their kimonos in fits of jealousy. But the Japanese theater has not only preserved the gestures and signs of amorous passion in family dramas, it has also preserved much else: the court ceremonies, the rituals of receiving vassals, the dispatch of envoys with secret letters, the acts of allegiance and betrayal. Just as in Shakespeare's royal tragedies the battles of entire armies are presented as pageant and action. On the stage of the kabuki, two great samurai armies, cavalry and infantry, are represented by four, maybe eight, warriors. They wear the same leather helmets and move in the same easy steps; they draw their bows and shoot with a simultaneous gesture. The two armies differ only in the color of the large streamers attached like wings to their shoulders.

Lear's three daughters, as I've said, are replaced by Hidetora's three sons. The theme is fratricidal war. The castle gates are rammed open. The red troops pour in like rivers of ants while the blues pour out in another stream. Nothing but arrow-studded bodies remain on the ramparts and turrets of the castle, nothing but bodies are left speared to the floor. Kurosawa is a peerless master of battle scenes. Even the cruelest of them makes you gasp in amazement. They are a vision of the apocalypse rendered with the highest artistic perfection.

The enormous castle constructed of wooden beams that Hidetora had attacked and conquered years ago, the castle in which he murdered every last man, is now set afire. Hidetora remains in it alone. His guards have been shot or speared. The bodies of concubines, who ran themselves through with daggers, litter the floor of the neighboring room. Flames approach the throne where Hidetora sits. He runs to the roof of the fortress where he sees the fields covered with his son's armies. Hidetora runs down into the courtyard. The soldiers step aside for the old man who runs like a ghost out of the flames. The son takes out his sword. But neither he nor his generals have the heart to kill the old man.

Hidetora steps out through the gates of the fortress into the green fields. His last journey leads him through these green hills and fields. The faithful exile and the Jester, the two nurses of the madman, will serve him until his death. The Jester puts a crown of reeds on his head. Hidetora crawls through the rushes like a large child, on all fours, picking flowers. The two armies, the red and the black, occupy their starting positions on opposing hillsides.

From then on, everything happens as in Shakespeare. Except that the youngest of his sons, not Cordelia, finds Hidetora. But briefly. The youngest son dies in an ambush arranged by his older brother. And, as in Shakespeare, the Japanese Lear dies holding the expiring body in his arms. "As flies to wanton boys are we to th' gods; / They kill us for their sport." The lines uttered by Gloucester at the height of his experience are spoken by Kurosawa's jester.

A few years ago during a break at a conference on Shakespeare, I asked two of my colleagues, "Who succeeds Lear?" "The Duke of Albany is still one of the titles of English kings," said the first colleague, "and it is clear to every civilized Englishman that Goneril's husband, the Duke of Albany, would inherit the throne after Lear." "Even my grad students," said my Italian colleague, "who have just scanned Aristotle, think it obvious that noble Edgar must succeed Lear, in keeping with the logic of a tragedy." "Every Pole," I said, "in keeping with his personal and historical experience, is certain that no one will succeed Lear. The world in which Lear lived has been torn asunder and it will never grow back together again."

"Ran" means "fury," "revolt," "madness" in Japanese. In the last scene, a blind man feels his way along the threshold of the gutted castle to the edge of a precipice. In fleeing the assassins, he has left his flute behind. His sister goes back to find his flute, leaving him meanwhile with a roll of parchment on which appears a picture of the Buddha. Kurosawa understood that in the architectonics of *Lear,* even in the most remote adaptation, Cordelia's place could not remain completely vacant. The eyes of this Buddhist brother of Cordelia have been put out. Hidetora orders the rest of her family murdered. Later Hidetora marries her off to his middle son. She alone does not hate. But perhaps in the broader perspective in which nothing at all survives, pity and hate are equal.

Yet not even she is left alive. When she returns for the flute her head is cut off. The wife of Hidetora's eldest son, who had asked for her head, is also dead. Hidetora himself is dead, as are all his sons. The blind man feels his way to the edge of the abyss. The parchment falls from his hands and unrolls over the bluff where the wind gently rocks the likeness of the smiling Buddha. The sky is light blue, streaked with gentle, slow-moving clouds. The blue sky is completely empty.

This is also the color of the winter sky in Santa Monica, where I now live. Some miles southeast of Santa Monica, in Irvine, the sky is perhaps even bluer. Coral trees bloom bright red and give off a strong fragrance even in February. The Irvine campus is one of the largest in the United States. It seems to be empty, because it is part of an enormous garden, almost a forest, and the campus stretches imperceptibly into the desert. There at the edge of the campus, Jerzy Grotowski has a wooden shack that houses the last of his theater-laboratories. The shack is empty, furnished only with a torn drum. Next to the shack Grotowski has built a Siberian yurt or hut out of a light, still fragrant wood. The floor in the yurt is waxed, and those entering it remove their shoes. The yurt is also bare except for a crude table that stands against one wall.

Grotowski's "Poor Theater" has not existed for years. Three of the actors have died, all the others—actors, co-workers, and students—are scattered throughout the world. Behind the yurt stretches a green meadow, where horses graze as if in a painting by Gauguin. Beyond that is the desert. At night, coyotes come as close as Grotowski's yurt. At noon, when the sun is hottest, you can hear the clattering whir of rattlesnakes.

Ran and the Tragedy of History

BRIAN PARKER

Fourteen years ago, at the first World Shakespeare Congress in Vancouver, I invited the Russian director Grigori Kozintsev to speak for a panel I was organizing on "Shakespeare in Modern Production." He gave a fine talk on the creative thinking behind his films of *Hamlet* and *King Lear,* and, as a bonus, brought with him the first copy of his *Lear* film to be seen outside Russia, the screening of which brought the members of the Congress to their feet applauding. I mention this not out of vainglory but because at the same time I tried to invite Akira Kurosawa but could not manage to contact him. When I mentioned this to Kozintsev, his reply was: "What a pity! He was staying with me and would have loved to come." Kozintsev was also a personal friend of Peter Brook, the English stage and screen director; and it is these three men who have made the most interesting modern film versions of *King Lear.* A brief comparison of their approaches can illuminate Kurosawa's unique achievement in *Ran.*

I

In both Kozintzev's books, *Shakespeare: Time and Conscience* (1966) and (especially) *King Lear: The Space of Tragedy* (1977), there is very generous praise for Peter Brook's stage version of the play; and earlier, in a 1967 article in *Sight and Sound,* Brook was equally laudatory about Kozintsev's film of *Hamlet.* The two men discussed the problem of filming *King Lear* at a meeting in Paris in 1967, began to shoot it simultaneously, the one in Northern Jutland, the other in the Crimea, and exchanged very interesting letters about their theories and experiences, some of which Kozintsev has reprinted in his *Lear* book.

They agreed that, in translating the play to the medium of film, it was not their job just to illustrate the text but to find visual equivalents for its highly metaphoric language. This concern focused first of all in a common desire to find a non-specific location for their films, full enough of precise detail to be imaginatively convincing but not based on any particular historical place or period. They also agreed that colour was totally inappropriate for *King Lear;* only black and white could avoid a vulgar interest in verisimilitude and convey the play's great moral and emotional extremes: "I do not know what colour grief is," writes Kozintsev, "or what shades suffering has."[1] Setting, they agreed, must be a universal "country of the mind"; so both rejected any

Reprinted from *University of Toronto Quarterly* 55, no. 4 (Summer 1986): 412–23. Copyright © 1986 University of Toronto Press. Reprinted by permission of University of Toronto Press.

interest in either historical authenticity or décor that was visually attractive in its own right.

They also agreed on the importance of close-up shots to capture what Brook would no doubt have called the "psychological" and Kozintsev the "spiritual" heart of the play. The advantage of film, says Kozintsev (echoing Pudovkin), is not that it enables you to bring on real horses but that you can look into a man's soul through his eyes. Kozintsev thought Brook overemphasized close-ups, however, and pointed out that the facial intensity of a silent film such as Dreyer's *Jeanne d'Arc* (which Brook was citing as his model) depended on having no dialogue: with sound a much greater variety of distance is required, and in *King Lear* particularly the hero's subjective experience needs to be "placed" within wider social and natural contexts.

Each also agreed that the storm should not be treated in a spectacularly literal way because it is Lear's reaction to the storm rather than the weather itself that the director should try to convey; but they went about this in rather different fashions. For Kozintsev, the heart of the storm was Lear's experience in Poor Tom's hovel, where he is represented as just one among many hapless "naked wretches" whose misery he had ignored as king. Brook, on the other hand, in his search for a visual equivalent of the multi-valency of Shakespeare's language—its ability to say many things simultaneously at different levels—used the storm to show Lear's mental breakdown, mingling factual images and phantasmagoric horrors in the flashes of lightning, with distorted, displaced, and overlaid images, and frames that were completely white or black.

This difference reflected their polarized interpretations of the play. Brook, under the influence of Jan Kott, saw *King Lear* as a play about absurdist despair whose central scene was the Beckett-like encounter between the blind Gloucester and the mad, Tolstoyan Lear in the leached-out, stony emptiness of Dover beach; Kozintsev, on the other hand, saw it as a Christian-Marxist parable about the retribution that follows irresponsible government, which nevertheless cannot stifle family love or the resilience of human nature. For him the episode of the reconciled Lear and Cordelia going uncowed to prison was the key scene of the play, and at the end, says Kozintsev, "Life—a none too easy one—goes on."[2] Between them, the two interpretations set up a dialectic between negative and positive that seemed to cover the whole critical response to *King Lear* as a tragedy, leaving precious little that was new for any subsequent director to say. Something they did not cover, however, was the fact that in its original quarto editions as well as in a 1607 entry in the Stationers' Register *King Lear* was described not as a tragedy but as a chronicle history; and it is here that Kurosawa's interpretation, *Ran* (Chaos), comes in.

Both Brook and Kozintsev praised Kurosawa's version of *Macbeth, The Throne of Blood* (to give its English title), as the best Shakespeare film so far made; both expressed keen interest in the lyrical compression, symbolism, and subtlety of Noh drama, which has always been a major influence on Kurosawa; and Kozintsev's second chapter in *King Lear: The Space of Tragedy* is an account of his visit to Japan while planning his film, and his reactions to Zen-inspired art and the Noh play in particular. But the irony is that this film-maker whom they praised so much and were so eager to learn from contra-dicts in *Ran* all the principles they had agreed on for the filming of *King Lear*.

Technically, for example, Kurosawa opposes close-ups and favours long shots. Far from letting you look into a character's soul, he argues, close-ups merely encourage an actor to be lazy and not to act with his whole body, and without such total commitment the representation will, in fact, lack soul; moreover, close-ups would expose the elaborate makeup of his Lear-character, Hidetora; and, most important of all, long shots flatten char-acter so that a Noh-like objective aloofness is maintained, in the same way that Noh masks impose a surrender of subjectivism upon the actors wearing them. The characters of *Ran* are less concerned with intrinsic identity, with "Who is it can tell me what I am?" than with their positions in society.

Similarly, whereas Kozintsev insisted that the décor and costumes of his *Lear* film must not themselves be attractive, Kurosawa states firmly that "What is of prime importance is the quality of the décor, of the objects or the beauty of the countryside in which the film is shot,"[3] and, in opposition to Brook's concern for self-conscious camera-work (metacinema), he insists that the camera must *not* draw attention to itself, because "Beauty comes from what is filmed, not how."[4] Thus, instead of moving his cameras about independently of the actors, in *Ran* he goes so far as to stop all camera movement whenever the characters stop moving;[5] and editing each day's take immediately (as is his habit) enabled him to ensure smooth transitions for the seamless flow and dreamlike rhythm of Noh, rather than drawing attention to the joins with discontinuities, jump cuts, and odd camera angles as Brook strove so deliberately to do. In particular, Kurosawa often puts a shot of clouds between the major joins or uses the continued line of a ges-ture as a bridge across frames, techniques he may have learned from thir-teenth-century Japanese scroll painting.

Where Brook and Kozintsev eschew spectacle, Kurosawa revels in it. For example, in the two black-and-white films the battle scenes are marginally represented: as occasional small-scale skirmishing round the unconscious Lear's stretcher in Kozintsev, with burning buildings and refugees showing the effects of war rather than war itself; and in Brook even more abstractly as mere sounds heard by blind Gloucester, whose out-of-focus, listening face is all that can be seen. In Kurosawa, on the other hand, battles are fully repre-sented with enormous virtuosity of detail and a cast literally of thousands, not to speak of two hundred horses. And then, of course, there is his vivid and beautiful use of colour, which Brook and Kozintsev both thought inap-propriate for *Lear*. *Throne of Blood* was in black and white too, but this was not for theoretical or ideological reasons but merely because Kurosawa considered the colour process at that time (1957) not sensitive enough to record the range of colour he required. Kurosawa began his career as a painter, in fact, and goes to considerable trouble to paint elaborate colour sketches of his films as a guide to his designers and as a way of clarifying his own conceptions. Because of its ten-year production delay, he had time to make more than one hundred colour sketches for *Ran* in a vivid style reflecting his admiration for van Gogh, Lautrec, and Rouault, and portfolios of these sketches were distributed to all his co-workers on the project. He also designed, and even painted, many of the kimonos and some of the armour used in the film, and during the shooting enhanced their colours not only with gels but also by the use of coloured light reflectors. Colour is an essential part of the imagery of *Ran,* in fact, and, as in Noh drama, it is used as a notation for immediate symbolic effect.[6]

Because Kurosawa literally thinks in images (as he has said), he is very far from taking the reverential attitude to Shakespeare's language of Kozintsev and Brook. He complains that Shakespeare is always too wordy, and hazards the explanation that the original actors must have egotistically inflated their parts. He habitually writes his own scripts, in which characters speak only when they cannot communicate in other ways, and then in language that is terse and almost brutally functional; and, of course, he takes great liberties with the original: "I had no wish for a literal transposition," he says, "I looked mainly for a perspective."[7] In fact, he insists that *Ran's* relation to *King Lear* is really secondary: "I started out to make a film about Motonari Mori, the 16th-century warlord whose three sons are admired in Japan as paragons of filial virtue. What might their story be like, I wondered, if the sons had not been so good? It was only after I was well into writing the script about these imaginary unfilial sons of the Mori clan that the similarities to Lear occurred to me. Since my story is set in medieval Japan, the protagonist's children had to be men; to divide a realm among daughters would have been unthinkable."[8] This approach reminds one of Brecht in *The Messingkauf Dialogues,* who argues that if one is going to adapt, one must never merely tinker but be sure to change enough.

The non-Shakespearean influence also points to the most striking difference between Kurosawa and his two admirers. Whereas Brook and Kozintsev insist on an unlocalized time and place for *King Lear,* Kurosawa places *Ran* very firmly and precisely in the Japanese Middle Ages, a period towards the beginning of the sixteenth century when central government had utterly broken down and Japan was ravaged by the continual strife of war-lords—a period not unlike that of Shakespeare's War of the Roses. Kurosawa had depicted this period in such previous films as *The Seven Samurai, Throne of Blood,* and *Ran's* immediate predecessor, *Kagemusha,* and seems to be attracted to it not only because of his own samurai descent but also because, like Brecht and the Elizabethans, he sees history as an ominous mirror of the present.

His view of history is very close to Shakespeare's, in fact; he sees it as an endless chain-reaction of wars and depositions, what Jan Kott, commenting on Shakespeare's first tetralogy, has called the "Great Machine": "When I look at Japanese history," Kurosawa is reported to have said, "what I see is how man repeats himself over and over again."[9] Once this is grasped, other aspects of *Ran* become clear. What is arbitrary and irrational in *Lear* is given a moral and historical explanation. "What has always troubled me about *King Lear*," says Kurosawa, "is that Shakespeare gives his characters no past. We are plunged directly into the agonies of their present dilemmas without knowing how they come to this point. Without knowing his past, I've never really understood the ferocity of his daughters' response to Lear's feeble attempts to shed his royal power. In *Ran* I've tried to give Lear a history. I try to make clear that his power must rest upon a lifetime of bloodthirsty savagery. Forced to confront the consequences of his misdeeds, he is driven mad. But only by confronting his evil head on can he transcend it and begin to struggle again toward virtue."[10] Similarly, Kurosawa explains Hidetora's sudden wrath at his youngest child by the latter's breaking of the three arrows with which the old man has tried to demonstrate the strength of brotherly unity, and "In this respect," says Kurosawa, "I feel my work is very different from Shakespeare's play."[11] Disaster and cruelty no longer have the mysterious, cosmic arbitrariness postulated by *Lear* but are shown always as the direct result of human error or evil.

There are also specific details in *Ran* which may have been suggested by acquaintance with the Shakespeare history plays. Hidetora's descent from the burning keep, for example, is like Richard II's descent into the base court and subsequently into madness; and Lady Kaede, who has been described as an amalgam of Goneril, Regan, Lady Macbeth, and Edmund, is even more like Queen Margaret in the *Henry VI* plays in that she "acts as [Hidetora's] past"[12] with destructive sexuality and an unwavering purpose of revenge, and her demonic reaction to victimization is contrasted to the saintly Lady Sué's as Margaret's is to Henry VI's.

This relation to the Shakespeare history cycles can be clarified by a closer look at the ways that Kurosawa works his story out in terms of visual imagery.

II

Reviewing *Throne of Blood*, Professor Blumenthal has remarked on Kurosawa's "ability to imbue a place with such deep moral meaning that the place often seems to take charge and structure the narrative on its own."[13] In *Ran* it is the castles that chiefly have this function, representing as they do man's power over nature and his fellow men. Hidetora divides the three castles of his realm among his sons. The first, which originally belonged to Lady Kaede's family, is given to her husband Taro, Hidetora's eldest son, and is the most sophisticated and elaborate, with a white-walled keep, elaborately cut stone, and green metal hinges on its gates; the second, given to Jiro and his wife Sué, has rougher stone and dark polished wood, with red hinges on the gates; and the third, where Hidetora's conquests started from and where he suffers final defeat, is smaller, with rough stone work, weathered wood, and no metal on the gates: it is given to Saburo but never occupied by him. There is also a fourth castle, which stands in ruins in the volcanic desert of Azusa: it belonged to the family of Sué and her brother Tsurumaru before Hidetora defeated them, and its ruins are a bleak reminder of the transitoriness of power.[14]

The castle gates (which Kurosawa unhistorically enlarged so that horsemen with banners could ride through) are important locales of action. When Taro's treacherous garrison closes the gates of the third castle behind Hidetora's party with a double crash, one feels a trap has been sprung; and gates—as the boundary between raw nature and man's area of imposed control—are emphasized by such scenes as Hidetora's wrathful passage of the gates from Jiro's castle (when again they crash to behind him), and especially by Hidetora's dazed exit from the third castle into empty heath and storm, dressed only in his sleeping kimono. At the centre of each castle is a keep, which is the place of power and honour. Part of Hidetora's resignation of power is to cede the keep of the first castle to Taro and Kaede, and later he is burned out of the keep of the third castle in which he had taken refuge. Like the "crowns" of the castles, it is the keeps which burn, while the massive stone substructures, like human nature itself, endure, so that Hidetora, Tango, and the fool, Kyoami, can find refuge in a cellar of the ruined castle. Stones are used as a visual emblem of power and authority in a world otherwise neutral: "Empty skies above the walls," says the mad Hidetora in the ruined castle. So in the argument between Jiro and Hidetora, the son stands in the position of power with a massive stone wall behind him. This contrasts to the flimsiness of Tsurumaru's hut, where the wall collapses literally under the weight of Hidetora's guilt.

Characters attempt to find a similar sense of strength and protection in the stones of nature, but this is delusory. As the disabused Hidetora sits with his followers on a platform of white clay, dazed by the blazing sun from which he has no such leafy shelter as his youngest son provided in the opening bivouac sequence, there is a rough wall of rocks behind him which affords no real protection: flowers grow from its crannies, as they grow in the ruined castle walls. Similarly, in the scene where the fool makes Hidetora a reed helmet (like the lordless knight's sedge hat in *Ronin Sakazuki* or Lear's crown of flowers), the bereft old man sits with his back against huge rocks; and in the scene at the end, where he objects to being rescued from his "grave," he tries desperately to burrow beneath a rocky slab.

Nature, in fact, is seen as both a contrast and a parallel to human behaviour. Its beauty contrasts with man's savagery in the surpassingly lovely opening shots, where mounted samurai, bristling with arrows, stare watchfully over the green, round slopes of Mount Fuji; the mad war-lord and his fool wander in lush grass vivid with brilliant flowers; and later the verdant valley where the armies of Jiro and Saburo fight provides a contrast to the carnage enacted in it. On the other hand, there is also considerable use of "pathetic fallacy," with nature reflecting human moods. As might be expected in a work associated with *King Lear,* there is a vein of animal imagery in the film (though not to the same extent as in Brook and Kozintsev). The initial boar hunt symbolically recapitulates the violence of Hidetora's past (he later uses the same bow to kill an officer of Taro); Kyoami's *kyogen*-like song identifies the two vassal lords as hares; Jiro's followers see themselves jocularly as hunting dogs, with Hidetora now the boar; and, most striking of all, Jiro's lieutenant, Kurogane, compares Lady Kaede to a traditional demon-fox, presenting her with the stone head of Inari from a desecrated Shinto fertility shrine instead of the head of the true wife, Sué. During her simulated weeping, Kaede callously crushes a butterfly, traditional symbol of the soul, and the *shudo* (homosexual) fool, Kyoami, it should be noted, has dragon-fly decorations on his robe.

Weather is also used to reflect mood. To Kurosawa's delight, a typhoon fortuitously came up for Hidetora's passage into the wilderness, though it is not nearly as striking as the storm in Brook or Kozintsev. Earlier the war-lord's dazed silence under the noon sun conveyed the nonplus to which his sons' defection had brought him. And throughout, like punctuation, there are frequent shots of cloud: accelerated shots of cumulus boiling up like the cloud at Hiroshima when Hidetora decides to split his kingdom; gathering thunderheads after his banishment of Saburo and Tango; and, most subjective and "internalized" of all, an unearthly pale green sky with scudding shreds of cloud when he is awakened from his "grave" and thinks himself in Paradise. At the peak of his insight and madness, however, the sky is vivid blue, with other colours standing out brightly against it; and there are several important sunset scenes, the most notable being that on the second castle's wall where Hidetora fails to understand the pious Sué's lack of hatred, then confronts the unfilialness of Jiro, while the light changes from gorgeous red and orange to dark grey streakiness as the sun goes down (another example of Kurosawa's ability to exploit happenstance), and the final shot of blind Tsurumaru on the lip of a sheer drop, silhouetted against a smoky sunset. Other examples of this imagistic use of setting are the tumultuous long grasses in the storm that are associated with the unquiet ghosts of Hidetora's victims, the burnt-out desert into which Hidetora flies rather than face Saburo and where he dies, and the crossing of the river by Saburo's cavalry on their mission of succour.

As has been mentioned, elaborate battle scenes are as central to *Ran* as they are to some of Shakespeare's history plays. The film has Kurosawa's favourite sonata form: the *prelude* of the boar hunt is followed by a statement of the *first theme,* the dividing of the kingdom; then the insulting of Hidetora provides an important *bridge* to the statement of the *main theme* (which is always a complex of ideas) represented by the first battle, the destruction of Saburo's castle, and Hidetora's descent into madness; the encounter with blind Tsurumaru and Lady Kaede's seduction of Jiro and scheming against Sué then provide the *complication;* which leads to the *recapitulation* by a second elaborate battle sequence and the death of Hidetora; and an ironic *coda,* speeded up like the final sequences of a Noh play, shows the army of the vassal lord Ayabe investing the first castle, which is also now in flames: the cycle of carnage will obviously continue. These battles are so extended that they take over the symbolic importance of the storm scenes in *King Lear,* the storm itself being so mild; and three quarters of the first battle is conducted in silence, with only somber music behind, until the treacherous gunshot which hits Taro in the back unleashes an avalanche of noise. The result is to make this battle a "resonator of human folly," according to Kurosawa,[15] a dreamlike collage of ferocious imagery— a man holding his own severed arm, another with an arrow in his eye, Hidetora's concubines committing mutual suicide with knives; and everywhere galloping horses, blood, bodies porcupined with arrows, and ranks of rushing foot-soldiers. Normally, Kurosawa prefers natural sound to music (which he thinks can distract from the visuals): the thud of hooves, the swish of arrows or of Kaede's silk kimonos over the matting, or the maddening tumult of cicadas; and he makes impressive use of prolonged silence. Besides the music behind the first battle, the only other striking musical moments are the fool's songs and, especially, the plangent flute-playing of Tsurumaru in the middle of the film as Hidetora realizes his own guilt. This same mournful flute music underscores the opening boar hunt and closes the film beneath the cortège of Hidetora and Saburo and the long shot of Tsurumaru abandoned at the very edge of his family's ruined keep.

At first sight, the battle scenes strike one as realistic, and Kurosawa's debt to John Ford, Howard Hawks, and George Stevens is easily traced in the crossing-of-the-river scene or the cement-dust clouds kicked up by Jiro's cavalry; but a more important influence is the *musha-e* scrolls of the Kamakura period (1185–1333), such as the thirteenth-century scroll of "The Burning of the Sanjo Palace," of which Kurosawa seems to have made a special study. The horizontals and diagonals of soldiers charging with banners, Hidetora's long diagonal exit from the third castle between rows of milling foot-soldiers and flickering red and yellow flags, and Jiro's blurred cavalry charges in the second battle derive directly from these scrolls; and colour coding is an essential clue for understanding their composition. Taro's men are in yellow, Jiro's in red, Saburo's in blue, the good vassal lord's in white, the bad one's in black; Hidetora's colours—a yellow sun and moon on a black ground, displayed strikingly in the bivouac that follows the boar hunt—sum up the colour shift of dominance in the film from yellow to final black.

The other kind of picture favoured by the scroll artists was quiet indoor scenes where the lucid, fragile geometry of classic Japanese domestic architecture was especially associated with the ceremonial activities of women, in contrast to the turmoil of the battle scenes. There is a sense of this elaborate etiquette in the bivouac scene which follows the boar hunt, but its ironic embodiment is the scenes dominated by the Lady Kaede, whose air of still, controlled violence perverts their ceremony to destruction. She is first glimpsed at the head of a ninety-person procession (contrasting to Hidetora's diminished train), insisting that the procession of her father-in-law's concubines yield way to her; but most of her activity is set in the "gold room" of the first castle. In this room low platforms are visually important to show social dominance—Hidetora initially objects to sitting below his son and daughter-in-law; and eye contact, or its avoidance, subtly conveys relationships, as the estranged Taro and Kaede gaze different ways from their sitting positions, and Jiro and Kaede avoid looking at each other after love-making. And Kurosawa went to extraordinary pains to ensure that methods of kneeling, positioning the hands, closing the sliding doors, serving saki, and Kaede's susurrating heel-to-toe walk conformed to aristocratic etiquette. This apparently serene control is all a sham, however. We hear that Kaede's mother committed suicide in this room; she herself violently attacks, then violently seduces Jiro there; she unwraps what she thinks will be the severed head of Sué there; and its final desecration comes when she is herself beheaded with a single stroke, to fall where her mother fell, with blood covering the wall where Hidetora's insignia once hung and where the Buddhist scroll of the Bodhisattva which hypocritically replaced it eventually curls into ashes.

The major influence on these "gold room" scenes is the Noh drama (about which Kurosawa is currently making a documentary). This can be seen superficially in the mannered staging of the Kaede scenes, her stylized behaviour and the symbolic gift of the stone fox head (the substitute-head and the fox-in-human-shape are frequent Noh themes); her facial appearance is also modelled on a Noh mask, as is Hidetora's elaborate makeup— his scowl of avenging justice, his open-mouthed, round-eyed expression of terror, and an increasing blue tinge in his facial powdering to signify growing madness. Besides the Kaede scenes, the other most striking Noh borrowing is the scene of Tsurumaru's mysterious hut (compare the witch's hut in *Throne of Blood*). Tsurumaru himself is an enigmatic image with his loose white kimono, long dark hair, and epicene low voice.[16] Tango mistakes him for a woman, but the main impression is ghost-like, with his eerie flute-playing awakening Hidetora's recognition of guilt for his blinding. The idea of vengeful ghost-figures is very common in Noh, and in the film is also represented ironically by Sué, when Hidetora sees her like a white angel on the battlements of the ruined castle and imagines himself in hell, and by Hidetora himself, emerging like the walking dead from the burning keep, and driving panic into the hearts of the two traitors whom Tango is challenging when he appears suddenly above them on the skyline.

This overlaps a more profound influence of Noh. Both it and *bushido,* the samurai code of honor, derive from Zen Buddhism, which sees the world as essentially an impermanent stage for repeated actions, the wheel of recurrence. "According to Buddhist belief, all those who engaged in battle would, after death, be condemned to an eternity in Naraku, an inferno of fighting and bloodshed presided over by the deity Asura. Naraku is a place of torture and chaos [N.B.] where strong castles crown mountain tops and where warriors are forced to fight continuously amid a shower of arrows" and fire.[17] There is a group of Noh plays called *Shuramono* about the ghosts of warriors who recount this torment and beg for prayer to relieve them. In the film both the burning keep and the ruined castle are specifically identified as hell, and Hidetora assures Sué that it is Asura, not Buddha, who rules this world. The Buddhist alternative to such unending violence is a moral one, compassion, forgiveness, the refusal to hate. Sué disconcerts Hidetora by refusing to hate him for his victimization of her family; Tsurumaru says he is trying to imitate her; and the same assurance is repeated by Saburo to his father at the end. "I do not hate you"—a spiritual generosity Hidetora finds it much more difficult to accept than death. This does not stop violence recurring—Sué is brutally decapitated, Saburo is ambushed, Hidetora dies of grief, and Ayabe's attack on Jiro's castle ensures that warfare will continue—but for the individual soul the doctrine offers hope.

Kurosawa insists that he has no didactic intention in *Ran;* as with the Noh, the audience must learn what it can from the film. But our time, he says, is a tragic one, whose reality must nevertheless be faced;[18] and he hopes that his work may "be able to create hope somewhere."[19] Hidetora's death, he thinks, is "perhaps the one that contains the greatest plea for human understanding, . . . the most pitiful and at the same time the most magnificent that I feel I have been able to conceive in my films."[20] But his conclusion is one consistent with Buddhism and the samurai code, very different from Brook's nihilist existentialism or the Christian-Marxism of Kozintsev. It assumes the tragedy of human history itself—the old age of mankind, which can only be escaped from by individual spirituality; and this is not very far from the implications of Shakespeare's own history plays.

Hence the poignant, elegiac but uncertain last image of the film: a long shot of Tsurumaru, who has lost hold of his sister's scroll of Buddha, groping alone with his stick at the edge of a precipitous fall, silhouetted against a glowing, peach-coloured sunset which he cannot see, to the sound of his own lost flute. Here is the Buddhist sense of *"mono no aware,"* of beauty in the very sadness of life, of tranquillity before the terrible fact that human power fails.[21]

Notes

1. Grigori Kozintsev, *King Lear: The Space of Tragedy,* trans. Mary Mackintosh (London, 1977), 37.

2. Grigori Kozintsev, *"Hamlet* and *King Lear:* Stage and Film," in *Shakespeare* 1972, ed. C. Leech and J. M. R. Margeson (Toronto, 1972), 198.

3. Bertrand Raison and Serge Toubiana, *Le Livre de Ran* (Paris, 1985), 14; "Ce qui est primordial c'est la qualité du décor, de l'objet ou la beauté du paysage que vous voulez filmer."

4. Ibid., 4.

5. See Michael Healy, "Kurosawa's Long Answer Said a Lot," *Denver Post,* Sunday, 6 Oct. 1985, 11.

6. Ironically, Brook seems to have foreseen this. In an article he submitted to *Sight and Sound* while he was still a student at Oxford he argued that the use of colour would eliminate the subjective point of view imposed by black-and-white cameras, because the eye is always attracted to various parts of a coloured picture, and that the logical development then would be what he called the "Long Screen," by which he meant the "wide screen," as used so brilliantly in *Kagemusha* and *Ran.* The article was rejected as too fanciful, but is mentioned as a wry afternote to his later piece on "The Filming of Shakespeare," *Sight and Sound* 34 (1965): 70.

7. Raison and Toubiana, 13.

8. See Peter Grilli, "Kurosawa Directs a Cinematic *Lear,"* *New York Times,* Sunday, 15 Dec. 1985, 1.

9. See Donald Richie, *The Films of Akira Kurosawa* (Berkeley, 1965), 115.

10. Grilli, 1.

11. Healy, 11.

12. Raison and Toubiana, 11. Ian Buruma, *Behind the Mask: On Sexual Demons, Sacred Mothers, Transvestites, Gangsters and Other Japanese Cultural Heroes* (New York, 1984), chap. 4, "Demon Woman."

13. J. Blumenthal, *"Macbeth* into *Throne of Blood,"* *Sight and Sound,* 34 (1965): 191.

14. One of Kurosawa's co-scriptwriters, Hideo Oguni, considered the film weakened because it contained no peasants, the people who farmed the land. Kurosawa's reply was that "It is not a story that concerns peasants, one can't describe everything" (Raison and Toubiana, 138–39, 12). There was to have been a scene of the burning of an abandoned village, but this was cut in the interests of economy.

15. Raison and Toubiana, 16.

16. Sexual ambivalence is an important element in the Buddhist tradition, as Lévi-Strauss explains in *Tristes Tropiques:* "[Buddhism] expresses a placid femininity which is also suggested by the temple priests whose shaven heads make them indistinguishable from the nuns, with whom they form a kind of third sex . . ."—quoted in Buruma, 115. Buddhist sculpture often expresses a kind of androgyny, transcending the sexes, and this is clearly one element (though only one) in the casting of Kyoami, who combines Lear's fool with aspects of Cordelia ("my poor fool").

17. Ana Laura Zambrano, *"Throne of Blood:* Kurosawa's *Macbeth,"* *Literature/Film Quarterly,* 2 (1974): 270.

18. Healy, 1.

19. Dan Yakir, "The Warrior Returns," *Film Comment,* 16 (Nov.–Dec. 1980): 57.

20. Healy, 10.

21. A version of this paper was delivered at the Third World Shakespeare Congress, West Berlin, April 1986. I wish to thank David Waterhouse and Chandrabhanu Pattanayak for helpful suggestions about Shinto and Buddhist motifs.

[Review of *Dreams*]

TERRENCE RAFFERTY

T HE STRANGEST thing about *Akira Kurosawa's Dreams* is that not one of its eight segments feels like a real dream. What Kurosawa calls dreams are more like poetic *tableaux vivants:* meticulous formal elaborations of imagery that could have originated in the mind of someone dreaming. And although Kurosawa's style is unmistakable, we never get the sense that he's truly revealing himself here; the movie has an eerily impersonal quality. Ostensibly, the filmmaker is serving up the very stuff of his unconscious. Actually, he's doing something quite different: attempting to refine and abstract unconscious material to the point of absolute purity—the purity of ritual. The kind of power that Kurosawa aims for, and intermittently achieves, in *Dreams* is less oneiric than ceremonial. The film is a succession of sweeping dramatic gestures and lofty incantations performed in an atmosphere of hushed solemnity.

The high-priestly tone of Kurosawa's direction is an extension of the stately, imperious manner of his later films (like the 1980 *Kagemusha* and the 1985 *Ran*). This sort of style can be irritating: every effect is huge; every composition seems to strain for transcendence; every statement sounds like the word of God. As Kurosawa approaches the end of an extraordinary filmmaking career—he is eighty years old—his work has taken on the burden of metaphysics, but he is no philosopher, and never has been. What he has always been is a great maker of images, and his attempt to tap into the mysteries of the universe is primarily an exploration of the power of visual form: the arrangement of colors and shapes in the vast space of the movie screen. In temperament, Kurosawa's recent work resembles nothing so much as the late paintings of Mark Rothko, with their gigantic, looming shapes set against —and dissolving into—even larger fields of uniform color: canvases that mean to induce in us a kind of spiritual shiver, to chill us with intimations of infinity. To try to make art of this kind is, of course, an act of hubris, and if you fail you look like a windbag, an arrogant fool. Kurosawa has never been afraid to embarrass himself by overreaching. When he adapts a work of literature, he invariably chooses something of the most daunting complexity, like *The Idiot* or *King Lear* (the main source of *Ran*); his action films, like *The Seven Samurai* and *Yojimbo,* are conceived on the scale of epics. And even when he has worked on stories of apparently less ambitious scope, with a smaller cast of characters or a more confined setting (as in *Rashomon,*

Reprinted from *The New Yorker,* 10 September 1990, 101–3. Reprinted by permission; © 1990 Terrence Rafferty. Originally in *The New Yorker.*

Ikiru, The Lower Depths, High and Low, Red Beard, Dodeskaden), he has always tried to extract from the material some statement of universal significance—to turn these modest dramas into moral epics. In his films Kurosawa is immodest to the core, as Griffith was, as Abel Gance was; and, like them, he's unsubtle—prone to grandiosity, sentimentality, didacticism, all kinds of pompous folly. And there isn't a filmmaker alive whose art so persistently strives for exaltation or so frequently produces it.

So let's cut Kurosawa some slack, and pass quickly over the four tedious, overblown segments that make up the second hour of *Dreams.* The fifth episode, "Crows," a fantasy encounter with van Gogh, is perhaps the dopiest sequence Kurosawa has ever put on film: paintings become real, natural backgrounds turn into paintings, and van Gogh (played by Martin Scorsese) mumbles a few truisms about the nature of art. It's a thin conceit, and neither the grandeur of van Gogh's paintings nor the cleverness of Kurosawa's recreations of them can disguise its preciousness. The next two segments, "Mount Fuji in Red" and "The Weeping Demon," are cautionary fables about nuclear devastation. In the first, a nuclear-power-plant explosion has caused Mount Fuji to erupt; the few survivors gather by the sea, and make speeches about who's responsible for the disaster until bright-colored radioactive clouds overcome them all. In the second, a solitary traveler (Akira Terao, who plays the dreamer in all but the first two segments of the film) wanders through a blasted postapocalyptic landscape and comes upon a grotesque, tattered old man, who gives him a guided tour of a nightmarishly mutated world, full of ominous giant dandelions and wailing humanoid demons. The final segment, "Village of the Watermills," is a pastoral idyll in which a very old man (Chishu Ryu) extolls the virtues of living in harmony with nature. This segment is meant, of course, as a corrective to the science-fiction horrors of the two previous ones; it's Kurosawa's prescription for all that ails us. The trouble with this sequence, as with the two before it, is that we get the idea of each very quickly, and the idea is neither startling enough to resonate nor complex enough to develop. Even though they last only fifteen minutes or so apiece, these episodes seem static and overlong. And they feel *willed,* self-conscious; homilies are not the stuff of dreams.

In the four earlier segments, Kurosawa keeps his aesthetic and moral impulses in better balance: when he's at his best, the impulses are indistinguishable. The opening segment, "Sunshine Through the Rain," is the vision of a small child, and it seems to have sprung from a strong image—if not a dream, then a memory—rather than from a didactic urge. A five-year-old boy stands at the gate of his house watching rain fall on a sunny day; his mother tells him that in this sort of weather foxes hold their wedding processions, and the boy goes into the forest and spies on the animals' ceremony. The foxes' wedding—performed by dancers in masks—is a thing of solemn beauty, made even more magical by the sight and sound of shimmering rainfall: the light has an unearthly quality, and gives the images a sort of translucent clarity. When the boy returns home after witnessing this dazzling spectacle, his mother scolds him and refuses to let him back in the house; by watching the procession, she says, he has angered the foxes, and unless they forgive him he'll have to kill himself. She shuts the gate, and he wanders off again; in the segment's final image, he sees a rainbow, which is the sign of the foxes' forgiveness. This resolution is also a sign that "Sunshine Through the Rain" is something other than a literal transcription of a dream: a real dream would end with the shutting of the gate, not with the redemptive rainbow. But there is greatness in this sequence—a wholly original sense of the rapturous fear and awe we feel when we first come upon the wonders of the natural world.

The ecstatic pantheism of the opening episode is slightly blunted by the second, "The Peach Orchard," which is also a childhood dream about nature; it's lovely, but its mood and pace are too similar to those of the first, and its respect-for-living-things message is more explicit, and therefore weaker. The third episode, "The Blizzard," is a radical departure from the green childhood world of the first and second. There's virtually no color in this sequence. Four men are trapped in a ferocious snowstorm on the side of a mountain, and all they can see is white; they're the only things alive in the middle of a fierce blankness, and if they give up they'll become part of it. Characteristically, Kurosawa turns what seems to be an exercise in minimalism into something excessive, hyperbolic: he lays on the (fake) snow, the howling-wind effects, and the bleak, undifferentiated vistas of despair until we feel like screaming from the sheer hopeless monotony of it all. And then he pulls a miracle out of the white void: a woman (Mieko Harada, who played the ravishing, murderous Lady Kaede in *Ran*) appears to the party's leader as he battles sleep. She has long black hair and wears diaphanous robes, and Kurosawa performs wonders with that hair and those robes: they whip and swirl around her so that her image remains fluid, changing, ungraspable. We can't take our eyes off her, and we're never quite sure what she's meant to represent. She is beautiful—impossibly, indefinably beautiful—and this is perhaps the most piercing image ever made of the desires that keep people from surrendering to death: *this* is a spirit to leap out of your deathbed in pursuit of. And it's the sort of transcendent image that undoubtedly keeps Kurosawa going, too.

The inspiration that radiates from the final few minutes of "The Blizzard" carries over to the next episode, which is called "The Tunnel." Here the dominant color is black. The dreamer, in a military officer's uniform, walks along a deserted road toward a tunnel. He approaches it slowly, as if he dreaded having to pass through it; a dog emerges from the darkness, barks and growls at him, and then backs off, and he continues, his footsteps echoing rhythmically as he walks through the tunnel and finally comes out into the light on the other side. Then he hears footsteps behind him and turns to face the blackness again, and as the steps grow louder a figure emerges: a man with an ash-white face, in the uniform of a private. He stops and stands at attention: the dreamer was his commanding officer. Respectfully, this apparition—who is as alarming and as poignant as the gaunt soldier who dies in front of young Henry in *The Red Badge of Courage*—tells his superior, "I can't believe I'm really dead." He points to a single light on a distant hillside: "That's my home." He presents arms, wheels, and returns to the tunnel, and then the rest of the platoon—all white-faced, all dead—march out to face the commander. The dreamer acknowledges responsibility for sending them to their deaths, expresses guilt at having survived them, then dismisses them back to the tunnel; as he turns away from the darkness for the last time, the dog appears again, snarling at his feet, and the sequence ends. The idea of this segment may be banal, but "The Tunnel" is a brilliant, hypnotic piece of filmmaking. Its images are simple, stark, and resonant, its dramatic shape is lucid and classically satisfying, and its rhythm is overwhelming, unstoppable: it moves with a sorrowful marching pace, the rhythm of grief.

If *Dreams* had ended there, with that menacing dog, it might have seemed a masterpiece; it would have seemed more dreamlike, too. But the world isn't perfect, and neither is Kurosawa. Forget about the feeble sermonizing of the second half. Kurosawa has more than earned our forgiveness for his lapses. At its best, his work has a grace and a strength that few other film artists have achieved; in long passages, and sometimes in whole movies, he has come within shouting distance of the sublime. And even when he's just huffing and puffing and lumbering around, he huffs and puffs and lumbers like a giant.

[Review of *Rhapsody in August*]

VINCENT CANBY

K UROSAWA DIRECTED his first film in 1942 and appears to be in the midst of a vigorous Golden Age. It's a measure of the true originality of *Rhapsody in August* that it has not been a major festival hit. It doesn't cater to an audience's preconceptions of the new. It's not self-consciously inventive in the way of the films of Werner Schroeter, Lars Von Trier, and the other avant-garde directors who come to Cannes.

Instead, it is distilled, utterly direct, abrasive. It reflects the manner of a man who is no longer interested in superficial effects, only in expressing what is on his mind as efficiently as possible. The film is a message from a director who was born four years before the guns of August were fired in 1914. It is a report from that generation of directors who are supposed to be dead or at least retired and modestly grateful for honorary awards.

Like *Akira Kurosawa's Dreams,* shown out of competition at last year's Cannes festival, *Rhapsody in August* is visually splendid. Unlike *Dreams,* though, it is almost willfully austere. It suggests something of the rigor of Roberto Rossellini's late films, though the two men otherwise don't have much in common. It is also a movie that could prompt righteous outrage in some quarters of the United States. At one point or another, there is something in it to offend everybody, including me. Mr. Kurosawa doesn't make it easy to accept man's higher nature, at least in part because the movie doesn't work in the way he seems to have intended.

Rhapsody in August, adapted by the director from a Japanese novel, *Nabe no Naka,* by Kiyoko Murata, is about the dropping of America's second atom bomb, on August 9, 1945, on the city of Nagasaki. Unlike Shohei Imamura's *Black Rain* (1989), in which the effects of the Hiroshima bomb are explicitly detailed, *Rhapsody in August* avoids any attempt to recreate the spectacle of atomic holocaust.

The time is now, and the setting is an idyllic farm on the far side of the mountains outside Nagasaki. Four teen-age children have been parked for the summer with their grandmother, widowed long ago in the Nagasaki raid, while their parents go off to Hawaii to visit the grandmother's dying brother, who became rich in Hawaii as a pineapple planter.

The Hawaiian household includes the half-American children of the grandmother's dead sister. Kane, the grandmother, now mentally confused

Reprinted from "Madonna and the Master at Cannes," *The New York Times,* 19 May 1991, H 13, 17. Copyright © 1991 by the New York Times Company. Reprinted by permission.

in her old age, had ten brothers and sisters and has trouble keeping them straight, as does the audience, though that's not important.

When Kane and the children are invited to join the others in Hawaii, she refuses. She doesn't hate all Americans, she says, but she doesn't especially cherish them. Little by little, she begins to tell the children stories about the bombing. Some are grimly factual; some sound like myth.

She had a younger brother who, though not caught directly in the raid, lost all his hair from the effects of radiation. He was so embarrassed that he spent the rest of his life in his room in the farmhouse. He was a painter, but his sole subject was a large eye, which Kane describes as "the eye of the flash" they saw on the far side of the mountain on the morning of the raid.

At a key moment, Mr. Kurosawa shows the audience that eye. It is large and red and fills the sky. The effect is both shocking and magical. It's not an evil eye; neither is it good. It is a presence that hovers over their lives. The youngest grandson later sees the eye in a snake he finds in the mountain pool where Kane's bald brother used to swim at night.

Kane remembers when a skinny-legged, dwarfish creature showed up at the farmhouse, having fished her nearly drowned brother out of the mountain pool. "A kappa," she says, as if describing a village policeman, "a water spirit." According to Kane, kappas do that occasionally.

Rhapsody in August vividly recalls the atomic holocaust, but entirely by indirection. Though Mr. Kurosawa says he intended that the movie should be about the awakening of the children to the bomb's meaning, the children are less important to the movie than the indirectly evoked bombing itself and the vision of the apocalypse.

The children, who range in age from late to early teens, remain largely uncharacterized. At first they miss television and the other pleasures they left at home in Tokyo. They are generic children, differentiated only by age, sex and the M.I.T. and U.S.C. T-shirts they wear.

Somewhat too quickly and obligingly, they begin to explore Nagasaki on their own, looking for evidence of the August 9 raid. It's as if Mr. Kurosawa didn't have time to waste in creating especially compelling children.

Yet this doesn't interfere with Mr. Kurosawa's extraordinarily heartfelt recollection of the war and what it meant to the generations that survived it. Where the film gets tricky, and even ticklish, is when Richard Gere shows up as Kane's half-American nephew from Hawaii, who has come to pay his respects to his Japanese cousins and to apologize for the war.

Mr. Gere gives a good, self-effacing performance in a role that's a little unreal. He speaks his own Japanese dialogue easily and is at the center of one of Mr. Kurosawa's most breathtaking moments.

During a ceremony honoring the bomb victims, the camera shifts away from the shrine to show a line of ants making a purposeful ant-line toward a rosebush. The ants climb the bushy stalk, single file, to arrive at the magnificent blood-red bloom.

This may suggest that the ants, like the bomb's victims, have found their peace. However, it is far more effective if left uninterpreted. The film is full of such moments that might have pleased Luis Buñuel.

When the movie's politics were questioned at a post-screening news conference, Mr. Kurosawa denied any intention to sidestep Japanese responsibility for the war. "We Japanese," he said, "were also the victims of Japanese militarism." The subject of the film, he insisted, is not guilt and responsibility but the horrors of war, in particular of the bomb, which has made possible the absolute end of everything.

It is, indeed, a subject about which he has been ruminating for years, most memorably in the 1955 *I Live in Fear [Record of a Living Being]*, about a man obsessed by atomic destruction, and the wildly garish end-of-the-world nightmare sequence in *Dreams* last year.

Later, at lunch at the Hôtel du Cap in Antibes, sitting on a sun-drenched terrace, looking at the Mediterranean, Mr. Kurosawa expressed satisfaction with the film's reception here. The film maker looks a good ten to fifteen years younger than his age and is ready for a new project.

He noted that his longtime associate, Ishiro Honda (the director of *Godzilla* and other Japanese sci-fi classics), had directed the stunning ant sequence in *Rhapsody in August*. Ants, it seems, are more difficult to direct than dogs, cats, and children. Mr. Kurosawa doesn't have the patience for it.

Nor did he have patience for several grimly insistent autograph hunters who suddenly turned up on the closely guarded hotel terrace. He signed the first sheet of a paper shoved in front of him, then erupted in the formidable style of the man who is called "sensei" ("master") on the set. It was a ferocious but short outburst, after which the appetite, the charm and the concentration returned.

Zen and Selfhood: Patterns of Eastern Thought in Kurosawa's Films

STEPHEN PRINCE

T HE RELATIONSHIP of Kurosawa's films to patterns of Japanese culture, and to Zen in particular, is not simple or straightforward. Kurosawa has always spoken to Japan with several voices, and in his attempts to address the inequities of Japan's feudal heritage, he has found some Western perspectives and norms of value. This is why his relation to Zen is so complex. Kurosawa has borrowed and altered, shifted and inverted many of the formal and philosophical values of Zen, so that to trace this influence means coming to terms with the dialectical manner in which Kurosawa has addressed Japan and the Japanese by way of the West. Zen has profoundly influenced Kurosawa's films. Sometimes the influence is clear and easily grasped. Other times, it must be seen as a residue left by Kurosawa's search for a meeting point for East and West.

Before I deal with Zen, however, I wish to consider some more general ways that Kurosawa has sought to conjoin Eastern and Western perspectives. This may be accomplished through a sketch of the thematic structure of his films, so that the influence of Zen may then be examined in terms of both Kurosawa's themes and visual style. (A note on gender: Throughout this essay, such gender terms as *he, him, himself* refer to the male of the species. Kurosawa's is a male-centered vision, in which he clearly intends that the male should stand for humanity.)

Throughout his films, Kurosawa is critical of feudalistic normative structures, whereby social identities generated by the family, village, corporation, or state, and the bonds of obligation owed these groups, constrain the self. Feudalism rigidly stratified personal and social life and helped discourage the emergence of individualist social values. The system was perpetuated for centuries, generating social norms of joint responsibility, group sanctions for individual behavior, and a system of limitless, interlocking obligations that defined and directed the individual's personal life. One result, Yazaki Takeo suggests, was a cultural lack of regard for individual autonomy.[1] And by the 1930s in Japan, a virulent form of fascism, obliterating the individual in favor of a militarist mysticism, had taken root in a cultural soil made favorable by the long feudal heritage.

Referring to the chaotic condition of Japan's culture and economy immediately following the Second World War, Kurosawa remarked, "I believed at

Reprinted from *Post Script* 7, no. 2 (Winter 1988): 4–17, by permission.

that time that for Japan to recover it was necessary to place a high value on the self. I still believe this."[2]

This strength of self Kurosawa emphasizes is realized in the films through the capability of the heroes to confront a world dominated by predators, a world of exploitation and oppression. The town in *Yojimbo* (1961) is a microcosm of feudal society and is controlled by criminals and merchants who are slowly annihilating each other in a struggle for markets. The town's citizens flee or hide timidly in their dwellings to escape the violence of a world they cannot control, where the strong prey upon the weak. The wandering samurai hero decides the world would be better if all these wicked gangsters and merchants were dead. Similarly, the corrupt corporations in *The Bad Sleep Well* (1960) are ravaging Japanese society, murdering and blackmailing those who oppose them, and the hero Nishi dedicates himself to overthrowing them "for all the people too weak to fight back."

Aware of the profound and prolonged brutalities of feudal life, Kurosawa is given to a dark view of human society. An impoverished and dying woman in *The Lower Depths* (1957) believes she has lived in hell all her life. Someone tells her that the next world must be better, but she doubts this. She grows terrified at letting go her hold on life for the next world might be worse.

This perspective of universal suffering is similar to the Buddhist view of the eternal cycle of pain that defines existence.[3] As a means of escape from the inevitable trauma of life, the Buddhist seeks to dissolve a sense of self into the void, to lose consciousness of corporeal corruptibility by merging into the great emptiness that lies behind the material world. The Buddhist perspective, including its Western disciples like Schopenhauer, views the will as the source of all suffering, since every action must end in disappointment. Achievement is short-lived and falls short of the intention.[4]

Kurosawa, however, does not view the will in the same manner as the Buddhist, nor does he ever seek in his films to resign individuals to their fate. On the contrary, the director insists on the power of the self, the effort of will, designed to strike back at oppressors.

Kurosawa sees the larger context of established Japanese society as corrupted by a pursuit of position, wealth, or property. In each film, the hero must struggle against a facet of this society: in *Ikiru* (1952), against governmental bureaucracy whose stratified and hierarchical organization encourages feudalistic behavior; in *Red Beard* (1965), against a culture that encourages doctors to get rich by curing the aristocracy of cataracts and calluses; in *Seven Samurai* (1954), against a class heritage which demands that samurai refuse to help farmers and allow them to perish at the hands of bandits. And in *No Regrets for Our Youth* (1946), *Record of a Living Being* (1955), *Ikiru*, *The Bad Sleep Well*, *Yojimbo*, and *Red Beard*, the central institution of the family is viewed as cold, malignant, or repressive.

Kurosawa's regard for the individual is, then, a departure from traditional cultural norms. His heroes must break from traditional social groups, such as family and state, to discover a regard for human dignity. But Kurosawa does not lapse into a Western nihilism because his characters never break completely from society. They re-enter the social world to build parks, to defend farmers, to mitigate the general oppressiveness of things.

Kurosawa's is a dialectical use of East and West. His valuation of the self is not only or essentially Western, for Kurosawa's heroes are also generated and informed by the ideals of the samurai warrior. *Bushido* was an unwritten code that defined the proper conduct of the samurai, and Kurosawa's heroes manifest many of the principles of this code. *Bushido* emphasized individual courage, integrity, strength, fortitude, and fealty.[5] The warrior ideal focused on the development of the individual's capabilities for strength: physical, moral, and spiritual. The ideal samurai combined physical prowess with moral courage and unswerving allegiance to his lord. His physical skills received continual test in battle, and his moral development was expected to be no less rigorous.

Bushido achieved an imaginative and cultural dominance in Japanese life, and this mythic significance Kurosawa draws from in creating his heroes. All of the best qualities of the warrior have been spiritualized by Kurosawa in his art. The Kurosawa hero is always strong as the ideal samurai. This strength may be physical, as in the samurai heroes of *Seven Samurai, Yojimbo,* and *Sanjuro* (1962). But the hero may also be a person of ordinary or inferior physical capabilities, as in *Drunken Angel* (1948), *High and Low* (1963), *Dersu Uzala* (1975), *No Regrets for Our Youth, Ikiru,* and *Record of a Living Being.* Their great strength is moral. Their will to create good is overwhelming, and this obsessive dedication enables them to triumph, rather than any use of physical might. To the emphasis on individual willpower and physical might, Kurosawa adds a deep compassion for mankind and the necessity for the hero to serve others. Kurosawa thus translates the samurai's obligation to serve his lord into the hero's obligation to serve humanity. Both figures are bound by a duty of fealty, and the endurance of both is severely tested: the samurai in battle and in the bonds which link his fortunes to those of his lord, the Kurosawa hero in the conflict and struggle to humanize a corrupted society.

The samurai as a class were attracted to Zen, and Kurosawa's sympathies for samurai ideals may account for the place of Zen in his films. Kurosawa never merely borrows from an aesthetic heritage without also transforming and reconstructing it. As with other aspects of Japanese culture, Kurosawa's is a pattern of acceptance and rejection. He both affirms and rejects the principles of Zen.

A product of Indian Buddhism and Chinese Taoism, Zen entered deeply into all facets of Japanese culture, in part because the Zen monasteries became centers of teaching and learning and advanced cultural knowledge.[6] In contrast to Western intellectual traditions, Zen is not a philosophy in the strict sense because it values direct experience over conceptualizing about experience. It is, instead, a loosely-formulated perspective on the world that proceeds from distinctively Eastern assumptions. Zen posits a benevolent force or presence that suffuses all of existence, and the discipline stimulates within individuals a frame of mind that approximates this positive emptiness or benevolent void. Zen as a discipline is an attempt to get in touch with the oneness in the midst of multiplicity and the many within the one. Zen's doctrine of the interpenetration of this oneness or Tao with phenomena is in contrast to the Western dualities of mind and matter, body and spirit, good and evil. Zen distrusts conceptualization because language is thought to foster such artificial distinctions within a world that is whole in spirit. For this reason, Zen favors action over words, and the discipline is distinguished by its directness. Thus, it appealed to samurai warriors whose proximity to death in battle lent itself to a mode of experience that favored instantaneous action.

Zen characterizes itself as *wu-hsin* (no-mind) and *wu-nien* (no-thought).[7] The mind is emptied of linguistic structures so that it might partake of the positive emptiness of the universe. The celebrated Zen *mondo* is a method of "direct pointing" used to test the depth of a pupil's insight. The *mondo* sounds semantically absurd; this is precisely its purpose. It indicates, for followers of Zen, the limitations of conceptualizing and stimulates an instantaneous awakening or *satori* in the pupil.

> — What is the Tao?
> — Your ordinary mind is the Tao.
> — How can one return into accord with it?
> — By intending to accord you immediately deviate.
> — But without intention, how can one know the Tao?
> — The Tao belongs neither to knowing nor not knowing. Knowing is false understanding; not knowing is blind ignorance. If you really understand the Tao beyond doubt, it's like the empty sky. Why drag in right and wrong?[8]

Satori cannot be attained by seeking it nor through a deliberate non-seeking, since not-seeking-it is just as much an intention as to seek. Instead, one must become of no-mind, allowing the Tao or the Buddha within one to emerge. The human being is thus seen by Zen as a fundamentally spiritual creature, not as the debased fallen one of Christian tradition. Zen says that it does not seek to render the mind a vacuum, but to allow one's inherent spirituality and intelligence to emerge.[9] Enlightenment must come from within each person. It cannot be implanted from without. Accordingly, the Zen instructor does little teaching aside from the direct pointing of the *mondo* and will even disclaim his own role as a teacher. The pupil must discover himself.

This restrained relationship between teacher and pupil that is character-istic of Zen reveals itself in Kurosawa's films because what occurs in each film is a model of Zen instruction, whereby a master allows a pupil to observe and learn without overt guidance.[10] In *Seven Samurai*, Kambei teaches the young samurai Katsushiro by allowing the young man to travel in his company. Kambei observes Katsushiro's rites of passage: the youngster's first experience with a woman and with the violence of battle. But the elder samurai tells Katsushiro, "I have no disciples," and allows him to make what he will of his experiences with Kambei. Similarly, Dersu Uzala rarely gives explicit moral lessons to Arseniev, yet the Russian explorer is a wiser man for his friendship with Dersu and reaches a new understanding of the spiritual power of nature.

Just as Zen emphasizes inner enlightenment, Kurosawa insists that knowl-edge must come from within each person, not be implanted from without, and the pattern whereby his heroes must separate themselves from estab-lished social groupings is a structural embodiment of this inner discipline. Enlightenment will not be found within an oppressive society, but only through the individual's separation from that social order, although Kuro-sawa will also insist that his heroes, having attained enlightenment, return to the social order and attempt to humanize it. For such a philosophical direc-tor, few scenes occur in the films in which a character speaks about what he or she has learned. Instead, as Zen maintains, knowledge is revealed through action. When Watanabe attains his enlightenment in *Ikiru,* he does not speak, but returns to work to push the park project through to comple-tion. His new behavior and its concrete symbolization in the slum play-ground he helps erect are the correlatives of his enlightenment.

Zen's disdain for intellectualizing one's morality into being is revealed in Kurosawa's insistence that his heroes act. Knowledge is only gained through experience and validated by acting. Through movement and action, moral-ity is revealed. In its broadest sense, movement in Kurosawa's films is a moral metaphor—and this has influenced his visual style. A person is what he or she does: it sounds so Western but here it is particularly Eastern. The Tao at the center of things delivers itself up through experience, and by car-ing for the sick, by building parks, by defending villages, a person reveals true knowledge and spirituality. This is not simply charity for others, but a redemption of oneself and of the world. For through one's enlightened actions flows the benevolent spirit of the universe, which may bring one into unity with all things.

That unity extends especially to the world of nature. Zen is informed by a reverence for nature quite unlike the perspective of the Western world, wherein nature is something to be conquered and dominated by human beings. For Zen, one does not dominate nature and expect to live in a truly spiritual fashion. *Satori* flows from living in harmony with the natural world.[11]

Zen's reverence for nature has influenced the traditional arts in Japan, including the tea ceremony.[12] The ideal of the art of tea is to contemplate and draw closer to nature. During the ceremony the participants may speak, but they maintain a pensive attitude while the rituals of the ceremony and the landscape outside remind them of the significance of the natural world. The ritual is a formal symbolization of the human place in that world. Boiling water sounds like a breeze passing through pine needles. Pouring a dipperful of water from a kettle is reminiscent of the flow of a mountain stream.

Like the tea ceremony, other Japanese arts exhibit the reverential attitude of those who seek harmony with the world of snow, moonbeams, and mountain streams. The *haiku* is a seventeen-syllable poem that uses the Eastern conception of emptiness as a positive quality and the glory of nature even in its smallest creatures.

Like these arts, Kurosawa's films are filled with representations of the interconnectedness of human life and the natural world. Kurosawa devotes a detailed cinematic attention to the presence and forms of nature. One entire track of the stereophonic soundtrack of *Red Beard* functions to establish the physical presence of nature.[13] It is filled with the rustle of leaves, the drip of water, the creak of settling wood. But, beyond the merely descriptive level, the films visualize the natural world as an extension and elaboration of human conflict. Rain, snow, and windstorms are indices of human passion in Kurosawa's films. At moments of moral conflict, the hero's inner turbulence is manifested by climactic gusts of wind which may be seen or heard on the soundtrack. At the climax of *Yojimbo,* the extremity of the samurai hero's predicament is visualized in the violence of the elements. Seeking vengeance, the samurai has returned to town, and as he faces a horde of enemies, frenzied bursts of wind scatter enormous clouds of dust about the combatants.

In *Red Beard* the cycles of nature become metaphors for the moral alterations the young doctor Yasumoto undergoes during his education at the clinic. The narrative opens in spring, when he arrives at the clinic, full of pride and ambition, egocentric and naive. As he is confronted with endless suffering, the film's tone darkens and the world freezes with snow and winter storms. But when Yasumoto attains enlightenment and is able to nurse a battered young girl back to health, Kurosawa shows us the melting of the snows and the gradual thawing of the world, even as Niide warns Yasumoto that hard times and more winters lie ahead. In *Red Beard* the rhythms of the seasons are the film's governing metaphor for the moral transformation of the material world.

Finally, in the symbolization of nature *Dersu Uzala* is the consummate work. This hymn to nature is the ultimate synthesis of Kurosawa's individualist morality with the Eastern reverence for nature. Here nature is portrayed as the measure of human beings and the tangible force that creates moralities. Dersu has been raised in the forest and is portrayed, therefore, as an inherently moral man. His sagacity and spirituality impress the explorer and urbanite, Arseniev. Dersu dies at the dawn of the industrial age, when human beings begin to isolate themselves from the world of mountains and forests and attempt to subjugate it. The film opens and closes by Dersu's grave, thus achieving a formal closure and an unbearable sadness indicating Kurosawa's awareness of the remoteness of his ideals to an over-developed, over-polluted contemporary Japan.

These films indicate one of Kurosawa's strengths: a talent for making environments and characters reciprocal units of expression. As in Zen, human life and the natural world interpenetrate.

But just as he touches and then withdraws from the Japanese conception of community and the social sanctions for behavior, Kurosawa's reliance on the individual necessitates a partial withdrawal from Zen. Kurosawa accepts Zen's maxim that truth comes from within each person, but Zen teaches a passivity and resignation before events that Kurosawa rebels against. His films are cries that people do not have to meekly submit to injustice and to poverty of the spirit. Zen is a letting go of one's hold upon the world to allow the spirit behind all things to be felt. Zen teaches one not to strive, not to seek, for these are intentions which will interfere with *satori*. In contrast, the Kurosawa hero grasps events tightly and demands that they conform to his will. There is no resignation to events behind Watanabe's desperate effort to build the park. Watanabe's quest is a denial of death, a rejection of the void which, to Zen, is part of the benevolent world-spirit and a necessary part of life which must be accepted. The instructor Lin-chi observed:

> There is no place in Buddhism for using effort. Just be ordinary and nothing special. Relieve your bowels, pass water, put on your clothes, and eat your food.... As you go from place to place, if you regard each one as your home, they will all be genuine, for when circumstances come you must not try to change them.[14]

This resignation to fate and indifference to political and social conditions—which should be regarded as a major shortcoming of mystical outlooks—is what the Kurosawa hero seeks to overcome. His characters attempt to transform the world into more just terms, rather than resign themselves to the existing oppression and corruption. Activity, vitality, and aggression are the attributes of Kurosawa's characters, not resigned acceptance of a disillusioning world.

The energy of this protest has affected Kurosawa's film style. His handling of movement often functions as a metaphor for the spiritual or emotional capabilities of a character. Just as the enlightenment of Zen is visible only through the actions of one who has become a Buddha, the moral ideals of Kurosawa's cinema are realized through the director's peculiar articulation of movement on screen. Kurosawa's distinctive realization of cinematic space and its compositional organization work to define the position of characters within his thematic-moral system.

To understand how Kurosawa deals with movement on screen, we must grasp properties of lenses of long focal length, since such "long" lenses are a fundamental feature of Kurosawa's visual style. The expressive characteristics of these lenses are linked to the intent of his cinema, which is to study on-screen movement by heightening its presence. The long lens for Kurosawa abstracts and purifies movement by plucking action from a spatial context. It makes movement a subject to be studied and contemplated as well as an element of style. How does this abstraction and elevation of movement occur?

In Kurosawa's post-1940s films, an enormous compression of depth occurs within the frame, effected by the long lens. Kurosawa uses the long lens to radically compress and flatten space. Thus, his filmic space exists on a two-dimensional plane, a horizontal-vertical axis, rather than in three dimensions as in most other narrative films. The illusion of three-dimensional space, basic to cinema, becomes for Kurosawa a planar conception of space. For him, space is a plane, not a volume.

In films shot with moderate or short focal length lenses, the illusion of spatial depth is primary, as something within which the characters may be placed or through which they may move. But in Kurosawa's films, this is no longer true. Here one cannot speak of movement *through* space, for space no longer exists within the frame as a volume in which to inscribe the movements of a character. When a horseman gallops toward the camera in a Kurosawa film shot with long lenses, that movement does not occur from point A to point B within a volume of space. It is a dislocated movement.

The galloping horseman does not travel through a depth of space toward the camera, but, instead, as he moves, his actions are suspended from spatial considerations, or, more precisely, a spatial context defined by depth perspective no longer serves to contain the movements of the character. Paradoxically, movement is foregrounded by being flattened, and motion in Kurosawa's cinema thus becomes highly stylized, abstracted, and heightened.

But having discovered the resources of the long lens, Kurosawa mitigates and modulates the space-compressing ability of this lens by using patterns of movement to suggest a field of space. A dialectical relationship occurs here between Kurosawa's choreography of movement and his use of the long lens. One element of style works to dissolve spatial relations while the other element suggests those relations. By considering Kurosawa's creation of a spatial context through the choreography of object and camera movement, we will encounter ways he uses visual design to place his characters in thematic and moral relationships with each other.

The choreography of converging zones of movement is one strategy that enables Kurosawa both to reorganize the constraints imposed upon his spatial fields by the long lens and to reveal emotional or moral qualities about his characters through formal means. In *Stray Dog* (1949), during a long montage sequence, the young detective, Murakami, searches with determination through the hot cities of Asakusa and Ueno for his stolen gun. The context is post-war Japan, an era in which blackmarket dealings in guns, drugs, and sex are rife. Murakami had once faced the same deplorable living conditions endured by residents of the slum sections he is searching. Like the father in *Bicycle Thieves* (1948), Murakami had been sufficiently brutalized by the post-war social collapse that the temptation to commit crime was strong, but, unlike De Sica's hero, he chose not to steal and rob. He made a moral choice which set him apart from the criminals in whose world he now searches. This moral separation is expressed by a shot in which Murakami walks from the foreground to the background of the image while a mass of people engulf him as they rush toward the camera. The organization of movement expresses the loneliness and isolation of the Kurosawa hero, the tension between himself, seeking enlightenment and responsible action, and the weaker, more indistinct masses of people representative of that residual element of feudalism in Kurosawa's thinking. This metaphorical shot organizes zones of movement so that a spatial field, foreground and background areas, is established in tension with the telephoto lens, which works toward compressing and therefore dissolving foreground and background. Having compressed space with his lenses, Kurosawa uses object movement to reconstruct it in a form that contains and defines his characters.

Kurosawa will also use his most famous and recognizable element of style, the tracking camera, to render movement morally significant and to create spatial zones in tension with the effects of the long lens. His tracking shots may reveal the state of mind of a character or be a synecdoche, standing for the larger thematic or moral perspective of a film. In the flamboyant early sequences of *Rashomon* (1950), the tracking camera pursues a woodcutter strolling through the forest. This character is in a purely emotional state, sensually responding to his environment. Feeling a oneness with nature, the woodcutter appears to be in a trance, intuitively responding to the rhythms of the forest by leaping a river, ducking a branch, crossing a bridge. He does not recognize these objects consciously, but glides over them in a Zen-like state. He appears so calm because his intellect has been suspended while he merges with the natural world.

The lyrically tracking camera simulates the rhythms of his walk and the topography of the forest and is, therefore, a formal indicator of this emotional state. The camera tracks beneath the character as he crosses a log over a stream, and, when he brushes away branches from his head, the camera moves to a higher angle just above his shoulders.

But the woodcutter's reverie is interrupted when he discovers evidence of a crime. He finds a hat lying on the ground, and he begins to walk faster, more anxiously. He finds a discarded sword, and scuttles about with fear. Finally, he stumbles across the body of a dead samurai.

All the shots in the sequence had been moving camera shots until the woodcutter discovered the hat, and then the tracking movements diminished and finally stopped. The woodcutter's discovery made him alarmed and rational. His thinking mind was switched on, and his sensuous, intuitive response to the forest was lost. This change is reflected in the shift from a moving camera to the stationary shots which record the discoveries of the clothes and the dead man. The sequence has shifted on a formal and a dramatic level from sensuous movement to a fixed, narrowed perspective of interest, from the intuitive responses of the Zen state to the divided and rigid perspectives of the rational mind. Kurosawa is thus treating emotions on a formal level, and this is one of the keynotes of his cinema: an attempt to find, in filmic terms, equivalent emotional forms.

In *Ikiru,* Watanabe has gone through several stages of despair upon learning that he will die, and he finally decides that he can redeem his life by building a park for slum children. He re-appears at his office and, as several co-workers gather about him, he explains what must be done. Watanabe sits at his desk in the background of the shot while two co-workers stand in the foreground on each side of the frame so that their bodies visually entrap the dying clerk, the entire composition flattened by the telephoto lens. As he tells his associates that he has decided to act upon a petition for a park, the camera slowly dollies forward, between the co-workers who disappear off the edges of the frame, toward Watanabe who now dominates the frame by himself. The camera movement has altered the composition so that Watanabe shifts from being a submissive to a dominant visual element. His newly-found moral strength liberates him from the deadening bureaucratic world, and the camera celebrates this change in one of the most joyous movements in Kurosawa's cinema.

Kurosawa's camera has drawn closer to the individual and has found methods to discriminate, at the level of the image, the worth of the self from the deadening despair and passivity of the social order, where predatory corporations, gangsters, the threat of atomic war, and an ethic of selfishness are in command of the world. Kurosawa's camera has described the possible relations between the enlightened individual and a violent and self-destructive world. In examining the structures and forms of humanizing behavior, Kurosawa has sought to bring together what he finds of greatest value in the cultures of East and West, in order that the deficiencies of both might be rectified, and in doing so, he transforms the contexts and reference points of Eastern and Western thought. If he has used a Western valuation of the individual to redress an oppressively feudal heritage which had proven quite compatible with fascism in the contemporary world, he has embedded this individualist emphasis within the spiritual framework provided by Zen. The encounter of East and West has also led to Kurosawa's softening of the codes of *bushido* and to the emphasis upon inner enlightenment. It is responsible as well for his fascination with making character and camera movement carry moral and psychological significance. That his films should be so full of energy and so relentlessly equate movement in theme and form with personal enlightenment is in accord with his view of life as a dynamic event. His perspective is not one of stasis, of silence, of emptiness, though he will at times engage these qualities. Watanabe's climactic action of self-affirmation is made in negation of the void into which he has so deeply peered and in which Zen finds such comfort. The Kurosawa character is most alive when he does not yield to stasis, silence, or emptiness, but when he defiantly rejects them. Herein lies Kurosawa's relevance: the attention and urgency given to this life, to this world, because that is all we will have.

Notes

1. Yazaki Takeo, "The Samurai Family and Feudal Ideology," in *The Japan Reader: Imperial Japan 1800–1945,* eds. Jon Livingston, Joe Moore, and Felicia Oldfather (New York: Pantheon, 1973), 60.

2. Cited in Audie Bock, *Japanese Film Directors* (New York: Kodansha International, 1978), 167.

3. For a discussion of this, see Ernst Cassirer, *The Philosophy of Symbolic Forms,* vol. 2: *Mythical Thought,* trans. Ralph Manheim (New Haven, Conn.: Yale University Press, 1977), 245–47.

4. See the discussion of the will and of happiness as a negative quality in Arthur Schopenhauer, *The World as Will and Representation* (New York: Dover, 1969), vol. 1: 306–26.

5. For a detailed discussion of the samurai's martial code, see Daisetz T. Suzuki, *Zen and Japanese Culture,* Bollingen Series no. 64 (Princeton, N.J.: Princeton University Press, 1973), 89–136.

6. Ibid., 21, 28.

7. Alan Watts, *The Way of Zen* (New York: Vintage, 1957), 23, 93, 100.

8. Ibid., 98.

9. Ibid., 21.

10. This has also been noted by Akira Iwasaki, "Kurosawa and His Work," *Japan Quarterly* 12, no. 1: 60.

11. Suzuki, 345–67.

12. Ibid., 271–314.

13. Donald Richie, *The Films of Akira Kurosawa* (Berkeley and Los Angeles: The University of California Press, 1965), 179.

14. Watts, 101.

Method, Technique, and Style

DONALD RICHIE

K UROSAWA HAS said that he could not possibly define his own style, that he does not know what it consists of, that it never occurs to him to think of it. While quite ready to talk about lenses, or acting, or the best kind of camera-dolly, he is unwilling to discuss meaning or aesthetics. Once I asked what a certain scene was really about. He smiled and said: "Well, if I could answer that, it wouldn't have been necessary for me to have filmed the scene, would it?"

Perhaps the reason for his reluctance to talk about meaning, about aesthetics, is that they are not *real,* they have no visible actuality. Aesthetics presume a system, and style presumes an expression and a reflection of the man himself. Neither are of any interest compared to the *actuality* of the new film to be made, the new script to be written. A man concerned with his own style is a self-conscious man, and Kurosawa is self-contained. Each film is a direct expression of himself, it is true, but, far from wanting to trace parallels or seek comparisons among his pictures, he has an aversion against seeing himself as he was. Just as he insists that his heroes neglect their past and live continually in the present, so he himself is uninterested in anything that *has* happened to him. "A director always likes his current picture the best. If he doesn't, he cannot direct it," he once said, and because the present is of such importance, his attitude toward past accomplishments has been both neglectful and cavalier.

He is particularly distrustful of any discussion of aesthetics because he dislikes generalization. He finds it a very clumsy tool. The abstract statement is not true because it must try to handle life, and life—as his films have indicated—should be shown subtly and delicately, and not handled at all. Theories, comparisons, generalizations, parallels, rules-of-thumb, these are destroyers of life and he refuses to use them.

You cannot sum up a living person; you can only sum up the dead. It is easy to speak of a director's past films; it is difficult to speak of his continuing style. Kurosawa is profoundly disinterested in his own style because he is so alive. He is, on the other hand, quite ready to talk about methods, about techniques. These are tools. These are *real.*

Excerpted and reprinted from *The Films of Akira Kurosawa,* rev. ed. (Berkeley: University of California Press, 1984), 214–18, 228, by permission. Copyright © 1984 The Regents of the University of California.

All Kurosawa films are about the same thing. In simplest terms, and shorn of all philosophy, his pictures are about character revelation. One of the reasons he has made so many suspense films either directly (*Stray Dog, The Bad Sleep Well, High and Low*) or indirectly (almost all the others, particularly *Rashomon* and *Ikiru,* with *Dodeskaden* and *Dersu Uzala* representing departures from this tendency) is that the suspense-story, like the detective-story, is about revelation. Kurosawa takes the "crime" (the unrealized life or the problem of choosing among evils) and works out a "solution." The solution is usually the hero himself and his character; this is what gives the film its final form.

Or forms, because Kurosawa has several favorites. One of them, for lack of any better name, I will call "sonata-form." The other (for the same reason) the "theme with variations." The latter is the simpler, and *Rashomon* is an example. So, however, is *One Wonderful Sunday;* so is *Ikiru;* and so is *Dodeskaden.* The sonata-form is more common in the later films and usually consists of (1) an introduction or prelude, which usually sounds the major theme, (2) a bridge, which is usually of major cinematic importance, (3) the main theme or *Hauptsatz* (whether there is a *Seitensatz* or not depends on the film), which is not as much a first "subject" as a complex of related ideas; it leads into (4) the development, of which it is also itself a part, and into (5) a recapitulation, which may be separate from the (often ironic) (6) coda.

This sonata-form need not be insisted upon, but it is interesting that so many of the films exhibit the same pattern. Perhaps it is because these films are based on conflict in a way that ordinary pictures are not. Since the conflict is usually one of character rather than of situation, it naturally follows that a "recapitulation" (that is, a testing of the hero) would bring back to the film its own major idea in a new, different, or expanded form. The reason one may refer to the form as similar to first-movement sonata-form is that both are about conflict. Music has never found a better way of presenting conflict than through the sonata-form, and the fact that Kurosawa's pictures fall into a somewhat similar pattern is another example of its validity.

Another aspect of form seen in many of Kurosawa's pictures is that of the full circle, or the spiral, the return to the beginning with a difference, the cyclic.

The circle appears in various ways. The theme-and-variation form (seen in *Rashomon* and *Stray Dog*) leads us back to the beginning (with a difference), and within the films themselves circular forms are often seen. The triangle in *Rashomon* is visual and the composition enforces it; the horse in *The Throne of Blood* runs round and round in a circle; the farmers in *Seven Samurai* always gather in a circle, as do Arseniev and his company around their campfire in *Dersu Uzala.* Circular images are stronger and more frequent in Kurosawa's films than they are in the pictures of most directors.

Likewise common is the form of the return. This is often inherent in the theme, since so many of Kurosawa's pictures are about the difference between theory and practice or the difference between illusion and reality. We see theory or illusion and then contrast and compare with practice or reality. This often has the effect of seeing the same thing twice (with enormous differences, of course), and this in turn creates the feeling of the return. In its simplest form this is seen in the many "practice" scenes that occur in Kurosawa's films. In *Sugata II* the teacher practices judo throws using a jug on a rope; these later become very real throws. During the practice he mentions one of Sugata's vices with every kick; during the fight Sugata—engaged in the real thing—discovers the reality of his own vices. In *Seven Samurai* Chiaki's wood-chopping (with its references to man-chopping) turns before our eyes into man-chopping during the film itself. In *Yojimbo* the practice with the knife (impaling dry leaves) becomes the real thing (impaling men). A variation on this motif, moving from reality to fantasy, occurs at the end of *Dodeskaden* when with a cut, the flashing light of a real trolley becomes the lamp that Rokuchan straps to his waist as he runs his imaginary streetcar at night. An example of the full return is also found in *Yojimbo*. The coward son returned home cries "mother" and she slaps him, and this is seen as funny; when he sees her killed he cries "mother" again and this is not so funny; when a swordsman drops his sword and dies shouting "mother," this extreme cliché from the period-film is given back all its horror and is extremely chilling, not funny in the slightest. A fine example of circular continuity is seen in *No Regrets for Our Youth*. A sequence opens with Fujita having a drink in a public bar. Some students are singing. This is followed by the dinner scene at the girl's home. She walks part of the way to the station with the guests—including Fujita. In the distance is a group of drunken students, obviously the same boys from the opening scene, still singing the same song. The next sequence opens with a title ("1938") and five years have passed. The opening scene is a group of young men going off to war. Though quite sober, they are singing the same song. The full return also defines the parameters of *Dersu Uzala*, where landscape reflects and merges with character. The two gigantic Siberian cedars between which Dersu Uzala was buried are missing from the opening scene but reappear in the final sequence when industrialization, if clearly imminent, has not yet engulfed the Taiga.

One could just as well see this as a process of metamorphosis, things changing with circumstances and yet, somehow, remaining the same; things viewed, as it were, from different angles, as though the director himself were circling around the object of his film.

Metamorphosis, the feeling for the circle, the sense of return, the recapitulation—all contribute to the form of the Kurosawa script and give the pattern of the picture. There are doubtless very personal reasons why this should be so, but another reason would be that Kurosawa is interested in the totality of a character, the totality of a situation. One of the few ways a narrative art may encompass a character is to circle the character, to reveal one facet after another, to return continually to what is already known, to contrast what we saw then with what we know now. The most revealing of psychological fiction (Proust, for example) continually circles and returns. Kurosawa's interest in character revelation insists upon a like movement—with the result of a like pattern.

Kurosawa comes from samurai stock; his father was one of the last of the old military-educators. Whatever part heredity and environment may have played, Kurosawa himself embodies a number of these earlier qualities. In particular, in him is seen in a very pure form the old-fashioned virtue of compassionate steadfastness, complete moral honesty, inability to compromise, and action through belief—all of which come under that single much-maligned term: *bushido.*

Nowadays all one sees of it is in the *chambara* or the Kabuki, and in a very debased form indeed. It usually has to do with obligation, personal honor, self-sacrifice, and other uninteresting attributes. Originally, however, it was a code of ethics, based in part on Zen teachings, which in its finest form became a philosophy, part of which might be paraphrased (from one of the original teachings) as: "If your mind is clean, orderly, likewise will your environment be clean, orderly." The follower of *bushido* could not blame environment for any lapse. He had to take full responsibility for wherever he was and for those with whom he was. Their state commented directly on his own. He was the center of his universe and if it was less than habitable then this was his own doing. Consequently early *bushido* had much to do with spiritual enlightenment, with an acute sensitivity to things as they are, and was of an innate practicality.

Another maxim of the time was: "Face both man and nature and learn." Thus the man adhering to *bushido* was a continual student in the face of the world and his test lay never in what he planned or thought but in what he did. If the *chambara* now has a large stock of heroes, it is because most heroes believe that a man is solely and entirely what he does. Consequently, the samurai who understood *bushido* was no sword-slinger. Action is far too precious to waste. Further, any action that could not in some way be corrected (a way of fighting, a way of thinking) was valueless. The reason was not, as might be thought, that perfection ought to be attained; rather, it was that *bushido* as a philosophy insisted on the fact that perfection was not only impossible, it was also a chimera, and a dangerous one at that. *Bushido* led nowhere, that is, it had no goal. It was just what the name implies, a way—a way of living, a process rather than a state. Therefore, anyone who thought himself past correction would be a fraud, because in *bushido* one could never attain the status of an end-result, an accomplished thing. Accordingly, *bushido* could only be expressed through action, and the most profound of the samurai maxims was: "To know and to act are one and the same."

The application of *bushido* tenets to the films of Kurosawa is obvious. His heroes are always completely human in that they are corrigible. The Kurosawa fable shows that it is difficult indeed "to know"; but at the end of the picture the hero has come to learn that "to know and to act are one and the same." The Kurosawa villain is the man who thinks he knows, who thinks he is complete.

Perhaps nowhere more completely do these tenets of *bushido* define the Kurosawa hero than in *Dersu Uzala,* where Dersu himself is a living example of a person who embodies the maxim "face both man and nature and learn." He is, ironically, an isolated Siberian hunter and not a samurai; yet through Dersu Kurosawa has created a man who exemplifies the pure way of life in harmony with self and nature, in humble acknowledgement of man's small-ness before the world. In having discovered the balance between the self and the demands of the environment, Dersu, although he carries no sword, is as ideal a warrior as Kambei of *Seven Samurai* himself. Like the samurai he cares nothing for material things, content to take from the world only what he requires for his own sustenance. His ethical code and his way of life are indeed identical.

Since the similarities between Kurosawa's heroes and Kurosawa himself are many, one may observe the old-fashioned virtues of *bushido* in the direc-tor himself—which is just what we have done throughout this book. With his ascetic face, his swordsman's hands, Kurosawa might be thought of as the last of the samurai.

In contemporary Japan, *bushido* is completely debased; the fury of the critics, to whom (in Japan more than elsewhere) compromise is a way of life, might be caused in part by Kurosawa's commitment to its virtues. At the same time, certainly, part of the success of *Seven Samurai, Yojimbo, Kage-musha,* and even the foreign-made *Dersu Uzala* with the Japanese audience is that these films present this ethic at a time when it is almost forgotten, yet still retains its part—however small—in the national character. When Kurosawa says he makes his films for the young people, he also says that he is bringing back to them a spiritual heritage that was once theirs. Like all creators, Kurosawa is a moralist; like all stylists, he manages to hide that fact superlatively well.

Akira Kurosawa

NOËL BURCH

KUROSAWA (BORN 1910) may be regarded as the direct heir of Eisenstein in so far as he returned the shot-change to its true function as a *visible, avowed parameter* of filmic discourse and was the first to apply consistently the Russian master's principle of montage units, with its dialectics of "correct" and "incorrect" matches. This assertion of direct affiliation is, however, something of an over-simplification in that several Japanese masters (Ozu and Naruse in particular) whose careers began a good decade prior to Kurosawa's, displayed almost from the outset a keen awareness of the necessity for the "intra-sequential" shot-changes being *seen,* both as an essential part of the film's abstract texture and as a contrapuntal component of its dramaturgy.

Now in Ozu's and Naruse's pre-war films, the anti-illusionist attitude which holds that there is nothing wrong about a shot-change being seen is especially noticeable in their almost total disregard for eyeline matching. Nearly every reverse-field set-up in the films which Ozu made during the middle 1930s was "wrong" from the normative standpoint of Western motion pictures, which by then had established very strict rules governing eyeline-direction and screen-position matching. The argument that this anomaly is merely Japanese naïveté, an aftermath of that historical lag observed during the previous period, is quite explicitly rebutted by the fact that Ozu's early comedies, up to about the time of *Tokyo no Gassho (Chorus of Tokyo,* 1931), contain a far greater proportion of "correct" (invisible) continuity matches than the films of the 1930s and early 1940s in which the director scarcely ever misses an opportunity for a "bad" match. These mismatched eyelines are part of a whole context of discontinuity in which "illogical" reversals of screen direction, startling ellipses, and a disruptive type of cutting of movement also abound.

Kurosawa's partial acceptance of his elders' attitude towards matching was undeniably a *choice,* essential to his mature formal conception, occurring as it did when he had been directing for nearly a decade. Indeed, during his first period (1942–51), Kurosawa ascribed far more importance to continuity than those elders had ever done, throughout a series of films which, though not always "transparent" (i.e., devoid of formal preoccupations, reducible to plot and dramaturgy), were undeniably illustrative, both

---

Excerpted and reprinted from *Cinema: A Critical Dictionary,* ed. Richard Roud (London: Martin Secker & Warburg, Ltd., 1980), 573, 575–77, by permission.

241

ethically and aesthetically, of the then worldwide concern with "social realism" as exemplified by the notoriously transparent school of post-war Italy.

It was not until *Rashomon* (1950) and above all *Ikiru* (U.K.: *Living;* U.S.:
To Live, 1952), that a resolutely "brutal" approach to the shot-change
became a permanent, fundamental option in Kurosawa's work. However,
while he employs many devices to emphasize and *use* the discontinuous
nature of the shot-change, attributing a "rhythmic," i.e., *structural* role to
the varying degrees of impact produced upon the spectator's perceptual system by those artificial caesuras in the continuity of the "action," there is one
important respect in which he diverges from Ozu and early Naruse. For,
while he often skillfully violates the "screen-positions rule" (and therefore
incidentally the eyeline rule) when cutting from two-shot to two-shot in
reverse-field set-ups, he never allows himself a "bad" eyeline match when
one or the other of his characters is alone in his or her respective shots. The
basic difference between these two kinds of "error" is that the one produces
an open, unresolved, "monolithic" disorientation, and the other is more
richly dialectical in that it offers both an immediate contradiction and its *de
facto* resolution through the patently visible reversal of positions. We may
surmise that Kurosawa's rejection of the "incorrect" eyeline match—in the
case, for example, of successive close-ups—is motivated by an awareness
that within a context of continuity, even if only partially *assumed,* such a
device is not productive of dynamic structure.

Probably the first film in which Kurosawa harks back to Eisenstein's all
but forgotten principle of montage units is *Ikiru.* Two of the film's key
tête-à-tête scenes—the condemned Watanabe's meeting with the writer in
the drinking stall, and his restaurant dinner with the girl Toyo—are built on
what might be called a mixture of two montage units. Now if these scenes
were simply alternations of mismatched field and reverse-field—as was the
case in the early films of Naruse and in Ozu's films—it would be stretching
a point to refer to them as being structured....

It is perfectly legitimate to put a dramaturgical interpretation on the
morphology of these sequences, asserting that the second, bracketed as it is
by "correct" matches, has a "closed" quality about it which metaphorically
reflects the fact that Toyo has no intention of seeing Watanabe again (as
indeed we discover in the subsequent scene outside the toy factory). Similarly, the fact that the scene with the writer involves only one such match
(at the beginning) may be regarded as leaving the scene "open" for Watanabe's pathetic night on the town, to which it is the prelude. Invariably, this
kind of *correspondence* between narrative organization and the material
options of set-up and editing will be encountered in any organically structured film—such symbiotic relationships abound in Ozu, Naruse, and
Mizoguchi—since an artist evolving a work with two or more structured levels will always tend to interweave them. The important thing is to guard
against reducing the one to the other, against regarding as most important

the level which superficially seems to communicate directly with our daily experience.

For the notion that structure is by definition a *code,* a configuration of signs which stand for "something else," be it "metaphysical," psychological, or merely behavioural, seems very much open to question today. It would, for example, lead to the dubious conclusion that this or that piece of scoring in a Wagner opera is predicated on purely dramaturgical considerations, whereas even if we are dealing with a leitmotiv which does, melodically analysed, have definite, codifiable bearings upon the libretto, the *totality* of the co-ordinates assigned to it (tonal, harmonic, rhythmic, instrumentational, etc.) sets up relationships with the overall formal conception of the work which are at least as important as its participation in the narrative discourse. And to take an even more familiar example, this same notion has also led to the kind of secondary school "close reading" of English Romantic poetry which reduces form to a series of dramaturgical, "expressive" effects, always in the name of the "higher" human values.

Thus, in *Ikiru,* the organization of these two sequences, while incontrovertibly "attuned" to the film's narrative dimension, is to at least an equal extent involved in the total formal scheme (which in this case is essentially based on narrative modes!). It is also closely related to the general demand for what I can only call "textural awareness" which all Kurosawa's major works place upon their audience, through the emphasis on shot-change *per se.* The difficulty with motion pictures, as Kurosawa and a few others have directed them, is that they are implicitly asking us to cope simultaneously with statements of several different species: we are being told a story and, at the same time, we are witnessing a kind of re-working of that space-time continuum which is occupied ideally (i.e., in our "mind's eye") by that story. The re-working is as much a statement as the story itself; however, the simultaneous perception of both demands what the specialists call a "good *Gestalt*"; in films this means a parallel awareness of both correspondences and variances, of likenesses and contrasts. In the present instance, it means recognizing these sequences as, indeed, "open" and "closed" in terms of the script movement, but also seeing them as structurally related in one respect (the repetition of the right-left reversals inherent in "bad" matches), unrelated in others (the cutaway to the stray dog in the first, the presence, in the second, of a second "correct" match).

Let us now examine the other ways in which Kurosawa "drives home" the shot-change; for, taken together with the Eisensteinian "mismatching" just discussed, they constitute in themselves a kind of vast, single variation form running through all his mature films, with the emphasis laid now on one mode, now on another. In *Rashomon* the emphasis is on radical oppositions between long-shot and extreme close-up; concomitantly, the 180-degree reversals, in which the film abounds, involve great "depth of field" (actually exaggerated perspectives through the use of wide-angle lenses). Another, more general strategy, though closely related to the 180-degree reversals and to their corollary, mis-matched screen-positions, consists of broad displacements, from one shot to the next, of the main object of screen-attention, generally from one edge of the frame to the opposite. This is, of course, especially remarkable in the wide-screen films, starting with *Kakushi Toride no San Akunin* (*The Hidden Fortress,* 1958), and culminating in the masterful *Tengoku to Jigoku* (*High and Low,* U.S. alternative title: *The Ransom,* 1963). Here, the whole first half of the film, shot in the living room of a wealthy shoe manufacturer whose chauffeur's son has been mistaken by a kidnapper for the industrialist's own boy, is built upon wholesale permutations and reversals of the characters on the screen (at times as many as seven or eight) from one shot to the next, and constitutes one of the most highly developed variation structures in Kurosawa's work.

It is interesting to note, in connection with this remarkable "cloistered" section, that the film in which the editing is most "brutal," in which the shot-changes ring out like so many pistol-shots in the mind's ear, is also the most claustrophobic of them all: *The Lower Depths,* drawn from the Gorky play. Over half the film takes place in one large room, and there is a heavy preponderance of 180-degree reversals among the shot-changes. Here, moreover, the limited range of shot-sizes allowed by the room makes these "jarring" shot-changes all the more dissonant, as opposed to the emphatic size-oppositions in *Rashomon,* which had a more conventionally "satisfying," resolved quality about them.

There is an interesting extension of Kurosawa's tendency to lay bare the reality of the shot-change: his use of hard-edge wipes in preference to dissolves. His one great "samurai" film, *Kumonosu-jo* (*Throne of Blood,* 1957), based on *Macbeth,* is particularly rich in examples of this, the least transparent of all "punctuation devices." It is no doubt just this quality, moreover, which caused it to be so quickly abandoned, after the orgy of ornamental use to which it was put following its invention in the early 1930s: the "sophisticated" directors of the 1940s saw only too well that this key, *par excellence,* to the essential artifice of films—the frameline itself crossing the spectator's effective field of vision and acting, besides, as a material embodiment of the shot-change—could unravel the illusionist tissue and give the whole game away. And it is in this light that Kurosawa's use of the wipe seems to me highly significant.

Aside from this basic emphasis on shot-change and the modal variation associated with it (differing degrees of obviousness, different ways of achieving it), there are other essential orientations which inform the works of Kurosawa. One of these is the idea of singularizing a certain figure or type of material. The long sequence-shot in *The Lower Depths* contrasting sharply with the fragmented texture of the rest of the film, making the most of the compositional possibilities afforded by the first really "open-air" shot in the film and constituting a pivot and a breathing space on which the whole film may be said to rest, is one good example of this principle. Another is the pair of color shots (showing the pink smoke which rises when the kidnapper burns the ransom brief-case) which intrudes stunningly upon the otherwise black-and-white context of *High and Low* and which also acts as a pivot: the film suddenly swings from the last of the long, static waiting scenes in the tycoon's lounge to the frantic chase across Tokyo with which all the rest of the film is concerned.

Different in substance and function, but related to the same attitude, are the three widely spaced interventions in *Ikiru* of an off-screen narrator, each shorter than the last, which break off entirely two-thirds of the way through the film on the words "Five months later the hero of our story died." Aside from their rarity, these passages are singularized in another way: all are associated with the heavily satirical setting of Watanabe's office in the city hall (they serve, in this context, to create a chastening "distance" effect); and in this connection, one may further observe that the first line of the initial intervention (which is divided into several subsections) is spoken over the X-ray negative of Watanabe's stomach, an even more radical "distance" device which destroys all conventional suspense and, at the same time, links this shot to the single other close-up of the X-ray, in the hospital consultation room.

Less significant perhaps, but nevertheless attesting to Kurosawa's sensitivity to the importance of this strategy, are the two slow-motion shots near the beginning of *Seven Samurai,* and the soundtrack cut near the end of *Tsubaki Sanjuro (Sanjuro,* 1962) as the two antagonists face each other before the final draw. This last scene, in which the interminably tense wait ends explosively in a single, lightning sword-stroke and a three-foot fountain of gushing blood, may be said to epitomize the last general construction principle which I should like to point out in Kurosawa's work: a systematic opposition between paroxysmic violence and protracted, sometimes lyrical, sometimes static scenes, from which narrative is momentarily evacuated but in which the tension builds.

Figures, or the Transformation of Forms

GILLES DELEUZE

ISENSTEIN WAS fascinated by Chinese and Japanese landscape painting, because he saw in it a prefiguration of the cinema.[1] But in the Japanese cinema itself, each of the two great directors closest to us has given priority to one of the two action spaces. Kurosawa's work is animated by a breath which fills the duels and battles. This breath is represented by a single stroke, both as synsign of the work and as Kurosawa's personal signature.[2] Imagine a thick vertical line which runs from top to bottom of the screen, which is crossed by two thinner horizontal lines, from right to left and from left to right. In *Kagemusha* this is the envoy's magnificent descent, constantly diverted to left and right. Kurosawa is one of the greatest film-makers of rain: in *The Seven Samurai* a dense rain falls while the bandits, caught in a trap, gallop on horseback from one end of the village to the other and back again. The camera angle often forms a flattened image, which brings out the constant lateral movements. We can understand this great breath-space—whether expanded or contracted—if we refer to a Japanese topology. One does not begin with an individual, going on to indicate the number, the street, the locality, the town; one starts off, on the contrary, from the walls, the town, then one designates the large block, then the locality, finally the space in which to seek the unknown woman.[3] One does not move from an unknown woman to the givens capable of determining her: one starts off from all the givens, and one moves down from them to mark the limits within which the unknown woman is contained. This, it would seem, is an extremely pure SA formula: one must know all the givens before acting and in order to act.[4] Kurosawa says that the most difficult time for him is "before the character starts to act: to get to that point I need to think for several months."[5] But, indeed, this is only difficult because it is difficult for the character himself: he first had to have all the givens. This is why Kurosawa's films often have two clearly distinct parts; the first, a long exposition and the second when senseless, brutal action begins (*Stray Dog, Heaven and Hell*). This is also why Kurosawa's space can be a contracted, theatrical space where the hero has all the givens before him and keeps them in view in order to act (*The Bodyguard*).[6] This is why, finally, the space expands and forms a great circle which joins the world of the rich and the world of the poor, the heights and the depths, heaven and hell. An exploration of the lower depths must take place at the same time as an exposition of the heights in order to trace this circle of the large form, crossed laterally by a diameter in which the hero is and moves (*Heaven and Hell*).

But, if there were nothing else, Kurosawa would merely be a distinguished director who developed the large form and could be understood according to the Western criteria which have become classical. His exploration of the lower depths might correspond accurately to the criminal or "miserabilist" film. His great circle of the world of the poor and the world of the rich might reflect the liberal humanist conception which Griffith was able to impose both as a given of the Universe and as a foundation of montage—and, indeed, this Griffithian version exists in Kurosawa: there are rich and poor, and they ought to understand each other, come to a mutual agreement.... In short, the requirement of an exposition before the action would correspond exactly to the SA formula: from the situation to the action. Within the context of this large form there are, however, several aspects which bear witness to a profound originality which can certainly be linked to Japanese traditions, but which may also be attributed to Kurosawa's own genius. In the first place, the givens, of which there must be a complete exposition, are not simply those of the situation. They are the *givens of a question* which is hidden in the situation, wrapped up in the situation, and which the hero must extract in order to be able to act, in order to be able to respond to the situation. The "response" therefore is not merely that of the action to the situation, but, more profoundly, a response to the question, or to the problem that the situation was not sufficient to disclose. If there is a certain affinity between Kurosawa and Dostoevsky, it is precisely on this point. In Dostoevsky, the urgency of a situation, however great, is deliberately ignored by the hero, who first wants to look for a question which is still more pressing. This is what Kurosawa loves in Russian literature, the connection which he establishes between Russian and Japan. One must tear from a situation the question which it contains, discover the givens of the secret question which alone permit a response to it and without which even the action would not be a response. Kurosawa is thus in his own way a metaphysician, inventing an expansion of the large form: he goes beyond the situation towards a question and raises the givens to the status of givens of the question, no longer of the situation. Hence it matters little that the question sometimes appears disappointing, bourgeois, born of an empty humanism. What counts is this form of the extraction of an any-question-whatever, its intensity rather than its content, its givens rather than its object, which make it, in any event, into a sphinx's question, a sorceress's question.

He who does not understand, he who is in a hurry to act because he believes he possesses all the givens of a situation and is content with this, will perish, by a wretched death: in *The Castle of the Spider's Web* [*Throne of Blood*] the breath-space is transformed into a spider's web which entraps Macbeth because he has not understood the question, whose secret was held by the sorceress alone. In a second case, a character believes it is enough to grasp the givens of a situation: he even proceeds to draw all their consequences, but notices that there is a hidden question, which he suddenly understands and which changes his decision. Thus, *Red Beard*'s deputy understands the situation of sick people and the givens of madness scientifically; he prepares to leave his master whose practices seem authoritarian, archaic, and barely scientific. But he meets a madwoman and in her complaint apprehends what was nevertheless already present in all the other madwomen, the echo of an insane, unfathomable question, which goes infinitely beyond any objective or objectifiable situation. He suddenly understands that the master "understood" the question, and that his practices explored its basis; he will therefore stay with Red Beard (in any case, no flight is possible in Kurosawa's space). What was particularly in evidence here was that the givens of the question in themselves implied the dreams and nightmares, ideas and visions, impetuses and actions of the subjects involved, while the givens of the situation merely contained causes and effects against which one could only struggle by wiping out this great breath, which bore both the question and its response. In reality, there will be no response if the question is not preserved and respected, even in the terrible, senseless and puerile images in which it is expressed. This is the origin of Kurosawa's oneirism, such that the hallucinatory visions are not merely subjective images, but rather figures of the thought which discovers the givens of a transcendent question, in so far as they belong to the world, to the deepest part of the world (*The Idiot*). The respiration in Kurosawa's films does not solely consist in the alternation between epic and intimate scenes, intensity and respite, tracking-shot and close-up, realistic and unrealistic sequences, but to an even greater extent in the manner in which one is elevated from a real situation to the necessarily unreal givens of a question which haunts the situation.[7]

In a third case it is clearly necessary that the character should absorb all the givens. But, since it refers to a question rather than a situation, this respiration-absorption differs profoundly from that of the Actors Studio. Instead of absorbing a situation in order to produce a response which is merely an explosive action, it is necessary to absorb a question in order to produce an action which would truly be a considered response. Consequently, the sign of the impression had an unprecedented development. In *Kagemusha* the double must absorb everything surrounding the master, he must himself become impression and pass through the various situations (the women, the small child, and above all the horse). One might say that Western films have taken up the same theme. But, in this case, the double has to absorb all the givens of the question that only the master knows, "fast as the wind, silent as the forest, terrible as fire, immobile as the mountain." This is not a description of the master; it is the enigma whose response he possesses and carries off. Far from making imitation of him easier, it is this which makes him superhuman or secures for him a cosmic relevance. Here, it seems, we run up against a new limit: he who absorbs all the givens will merely be a double, a shadow in the service of the master, of the World. Dersu Uzala, master of the forest impressions, slips into the state of shadow himself when his eyesight fails and he can no longer hear the sublime question which the forest asks men. He will die, although a comfortable "position" has been arranged for him. And *The Seven Samurai:* if they take so long to gather information on the situation, if they absorb not merely the physical givens of the village but the psychological givens of the inhabitants, it is because there is a higher question which can only be extracted gradually from all the situations. This question is not "Can the village be defended?" but "What is a samurai today, at this particular moment of History?" And the response, which comes with the question, once it is finally reached, will be that the samurai have become shadows who no longer have a place, either with the rich or with the poor (the peasants have been the true victors).

But in those very deaths, there is something appeased which allows a more complete response to be presaged. A fourth case, in effect, allows us to recapitulate the whole. *To Live* [*Ikiru*], one of Kurosawa's finest films, asks the question, "What is a man who knows he is allowed only a few more months of life to do?" Everything depends on the givens. Should we understand it to be, "What should one do to know pleasure at last?" The man, astonished and inept, duly does the rounds of the haunts of pleasure, bars and strip-clubs. Does this give the real givens for a question? Is it not rather a restlessness which obscures and hides it? Feeling a strong affection for a girl, the man learns from her that neither is it a question of a last-minute love affair. She cites her own example, explains that she makes little mechanical rabbits on a production-line, and is happy knowing that they will fall into the hands of unknown children, and in this way pass around the town. And the man understands: the givens of the question "What is to be done?" are those of a useful task to be performed. He therefore takes up his plan for a public park again and before he dies overcomes all the obstacles to it. There again, one might say that Kurosawa is giving us a fairly mundane humanist message. But the film is something quite different: the dogged search for the question and its givens through the situations. And the discovery of the response, gradually as the search progresses. The only response consists in providing givens again, re-stocking the world with givens, putting something into circulation, as much as possible, however little it may be in such a way that through these new or renewed givens, questions which are less cruel arise and are disseminated, questions which are more joyful, closer to nature and to life. This is what Dersu Uzala was doing when he wanted the hut to be prepared and a little food left around, so that the next travellers might survive and circulate in their turn. Then one may be a shadow, one may die: but one will have given back some breath to space, one will have regained the breath-space, one will have become park or forest, or mechanical rabbit, in the sense in which Henry Miller said that if he had to be reincarnated, he would be reincarnated as a park.

The contrast between Kurosawa and Mizoguchi is as well known as that between Corneille and Racine (the chronological order being reversed). Kurosawa's almost exclusively masculine world is opposed to Mizoguchi's feminine universe. Mizoguchi's work belongs to the small form, as much as Kurosawa's belongs to the large; Mizoguchi's signature is not the single stroke, but the wrinkled stroke, as on the lake in *Chronicle of the May Rain*, where the wrinkles of the water occupy the whole image. The two directors provide evidence for a clear distinction between the two forms, rather than for the complementarity which converts one into the other. But Kurosawa, through his technique and his metaphysics, subjects the large form to a broadening which operates as a transformation on the spot. On the other hand, Mizoguchi subjects the small form to a lengthening, a drawing-out which transforms it in itself. It is obvious from several points of view that Mizoguchi starts off from the second principle: no longer is it the breath, but the skeleton, the little fragment of space which must be connected to the next fragment. Everything starts out from the "background," that is, the fragment of space reserved for women, "the part of the house which is furthest back," with its delicate framework and veils.

Notes

1. Cf. in particular, *La non-indifférente Nature*, trans. Luda and Jean Schnitzer (Paris: 10/18, 1976), vol. 2: pp. 71-107. However, Eisenstein is interested less in different spaces than in the form of the "rolling pictures," which he compares to a pan shot. But he notes that the first rolling pictures constitute a linear space, and evolve in the direction of a tonal organisation of surfaces, animated by a breath. There is even a form where it is no longer the surface which is rolled up, but the image which is rolled on to the surface in such a way as to constitute a whole. Thus we rediscover the two spaces. And Eisenstein presents the cinema as the synthesis of the two forms.

2. [Ed. note: *Synsign* is a term Deleuze uses to designate the set of qualities and forces that are actualized in a particular milieu or situation.]

3. Akira Mizubayashi, "Autour du bain," *Critique*, no. 418 (Jan. 1983): 5.

4. [Ed. note: *SA* stands for Deleuze's formulation "from the situation to the action."]

5. Kurosawa, "Entretien avec Shimizu," *Etudes cinématographiques* nos. 30–31 (1964), 7.

6. Luigi Martelli, *"Yojimbo," Etudes cinématographiques*, nos. 30–31 (1964), 112: "All the episodes are placed in view of the main character . . . [Kurosawa] has sought to give priority to camera angles which contribute to flattening the image, and in the absence of depth of field, to inducing an impression of transversal movement. These technical processes play a fundamentally important role to the extent that they tend to represent a critical judgment, that of the hero who follows history through eyes with which we identify." [Ed. note: *The Bodyguard* is an alternate title under which *Yojimbo* (1961) was distributed in the West, and *Heaven and Hell* is another title for *High and Low* (1963).]

7. Cf. Michel Estève, *"Hakuchi (L'Idiot):* Une pureté Fascinante," *Etudes cinématographiques*, nos. 30–31 (1964), 50–54, and Alain Jourdat (*Cinématographe*, no. 67, May 1981), who analyse some of the great scenes of *The Idiot* in this connection: the snow, the skaters' carnival, the eyes, and the ice, where the oneirism does not alternate with, but is extracted from, the realism of the situation.

[The Heroic Mode of Kurosawa's Cinema]

STEPHEN PRINCE

"Reading and writing should become habitual."—AKIRA KUROSAWA[1]

W E ARE now in a position to consider the general contours of the heroic mode of Kurosawa's cinema. The films examined [in the previous chapter] advance a particular model of the world that tries to engage aspects of the postwar cultural landscape. It is important to consider the terms of this model because they show Kurosawa's highly selective use of cultural materials. But this model must also be understood so that its disintegration in later films may be grasped. In Kurosawa's cinema, we are dealing with twin impulses. The postwar imperative to engage history and remake society will be offset in later films by a contrary inclination to conceive the temporal process as fate and human life as an insubstantial shadow in a world of tears. This latter impulse is in marked contrast to the social optimism of the early films like *No Regrets for Our Youth* and *Stray Dog*. The chapters that follow explore different facets of these contrary qualities, while in the present discussion I attempt to clarify some cultural bases for Kurosawa's conception of heroism.

Kurosawa's films valorize qualities of strength, discipline, courage, and determination in their portrait of the hero's engagement with the social world. Kurosawa deeply admires spartan attributes and the strength of character they disclose. He says the home in which he grew up possessed "a samurai atmosphere."[2] His father was a military instructor whose "educational principles were terribly spartan."[3] He reports that under his father's influence, he approached such sports as judo and kendo swordfighting with single-minded devotion. Kurosawa portrays not only his father but also his mother in these terms. He relates a remarkable incident that displayed her strength of spirit, and in its use of crisis to reveal character, the anecdote could have come from any of his films:

My mother's strength lay particularly in her endurance. I remember an amazing example. It happened when she was deep-frying tempura in the kitchen one day. The oil in the pot caught fire. Before it could ignite anything else, she proceeded to pick up the pot with both hands—while her eyebrows and eyelashes were singed to crinkled crisps—walk calmly across the tatami-mat room, properly put on her clogs at the garden door, and carry the flaming pot out to the center of the garden to set it down.[4]

Reprinted from Stephen Prince, *The Warrior's Camera: The Cinema of Akira Kurosawa* (Princeton: Princeton University Press, 1991), 114–24, by permission. Copyright © 1991 Princeton University Press.

Afterwards, the doctor arrived and peeled away the scorched skin from her hands. Kurosawa says he was unable to watch this, but that his "mother's facial expression never betrayed the slightest tremor. Nearly a month passed before she was able to grasp something in her bandaged hands. Holding them in front of her chest, she never uttered a word about pain; she just sat quietly."[5] He adds, with deep respect, "No matter how I might try, I could never do the same."[6]

In foregrounding such qualities, Kurosawa's films display a warrior ideal, regardless of the historical era in which they are set. For one of the duties of a warrior was the injunction to maintain severe discipline. "[T]he true master of the way of the warrior is one who maintains his martial discipline even in time of peace," Tokugawa Ieyasu, one of the unifiers of Japan, is reported to have proclaimed.[7] In a world perceived as a place of violence and strife, a person of honor is obligated to choose a side and enter the battle. Kurosawa's world is an arena where his characters must be tested, where they must be victorious in their goals or must be broken and defeated. Passivity, acquiescence, and conformity to social norms are eschewed. The true life is one of conflict and even violence. The world through which the heroes move is often a frightful and terrible place and against which they must struggle. The environment—the deadening bureaucratic world that nearly claims Watanabe in *Ikiru* or the elements of rain and wind against which the seven samurai battle in their final fight—is at odds with the actions of the heroes. The world in these films admits of no kindnesses. The hero must fight to create humane perspectives.

It is through the terms of this fight that Kurosawa's ethical manifesto is presented. The strength of self he emphasizes is realized in the films through the capability of the heroes to face a society dominated by predators, where exploitation and oppression are the rule. Both Sanada and Watanabe confront gangsters, whose black market activities thrive in the postwar environment "like bamboo shoots after a rain."[8] Similarly, the corrupt corporations in *The Bad Sleep Well* are ravaging society, murdering and blackmailing those who oppose them, and the hero Nishi dedicates himself to overthrowing them, as he says, for all the people too weak to fight back. Here may be located a major distinction between Kurosawa and the American director with whom he is often compared, John Ford. The Fordian heroes in films like *My Darling Clementine* or *How Green Was My Valley* are strong supporters of conservative values. The latter film is a ringing affirmation of the family, with Donald Crisp the ideal patriarch. Ford creates a warm portrait of family life without admitting the ways that the patriarchal family can be a repressive extension of the state. In the early optimistic films, as well as in his later, darker works. Ford insists that his hero serve the institutions of the family, nation, or military. Films like *The Searchers* and *The Man Who Shot Liberty Valance* display a greater recognition of the cost these institutions exact, but their full meanings are not analyzed. That which Ford affirms, or cannot deny, of course, are those groups that the Kurosawa hero must reject: the state, corporation, and family.

In his films, Kurosawa views the larger context of established society as corrupted by the pursuit of position, wealth, or property. Keiko McDonald sees the basic question of the narrative of *Red Beard* as "How can one act in the face of a hostile social environment?"[9] In fact, this is a basic question of Kurosawa's narratives in general. The heroes struggle against their society: in *Ikiru*, against governmental bureaucracy whose stratified and hierarchical organization encourages submission and passivity; in *Red Beard*, against a culture that encourages doctors to get rich by treating a constipated aristocracy; in *Seven Samurai*, against a class heritage that demands that samurai refuse to help farmers and allow them to perish at the hands of bandits. And in *Record of a Living Being, Ikiru, The Bad Sleep Well, Yojimbo*, and *Red Beard* the central institution of the family is frequently viewed as cold, malignant, or repressive. Kurosawa's characters must break from these social groups to discover a regard for human dignity. But his work does not lapse into nihilism because the characters never reject the basic reality of human interconnectedness. The interactionist self is not abandoned, but in the films its field is reduced so that a space for autonomy can be opened. In acknowledging the interactionist self (i.e., insisting that the hero serve humanity), Kurosawa's films illustrate a cultural attitude described by Hajime Nakamura as dedication to the "human nexus": "The people to whom a human nexus is important place great moral emphasis upon complete and willing dedication of the self to others in a specific human collective. This attitude, though it may be a basic moral requirement in all peoples, occupies a dominant position in Japanese social life. Self-dedication to a specific human nexus has been one of the most powerful factors in Japanese history."[10]

Thus, although they pay great attention to the individualized self, Kurosawa's films also draw from this cultural basis in constructing their narratives and ethic. The characters embark upon a solitary path. Yukie, Sanada, Watanabe must climb their own mountains, and the price of this determined individualism is a profound loneliness that is the "other side" of individualism.[11] They are, however, rescued from nihilism or despair by their dedication to a human community. They reenter the social world to build parks, to defend farmers, to mitigate the general oppressiveness of things. It may be in this regard that Kurosawa's fondness for adventure stories should be understood. They permit him to construct a cinema of ideas in which human capabilities are defined as open-ended and developing, rather than closed, sealed by sets of institutional and social roles. Human life is portrayed as potential, as powerful energy flowing in new and sometimes frightening directions. Mikhail Bakhtin has pointed out that the adventure story "does not rely on already available and stable positions—family, social, biographical; it develops in spite of them."[12] The story is merely "clothing draped over the hero" that can change as often as he does. "It places a person in extraordinary positions that expose and provoke him, it connects him and makes him collide with other people under unusual and unexpected conditions precisely for the purpose of testing the idea and the man of the idea."[13] For Kurosawa, the adventure story becomes a metaphorical form probing the boundaries of the social world, the construction of the self, and the horizons of human development.

In this cinema of ideas, however, Kurosawa's valuation of the self should not be regarded as strictly the result of Western influences. As noted, his heroes are generated and informed by the ideals of the samurai warrior. Richie has described Kurosawa himself as "the last of the samurai."[14] The codes of *bushido* defined the proper conduct of the warrior, and the director's protagonists manifest many of its principles. *Bushido* emphasized courage, integrity, fortitude, and fealty.[15] The warrior ideal focused on the development of the individual's capabilities for strength: physical, moral, and spiritual. The ideal samurai combined athletic prowess with moral courage and unswerving allegiance to his lord. His martial skills received continual test in battle, and his moral development was expected to be no less rigorous. *Bushido* achieved an imaginative and cultural dominance in Japanese life, and Kurosawa draws from this mythic significance in creating his heroes. All the best qualities of the warrior have been spiritualized by Kurosawa in his art. The hero is always as strong as the ideal samurai. This strength may be physical, as in the samurai heroes of *Seven Samurai,* *Yojimbo,* and *Sanjuro.* But the protagonist may also be a person of ordinary or inferior physical capabilities, as in *Drunken Angel, No Regrets for Our Youth,* and *Ikiru.* As Tadao Sato remarks, their great strength is spiritual rather than physical.[16] Their will to create good is overwhelming, and this obsessive dedication, rather than any use of physical force, enables them to triumph. To the emphasis on individual willpower and physical might, Kurosawa adds an abiding commitment to securing the basic needs of other human beings. He thus translates the samurai's obligation to serve his lord into the hero's obligation to serve humanity. Both figures are bound by a duty of fealty, and the endurance of both is severely tested: the samurai in battle and in the bonds that link his fortunes to those of his lord, the Kurosawa hero in the conflict and struggle to humanize a corrupted world.

The samurai as a class were attracted to Zen,[17] and the director's sympathies for samurai culture may account for some features of the films that are analogous to certain Zen ideals. As Donald Keene remarked in a different context, however, direct influence is difficult to prove, and it may be more accurate to say that these features "coincide" with Zen.[18] A comparison of Kurosawa's narratives and characters with the model of enlightenment posited by Zen Buddhism can be instructive and can help us to understand some of the ways that Kurosawa's work resonates with a Japanese cultural heritage.

Introduced to Japan from China, Zen was one of a number of Buddhist schools that gained in popularity during the Kamakura and Ashikaga eras. In contrast to the older Tendai and Shingon sects, the Pure Land, Nichiren, and Zen sects emphasized the certainty of salvation and its potential availability to all.[19] Furthermore, Neil McMullin points out that each of these salvationist sects had a pragmatic, empirical emphasis upon *this* world, as opposed to the next.[20] For example, "Zen Buddhism so identifies the transcendent with the immanent, the 'other shore' with 'this shore,' that there is no reason for people to raise their vision above the level of this empirical world."[21]

Whether seeking wisdom via zazen (sitting meditation) or via koan exercises, the Zen initiate seeks to discover a potential for enlightenment that is inherent in all beings. "The Zen disciple . . . does not seek the Absolute outside himself; . . . he finds in himself the Buddha-nature as the foundation of his own being."[22] Since Buddha-nature is inherent in all things, enlightenment is truly the natural way of things, and it may be achieved by penetrating beyond the veils of illusion that attach to corporeal bodies and the material world. Worldly desires must be transcended to achieve enlightenment, but paradoxically, real-world consequences flow from this wisdom as it is applied to ameliorate human life. "To Zen, the enlightened mind is the truly natural mind, the mind allowed to be itself apart from all delusion or desire. It is awakened in meditation but is ultimately demonstrated in all arenas of life: work, caring for others, artistic creativity."[23]

In Zen there is a distrust of conceptualization because language is thought to foster artificial distinctions within a world that is whole in spirit. The "inner relationship between word and reality" is denied.[24] For this reason, action is favored over words, and the discipline is distinguished by its directness. The koan, riddles, and word puzzles are meant to test the depth of a pupil's insight. The questions or answers may sound semantically absurd, but this indicates the limitations of conceptualizing and, by rupturing the boundaries of language, can stimulate in the pupil enlightenment or *satori*, which in the Rinzai school can occur instantaneously.

Suzuki describes Zen as a religion of "self-reliance." Instruction about the experience of enlightenment is futile. "Satori must be the outgrowth of one's inner life and not a verbal implantation brought from the outside."[25] There is an emphasis on the individual's unique and private search for wisdom, which can be realized only through experience. Accordingly, the Zen instructor does little explicit teaching and will even disclaim his own role as a teacher. For the Zen master Dogen, "purposelessness" was essential to achieving enlightenment.[26] Thoughts, attachments, and the desire for enlightenment were to be discarded. The pupil must discover for himself or herself, but without intention or conscious goal.

Kurosawa's films demonstrate a fascination with a similar mode of instruction, appearing as a recurrent feature of narrative structure. In *Sanshiro Sugata, Drunken Angel, Stray Dog, Seven Samurai, Red Beard,* and *Derzu Uzala,* a master allows a pupil to observe and learn through experience, and the shocks that Matsunaga and Murakami undergo, shocks that are central to the experience of all Kurosawa heroes, are the necessary means toward enlightenment and are conceived as phases of moral transformation.[27] These shocks, in the words of a Zen priest, are "a trial to the soul, and can shatter the conventional lies with which it surrounds itself."[28] Kurosawa views enlightenment and spiritual development as necessarily predicated upon shock, and the narrative of his autobiography, like those of his films, is cast in this form. The events he recalls from his youth are often quite traumatic: nearly drowning several times as a boy, confronting mountains of corpses after the great Kanto earthquake of 1923 (an experience he describes as like "standing at the gates of hell"[29]), observing a young girl bound and tortured by a stepmother who, on the street, was the model of politeness. Of his memories, Kurosawa remarks, "The clarity of my memory seems to improve in direct proportion to the intensity of shock I underwent."[30]

The other component to this model of enlightenment is the unimportance of verbal instruction. Experience, often of a baffling, bewildering sort, is the guide. Kurosawa recalls his brother treating him with what seemed senseless cruelty—insulting him on the way to school, pushing him into a river when he could not swim—only to realize afterward that these harsh treatments were meant to contain a lesson and that, during moments of real crisis, his brother was always there to intervene on his behalf.[31] Throughout the autobiography, this brother assumes the role of a spiritual guide and a master. Indeed, for Kurosawa it is clear that this brother, Heigo, seems to live in a way that bursts the bounds of normal social life and may be a source for all the Kurosawa characters who do likewise.[32] As Kurosawa apparently did in life, his characters learn through similar examples.[33] In *Seven Samurai*, Kambei teaches the young samurai Katsushiro by allowing the young man to travel in his company, but it is a silent, wordless instruction, forged through experience and example. Similarly, Dersu Uzala rarely gives explicit moral lessons to Arseniev, yet the Russian explorer is a wiser man for his friendship with Dersu and reaches a new understanding of the spiritual power of nature. Though no master-pupil relationship exists in *Ikiru,* Watanabe's sudden realization of the path he must follow is precisely the kind of instantaneous awakening extolled in Zen, and it transforms his life, as it does the lives of the other heroes. (A similar literal rendition of *satori* occurs in *Sanshiro Sugata.*) "Satori is emancipation, moral, spiritual, as well as intellectual."[34]

Just as Zen emphasizes inner enlightenment, Kurosawa insists that spiritual awakening is a personal affair, that it cannot be imposed from without, and the pattern whereby his heroes must separate themselves from established social groupings is a structural embodiment of this inner wisdom. Enlightenment will not be found within an oppressive society but only through the individual's separation from it, although Kurosawa will also insist that his heroes, having attained enlightenment, return to the social order and attempt to reform it. That is, the enlightenment mind demonstrates itself "in all arenas of life." For such a philosophical director, few scenes occur in the films in which a character speaks about what he or she has learned. Instead, knowledge is revealed through action. When Watanabe attains satori in *Ikiru*, he does not speak but returns to work to push the park project through to completion. His new behavior and its concrete symbolization in the slum playground he helps erect are the correlatives of this wisdom.

Kurosawa's model of devotion to the "human nexus" acknowledges the parameters of the interactionist self, while limiting that acknowledgment through characters who are obsessive in their lonely individualism. Kurosawa seems to accept the maxim found in Zen that truth is a private matter, but Zen posits enlightenment upon a renunciation of the ego and desire.[35] The goal of enlightenment may be attained, but the caveat is that it be achieved through a deliberate nonseeking. Zen's model of self-liberation is based on a posture of humility and reverence. "There is here no Promethean struggle for the liberation and elevation of human nature."[36] By contrast, epic, Promethean struggles abound in Kurosawa's films and are, in fact, the model of heroic, human relations that his work constructs. Watanabe's rebellion against the stultifying bureaucracy is an act of stealing fire, as is Yukie's forfeiture of a conventional class identity. Kurosawa's postwar films are cries that people do not have to submit meekly to injustice and to poverty of the spirit. Zen acknowledges that letting go of one's hold upon the world is necessary to allow the spirit behind all things to be felt. In this context, one is taught not to strive (while, paradoxically, striving), nor to seek (while, enigmatically, seeking), for these are intentions that will interfere with the goal of *satori*. By contrast, this paradoxical relation between striving-while-not-striving is absent from Kurosawa's films. His heroes fight to transform the world into more just terms.

A major paradox must now be acknowledged, which lies within the more general Buddhist orientation to the world, of which Zen is merely one variant. (And Buddhism, in turn, is but one component of the Japanese religious tradition, which, because of its diversity, has been described as a "syncretic" one, an admixture of Shinto, Buddhist, Taoist, and Confucian elements.[37]) Buddhist doctrine seems to point to a quietistic outlook, an extinction of desire, withdrawal from the world, and contemplation of spiritual matters. The implications of such a stance might seem to "support an uncritical acceptance of social and political institutions."[38] As a character remarks in *The Tale of Genji*, "Our life is far too short and uncertain for anything in this world to have much importance."[39] A character in the Noh play *Obasute* observes, "Ah, well, this world is all a dream—best I speak not, think not."[40] The apparent fatalism of such a perspective partly involves the doctrine of karma, which regards the events of one's life as being predetermined by the deeds of previous lives. If misfortune befalls one, it must be because of some sin one committed in an earlier life or the transgression of a family member. "All relations with other people spring from some past act, however trivial. To drink from the same stream as another, to touch with your sleeve the sleeve of another even these acts are determined by some relationship in another life."[41] The destruction of the Taira clan by the Minamoto is attributed, in Japan's warrior epic *The Tale of the Heike,* to the effects of karma: "Their suffering was in retribution for the evil deeds of Kiyomori, the leader of their clan. He had held in his palms both heaven and earth; but to the throne above he paid no respect, and to the people below he paid no heed. He had put many men to death and had exiled many others at his whim, ignoring the mood of the people. None of his descendants could escape retribution for his crimes."[42]

Nirvana, the state of enlightenment and deliverance from worldly woes, from the cycle of rebirths, avidly sought by Buddhists, has been described as signifying a state of "motionless rest, where no wind blows, the fire is quenched, the light is extinguished, the stars have set, and the saint has died.... Such words and images evoke the concept of complete annihilation."[43] Yet such negativism, Dumoulin points out, should not be understood as a kind of nihilism because it furnishes the basis for supreme wisdom and for a commitment to the world. "Though aware of the nothingness of all things and of the ultimate irrelevance of all exertions of the spirit, he [the Bodhisattva, who has achieved enlightenment yet forgoes entrance into nirvana] never ceases to work for the benefit of all sentient beings."[44] Thus, to the extent that enlightenment leads to a dedication to benefiting others, the apparent negativism of the doctrine is not to be understood negatively.[45]

Moreover, from a historical standpoint, Buddhism was not disengaged from social and political realities. In fact, Buddhist monasteries had become such centers of economic, political, and military power that their subjugation was perceived by Oda Nobunaga in the sixteenth century as a prerequisite for the emergence of national unification, and he accordingly undertook such a campaign.[46] Thus, to separate Buddhist doctrine from the political, military, or economic power of the estates, or to regard the latter as of subordinate importance, is to risk losing sight of the this-worldly emphasis of Japanese Buddhism, especially of the salvationist sects such as Zen. Hajime Nakamura points out that Japanese Buddhism is "strongly imbued with an activistic behaviorism and practical tendency, which is tied up with its this-worldliness."[47] Religion and worldly affairs, religion and politics, were not separated in premodern Japan during the great periods of Buddhist power.[48]

> To separate the doctrinal and institutional dimensions of Buddhism, or to consider the former dimension to be more purely Buddhist than the latter, is to impose a false distinction on both the Buddhist and the Japanese traditions. The Buddhist tradition was never, least of all in Japan, simply a set of doctrines and religious practices. Rather, it was a complex economic, ethical, philosophical, political, and social phenomenon that wielded immense influence for over a millennium."[49]

With this important qualification in mind—that Japanese Buddhism played a powerful institutional, pragmatic role in worldly affairs—it may now be suggested that Kurosawa's films often seem drawn to formulations akin to the doctrinal negativism of the Buddhist outlook. His films insist that human beings grasp events tightly and make the conditions of their lives conform to their will, that intervention against oppression is a moral necessity. Counterposed to this insistence, however, is an affinity to a perception of life as an insubstantial shadow. We are not yet in a position to see this, but several of the films treated in this chapter—*Rashomon, The Lower Depths,* and *Throne of Blood*—describe a vision diametrically opposed to that found in *No Regrets for Our Youth, Drunken Angel, The Quiet Duel, Stray Dog,* and *Ikiru.* In short, it will become apparent that one of the dialectics informing Kurosawa's works is a struggle between a belief in the materialist process—that human beings make their world and can change it—and an emphasis on dissolution, decay, and impermanence as fundamental truths of human life.

Notes

1. Kyoko Hirano, "Making Films for All the People: An Interview with Akira Kurosawa," *Cineaste* 14, no. 4 (1986): 25.

2. Akira Kurosawa, *Something Like an Autobiography,* trans. Audie E. Bock (New York: Vintage, 1983), 28.

3. Ibid., 17.

4. Ibid., 22.

5. Ibid.

6. Ibid.

7. Ryusaku Tsunoda, Wm. Theodore de Bary, and Donald Keene, eds., *Sources of Japanese Tradition* (1958; reprint, New York: Columbia University Press, 1964): 330.

8. Kurosawa, *Something Like an Autobiography,* 156.

9. Keiko I. McDonald, *Cinema East: A Critical Study of Major Japanese Films* (Rutherford, N.J.: Fairleigh Dickinson University Press, 1983), 72.

10. Hajime Nakamura, *Ways of Thinking of Eastern Peoples,* rev. trans. ed. Philip Wiener (Honolulu: East-West Center Press, 1964), 414.

11. Soseki described individualism this way in a lecture on the topic, according to Howard S. Hibbett, "Natsume Soseki and the Psychological Novel," in *Tradition and Modernization in Japanese Culture,* ed. Donald H. Shively (Princeton, N.J.: Princeton University Press, 1982): 309. Hibbett writes (346) that "For Soseki . . . individualism and alienation were the inescapable conditions of a modern consciousness." The observation also applies to Kurosawa's cinema, where, in a typical example, the birth pangs of Watanabe's enlightenment accompany the trauma of the alienated self.

12. Mikhail Bakhtin, *Problems of Dostoevsky's Poetics,* ed. and trans. Caryl Emerson (Minneapolis: University of Minnesota Press, 1984), 104.

13. Ibid., 105.

14. Donald Richie, *The Films of Akira Kurosawa,* rev. ed. (Berkeley: University of California Press, 1984), 228. Richie suggests that Kurosawa's own life and personality are lived in accordance with *bushido.*

15. For discussions of *bushido,* see Tsunoda et al., *Sources of Japanese Tradition,* 389–91, and Kenneth Dean Butler, "The Heike Monogatari and the Japanese Warrior Ethic," *Harvard Journal of Asiatic Studies* 29 (1969): 93–108. Daisetz T. Suzuki discusses the codes of samurai behavior as related to Zen and the cult of swordsmanship in *Zen and Japanese Culture* (1959; reprint, Princeton, N.J.: Princeton University Press, 1973), 89–214.

16. Tadao Sato, *Currents in Japanese Cinema,* trans. Gregory Barrett (Tokyo: Kodansha International, 1982), 28.

17. H. Paul Varley cautions against overestimating the scope of this attraction. He maintains that it was the samurai elite who were drawn to Zen, while much of the class looked instead to the salvationist sects of Buddhism. *Japanese Culture,* 3rd ed. (Honolulu: University of Hawaii Press, 1973), 94.

18. Donald Keene, *Landscapes and Portraits: Appreciations of Japanese Culture* (Tokyo and Palo Alto, Calif.: Kodansha International, 1971), 15.

19. Joseph Kitagawa, *Religion in Japanese History* (New York: Columbia University Press, 1966), 111.

20. Neil McMullin, *Buddhism and the State in Sixteenth-Century Japan* (Princeton, N.J.: Princeton University Press, 1984), 280–82.

21. Ibid., 280–81.

22. Heinrich Dumoulin, *A History of Zen Buddhism,* trans. Paul Peachey (New York: Pantheon, 1963), 167.

23. Robert Ellwood and Richard Pilgrim, *Japanese Religion: A Cultural Perspective* (Englewood Cliffs, N.J.: Prentice-Hall, 1985), 119.

24. Dumoulin, *A History of Zen Buddhism,* 50.

25. Suzuki, *Zen and Japanese Culture,* 10.

26. Dumoulin, *A History of Zen Buddhism,* 161–64.

27. Sato feels the recurrent master-pupil relations in Kurosawa's films are evidence of an anxiety over generational ruptures in postwar Japan (i.e., parent-child estrangement). *Currents in Japanese Cinema,* 124–31.

28. E. Steinilber-Oberlin, *The Buddhist Sects of Japan,* trans. Marc Loge (1938; reprint, Westport, Conn.: Greenwood Press, 1970), 139.

29. Kurosawa, *Something Like an Autobiography,* 53.

30. Ibid., 5.

31. Ibid., 10–12.

32. This point was suggested to me by Michael Jeck, whose company, R5/S8 Presents, distributes many of Kurosawa's early films in the United States.

33. Akira Iwasaki also notes the wordless quality of the masters' instruction in Kurosawa's films in "Kurosawa and His Work," in *Focus on Rashomon,* ed. Donald Richie (Englewood Cliffs, N.J.: Prentice-Hall, 1972), 24.

34. Suzuki, *Zen and Japanese Culture,* 16–17.

35. Dumoulin, *A History of Zen Buddhism,* 172–73.

36. Ibid, 173.

37. McMullin, *Buddhism and the State,* 275–76.

38. Peter Pardue, *Buddhism: A Historical Introduction to Buddhist Values and the Social and Political Forms They Have Assumed in Asia,* quoted in McMullin, *Buddhism and the State,* 280. Ivan Morris offers a negative view of the stress of Heian Buddhism upon evanescence and impermanence in *The World of the Shining Prince* (New York: Penguin, 1964), 121–35. He finds (130) the social consequence of this emphasis to be "a sense of helplessness and resignation, a reluctance to take things into one's own hands or improve the conditions of one's existence."

39. Quoted in Morris, *The World of the Shining Prince,* 126.

40. Quoted in Donald Keene, ed., *20 Plays of the Noh Theatre* (New York: Columbia University Press, 1970), 125.

41. George Sansom, *A History of Japan* (1958–1963; reprint, Stanford, Calif.: Stanford University Press, 1987), vol 1: 436.

42. Hiroshi Kitagawa and Bruce T. Tsuchida, trans., *The Tale of the Heike* (Tokyo: University of Tokyo Press, 1975), 781.

43. Dumoulin, *A History of Zen Buddhism,* 14.

44. Ibid., 25.

45. In his discussion of Saburo Ienaga's work, Robert Bellah points to the "complex dialectic" acknowledged by Buddhism between a sinful world and religious ideals. "Salvation

comes not through fleeing from the world but through 'facing it head on' and recognizing its sinful and suffering nature.... For Ienaga religion does not dissolve the tension between the real and the ideal—it offers no resolution at all on this level—but insists on remaining acutely conscious of it," Robert N. Bellah, "Ienaga Saburo and the Search for Meaning in Modern Japan," in *Changing Japanese Attitudes Toward Modernization,* ed. Marius B. Jansen (1965; reprint, Princeton, N.J.: Princeton University Press, 1972), 398. This passage serves quite well as a description of how Kurosawa's moral vision is working in *Ran.* Kurosawa has likened the film's view to that of a "Buddha in tears." He confronts what he regards as the world's essentially sinful nature, issues a lament that is the film, and finds a kind of salvation in this recognition.

46. McMullin examines this campaign and its effects on Buddhism throughout *Buddhism and the State.*

47. Nakamura, *Ways of Thinking of Eastern Peoples,* 367.

48. See McMullin, *Buddhism and the State,* 282.

49. Ibid., 5.

Selected Bibliography

Books Available in English

Anderson, Joseph L., and Donald Richie. *The Japanese Film: Art and Industry.* Princeton, N.J.: Princeton University Press, 1982.

Bock, Audie. *Japanese Film Directors.* San Francisco: Kodansha International, 1985.

Burch, Noël. *To the Distant Observer: Form and Meaning in the Japanese Cinema.* Rev. and ed. Annette Michelson. Berkeley: University of California Press, 1979.

Chang, Kevin K. W., ed. *Kurosawa: Perceptions on Life, An Anthology of Essays.* Honolulu: Honolulu Academy of Arts, 1991.

Desser, David. *The Samurai Films of Akira Kurosawa.* Ann Arbor, Mich.: UMI Research Press, 1983.

Erens, Patricia. *Akira Kurosawa: A Guide to References and Resources.* Boston: G. K. Hall, 1979.

Goodwin, James. *Akira Kurosawa and Intertextual Cinema.* Baltimore, Md.: Johns Hopkins University Press, 1994.

Kurosawa, Akira. *Complete Works of Akira Kurosawa.* [In Japanese and English] Trans. Kimi Aida and Don Kenny. Tokyo: Kinema Jumpo Sha, 1971. Vol. 1: *Dodeskaden;* Vol. 2: *Sanshiro Sugata* and *No Regrets for Our Youth;* Vol. 3: *One Wonderful Sunday* and *Drunken Angel;* Vol. 4: *Quiet Duel* and *Stray Dog;* Vol. 6: *The Idiot* and *Ikiru;* Vol. 9: *The Hidden Fortress* and *The Bad Sleep Well.* [The edition ceased publication after these volumes.]

———. *Ikiru.* Trans. Donald Richie. New York: Simon and Schuster, 1969.

———. *Ran.* Trans. Tadashi Shishido. Boston: Shambhala, 1986.

———. *Rashomon.* Ed. and trans. Donald Richie. New York: Grove, 1969.

———. *Rashomon.* Ed. and trans. Donald Richie. New Brunswick, N.J.: Rutgers University Press, 1987.

———. *Seven Samurai.* Trans. Donald Richie. London: Lorrimer, 1970.

———. *Something Like an Autobiography.* Trans. Audie E. Bock. New York: Vintage, 1983.

McDonald, Keiko I. *Cinema East: A Critical Study of Major Japanese Films.* Rutherford, N.J.: Fairleigh Dickinson University Press, 1983.

Mellen, Joan. *Voices from the Japanese Cinema.* New York: Liveright, 1975.

———. *The Waves at Genji's Door: Japan Through Its Cinema.* New York: Pantheon, 1976.

Nolletti, Arthur, Jr., and David Desser, eds. *Reframing Japanese Cinema: Authorship, Genre, History.* Bloomington: Indiana University Press, 1992.

Prince, Stephen. *The Warrior's Camera: The Cinema of Akira Kurosawa.* Princeton, N.J.: Princeton University Press, 1991.

Richie, Donald. *The Films of Akira Kurosawa.* Rev. ed. Berkeley: University of California Press, 1984.

———. *Japanese Cinema: Film Style and National Character.* Garden City, N.Y.: Doubleday, 1971.

———. *The Japanese Movie.* Rev. ed. New York: Kodansha International, 1982.

Richie, Donald, ed. *Focus on Rashomon.* Englewood Cliffs, N.J.: Prentice-Hall, 1972.

Sato, Tadao, *Currents in Japanese Cinema.* Trans. Gregory Barrett. Tokyo: Kodansha International, 1982.

Silver, Alain. *The Samurai Film.* Rev. ed. Woodstock, N.Y.: Overlook Press, 1983.

Svensson, Arne. *Screen Series: Japan.* New York: A. S. Barnes, 1971.

Tucker, Richard N. *Japan: Film Image.* London: Studio Vista, 1973.

A Kurosawa Filmography

1943: *Sanshiro Sugata* [*Sugata Sanshiro*]

PRODUCTION COMPANY: Toho

PRODUCER: Keiji Matsuzaki

DIRECTOR: Akira Kurosawa

SCREENPLAY: Akira Kurosawa, based on the novel by Tsuneo Tomita

PHOTOGRAPHY: Akira Mimura

MUSIC: Seichi Suzuki

CAST: Susumu Fujita (Sanshiro Sugata), Denjiro Okochi (Shogoro Yano, his teacher), Takashi Shimura (Hansuke Murai), Yukiko Todoroki (Sayo, Murai's daughter), Yoshio Kosugi (Saburo Momma, jujitsu teacher), Ranko Hanai (Osumi, Momma's daughter), Ryunosuke Tsukigata (Gennosuke Higaki), Akitake Kono (Yoshimaro Dan), Soji Kiyokawa (Yujiro Toda), Kunio Mita (Kohei Tsuzaki), Akira Nakamura (Toranosuke Niiseki), Sugisaku Aoyama (Tsunetami Iinuma), Kokuten Kodo (priest), Ichiro Sugai (police chief), Michisaburo Segawa (Hatta)

1944: *The Most Beautiful* [*Ichiban Utsukushiku*]

PRODUCTION COMPANY: Toho

PRODUCER: Hitoshi Usami

DIRECTOR: Akira Kurosawa

SCREENPLAY: Akira Kurosawa

PHOTOGRAPHY: Joji Ohara

MUSIC: Seichi Suzuki

CAST: Takashi Shimura (Goro Ishida, factory head), Soji Kiyokawa (Soichi Yoshikawa, general manager), Ichiro Sugai (Ken Saneda, production chief), Takako Irie (Tokuko Mizushima, dormitory mother), Yoko Yaguchi (Tsuru Watanabe, group leader), Koyuri Tanima (Yuriko Tanimura, assistant group leader), Sachiko Ozaki, Shizuko Nishigaki, Asako Suzuki, Haruko Toyama, Aiko Masa, Kazuko Hitomi, Toshiko Hashima (female workers)

1945: *Sanshiro Sugata, Part Two* [*Zoku Sugata Sanshiro*]

PRODUCTION COMPANY: Toho

PRODUCER: Motohiko Ito

DIRECTOR: Akira Kurosawa

SCREENPLAY: Akira Kurosawa, based on the novel by Tsuneo Tomita
PHOTOGRAPHY: Takeo Ito
MUSIC: Seichi Suzuki
CAST: Susumu Fujita (Sanshiro Sugata), Denjiro Okochi (Shogoro Yano), Ryunosuke Tsukigata (Gennosuke Higaki), Akitake Kono (Genzaburo Higaki), Yukiko Todoroki (Sayo), Soji Kiyokawa (Yujiro Toda), Masayuki Mori (Yoshimaro Dan), Seiji Miyaguchi (Kohei Tsuzaki), Kokuten Kodo (Kazuyoshi Saizuchi)

1945: *The Men Who Tread On the Tiger's Tail* [*Tora no O o Fumu Otokotachi*]
PRODUCTION COMPANY: Toho
PRODUCER: Motohiko Ito
DIRECTOR: Akira Kurosawa
SCREENPLAY: Akira Kurosawa, based on the kabuki drama *Kanjincho*
PHOTOGRAPHY: Takeo Ito
MUSIC: Tadashi Hattori
CAST: Hanshiro Iwai (Yoshitsune, lord), Susumu Fujita (Togashi, magistrate), Kenichi Enomoto (porter), Denjiro Okochi (Benkei, chief vassal), Masayuki Mori (Kamei), Takashi Shimura (Kataoka), Akitake Kono (Ise), Yoshio Kosugi (Suruga), Dekao Yoko (Hita-chibo), Soji Kiyokawa (Togashi's aide)

1946: *No Regrets for Our Youth* [*Waga Seishun ni Kuinashi*]
PRODUCTION COMPANY: Toho
PRODUCER: Keiji Matsuzaki
DIRECTOR: Akira Kurosawa
SCREENPLAY: Eijiro Hisaita and Akira Kurosawa
PHOTOGRAPHY: Asakazu Nakai
MUSIC: Tadashi Hattori
CAST: Denjiro Okochi (Professor Yagihara), Eiko Miyoshi (his wife), Setsuko Hara (Yukie, his daughter), Susumu Fujita (Ryukichi Noge), Kokuten Kodo (his father), Haruko Sugimura (his mother), Akitake Kono (Itokawa), Takashi Shimura (Dokuichigo, police inspector), Masao Shimizu (Professor Hakozaki), Haruo Tanaka, Ichiro Chiba, Isamu Yonekura, Noboru Takagi, Hiroshi Sano (students)

1947: *One Wonderful Sunday* [*Subarashiki Nichiyobi*]
PRODUCTION COMPANY: Toho
PRODUCER: Sojiro Motoki
DIRECTOR: Akira Kurosawa
SCREENPLAY: Keinosuke Uegusa and Akira Kurosawa
PHOTOGRAPHY: Asakazu Nakai
MUSIC: Tadashi Hattori

CAST: Isao Numazaki (Yuzo), Chieko Nakakita (Masako), Ichiro Sugai (black-marketeer), Midori Ariyama (Sono, his mistress), Masao Shimizu (dance hall manager), Aguri Hidaka (dancer), Sachio Sakai (black-market ticket man), Toshi Mori (apartment owner), Tokuji Kobayashi (receptionist in apartment), Shiro Mizutani (street urchin), Zeko Nakamura (shop owner)

1948: *Drunken Angel [Yoidore Tenshi]*

PRODUCTION COMPANY: Toho

PRODUCER: Sojiro Motoki

DIRECTOR: Akira Kurosawa

SCREENPLAY: Keinosuke Uegusa and Akira Kurosawa

PHOTOGRAPHY: Takeo Ito

MUSIC: Fumio Hayasaka

CAST: Takashi Shimura (Sanada, doctor), Toshiro Mifune (Matsunaga, gangster), Reisaburo Yamamoto (Okada, gang boss), Chieko Nakakita (Miyo, nurse), Michiyo Kogure (Nanae, Matsunaga's mistress), Noriko Sengoku (Gin, bar girl), Eitaro Shindo (Takahama, the doctor's friend), Choko Iida (old wet nurse), Taiji Tonoyama (shop owner), Katao Kawasaki (manager of the flower shop), Ko Ubukata (young hoodlum), Yoshiko Kuga (girl), Shizuko Kasagi (singer), Masao Shimizu (boss)

1949: *The Quiet Duel [Shizukanaru Ketto]*

PRODUCTION COMPANY: Daiei

PRODUCER: Sojiro Motoki and Hisao Ichikawa

DIRECTOR: Akira Kurosawa

SCREENPLAY: Senkichi Taniguchi and Akira Kurosawa, based on the play *Datai I* (The Abortion Doctor) by Kazuo Kikuta

PHOTOGRAPHY: Soichi Aisaka

MUSIC: Akira Ifukube

CAST: Toshiro Mifune (Kyoji Fujisaki), Takashi Shimura (Konosuke Fujisaki, his father), Miki Sanjo (Misao Matsumoto, Kyoji's girlfriend), Kenjiro Uemura (Susumu Nakada), Chieko Nakakita (Takiko Nakada, his wife), Noriko Sengoku (Rui Minegishi, nurse), Junnosuke Miyazaki (Horiguchi), Isamu Yamaguchi (Inspector Nosaka), Seiji Izumi (policeman), Shigeru Matsumoto (boy with appendicitis), Tadashi Date (boy's father), Etsuko Sudo (boy's mother), Hiroko Machida (Imai, nurse), Wakayo Matsumura (student nurse)

1949: *Stray Dog [Nora Inu]*

PRODUCTION COMPANY: Shintoho

PRODUCER: Sojiro Motoki

DIRECTOR: Akira Kurosawa

SCREENPLAY: Ryuzo Kikushima and Akira Kurosawa

PHOTOGRAPHY: Asakazu Nakai

MUSIC: Fumio Hayasaka

CAST: Toshiro Mifune (Murakami, detective), Takashi Shimura (Sato, chief detective), Kazuko Motohashi (Sato's wife), Ko Kimura (Yusa, criminal), Keiko Awaji (Harumi Namiki, his girl), Reisaburo Yamamoto (Honda, suspect), Noriko Sengoku (girl), Gen Shimizu (Nakajima), Yasushi Nagata (Abe), Reikichi Kawamura (Ichikawa), Eiko Miyoshi (Harumi's mother), Yunosuke Ito (theater manager), Minoru Chiaki (young man at theater), Masao Shimizu (Nakamura)

1950: *Scandal* [*Shubun*]

PRODUCTION COMPANY: Shochiku

PRODUCER: Takashi Koide

DIRECTOR: Akira Kurosawa

SCREENPLAY: Ryuzo Kikushima and Akira Kurosawa

PHOTOGRAPHY: Toshio Ubukata

MUSIC: Fumio Hayasaka

CAST: Toshiro Mifune (Ichiro Aoe), Yoshiko Yamaguchi (Miyako Seijo), Takashi Shimura (Hiruta, lawyer), Yoko Katsuragi (Masako, his daughter), Noriko Sengoku (Sumie, Aoe's model), Eitaro Ozawa (Hori, publisher), Bokuzen Hidari (drunk), Kokuten Kodo (farmer)

1950: *Rashomon* [*Rashomon*]

PRODUCTION COMPANY: Daiei

PRODUCER: Jingo Minoura

DIRECTOR: Akira Kurosawa

SCREENPLAY: Shinobu Hashimoto and Akira Kurosawa, based on the stories "Rashomon" and "In a Grove" by Ryunosuke Akutagawa

PHOTOGRAPHY: Kazuo Miyagawa

MUSIC: Fumio Hayasaka

CAST: Toshiro Mifune (Tajomaru, bandit), Masayuki Mori (Takehiro, samurai), Machiko Kyo (Masago, his wife), Takashi Shimura (woodcutter), Minoru Chiaki (priest), Kichijiro Ueda (commoner), Daisuke Kato (police agent), Fumiko Homma (medium)

1951: *The Idiot* [*Hakuchi*]

PRODUCTION COMPANY: Shochiku

PRODUCER: Takashi Koide

DIRECTOR: Akira Kurosawa

SCREENPLAY: Eijiro Hisaita and Akira Kurosawa, based on the novel by Feodor Dostoyevsky

PHOTOGRAPHY: Toshio Ubukata

MUSIC: Fumio Hayasaka

CAST: Masayuki Mori (Kinji Kameda), Toshiro Mifune (Denkichi Akama), Mitsuyo Akashi (Akama's mother), Setsuko Hara (Taeko

Nasu), Takashi Shimura (Ono), Chieko Higashiyama (Satoko, his
wife), Chiyoko Fumiya (Noriko, his older daughter), Yoshiko Kuga
(Ayako, his younger daughter), Kokuten Kodo (Junpei Kayama), Eiko
Miyoshi (his wife), Minoru Chiaki (Mutsuo, his older son), Noriko
Sengoku (Takako, his daughter), Daisuke Inoue (Kaoru, his young
son), Bokuzen Hidari (Karube), Eijiro Yanagi (Tohata)

1952: *Ikiru* [*Ikiru*]
PRODUCTION COMPANY: Toho
PRODUCER: Sojiro Motoki
DIRECTOR: Akira Kurosawa
SCREENPLAY: Shinobu Hashimoto, Hideo Oguni, and Akira Kurosawa
PHOTOGRAPHY: Asakazu Nakai
MUSIC: Fumio Hayasaka
CAST: Takashi Shimura (Kanji Watanabe, chief of the Citizens' Sec-
tion), Nobuo Kaneko (Mitsuo, his son), Kyoko Seki (Kazue, Mitsuo's
wife), Makoto Kobori (Kiichi, Kanji Watanabe's older brother),
Kumeko Urabe (Tatsu, Kiichi's wife), Yoshie Minami (maid), Miki
Odagiri (Toyo Odagiri, young woman in Watanabe's office), Kamatari
Fujiwara (Ono, assistant chief), Minosuke Yamada (Saito, subordinate clerk), Haruo Tanaka (Sakai, assistant), Bokuzen Hidari (Ohara,
assistant), Shinichi Himori (Kimura, assistant), Minoru Chiaki (Noguchi, assistant), Kin Sugai, Eiko Miyoshi, Fumiko Homma (house-
wives), Atsushi Watanabe (patient), Masao Shimizu (doctor), Yunosuke Ito (the writer), Yatsuko Tanami (bar hostess), Nobuo
Nakamura (Deputy Mayor), Kusuo Abe (city councillor), Fuyuki
Murakami (journalist), Seiji Miyaguchi (gang boss), Daisuke Kato
(gang member), Ichiro Chiba (policeman)

1954: *Seven Samurai* [*Shichinin no Samurai*]
PRODUCTION COMPANY: Toho
PRODUCER: Sojiro Motoki
DIRECTOR: Akira Kurosawa
SCREENPLAY: Shinobu Hashimoto, Hideo Oguni, and Akira Kurosawa
PHOTOGRAPHY: Asakazu Nakai
MUSIC: Fumio Hayasaka
CAST: Takashi Shimura (Kambei Shimada, leader of the samurai),
Toshiro Mifune (Kikuchiyo), Yoshio Inaba (Gorobei), Seiji Miya-
guchi (Kyuzo), Minoru Chiaki (Heihachi), Daisuke Kato (Shichiroji),
Ko Kimura (Katsushiro), Kokuten Kodo (Gisaku, the village elder),
Kamatari Fujiwara (Manzo), Keiko Tsushima (Shino, his daughter),
Bokuzen Hidari (Yohei), Yoshio Kosugi (Mosuke), Yoshio Tsuchiya
(Rikichi), Yukiko Shimazaki (Rikichi's wife), Keiji Sakakida (Gosaku),
Toranosuke Ogawa (grandfather), Yu Akitsu (husband), Noriko Sen-
goku (wife), Kichijiro Ueda, Shimpei Takagi, Akira Tani, Haruo
Nakajima, Takashi Narita (bandits)

1955: *Record of a Living Being* [*Ikimono no Kiroku*] (alternate English title: *I Live in Fear*)

PRODUCTION COMPANY: Toho

PRODUCER: Sojiro Motoki

DIRECTOR: Akira Kurosawa

SCREENPLAY: Shinobu Hashimoto, Hideo Oguni, and Akira Kurosawa

PHOTOGRAPHY: Asakazu Nakai

MUSIC: Fumio Hayasaka; finished by Masaru Sato

CAST: Toshiro Mifune (Kiichi Nakajima), Eiko Miyoshi (Toyo, his wife), Yutaka Sada (Ichiro, his first son), Minoru Chiaki (Jiro, his second son), Haruko Togo (Yoshi, his first daughter), Kyoko Aoyama (Sué, his second daughter), Masao Shimizu (Yamazaki, Yoshi's husband), Noriko Sengoku (Kimie, Ichiro's wife), Yoichi Tachikawa (Ryoichi, Nakajima's son by a former mistress), Kiyomi Mizunoya (Satoko, Kiichi's first mistress), Saoko Yonemura (Taeko, her daughter), Akemi Negishi (Asako, his current mistress), Kichijiro Ueda (her father), Takashi Shimura (Dr. Harada, dentist and member of family court), Kazuo Kato (Susumu, his son), Eijiro Tono (the landowner from Brazil), Ken Mitsuda (Araki, judge), Toranosuke Ogawa (Hori, lawyer), Nobuo Nakamura (psychiatrist)

1957: *Throne of Blood* [*Kumonosu-jo*] (Castle of the Spider's Web)

PRODUCTION COMPANY: Toho

PRODUCER: Sojiro Motoki and Akira Kurosawa

DIRECTOR: Akira Kurosawa

SCREENPLAY: Shinobu Hashimoto, Ryuzo Kikushima, Hideo Oguni, and Akira Kurosawa, based on the play *Macbeth* by William Shakespeare

PHOTOGRAPHY: Asakazu Nakai

MUSIC: Masaru Sato

CAST: Toshiro Mifune (Taketoki Washizu), Isuzu Yamada (Asaji, his wife), Minoru Chiaki (Yoshiaki Miki, his comrade), Akira Kubo (Yoshiteru, Miki's son), Takamaru Sasaki (Kuniharu Tsuzuki), Yoichi Tachikawa (Kunimaru, Kuniharu's son), Takashi Shimura (Noriyasu Odagura), Chieko Naniwa (witch)

1957: *The Lower Depths* [*Donzoko*]

PRODUCTION COMPANY: Toho

PRODUCER: Akira Kurosawa

DIRECTOR: Akira Kurosawa

SCREENPLAY: Hideo Oguni and Akira Kurosawa, based on the play by Maxim Gorky

PHOTOGRAPHY: Kazuo Yamasaki

MUSIC: Masaru Sato

CAST: Toshiro Mifune (Sutekichi, thief), Ganjiro Nakamura (Rokubei, landlord), Isuzu Yamada (Osugi, his wife), Kyoko Kagawa (Okayo, her sister), Bokuzen Hidari (Kahei, a priest), Minoru Chiaki (the "samurai"), Kamatari Fujiwara (the actor), Eijiro Tono (Tomekichi, tinker), Eiko Miyoshi (Asa, his wife), Akemi Negishi (Osen, prostitute), Nijiko Kiyokawa (Otaki, peddler), Haruo Tanaka (Tatsu, bucket maker), Koji Mitsui (Yoshisaburo, gambler), Kichijiro Ueda (Shimazo, police agent), Yu Fujiki (Unokichi), Fujita-yama (Tsugaru), Atsushi Watanabe (companion to Tsugaru)

1958: ***The Hidden Fortress* [*Kakushi Toride no San-Akunin*] (Three Bad Men in a Hidden Fortress)**

PRODUCTION COMPANY: Toho

PRODUCER: Masumi Fujimoto and Akira Kurosawa

DIRECTOR: Akira Kurosawa

SCREENPLAY: Shinobu Hashimoto, Ryuzo Kikushima, Hideo Oguni, and Akira Kurosawa

PHOTOGRAPHY: Kazuo Yamasaki

MUSIC: Masaru Sato

CAST: Toshiro Mifune (General Rokurota Makabe), Misa Uehara (Princess Yuki), Takashi Shimura (General Izumi Nagakura), Susumu Fujita (General Hyoe Tadokoro), Eiko Miyoshi (lady-in-waiting), Minoru Chiaki (Tahei), Kamatari Fujiwara (Matashichi), Toshiko Higuchi (farm girl), Kichijiro Ueda (slave-trader), Koji Mitsui (soldier), Rinsaku Ogata (young man), Tadao Nakamaru (young man), Ikio Sawamura (gambler), Shiten Ohashi (samurai), Kokuten Kodo (man at the signboard), Takeshi Kato (stray soldier)

1960: ***The Bad Sleep Well* [*Warui Yatsu Hodo Yoku Nemuru*]**

PRODUCTION COMPANY: Kurosawa Films

PRODUCER: Tomoyuki Tanaka and Akira Kurosawa

DIRECTOR: Akira Kurosawa

SCREENPLAY: Shinobu Hashimoto, Hideo Oguni, Ryuzo Kikushima, Eijiro Hisaita, and Akira Kurosawa

PHOTOGRAPHY: Yuzuru Aizawa

MUSIC: Masaru Sato

CAST: Toshiro Mifune (Koichi Nishi, secretary to Iwabuchi), Takeshi Kato (Itakura, his friend), Masayuki Mori (Iwabuchi, company president), Takashi Shimura (Moriyama, admistrative officer), Akira Nishimura (Shirai, contract officer), Kamatari Fujiwara (Wada, accountant), Gen Shimizu (Miura, accountant), Kyoko Kagawa (Keiko, Iwabuchi's daughter), Tatsuya Mihashi (Tatsuo, Iwabuchi's son), Kyu Sazanka (Kaneko), Chishu Ryu (Nonaka, prosecutor), Seiji Miyaguchi (Okakura), Nobuo Nakamura (lawyer), Susumu Fujita (commissioner), Koji Mitsui (journalist)

1961: *Yojimbo* [*Yojimbo*]

PRODUCTION COMPANY: Kurosawa Films
PRODUCER: Tomoyuki Tanaka and Ryuzo Kikushima
DIRECTOR: Akira Kurosawa
SCREENPLAY: Ryuzo Kikushima and Akira Kurosawa
PHOTOGRAPHY: Kazuo Miyagawa
MUSIC: Masaru Sato
CAST: Toshiro Mifune (Sanjuro Kuwabatake), Eijiro Tono (Gonji, the saké-seller), Kamatari Fujiwara (Tazaemon, the silk merchant), Takashi Shimura (Tokuemon, the saké merchant), Seizaburo Kawazu (Seibei, Tazaemon's henchman), Isuzu Yamada (Orin, Seibei's wife), Hiroshi Tachikawa (Yoichiro, their son), Kyu Sazanka (Ushitora, Tokuemon's henchman), Tatsuya Nakadai (Unosuke, Ushitora's younger brother), Daisuke Kato (Inokichi, Ushitora's brother), Ikio Sawamura (Hansuke), Akira Nishimura (Kuma), Yoshio Tsuchiya (Kohei, a farmer), Yoko Tsukasa (Nui, his wife), Susumu Fujita (Homma)

1962: *Sanjuro* [*Tsubaki Sanjuro*] (Sanjuro of the Camellias)

PRODUCTION COMPANY: Kurosawa Films
PRODUCER: Tomoyuki Tanaka and Ryuzo Kikushima
DIRECTOR: Akira Kurosawa
SCREENPLAY: Ryuzo Kikushima, Hideo Oguni, and Akira Kurosawa, based on the novel *Hibi Heian* (Day-to-Day Security) by Shugoro Yamamoto
PHOTOGRAPHY: Fukuzo Koizumi
MUSIC: Masaru Sato
CAST: Toshiro Mifune (Sanjuro Tsubaki), Tatsuya Nakadai (Hanbei Muroto), Yuzo Kayama (Iori Izaka, leader of the samurai), Akihiko Hirata, Kunie Tanaka, Hiroshi Tachikawa, Tatsuhiko Hari, Tatsuyoshi Ehara, Kenzo Matsui, Yoshio Tsuchiya, Akira Kubo (samurai), Takashi Shimura (Kurofuji), Kamatari Fujiwara (Takebayashi), Masao Shimizu (Kikui), Yunosuke Ito (Mutsuta), Takako Irie (his wife), Reiko Dan (Chidori, his daughter), Keiju Kobayashi (spy)

1963: *High and Low* [*Tengoku to Jigoku*] (Heaven and Hell)

PRODUCTION COMPANY: Kurosawa Films
PRODUCER: Tomoyuki Tanaka and Ryuzo Kikushima
DIRECTOR: Akira Kurosawa
SCREENPLAY: Eijiro Hisaita, Ryuzo Kikushima, Hideo Oguni, and Akira Kurosawa, based on the novel *King's Ransom* by Ed McBain
PHOTOGRAPHY: Asakazu Nakai
MUSIC: Masaru Sato
CAST: Toshiro Mifune (Kingo Gondo), Kyoko Kagawa (Reiko, his wife), Tatsuya Mihashi (Kawanishi, his assistant), Yutaka Sada (Aoki,

the chauffeur), Tsutomu Yamazaki (Ginji Takeuchi, the kidnapper), Tatsuya Nakadai (Inspector Tokura), Takashi Shimura (director, police headquarters), Susumu Fujita (commissioner), Kenjiro Ishiyama (Detective Taguchi), Ko Kimura (Detective Arai), Takeshi Kato (Detective Nakao), Yoshio Tsuchiya (Detective Murata), Hiroshi Unayama (Detective Shimada), Koji Mitsui (journalist)

1965: *Red Beard* [*Akahige*]

PRODUCTION COMPANY: Kurosawa Films

PRODUCER: Ryuzo Kikushima and Tomoyuki Tanaka

DIRECTOR: Akira Kurosawa

SCREENPLAY: Ryuzo Kikushima, Hideo Oguni, Masato Ide, and Akira Kurosawa, based on the novel *Akahige Shinryodan* (Tales of Red Beard's Examinations) by Shugoro Yamamoto

PHOTOGRAPHY: Asakazu Nakai and Takao Saito

MUSIC: Masaru Sato

CAST: Toshiro Mifune (Dr. Kyojio Niide, "Red Beard"), Yuzo Kayama (Dr. Noboru Yasumoto), Chishu Ryu (Noboru's father), Kinuyo Tanaka (Noboru's mother), Yoshio Tsuchiya (Dr. Handayu Mori), Tatsuyoshi Ehara (Genzo Tsugawa), Reiko Dan (Osugi), Kyoko Kagawa (the madwoman), Kamatari Fujiwara (Rokusuke), Akemi Negishi (Okuni), Tsutomu Yamazaki (Sahachi), Miyuki Kuwano (Onaka), Eijiro Tono (Goheiji), Takashi Shimura (Tokubei Izumiya), Terumi Niki (Otoyo), Haruko Sugimura (Kin), Yoko Naito (Masae), Ken Mitsuda (her father), Yoshitaka Zushi (Choji)

1970: *Dodeskaden* [*Dodeskaden*]

PRODUCTION COMPANY: Yonki no Kai / Toho

PRODUCER: Yoichi Matsue and Akira Kurosawa

DIRECTOR: Akira Kurosawa

SCREENPLAY: Hideo Oguni, Shinobu Hashimoto, and Akira Kurosawa, based on the story collection *Kisetsu no nai Machi* (The Town without Seasons) by Shugoro Yamamoto

PHOTOGRAPHY: Takao Saito and Yasumichi Fukuzawa

MUSIC: Toru Takemitsu

CAST: Yoshitaka Zushi (Rokuchan), Kin Sugai (Okuni, his mother), Junzaburo Ban (Yukicihi Shima), Kiyoko Tange (his wife), Michio Hino, Tatsubei Shimokawa, Keishi Furuyama (guests of Shima), Hisashi Igawa (Masuda), Hideko Okiyama (his wife), Kunie Tanaka (Kawaguchi), Jitsuko Yoshimura (his wife), Noboru Mitani (beggar), Hiroyuki Kawase (his son), Hiroshi Akutagawa (Hei), Tomoko Naraoka (Ocho, his wife), Atsushi Watanabe (Tamba), Shinsuke Minami (Ryo), Yoko Kusunoki (his wife), Tatsuo Matsumura (Kyota), Tsuji Imura (his wife), Tomoko Yamazaki (his stepdaughter), Masahiko Kametani (Okabe), Sanji Kojima (thief), Kazuo Kato (painter), Kamatari Fujiwara (old man)

1975: ***Dersu Uzala* [*Dersu Uzala*]**
PRODUCTION COMPANY: Mosfilm
PRODUCER: Nikolai Sizov and Yoichi Matsue
DIRECTOR: Akira Kurosawa
SCREENPLAY: Yuri Nagibin and Akira Kurosawa, based on the book by Vladimir Arseniev
PHOTOGRAPHY: Asakazu Nakai, Yuri Gantman, and Feodor Dobronravov
MUSIC: Isaac Swartz
CAST: Maxim Munzuk (Dersu Uzala), Yuri Salomin (Vladimir Arseniev), Svetlana Danielchenko (his wife), Schemeikl Chokmorov (Jan Bao), Piyatokov, Purohanov, Vladimir Bururakov, Alexander Filipenko, Yuri Chernov, and Alexander Alexandrov (members of the 1902 expedition team)

1980: ***Kagemusha* [*Kagemusha*] (The Shadow Warrior)**
PRODUCTION COMPANY: Kurosawa Films
PRODUCER: Akira Kurosawa and Tomoyuki Tanaka
DIRECTOR: Akira Kurosawa
SCREENPLAY: Masato Ide and Akira Kurosawa
PHOTOGRAPHY: Takao Saito and Masaharu Ueda, with the collaboration of Kazuo Miyagawa and Asakazu Nakai
MUSIC: Shinichiro Ikebe
CAST: Tatsuya Nakadai (Shingen Takeda and his double, the Kagemusha), Tsutomu Yamazaki (Nobukado Takeda), Kenichi Hagiwara (Katsuyori Takeda), Kota Yui (Takemaru Takeda), Hideji Otaki (Masakage Yamagata), Hideo Murota (Nobuharu Baba), Takayuki Shiho (Masatoyo Naito), Shuhei Sugimori (Tadamasa Kosaka), Noboru Shimizu (Masatane Hara), Koji Shimizu (Katsusuke Atobe), Daisuke Ryu (Nobunaga Oda), Masayuki Yui (Ieyasu Tokugawa), Mitsuko Baisho (Oyunokata), Kaori Momoi (Otsuyanokata)

1985: ***Ran* [*Ran*] (Chaos)**
PRODUCTION COMPANY: Greenwich Film / Herald Ace / Nippon Herald
PRODUCER: Serge Silberman and Masato Hara
DIRECTOR: Akira Kurosawa
SCREENPLAY: Hideo Oguni, Masato Ide, and Akira Kurosawa
PHOTOGRAPHY: Takao Saito and Masaharu Ueda, with the collaboration of Asakazu Nakai
MUSIC: Toru Takemitsu
CAST: Tatsuya Nakadai (Hidetora Ichimonji), Akira Terao (Taro, his oldest son), Jinpachi Nezu (Jiro, his middle son), Daisuke Ryu (Saburo, his youngest son), Mieko Harada (Lady Kaede, Taro's wife), Yoshiko Miyazaki (Lady Sué, Jiro's wife), Takeshi Nomura (Tsurumaru, Sué's brother), Peter (Kyoami, Hidetora's fool), Masayuki Yui (Tango Hirayama, Hidetora's retainer), Kazuo Kato (Ikoma, Hide-

tora's retainer), Jun Tazaki (Seiji Ayabe), Hitoshi Ueki (Nobuhiro Fujimaki), Norio Matsui (Ogura, attendant to Taro), Hisashi Igawa (Kurogane, counselor to Jiro), Kenji Kodama (Shirane, counselor to Jiro), Toshiya Ito (Naganuma, counselor to Jiro), Takeshi Kato (Hatakeyama, commander of Saburo's troops)

1990: **Dreams [*Yume*]**

PRODUCTION COMPANY: Kurosawa Films

PRODUCER: Hisao Kurosawa and Yoshio Inoue

DIRECTOR: Akira Kurosawa

SCREENPLAY: Akira Kurosawa

PHOTOGRAPHY: Takao Saito and Masaharu Ueda

MUSIC: Shinichiro Ikebe

CAST: Akira Terao ("I," the dreamer), Mitsunori Isaki ("I," the young dreamer), Mitsuko Baisho (the dreamer's mother), Martin Scorsese (Vincent van Gogh), Chishu Ryu (old man), Mieko Harada (the snow spirit), Yoshitaka Zushi (Private Noguchi), Toshie Negishi (woman with child), Hisashi Igawa (man at the nuclear power plant), Chosuke Ikariya (the demon)

1991: **Rhapsody in August [*Hachigatsu no Kyoshikyoku*]**

PRODUCTION COMPANY: Kurosawa Films / Shochiku

PRODUCER: Hisao Kurosawa

DIRECTOR: Akira Kurosawa

SCREENPLAY: Akira Kurosawa, based on the novel *Nabe no Naka* (In the Cauldron) by Kiyoko Murata

PHOTOGRAPHY: Takao Saito and Masaharu Ueda

MUSIC: Shinichiro Ikebe

CAST: Sachiko Murase (Kane, grandmother), Hisashi Igawa (Tadao, her son), Narumi Kayashima (Machiko, his wife), Tomoko Otakara (Tami, older granddaughter), Mitsunori Isaki (Shinjiro, younger grandson), Toshie Negishi (Yoshie, Kane's daughter), Choichiro Kawarasaki (Noboru, Yoshie's husband), Hidetaka Yoshioka (Tateo, older grandson), Mie Suzuki (Minako, younger granddaughter), Richard Gere (Clark)

1993: **Mada Da Yo (Not Yet!)**

PRODUCTION COMPANY: Daiei

PRODUCER: Hisao Kurosawa

DIRECTOR: Akira Kurosawa

SCREENPLAY: Akira Kurosawa, based on works by Hyakken Uchida

PHOTOGRAPHY: Takao Saito and Masaharu Ueda

MUSIC: Shinichiro Ikebe

CAST: Tatsuo Matsumura (Hyakken Uchida), Kyoko Kagawa (his wife), Hisashi Igawa, Joji Tokoro, Akira Terao, Tsugutoshi Kobayashi

Video and Rental Sources

video distributor (v); 16mm film rental source (r)

SANSHIRO SUGATA v Sony; r Films Incorporated

THE MOST BEAUTIFUL r R5/S8 Presents

SANSHIRO SUGATA, PART TWO r R5/S8 Presents

THE MEN WHO TREAD ON THE TIGER'S TAIL v International Historic Films; r Films Incorporated

NO REGRETS FOR OUR YOUTH v Connoisseur Video Collection; r East-West Classics

ONE WONDERFUL SUNDAY r R5/S8 Presents

DRUNKEN ANGEL v Ingram International; r Films Incorporated

THE QUIET DUEL r Films Incorporated

STRAY DOG v Sony; r Films Incorporated

SCANDAL r Films Incorporated

RASHOMON v Orion Home Video; r Films Incorporated

THE IDIOT v New Yorker Films; r New Yorker Films

IKIRU v Media Home Entertainment; r Films Incorporated

SEVEN SAMURAI v Orion Home Video; r Films Incorporated

RECORD OF A LIVING BEING (alternate English title: I LIVE IN FEAR) v Facets Multimedia; r Films Incorporated

THRONE OF BLOOD v Media Home Entertainment; r Films Incorporated

THE LOWER DEPTHS v Sony; r Films Incorporated

THE HIDDEN FORTRESS v Media Home Entertainment; r Janus Films

THE BAD SLEEP WELL v Sony; r Films Incorporated

YOJIMBO v Orion Home Video; r Films Incorporated

SANJURO v Embassy Home Entertainment; r Films Incorporated

HIGH AND LOW v Pacific Arts Video; r East-West Classics

RED BEARD v Media Home Entertainment; r Films Incorporated

DODESKADEN v Embassy Home Entertainment; r Films Incorporated

DERSU UZALA v Orion Home Video; r Films Incorporated

KAGEMUSHA v CBS-Fox Video; r Films Incorporated

RAN v CBS-Fox Video; r Orion Classics

DREAMS v Warner Home Video

RHAPSODY IN AUGUST r New Yorker Films

rental companies

East-West Classics
1529 Acton St.
Berkeley, CA 94702
415/526-3611

Films Incorporated
5547 N. Ravenswood Ave.
Chicago, IL 60640-1199
800/323-4222 ext 42

Janus Films
888 7th Ave.
New York, NY 10106
212/753-7100

New Yorker Films
16 W. 61st St.
New York, NY 10023
212/247-6110

Orion Classics
711 5th Ave.
New York, NY 10022
212/758-5100

R5/S8 Presents
1028 Poplar Dr.
Falls Church, VA 22046
202/452-1717

Index